# SECOND LIFE

## A Guide to Your Virtual World

## Brian A. White
### a.k.a Ansel Gasparini

800 East 96th Street, Indianapolis, Indiana 46240 USA

# SECOND LIFE
## *A Guide to Your Virtual World*

**Copyright© 2008 by Que Publishing**

ISBN-13: 978-0-3215-0166-0
ISBN-10:   0-3215-0166-7

*Library of Congress Cataloging-in-Publication Data:*
White, Brian A.
   Second Life : a guide to your virtual world / Brian A. White.
      p. cm.
   ISBN 0-321-50166-7 (pbk. : alk. paper)  1.  Second Life (Game)  2.  Shared virtual environments.
3.  Avatars (Computer graphics)  4.  Internet.  I. Title.
   GV1469.25.S425W545 2007
   794.8—dc22
                                        2007025725

Printed in the United States of America
First Printing: August 2007

## TRADEMARKS

## WARNING AND DISCLAIMER

## BULK SALES

Que Publishing offers excellent discounts on this book when ordered in quantity for bulk purchases or special sales. For more information, please contact
   U.S. Corporate and Government Sales
   1-800-382-3419
   corpsales@pearsontechgroup.com

For sales outside the U.S., please contact
   International Sales
   international@pearsoned.com

**EDITOR-IN-CHIEF**
Karen Gettman

**EXECUTIVE EDITOR**
Chris Guzikowski

**SENIOR DEVELOPMENT EDITOR**
Chris Zahn

**MANAGING EDITOR**
Gina Kanouse

**SENIOR PROJECT EDITOR**
Lori Lyons

**COPY EDITOR**
Chuck Hutchinson

**INDEXER**
Heather McNeill

**PROOFREADER**
Kathy Bidwell

**TECHNICAL EDITORS**
Kymberli Hemberger
Adam Bloch

**PUBLISHING COORDINATOR**
Raina Chrobak

**BOOK DESIGNER**
Anne Jones

**COMPOSITOR**
Jake McFarland

*To my wife, Kimberly—without your support and encouragement this book would never exist.*
*And to August and MacIsaac—these will be your worlds.*

# CONTENTS AT A GLANCE

TABLE OF CONTENTS

# PREFACE

I entered a traditional Japanese style house through a crawlspace between the roof and the ceiling. The ceiling was made of wood and rice paper. As I crawled forward, the ceiling collapsed under my weight, and I fell into a hallway. There were shoji screens on either side of me. Part of me wondered how this place had been created or scripted. As I hit the ground, several swordsmen appeared at the end of the hallway and started advancing. I turned and ran for the door, closely pursued. As I was preparing to teleport home, I awoke.

It was December 9, 2006, and I had experienced my first Second Life dream. My real-life self had been dreaming in my virtual body (or avatar). This experience left no doubt in my mind that all my time spent in SL working on this book had left its mark on my subconscious. It was as thrilling as it was unnerving.

Some think that SL is a game, but before you judge, give it a try. You will see that while there are many aspects of play, SL is something more than just a game. SL is a new world accessible only through the Internet. You don't need to buy anything to participate; it is free to join. You will find passion, history, art, politics, culture, government, and drama in SL. It has an aboriginal population (old-timers), and it has an ever-growing number of artists, explorers, entrepreneurs, settlers, designers, musicians, misfits, builders, vamps, scripters, furries, griefers, androids, dragons, and yes, even corporations.

The tapestry of creative potential and social possibility becomes deeper and richer as you learn more about the world and spend time there. I am convinced that SL or worlds like it will become another breakthrough technology that affects your real life just as the Internet has done since the early 1990s.

It is my sincere hope that this book helps you unlock your own potential in SL faster and with less frustration than those who have gone before you.

## WHAT IS THIS BOOK ABOUT?

This book is about Linden Lab's Second Life (SL). Imagine a place where you can explore landscapes that stretch to the horizon, enjoy beautiful sunsets on a beach or from your jet ski, buy land and plant a garden, give your girlfriend that tattoo she's always wanted, go skydiving, spend an evening at a club dancing the night away or at home relaxing by the fire with friends listening to some smooth jazz on your new stereo. Now imagine doing this all online with friends from around the globe.

SL is a virtual world construction set full of creative potential. The SL residents form its community. This book provides the keys to unlocking your own potential in this vibrant online world while avoiding its pitfalls.

You can think of this book as a travel guide for visitors, a relocation guide for someone looking to buy land and move in, and a home improvement guide for the serious architect/builder who has been in SL a while. It will teach you how to move, fly, see, communicate, build, texture, script, animate, and explore.

## WHY A BOOK ON SECOND LIFE?

To get acclimated to SL, you have a lot to learn. Practical information is hard to find and often unavailable. Existing tribal knowledge is scattered across online help, forums, knowledge articles, blogs, websites, and YouTube videos. You need to learn the software (SL viewer) to accomplish the basics of movement and communication, and to breathe life into your own creations. Equally important, you need to learn the social networks and cultural norms of SL to be accepted as an SL insider. Helping you acquire these basics quickly and easily is what I set out to accomplish with this book.

If you've spent time in virtual worlds, you might consider it a quaint idea to write a traditional paper-based book on the subject of SL. I mean, aren't we supposed to be all-digital nowadays? I believe a traditional book, even today, remains a great way to deliver a large amount of structured information to a reader anywhere and at any time, without consideration for connectivity, bandwidth, power, and startup time.

## WHO SHOULD READ THIS BOOK?

This book has been written to address a broad audience. I expect you will come back to it again and again as your

SL knowledge increases. If you're completely new to virtual worlds, this is a great place to start. Even if you've been in SL a long time, you will still learn a new thing or two. If you're a graphics professional or game developer, it's worth your time to learn a little bit about SL. SL or worlds like it will be key components in the future of your profession. Finally, if your interest in SL is purely professional, this is an essential guide to help you understand your target audience.

## Those New to Virtual Worlds

The availability of broadband Internet and good graphics cards now make it possible for you, even if you are not a gamer, to get involved in virtual worlds, which are shaping the future of online communities in creative and even lucrative ways. This book reduces the barrier to entry for new SL residents. Chapters 1—4 will be particularly valuable to you.

## Second Life Residents (Who Already Know the Basics)

Other books (at least as of this writing) have only scratched the SL surface. If you've been in SL for a while and are looking to take your knowledge to the next level or maybe learn a new skill like scripting, texturing, or animation, then this book is for you. Reviewers who have been in SL more than three years have all commented that they learned something new while reviewing this material. Chapters 7—10 will be particularly relevant.

If you're getting involved in a relationship in SL and are trying to figure out how the social scene works, check out Chapter 5 on SL relationships. This chapter is uniquely nontechnical, yet the information in it is just as important to know about SL as that presented in the other chapters.

## Graphics Professionals Learning About Second Life

Maybe you are a graphic artist, 3D modeler, texture artist, or game-level designer looking for the next big thing in your career. Chapters 6, 7, and 9 will unlock your ability to create your vision on the SL platform.

## Corporate Marketing and Other Professionals

Whether you are taking your company into SL yourself or planning to use another firm, please read this book. It's a small investment in time and money, and it provides you significant insight into SL's culture and creativity. Learn about your audience before you jump in. Chapters 1 and 5 are great places to start.

## Aspiring Second Life DJs, Musicians, Photographers, and Movie Makers

If you are a singer/songwriter looking to open up an international market of music lovers without leaving your home studio, you've come to the right place. I ended up with an entire chapter on the subjects of SL music, photography, and machinima because there was so much to say. This topic seriously needs a book of its own, but Chapter 11 is a great place to start with references where you can learn more.

## ORGANIZATION OF THIS BOOK

Learning enough to cover the breadth of SL's capabilities would have taken me years. One unique approach I took when writing this book was to incorporate information gleaned from over 100 in-world interviews of both experienced residents as well as new residents. The book flows between topic coverage to expert comments and tips to tutorials meant to be performed in-world. The book is structured such that you can read it offline and then enforce the learning process by following tutorials while online. The book is laid out in the following chapters.

## Chapter 1: Welcome to Second Life

Get answers to your basic questions in Chapter 1. This chapter answers questions new residents often ask and introduces the basic vocabulary of SL. You will discover answers to questions like the following:

- What is SL?
- Is SL a game?
- What can I do in SL?
- How do I make money in SL?

## Chapter 2: Exploring the New Frontier

Learn how to explore the world in Chapter 2. This chapter teaches you how to walk, run, and fly in SL (movement basics). In addition to movement, you learn how to see the world (using camera controls). Finally, you learn how to navigate the world's geography through teleports, maps, and mini-maps.

## Chapter 3: Communication and Social Networking

Learn how to talk to each other in Chapter 3. This chapter teaches you how to communicate in SL, both verbally and through gestures. You learn about common pitfalls and mistakes new residents make when communicating with others. You also learn about tools for communicating and networking with other groups of like-minded residents. Finally, this chapter wraps up with tips on doing presentations in SL.

## Chapter 4: Your Avatar, Your Virtual Self

Lose your newbie look in Chapter 4. This chapter teaches you all about your avatar and how to change your look. You learn how to change your shape, hair, eyes, and skin. Chapter 4 also covers how to create your own basic clothes and shop for new clothes. Finally, you get some ideas about the wide variety of SL avatars that other residents have created.

## Chapter 5: Second Life Culture and Relationships

Learn about SL relationships in Chapter 5. This chapter teaches you about some ground rules and guidelines for SL relationships. You learn how to read profiles and adjust your own profile to communicate what you want. You discover the pace of SL relationships and the reasons residents may decide to partner. Finally, you uncover the secrets of virtual sex and where to learn more if you are interested.

## Chapter 6: Building Basics

Learn how to create your own stuff in Chapter 6. This chapter teaches you the basics of the SL building system. You learn how to create new objects and link them together to create more complex objects. You also learn about basic texturing and object permissions. Finally, you learn how to create flexible objects and objects that cast their own light.

## Chapter 7: Advanced Textures and Clothing

Learn how to make your stuff look real or unreal in Chapter 7. This chapter teaches you how to apply "tex-tures" to objects to make them look real. You learn how to apply textures to different sides of an object. You also learn how to make objects bumpy, shiny, and transparent. Finally, you'll create your own brick patio, blackberry plant, and custom T-shirt.

## Chapter 8: Making the Magic: Scripting Basics

Learn how to bring your objects to life in Chapter 8. This chapter teaches you the basics of the Linden Scripting Language. Even if you have no programming experience, this chapter teaches you to use existing scripts and write your own scripts. You learn to create a scripted door, a notecard giver, and a teleporter. What you create after that is purely up to your own imagination.

## Chapter 9: Land Ownership, Terraforming, and Landscaping

Learn how to find, terraform, and landscape your own land in Chapter 9. This chapter teaches you the advantages and costs of owning land in SL. You learn the difference between renting and buying and how to find a new piece of land. Finally, you learn how to terraform your land, build a waterfall, and find your first home.

## Chapter 10: Particles, Vehicles, Animations, and Sculpted Prims

Unlock the mysteries behind advanced SL effects such as particles, animations, sculpted prims, and vehicles in Chapter 10. You learn how to create the magic behind smoke, candles, fireworks, fountains, falling snow, leaves, rain, and, of course, bling. You create a basic sit animation and learn how to place it into a pose ball. You will learn about the latest building innovation in SL—the sculpted prim. Finally, you build your own airplane and fly it away!

## Chapter 11: Photography, Music, and Movies

Learn about photography, SL music, and movie making (machinima) in Chapter 11. This chapter teaches you about the snapshot tool, picture sharing, and picture taking. You learn about the SL music scene and how you can participate. Finally, this chapter provides several pointers on how to be your own director of SL movies.

## Chapter 12: Practical Matters: Under the Hood of the Metaverse

Learn how SL works and how to avoid common problems in Chapter 12! This chapter teaches you the basics of how the SL technology works and how to troubleshoot performance or connectivity issues. You learn how to deal with residents who are out for trouble, called *griefers*. Finally, you learn how to tame the growing beast called your *SL Inventory*.

## CONVENTIONS

I'll keep this brief. All references to contributors and interviewees use in-world avatar names versus real-life names. If you want to know who someone is in RL, then go ask his or her avatar.

I settled on using PC conventions in this book primarily because I am a PC user. The SL Viewer is also available for both Mac and Linux operating systems. See the following knowledge article for Mac keyboard equivalents: secondlife.com/knowledgebase/article.php?id=345. Some sections written by contributors may include the Mac equivalents to PC conventions.

**SLURL** Where you see this icon, you will find a Second Life URL, or SLURL, which is a real-life way of indicating a virtual world location. To use a SLURL, you simply place the link into the address field of a traditional browser (for example, Internet Explorer or Firefox). You also need to have the SL viewer installed. More on SLURLs later.

Code items from the Linden Scripting Language appear in a monospaced font.

## THE COMPANION IN-WORLD SITE

Technical books often include a CD-ROM and/or a companion website. Well, not this book! CD-ROMs or RL websites are not really practical, useful, or desirable in the case of SL. For example, say I create a texture for a waterfall in SL. I download it and put it onto a CD. You load the texture off the CD. At this point, you need to upload this texture into SL. This costs you L$10. If thousands of readers also take this texture from the CD and pay L$10 to upload it, there are now thousands of copies of the exact same object consuming resources (not to mention everyone had to pay L$10).

Rather than do this, I have built an in-world site where you will find the content that would exist on a traditional CD and much more. I am deeply indebted to Ceera Murakami, who kindly assisted me in this build. Check out her sim-wide design and build business *Fox and Ground Construction*. I am also indebted to Julia Hathor for providing the unique flora that grows on the site. Check out her lovely sims by searching for *Creative Fantasy Home & Garden*. I would also like to thank Jopsy Pendragon for getting me started on the geyser.

The in-world companion site has all the landmarks referenced in this book kept up-to-date in case things move around. You can discover the book's key contributors in the contributor's gallery. You will find all the textures and objects created in the book's tutorials if you want to get a copy of the final product. Finally, this is where I may add new tutorials and other information over time.

Last, but not least, the in-world site is located on a great rugged coastline that offers soothing ocean sounds and phenomenal sunsets. Take the elevator launch tube kindly provided by *Seifert Surface* to the top and take in the view.

The companion site is located on the old mainland in the Humuli sim at this SLURL:

**SLURL** http://slurl.com/secondlife/humuli/222/123/29

If you are interested in updates, instead of a mailing list I have created an SL group named "Artists, Explorers, and Entrepreneurs." You'll learn about SL groups and how to join them in a bit.

## ABOUT THE COVER

The cover of this book was extremely important to me because I wanted it to convey the various things that attract people to SL. I want to thank Judi Taylor and Anne Jones for taking all of my feedback and working with me to produce such a great piece.

I also want to thank Nyla Cheeky of www.houseofnyla.com. Nyla is a Vancouver, BC, fashion designer who is bringing her designs into SL and was kind enough to share some of her promotional images. Her Russian Ballerina is featured on the cover. I would also like to thank SunshineBlonde Fairymeadow and Osiris Acropolis, who kindly shared many photos of their relationship and whose "beauty and the beast" photo was compelling enough to land them on the cover. I'd also like to thank Malcolm Sydney for his surfing picture and Anika Davison and MagnAxiom Epsilon for their wedding picture. Last, to all the members of Seattle's Second Life Meetup who joined me in avian flight over Bliss Basin.

## AUTHOR FEEDBACK

I welcome your feedback on this book, both positive and negative. All comments will be considered and incorporated into future editions. The best way to reach me is by email at ansel.gasparini@gmail.com. Please include "SL feedback" in the subject line to help me sort.

If you would prefer to leave me feedback in SL, you can find a place to leave a notecard at the companion site in Humuli, located at http://slurl.com/secondlife/humuli/222/123/29. Due to the volume of IMs I receive, I may not get back to you reliably if you send me only an IM, but feel free to IM me, Ansel Gasparini, nonetheless.

## ABOUT THE AUTHOR

In "Real Life (RL)" **Brian A. White** has more than 15 years of experience in defining, developing, marketing, and selling enterprise software solutions. He has worked for successful startups and companies such as IBM, Microsoft, and Rational Software. He is currently Vice President of Product Management for Opsware Inc. He is familiar both with the technologies driving Second Life as well as the real-life tools that perform similar modeling/texturing jobs, such as LightWave, Poser, Bryce, and Photoshop. He lives with his wife and two sons in Seattle, Washington.

In "Second Life (SL), he is **Ansel Gasparini**, host of *Ansel Gasparini on Second Life, (http://anselgasparini. blogspot.com/),* organizer of the first Seattle/Pacific Northwest Meetup for Second Life residents, and SL Instructor/Mentor.

## ACKNOWLEDGMENTS

I will start this Oscar-award-winning acknowledgments section by thanking those who brought the concept and the reality of SL into existence. They include visionary authors Neil Stephenson, Verner Vinge, and William Gibson. They also include the operational visionaries Philip Rosedale and Cory Ondrejka. I would also like to thank Julian Dibbell for opening my eyes to the social and economic complexities of virtual worlds in his books.

This book would never have happened had it not been for an act of faith on the part of Karen Gettman and Chris Guzikowski. For agreeing to take on this project and allow one of their very techie authors into the mainstream publication market, I thank you. Thanks go to Lori Lyons for taking me through the production process.

Credit for the real work goes to Chris Zahn, Adam Bloch (Chosen Few), and Kymberli Hemberger (Kymber Schnook) for the countless hours of review and feedback, which not only made the text easier to read and more accurate, but seriously improved the overall product beyond anything I could have done on my own. I must also call out Jeff Barr (Jeffronious Batra of Virtual Amazon Web Service fame), whose detailed reviews, early collaboration, and ultimately his agreement to write an entire chapter for me made the workload more manageable.

There are a few SL residents I must draw special attention to. These residents I now count as friends, and they provided countless hours of review, feedback, and insights about SL that helped shape this book. My deepest thanks for their efforts. They are Julia Hathor, Ceera Murakami, and Pannie Paperdoll.

A lot of value in this book comes from others sharing their expertise. I could not hope to become an expert in all things in the time required, and so I relied on the real experts to lend their voice. I want to thank all of those who were willing to repurpose their blogs, write tutorials from scratch, or turn over their SL class materials. I truly believe their contributions contain some of the most valuable content in the book. They are Jeffronius Batra, Johan Durant, Chosen Few, Amanda Levitsky, Gwyneth Llewelyn, Alina Mikadze, Cubey Terra, Robin Sojourner, Julia Hathor, Pannie Paperdoll, and Willow Zander.

Other contributors sat down with me for literally hours, answering my questions, and sharing details of their SL and their knowledge. These interviews, I feel, really bring the book to life and help expose the complexities and excitement of SL living. I wish I had room to include all of the interviews I did. My thanks to all of you. Special thanks to the following individuals: Craig Altman, JeuL Resistance, Circe Broom, Jade Steele, Stroker Serpentine, Jacqueline Trudeau, Lumiere Noir, Aries Mathilde, Jopsy Pendragon, Wise Clapsaddle, Anika Davison, Gillygirl Hoffman, SunshineBlonde Fairymeadow, Attim Hokkagai, Obscuro Valkyrie, and Starax Statosky.

Finally, I want to thank many others who had more than a passing influence on different aspects of this text. Sadly, I am sure this is not a definitive list; my heartfelt apologies if I left you out. They are Alvin Ziegler, Malcolm Sydney, Morris Vig, Seifert Surface, Thor Eldrich, Heather Goodliffe, Beineff Bunder, Rosedrop Rust, Ayla Holt, Herb Greenspan, Justy Reymont, Joshua Nightshade, Osiris Acropolis, Regina Lynn, Laydin Tripp, Komuso Tokugawa, Chip Midnight, Fabs McAlpine, Kaikou Splash, David Gwynneville, Gypsy Paz, Karamel Madison, Toneless Tomba, SCOTTis Stradling, Rockwell Ginsberg, MagnAxiom Epsilon, and Lila Utu.

# WE WANT TO HEAR FROM YOU!

As the reader of this book, *you* are our most important critic and commentator. We value your opinion and want to know what we're doing right, what we could do better, what areas you'd like to see us publish in, and any other words of wisdom you're willing to pass our way.

As an executive editor for Que Publishing, I welcome your comments. You can email or write me directly to let me know what you did or didn't like about this book—as well as what we can do to make our books better.

*Please note that I cannot help you with technical problems related to the topic of this book. We do have a User Services group, however, where I will forward specific technical questions related to the book.*

When you write, please be sure to include this book's title and author as well as your name, email address, and phone number. I will carefully review your comments and share them with the author and editors who worked on the book.

Email:    feedback@quepublishing.com

Mail:     Chris Guzikowski
          Executive Editor
          Pearson Education
          75 Arlington Street
          Suite 300
          Boston, MA 02116 USA

# READER SERVICES

Visit our website and register this book at for convenient access to any updates, downloads, or errata that might be available for this book: www.quepublishing.com/register.

*Congratulations to the whole SL community on reaching
1 Million residents signed up!! Second Life is growing
because together we are all building content,
welcoming new people, expanding the community,
and adding new capabilities to the system.*

**—Philip Linden**

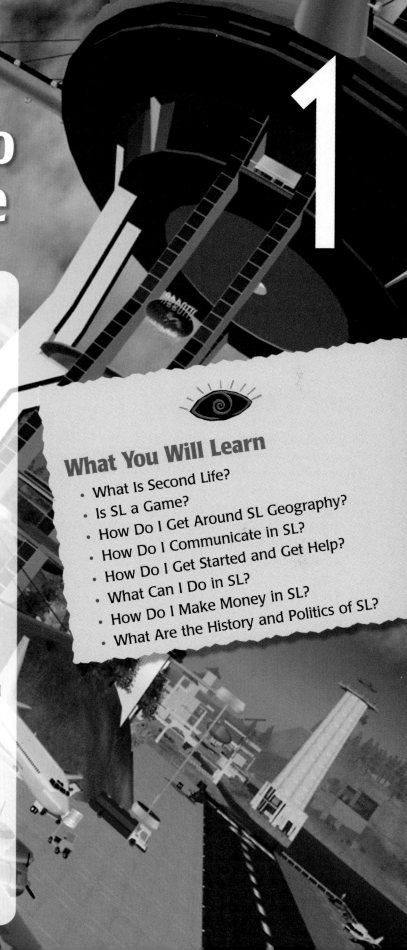

# Welcome to Second Life

1

**Second Life** (SL) is a new world accessible only through the Internet. You don't need to buy anything to participate; it's free to join. You will find passion, history, art, politics, culture, government, and drama in SL. It has an aboriginal population (old timers), and it has an ever-growing number of artists, explorers, entrepreneurs, settlers, designers, musicians, misfits, builders, vamps, scripters, furries, griefers, androids, dragons, and yes, even corporations.

SL is not a game of winners and losers or of heroic quests (although quests can be found). It is practically without boundaries and, just like **real life** (RL), you set your own course or drift directionless. It is a new frontier, sometimes thrilling, sometimes lawless, and sometimes exasperating. One thing it is not is short on opportunity and entertainment. Welcome to SL and your guide to success!

## What You Will Learn

- What Is Second Life?
- Is SL a Game?
- How Do I Get Around SL Geography?
- How Do I Communicate in SL?
- How Do I Get Started and Get Help?
- What Can I Do in SL?
- How Do I Make Money in SL?
- What Are the History and Politics of SL?

If you already have an avatar and understand things like *inventory*, *lag*, *rez*, *TP*, *prims*, *sim*, *L$*, *chat*, and *IM*, then you can skip ahead.

If you're new to SL and these terms are unfamiliar to you, then start here in Chapter 1. Here, I hit all the highlights of this new country in which you are about to arrive. I hope you enjoy it as much as I have.

In this chapter, we start a journey together to learn about SL and dig deep into both the fabric (platform) of SL as well as SL culture. This chapter answers many questions **newbies** ask (or *noobs*, short for *new residents*). OK, maybe it doesn't answer all questions, but at least it gives you a path to discovering your own answers.

# WHAT IS SECOND LIFE?

Second Life is not easy to sum up. It's kind of like the Blue Man Group (if you've seen it, you know what I mean). In the end, you define what SL is to you. Let me offer my own definition of SL, first as a platform and second as a community:

- The Second Life platform is an Internet-based, multi-user, 3D world construction set that emphasizes creativity, collaboration, socializing, and self-government.
- The Second Life community is a semi-self-governing group of residents who collaboratively create, live, and interact in a 3D online world owned and operated by Linden Lab.

You can participate in SL free simply by downloading the SL client from http://www.secondlife.com. It does not require a CD purchase from a store. SL does not have quests, winners, losers, experience, hit points, levels, and other things you might find in a massively multiplayer online role-playing game (MMORPG). If you have never heard of MMORPG, then forget about it! Welcome to the future of a 3D Internet that is strikingly like RL.

Let me offer the typical one-liners people use to describe SL so we can move past the first questions and into all the fun stuff:

- SL is like RL, only you can fly.
- SL is The Sims On-Line™ on steroids.
- SL is the latest incarnation of the "metaverse" as envisioned by Neal Stephenson in his novel *Snow Crash*.
- SL is an MMORPG, except there are no nonplayer characters (NPCs) or quests.
- SL is a glorified 3D chat room.
- SL is something created by Linden Lab.
- SL is a synthetic world (as described by economics researcher Edward Castronova in his book *Synthetic Worlds: The Business and Culture of Online Games*).
- SL is a virtual world (as described by Richard Bartle in his book *Designing Virtual Worlds*).
- SL is Web 3.0 or the 3D Internet.

Makes sense now? Probably not. As the cliche goes, "You've got to see it to believe it." In the future, you will not need to explain the concept of a virtual world to anyone, no more than you need to explain what the Internet is today. Until then, join the multitude of SL residents who try to explain it to their nonresident friends and family.

## WHAT IS LINDEN LAB AND HOW IS IT RELATED TO SL?

SL was created by and is hosted by **Linden Lab** (LL). As of this writing, Linden Lab (http://www.lindenlab.com) is a privately held firm headquartered in San Francisco, California. Founded in 1999 by Philip Rosedale (formerly VP and CTO of Real Networks), the company has a powerhouse of financial backers: Mitch Kapor, creator of Lotus 1-2-3; Pierre Omidyar, eBay founder; Jeff Bezos, Amazon CEO; and Ray Ozzie, Microsoft chief technology architect, to name a few.

Linden Lab represents the ultimate authority in SL, and you will find residents whose last name is Linden wandering about in SL. The best place to find them nowadays with SL being so large is in Linden Village.

In the company's own words:

> Linden Lab is a privately held company established to develop an extraordinary new form of shared 3D entertainment. Through its first product, 'Second Life,' Linden Lab offers a truly

collaborative, immersive and open-ended entertainment experience, where together people create and inhabit a virtual world of their own design.

## IS SECOND LIFE A GAME?

Whether SL is a game is a topic of great debate. Some would say SL is a game, in the same way that Sims On-Line or World of Warcraft is, whereas others would argue that SL is too open ended and without any artificially imposed goals to be classified as a game.

Those who say SL is not a game might argue it's no more a game than attending a friend's wedding is a game. I have attended weddings in SL and browsed the photo albums afterward. You are not there physically; the wedding itself is all enacted and presented virtually, but there are still two human beings on the other end of their computers making a commitment to each other.

Imagine you were confined to a wheelchair as a burn victim or you were housebound. What would it mean to you if you could interact with people all over the world on a social level where your RL attributes were not a consideration? What would it mean to walk like everyone else and even fly?

The answer to the question "Is SL a game?" boils down to your own definition of what constitutes work, leisure, and play and how you choose to approach SL.

David Kirkpatrick, *Fortune* magazine's senior editor, had this to say on the topic in his article "Second Life: It's Not a Game" (http://money.cnn.com/2007/01/22/magazines/fortune/whatsnext_secondlife.fortune/index.htm):

> Second Life is important not because it resembles a game, or because of how many people are signing up, or the big companies starting to do business inside it. What convinces me it is one of the most significant technology breakthroughs in history is that it is a platform on top of which users can create their own software and content, realize their ideas, and even make money.

Here is Philip Linden's take from a forum post on April 7, 2006. (Once you have your SL account, you will have access to all forum posts. The full text of Philip's post can be found at http:/forums.secondlife.com/showthread.php?postid=978622#post978622):

> I'm not a gamer, and SL isn't a game. From the start, we/LL observed that something like SL would have its first uses in entertainment, and then grow beyond those uses and people became more confident in the capabilities of the new platform/OS/whatever-we-want-to-call-it. So we focused on making SL very exciting and visceral and inspirational, but not on making it a game.
>
> The future that we are all most passionate about is creating a new version of the world with a fundamentally different and better set of capabilities, and then see what happens when we all move there. This means we want SL to be able to reach everyone in the world, to be able to scale to 100's of millions of users and millions of servers, and to remain an open decentralized system in which creativity rules.

I can tell you this much. The overwhelming response from all but one person I interviewed in the course of researching this book was "No, Second Life is not a game." Is it fun? Most definitely yes. Is it entertaining? Also a yes… But SL is something more.…

Just what SL will become remains to be seen.

And the secret is, it's up to you to decide!

## SL GEOGRAPHY AND GETTING AROUND

SL has a lot of geography to explore, and one of the first things you must learn is how to get around. You don't need to own land to enjoy SL, but if you decide you want your own plot, it will cost you.

### SL GEOGRAPHY

To give you an idea of the exploration potential, you need only look at the size of land available in SL. As of January 2007, SL contained virtual land that is the equivalent of over six times the size of New York's Manhattan Island.

Figure 1-1 shows a comparison of Google's aerial view map and SL's world map. The similarity may be shocking. Which is real and which is virtual? We come back to mapping in SL in Chapter 2, "Exploring the New Frontier."

**Figure 1-1**
*Second Life world map and Google maps.*

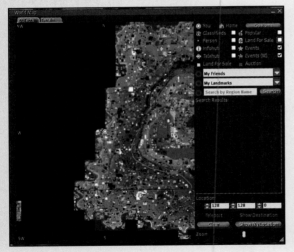

Land in SL is divided into **regions**. Regions are often called **sims**. *Sim* is short for *simulator*, referring specifically to the servers that simulate the SL world itself (there are other types of SL servers, which we get into in Chapter 12, "Practical Matters: Under the Hood of the Metaverse"). As of this writing, there are three **mainland** continents in SL and over 4,000 islands. Figure 1-2 shows the entire SL world zoomed way out and with all indicators active. The three continents are somewhat visible even at this range.

Mainland regions typically consist of many landowners living side by side just like in RL, with all its pros and cons.

Island estates are often owned by a single individual, corporation, or a group of like-minded residents and tend to be themed with more control over what you can and cannot build or do there.

A region has a name and 65,536 square meters of area. All locations in SL can be specified by the region name and x, y, z coordinates. You can reference SL locations in RL using a **SLURL** (Second Life uniform resource locator), which takes the following format:

SLURL **http://slurl.com/secondlife/<Region Name>/ <X>/<Y>/<Z>**

SLURLs can be broken down as follows; <Region Name> is the name of the region and <X>, <Y>, <Z> are the coordinates within that region. In this book, all locations in SL are indicated using this format. Think of SLURLs as the SL equivalent of RL addresses such as country, state, street, and home addresses or maybe a better analogy is that of global positioning system (GPS) coordinates. More on SLURLs in Chapter 2.

The geography or land of SL tends to be flat, +/– 4 meters in most mainland regions and +/– 100 meters on islands. However, the ground does not limit your building. Your home (or floating castle) may be up to 768 meters off the ground or underwater for that matter.

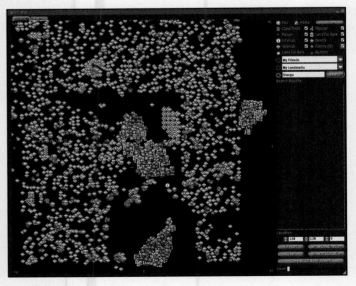

**Figure 1-2**
*The entire SL world.*

Land can be owned, rented, bought, and sold in SL. Land ownership has some very cool benefits, but you also start paying monthly fees to own land in SL. You learn more about owning and renting land, premium accounts, terraforming, and landscaping in Chapter 9, "Land Ownership, Terraforming, and Landscaping."

## GETTING AROUND IN SL

The typical way to move about within a region is to walk or fly from place to place. To get from region to region, the primary mode of transportation is the **teleport** (TP). You can teleport from location to location much more quickly than walking. You save locations in SL using **landmarks** (LM). Landmarks are basically a way to save and share locations by saving the region and coordinates.

To look around the world, you use a **mini-map** and **world map**. The mini-map is good for determining who is nearby and used locally within a region. The world map gives you a high-level view of the entire SL world. When I arrived in SL, I made it a practice every time I logged in to use the world map and teleport to a random spot. Try it a few times. You'll be happy you did. You will find interesting places and new people almost every time you teleport.

You learn how to get around in SL, teleport, create and share landmarks, and use the mini-map and world map in Chapter 2.

# SL CULTURE AND COMMUNICATION

RL people are represented in SL as **avatars**. Avatars are 3D visual representations of you as you exist in SL. That is, when others see you in SL, they see your avatar. When you join SL, you pick a default avatar, but you will want to quickly personalize your look. You learn all about avatars and how to make your avatar look the way you want in Chapter 4, "Your Avatar, Your Virtual Self." Figure 1-3 shows a small sample of avatar possibilities.

Once you know how to get around, you need to learn the mechanics of communicating and the cultural norms of SL. Let's touch on those next.

**Figure 1-3**
*A sampling of SL avatars.*

## COMMUNICATION

Communication between avatars in SL takes the form of a near real-time exchange of typed text. You do not audibly hear what someone types, nor do you hear that person's voice unless you're using some external means such as a phone call, voice over IP, or a conference call for larger groups. When someone "says" something, he is typing it into a chat window. When someone "hears" something, she is seeing the typed text in her own chat window.

There are two primary means of communication in SL: **chat** and **instant message (IM)**. Chat is public and heard locally by all nearby avatars, whereas IM is private and can be heard by those private parties no matter where they are in the world.

Chapter 3, "Communication and Social Networking," covers everything you need to know about SL communication including gestures, common mistakes, and even some tips on doing presentations in SL.

 NOTE

By the time you read this, SL will support voice. This is a major cultural change already sparking much debate about its pros and cons. We discuss this revolutionary change a bit more in Chapter 3.

## CULTURE

SL has its own culture and cultural norms. When you join SL, you agree to the Terms of Service (TOS) and a set of Community Standards (CS). The TOS and CS represent the legal and cultural norms enforced by LL. They apply any place in SL you go. We discuss more details about the TOS and CS in Chapter 12, "Practical Matters: Under the Hood of the Metaverse," and Chapter 5, "Second Life Culture and Relationships."

SL also has several thriving subcultures, each of which has its own cultural norms and social standards. These cultures include groups such as furries, vampires, and many sexual subcultures. To avoid becoming the SL police force, LL has given landowners a lot of power to allow or deny other avatars access to their land.

Many landowners have, therefore, established regional norms of behavior that are enforced. So, if you get involved in a SL subculture, it is worth learning the standards of behavior. They may be as simple as wearing a Guest tag when visiting or as complex as very specific requirements for how you dress, behave, and even talk.

You learn more about SL culture, SL relationships, and the steamy topic of virtual sex in Chapter 5.

## GETTING STARTED AND GETTING HELP

The following sections cover the basics of accessing SL and how to get help once you are **in-world** (or logged in to the SL client).

## GETTING THERE

Accessing SL is easy. The main problem with describing the process in a book is things change constantly. I can give you the general idea here, but expect your experience to be a bit different from what I have outlined.

### Step 1: Make Sure Your Computer Can Support SL

SL requires a pretty decent box. It requires a lot of CPU, a lot of memory (at least 512MB), and a modern graphics card. You also need a lot of bandwidth (broadband/DSL is best). You can check your PC, MAC, or even Linux box against the latest system requirements here:

http://secondlife.com/corporate/sysreqs.php

Julia Hathor notes: "Linden Lab's stated minimum requirements are generally thought (by the SL population) to be grossly inadequate. Any experience with this world will be either frustrated or facilitated by the quality of your computer and connection."

### Step 2: Create Your Account/Avatar

You create your account and avatar in SL by going to the main SL site and selecting Join Now.

http://www.secondlife.com/

### Step 3: Pick an Avatar Name

I suggest you give your avatar's name some serious thought. Your name is *not* among all the many things you *can* change in SL. Consider who you want to be in SL and what that person may be named.

People get to know you by your name, and the name you choose says something about who you are (or who you are role-playing). If you get into SL business, your name can quickly become your brand.

I picked my avatar name on a whim, Ansel Gasparini. I loved Ansel Adam's photography and my wife had nixed the name as an option for our first son, so I figured Ansel it was. Gasparini might imply I am Italian, but in all honesty, I don't remember why I picked it.

 NOTE

As of this writing, you may specify only a first name. You select from a list of available surnames. There is discussion about selling surnames (like domains), so maybe you will be able to buy your surname in the future.

### Step 4: Provide Credit Card Information

You may create an account for free! When you create a free or basic account, you may or may not provide a credit card. You might be asking, "Why would I provide a credit card for a free account?"

I strongly recommend that you provide credit card information. Allow me to explain: It used to be mandatory for individuals coming into SL to provide a credit card.

At some point, LL made it known the company was thinking about allowing new accounts to be created without providing any credit card information (removing the credit card requirement has increased international adoption). There were huge debates and quite a large uproar from many in the SL community. Some were concerned about **alts.** *Alts* (or *alternatives*) are additional avatars that are created and used by the same RL person. Another reason for concern was minors (children under 18 years old) coming into SL and being exposed to adults and adult content.

In the end, LL decided to proceed with allowing accounts to be created without a credit card. To address resident concerns, LL also enabled users to determine whether or not another avatar has provided credit card information and if this avatar has actually used that credit card.

Now, why would people want to know this? It turns out that a large number of **griefers** (residents who essentially bug other residents in some way or another) create accounts and do not provide any valid information—credit card or otherwise. So, some landowners use the lack of credit card information to ban these individuals from their land.

The bottom line is, if you do not have a credit card on file, you may be banned from some areas in SL solely for this reason.

## Step 5: Download and Install the SL Client

You need the SL client, software that you can download from the SL website, to begin. Download the SL client version that is right for your operating system. The client is free to use, and the source code is available as well if you are so inclined to use it.

http://secondlife.com/community/downloads.php

## Step 6: Arrive at Orientation Island

Once your account/avatar is created and you have the client downloaded and installed, you can log in and get started in SL. You start on Orientation Island.

Read on.

## GETTING HELP

The new resident experience is constantly changing as the SL population grows. A few key things will probably remain constant:

1. **Orientation Island:** You arrive first on Orientation Island, a small island with several instructional stations that explain the basics of SL. Current residents are not allowed on Orientation Island (except for SL greeters), so take your time and learn or just run on through. *"Look Mom, I'm running with scissors!"*

2. **Help Island:** The next stop is either Help Island or a welcome area. Help Island provides more of an SL atmosphere with additional objects, stores, tutorials, and **sandboxes** (areas to build in) for you to use.

3. **Welcome Areas:** Once you are through Orientation Island and Help Island, you arrive at a welcome area. These areas are often crowded with other new residents, but also older residents who like to hang out and help. Look out for those ready to exploit your newbieness. They may try to sell you something, get you to go somewhere, or get you to do something you don't want to do.

   Not all SL residents are like this, and you learn more about dealing with these bothersome individuals in Chapter 12.

4. **Greeters and Mentors:** Greeters and mentors are SL residents who enjoy or specialize in helping new residents get started. You will often find them on Help Island and in welcome areas. Feel free to approach these people and ask them questions or for help. You can tell who they are by looking above their avatar name.

5. **F1 Help:** The SL client comes with a pretty extensive help system. Press F1 and look for the answers to your questions.

6. **Live Help:** If all else fails, you can try Live Help. This connects you via IM to a volunteer support person (sometimes a Linden employee), who can help you address more technical issues. Live Help is not always manned.

Gwyneth Llewelyn's (see Figure 1-4) "Beginners' Guide to Second Life" has this to say about getting help:

**Figure 1-4**
*Gwyneth Llewelyn.*

> Welcome to Second Life! For all of you just starting, I hope you have lots of fun in this virtual world!
>
> My name is Gwyneth Llewelyn, and I'm a Mentor. This is a group of users—almost 1600 by now—who help newcomers to get started. You'll see them mostly at the Welcome Area—like on the Ahern complex, Waterhead or Plum, where most of you probably entered this world after leaving the Orientation or Help Island, or on one of the public sandboxes: Morris, Cordova, Goguen, Newcomb, Sandbox Island, etc.—places where everybody may freely build (but not sell items!). You can always ask Mentors for help, they are here for that!
>
> If your questions are very technical—mostly connected to objects or a bad/slow connection—you should get in touch with Live Help, an option you have on the Help menu on the top gray bar. They are also users, volunteering their time to answer your questions online. Finally, you may also find Liaisons. These are employees of Linden Lab, the company that runs this virtual world. You'll notice that all of them have the Linden surname. Lindens may sometimes be very busy answering questions of other players, so be patient if they don't reply immediately! Think of them as the in-world technical support staff of Second Life. They also have special tools not available to users to fix the most complex problems.

You can find the entire beginner's guide here and other great stuff at Gwyneth's Blog:

> http://gwynethllewelyn.net/

See her post on First Ever Questions:

> http://gwynethllewelyn.net/article125visual1layout1.html

## YOU AND YOUR INVENTORY

Before we go further, you need to know about one critical SL item and that is your **Inventory**. When you get started in SL, you already have some really cool stuff including different avatars, outfits, rocks, homes, a go-kart, fireworks, dominos, and so on. All this stuff lives in your Inventory.

Items in your Inventory remain there between logins or until you drag them out. Dragging items from your Inventory into the world or creating objects from scratch using building tools is called **rezzing**. If you take a basic building class, you'll often hear, "First, rez a cube."

You learn more about what's in your Inventory and how to use it throughout this book. You learn how to build your own items and save them in your Inventory in Chapter 6, "Building Basics." You learn about managing your Inventory as it grows larger and larger (as it will) in Chapter 12, "Practical Matters: Under the Hood of the Metaverse."

You open your Inventory using the Inventory button in the lower-right portion of your display, as you can see in Figure 1-5. Your Inventory contains two main folders: the Library folder, which contains everything that comes with SL; and a My Inventory folder, which is the place where all your stuff lives.

Now that you've arrived, let's explore what you can do here.

**Figure 1-5**
*Opening your Inventory.*

# WHAT DO I DO HERE?

Don't wait for me to tell you. There are no quests or structured play as you might find in a multiplayer game like Ultima On-line or Everquest. You need to find your own way. If you ask for help, there are many who are ready and willing to answer your questions. You might begin by searching for and finding an event or place that interests you.

We can only wish there was an SL travel guide. Most RL travel guides such as *Fodor's* or *Lonely Planet* need to be updated every year to keep pace with change. In SL, such a reference would need to be updated daily.

The Second Seeker and Second Tourist blogs are great starting points if you want exploration guidance:

> http://www.secondseeker.com/
> http://secondtourist.blogspot.com/index.html

Rather than explain what you could do here, I show you a few examples. Is it a definitive list? No. Is it the best of the best? Probably not. But again, I did not set out to write a travel guide. Try the ones you like, ignore the ones you don't, and search for the ones that are missing.

Do let me know when you've found something I should try myself!

## EXPLORING THE LANDSCAPE

Some really wonderful landscapes have been created in SL. They make you want to stop and just look around. One of the best known is Svarga.

SLURL Svarga can be found at **http://slurl.com/secondlife/ Svarga/128/128/0.**

In Figure 1-6, I'm roaming through a forest surrounded by a 100-meter sphere in the Dubia sim. You can find an interesting ruin here, and if you look hard, you may locate a cave as well. Will it be there if you go looking for it? Maybe. Maybe not. Things are not as permanent in SL as they are in RL.

**Figure 1-6**
*The forest in a sphere in the Dubia sim.*

SLURL The forest in Dubia can be found at **http://slurl.com/secondlife/Dubia/157/148/66.**

This SLURL gets you close to the sphere, but you're going to have to search to find it.

In Figure 1-7, I am standing next to a lava flow coming from the mountain above and meeting the sea in a steamy bath in the Chi sim. This sim has lot of surprises.

SLURL The Chi sim can be reached by going to **http://slurl.com/secondlife/Chi/132/109/52.**

**Figure 1-7**
*Lava meets the sea in the Chi sim.*

## SKYDIVING

There are many activities in SL, and new ones crop up all the time. One of the most fun (at least for me) is to go skydiving (see Figure 1-8). There are several locations where you can skydive, but one that has been around for a while is Abbotts Aerodrome.

While you can buy great skydiving gear such as the trailing smoke you see in Figure 1-8, you can start with free gear at the skydiving shop.

 Abbotts Aerodrome can be found at **http://slurl.com/secondlife/abbotts/ 160/152/71.**

**Figure 1-8**
*Skydiving at Abbotts Aerodrome.*

## HORSEBACK RIDING

Figure 1-9 shows my next-door neighbor riding over on horseback for a visit. In fact, you can ride just about any animal imaginable. How about riding an eagle, dragon, or dancing cow? There are many providers of animals to ride; use Search to find them.

In Figure 1-10 you can see me on a manta ray I designed and created. I really need some snorkel gear!

## VISITING MUSEUMS, MEMORIALS, AND ART GALLERIES

There are museums, memorials, and galleries to visit in SL. You may even take home a piece of virtual art for your virtual front yard. You visit the International Spaceflight Museum (see Figure 1-11) in Chapter 2.

**Figure 1-9**
*Horseback riding.*

 Drop in on the International Spaceflight Museum at **http://slurl.com/secondlife/Spaceport%20Alpha/ 94/125/75.**

The Oyster Bay Sculpture Garden is one of my favorite galleries because it's always changing. I had a Starax statue on loan there for a bit (see Figure 1-12). Yes, you heard me right, a virtual statue on loan to a virtual museum. Figure 1-13 shows Oyster Bay loaded up with resident-built hot air balloons ready for a launch festival. You can build and even fly your own hot air balloon in SL!

**Figure 1-10**
*Riding a manta ray.*

**Figure 1-11**
*Visiting museums: The International Spaceflight Museum.*

**Figure 1-12**
*Visit art galleries such as Oyster Bay.*

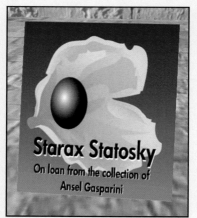

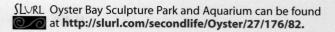
SLURL  Oyster Bay Sculpture Park and Aquarium can be found at **http://slurl.com/secondlife/Oyster/27/176/82.**

## GAMBLING AND GAMING

If gambling is your thing, there are many places to play casino games such as poker and slots. You can also find games that were created and popularized in SL such as Tringo, a kind of Bingo/Tetris hybrid (see Figure 1-14).

**Figure 1-14**
*Playing Tringo.*

> 👁 **NOTE**
>
> At the time of this writing, gambling in SL is still legal, but it is definitely coming under more scrutiny by the U.S. government and may become illegal by the time this book comes out.

## SAILING, SURFING, FLYING, AND RACING

You can surf, sail, fly, race, and even ice-skate in SL, all due to resident-conceived and built vehicles. You learn more about vehicles and how they are built in Chapter 10, "Particles, Vehicles, Animations, and Sculpted Prims." Figure 1-15 shows Malcolm Sydney catching a ride on Heather Goodliffe's scripted waves. Check out the Tropical Island Surf Shop for a rental board.

**Figure 1-13**
*Oyster Bay Sculpture Garden Balloon Festival.*

**Figure 1-15**
*Surfing in SL.*

*SLURL* Tropical Island Surf Shop can be found at **http:// slurl.com/secondlife/Quan%20Li/194/133/21.**

Figure 1-16 shows a sailboat race. You can purchase your own sailing yacht at Jacqueline's marina, shown in Figure 1-17. There are several other great locations to learn to sail in SL. Make sure to check out the classic flying Tako.

**Figure 1-17**
*Sailboats for sale at the marina in Eggar sim.*

*SLURL* Take this SLURL to Eggar sim:
**http://slurl.com/secondlife/Eggar/168/198/22.**

If go-karts or bumper cars grab you, see Figure 1-18 and accompanying SLURLs.

*SLURL* Go-kart racing can be found at
**http://slurl.com/secondlife/Igbo/79/233/351.**

*SLURL* Bumper cars are available at **http://slurl.com/ secondlife/Prim%20Hearts/134/31/29.**

## MEET OTHER NEW PEOPLE

If you just want to hang out and chat with other new residents, The Shelter is a great place. It is new resident friendly and can direct you to various classes in-world. You can see the house rules of The Shelter in Figure 1-19. You can also see the great pool and water slide available if you want to take a dip with new friends (see Figure 1-20).

*SLURL* The Shelter can be found at **http://slurl.com/secondlife/isabel/ 44/244/79/.**

**Figure 1-16**
*Sailing in SL.*

**Figure 1-18**
*Race some go-karts.*

**Figure 1-19**
*The Shelter House rules.*

**Figure 1-20**
*The Shelter poolside.*

## DISCUSSION GROUPS

You may also want to find a place with both new and long-time residents to discuss interesting topics. The Benicia Hill Community Center (see Figure 1-21) fits the bill for this. Whatever you want to discuss, you can find a group in SL doing it, and if you can't find the group, you can start your own!

SLURL The Benicia Hill Community Center is at **http://slurl.com/secondlife/Benicia/193/74/80.**

**Figure 1-21**
*Benicia Hill Community Center.*

## HAVE A DATE: DINNER, DANCING, AND THE TITANIC

If you want to do a date up right in SL, you can pull out all the stops and start with dinner. Yes, there is food in SL. Check out Karamel Madison's Kitchen Korner for a great selection of foods, wines, and other exotic fare (see Figure 1-22). Try preparing a meal at home for a nice surprise.

Next, go dancing. Search events or look for a club playing the music you like. You can meet in the formal attire-only Club Egret, as shown in Figure 1-24. I never dance the Tango in RL as well as I do in SL!

**Figure 1-22**
*Eating food.*

**Figure 1-24**
*Dancing at Club Egret: Formal attire only please.*

 Karamel Madison's Kitchen Korner can be found at **http://slurl.com/secondlife/ Kitchen%20Korner/203/ 68/42.**

Second, take a trip up to the top of a replica of Seattle's Space Needle for a view and a cup-a-joe (see Figure 1-23).

 The Seattle Space Needle is located at **http://slurl.com/ secondlife/Miramare/33/ 119/24.**

**Figure 1-23**
*Seattle Space Needle.*

 Check out Club Egret at **http://slurl.com/secondlife/ Gannet%20Island/125/129/24.**

Why not top off your date with something spectacular, like a visit to the bow of the Titanic for an "I'm on top of the world" moment, SL style (see Figure 1-25).

 You can find the Titanic at **http://slurl.com/ secondlife/Caribbean%20Wave/75/78/27.**

**Figure 1-25**
*A "top of the world" moment (visit the Titanic).*

## NIGHT LIFE AND MUSIC

One of my all-time favorite pastimes in SL is listening to the great live music performers in the wide range of venues. You can dance to the blues of Komuso Tokugawa live from Japan in your own living room (see Figure 1-26). You learn all about SL music and movie making in Chapter 11, "Photography, Music, and Movies."

**Figure 1-26**
*Dancing to live music.*

## ATTEND AN SL BIRTHDAY

Rosedrop Rust is a live performer in SL, and he hosted a great birthday. In SL, birthdays are celebrated on the year of your initial joining as an SL resident. Rosedrop did a reverse roast on all his friends and performed some exotic piano playing (or at least played on an exotic piano), as you can see in Figure 1-27.

**Figure 1-27**
*Rosedrop Rust's Babes on Grand.*

## CHILLING

You may just want to chill out, listen to the radio, and watch a sunset or moonrise in SL. There are plenty of places to do it. Figure 1-28 shows moonrise over my own land and an open air gazebo/roundhouse I built.

**Figure 1-28**
*Unwind by moonlight.*

## SHOPPING

Everyone wants to look good in SL, and there is a thriving clothing design industry with shops and malls galore to help you! I could fill a whole book with an SL shopping guide, but you will have to wait for that one. Use Search on Places to find what you're looking for. Even better, however, is to ask around. If you see someone with something you like, ask that person where he got it.

Stores in SL look a lot like stores in RL. Figure 1-29 shows Ayla Holt's Men In Action store. This is one of the best spots for hard-to-find good men's clothing. Just like in RL, the women have waaaay more options!

SLURL  The ::MIA:: Main Store can be reached at **http://slurl.com/secondlife/MIA/165/56/29.**

**Figure 1-29**
*Ayla Holt's Men In Action store.*

Figure 1-30 shows Calico Creations, a great store to buy an upgrade to your LL-issued hair.

SLURL  Visit Calico Creations at **http://slurl.com/secondlife/Calico%20Kitty/125/22/26.**

**Figure 1-30**
*Shopping at Calico Creations.*

## BUILD YOUR OWN STUFF

You can build your own things in SL, and, for me, this is one of the most enjoyable things about SL. Almost everything you see in the world was created by other residents just like you. If you can't find it, then build it! This book teaches you how, starting in Chapter 6, "Building Basics."

You learn about the basic building blocks of every object in SL called **prims**. *Prim* is short for *primitive*, which in 3D modeling lingo is the term for basic geometric shapes like cubes, spheres, cylinders, and tori. Prims in SL can be shaped, linked, and textured to form more complex objects.

We also cover some of the really cool SL prim properties like creating local lighting and using flexible prims for things like flags or bushes.

## CREATE TEXTURES, CLOTHING, AND SKINS

After you build what you want, you will want to add **textures** to make it look more realistic or surrealistic. Textures are 2D objects created in software like Photoshop to make things look real in SL. You can use textures to make something look rough, smooth, shiny, or even transparent.

You learn about texturing in Chapter 7, "Advanced Textures and Clothing." Also in that chapter, you learn how to use textures to create an avatar's skin and clothing. If you're interested in designing your own clothing, that is the place to start.

## BRING YOUR OBJECTS TO LIFE

Once you've built your house, you may want to add a door that opens, or perhaps you want your dragon to follow you around. SL offers a rich scripting language called the **Linden Scripting Language** (LSL). You don't have to be a scripter to get started with LSL. You learn the basics of scripting in Chapter 8, "Making the Magic: Scripting Basics."

## CREATE PARTICLES, VEHICLES, ANIMATIONS, AND SCULPTED PRIMS

If you have some background in computer animation, particle systems, physics, or 3D modeling, you may want to try your hand creating some of SL's more advanced objects and effects. You learn about all of these in Chapter 10.

# HOW DO I MAKE MONEY?

So, you've explored awhile, made friends, and built a few objects. You've collected a huge number of freebies in your Inventory, and now you want to go buy something cool. How do you get money without paying RL dollars?

Well, you can make money in SL, but let me be the first to tell you not to quit your day job! Before you even think about making money, you should first understand the currency you will be using.

Second Life has its own currency called **Linden Dollars**, abbreviated **L$**. You can use L$ to buy anything in SL, such as houses, yachts, animations, airplanes, fish, clothing, hair, skin, and sunglasses. You can also purchase land in SL using L$.

Unlike most multiplayer game companies that actively resist the buying and selling of virtual goods, Linden Lab has set up the Linden Exchange, or LindeX, where you can buy L$ with RL dollars and exchange L$ for RL dollars that show up in your PayPal account.

As one might expect, there is a currency exchange rate from virtual dollars to real ones, just like there is from one currency to another in RL. Figure 1-31 shows the exchange rate for September 2006 to March 2006. The L$ value as I write this is approximately 268 L$ to 1 US$.

Figure 1-31 also shows the cost of land charted at L$ per square meter. Land prices have risen quickly where the L$ exchange

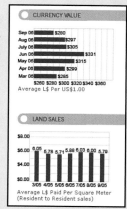

**Figure 1-31**
*Currency and land value charts.*

rate has remained relatively stable. There is, of course, a lot of variability based on location, location, location. For example, my latest land purchase in February 2007 cost me L$19 per square meter versus the average of L$6 per square meter in the chart. You learn about land ownership and why you might want to purchase land in Chapter 9.

So, back to the topic of how to make money in SL. The easiest way to get money in SL is to buy L$ using RL money. A little goes a long way. You can get a house for US $10, while a pair of jeans may run you 50 cents. But if you're looking for more of a challenge, you can earn money in SL by getting a job.

Be warned that to make money in SL, you really need to work for it. Just like in RL, there is no free lunch. The next section briefly describes common SL jobs.

## SL JOBS

Perhaps the first thing you should know about SL before you think about getting a job is that, unlike typical multiplayer games, in SL there are no character levels, and jobs are not a means to increase your character's skills. There are no quests or guided play in SL. You are who you are when you join, and you can choose to do whatever you like.

The hype cycle on making money in SL is in full swing, and before you set your hopes too high, be aware that very few people are making a RL living in SL. Some do make a living, and I am inclined to think there will be many more in the future, but doing this is about as extraordinary as becoming a rock star or a football player. You are more likely to make a living in SL by having a RL company hire you to do so. That said, if you're willing to work hard, you can afford all the cool stuff you want to buy. A more achievable goal, if you own land, is to be able to make enough at your SL job to cover the cost of your usage fees or "tier"—in other words, to make enough to fund your SL.

The needs of SL residents continue to evolve, and the need for specialized skills will follow suit. Therefore, the jobs in SL today may not be the same jobs in the future. For information on SL jobs, check out the Knowledgebase article "Guide to Jobs in Second Life" at http://secondlife.com/knowledgebase/article.php?id=077.

Here is a quick summary of common SL jobs:

- **Animator:** Create animations using Poser and Avimator for all the different things you can do in SL. Learn about how to do this in Chapter 10.

- **Builder:** Build things to sell or for others. Learn about building in SL in Chapter 6.

- **Business Owner:** Decide to create, market, and sell things in SL, including creating your own stores.

- **Couch Potato/Camping Chair:** Some people want your avatar to sit in their space (it increases the published "popularity" of their spot). They will pay you to sit or dance in one spot.

- **Dancer:** Many club owners would like to have dancers (typically female) dance in their clubs. You may be asked to do this with fewer and fewer clothes. If you're getting started, one perk of this job is that you may be provided with a freebie avatar makeover.

- **DJ:** If you have an audio stream or nice music library, you can DJ at clubs in SL just like you do in RL.

- **Escort:** Escorts in SL will show you around and show you a good time. This is a very high paying profession in SL, if you're willing to undress and do all (virtually). You will need to learn the subtleties of the trade, find a location, and get some pose balls (animations for avatars).

- **Event Host:** There are music events, weddings, and more serious nonprofit activities in SL. If you know how to draw a crowd and set up the acts, this may be the role for you. Learn a bit about hosting musical events in Chapter 11.

- **Fashion Designer:** Clothing design is H-O-T in SL. Whether you are already there or aspiring, you can make a name for yourself in the competitive field of fashion design.

- **Gambler:** Well, there are casinos in SL and slots. Maybe you can make your living here, but don't count on it.

- **Landlord:** Many residents are not too interested in locking into monthly land-use fees. Building apartments and renting may be for you.

- **Model:** All the fashion designers need models for their clothes (at least if they don't have alternative avatars, or alts, that they use for this purpose).

- **Musician:** If you can play, and you have an audio stream, you can play venues in SL. Avoid the mainstream music moguls and play for an international audience. Learn about music in SL in Chapter 11.

- **Real Estate Broker:** Well, as they say, it's location, location, location. If you can find a deal in SL, buy low, and sell high, perhaps you can make your money buying and selling land in SL.

- **Scripter:** Making the magic in SL often requires some development or scripting skills. Pair up with a builder or texture artist and you may find your path. Learn more about this in Chapter 8 and Chapter 10.

- **Shop Staff:** Sometimes business owners just need a helping hand. They may want you to help people shopping, or they may want you to be a bouncer in their bar.

- **Texture Artist:** Everything in SL boils down to textures. If you are highly skilled in Photoshop, you may want to pair up with builders to take their builds to the next level.

This is by no means a comprehensive list! Part of SL's appeal is the possibilities for new jobs that are invented every day.

# HISTORY, POLITICS, AND GOVERNMENT

SL V1.0.0 was released on July 23, 2003. LL published subscriber data, which indicated that in April 2001 there was one registered resident in SL. What a lonely existence it must have been as compared to today. SL already has a rich history for being around such a short time. You can find out quite a bit on the SL history wiki at http://slhistory.org/.

The wiki includes, among other things, the release notes for all SL versions. Figure 1-32 shows a screenshot from the beta version of SL. You can find an interesting article on the alpha version with screenshots at http://archive.gamespy.com/previews/december02/secondlifepc/.

**Figure 1-32**
*SL beta screenshot.*

There has been a string of firsts in SL chronicled in the SL history wiki. A few interesting ones are listed here:

- **First Sim/Region:** Da Boom; **Current Owner:** Rockwell Ginsberg

- **First privately owned region on the mainland:** Indigo; **Owner:** FlipperPA Perigrine

- **First Private Island:** Elysian Island (Cayman)

- **First Sim/Region Auctioned:** Then Island now Avalon; **Winning Bidder:** Fizik Baskerville

- **World Turns a Year Old: MP3 of Philip Linden's speech** (http://www.slinked.net/slmedia/ PhilipLinden-SecondLife1YearAnniversary- 20040626.mp3) "OK, testing one, two, three…my gosh it seems like this thing actually works."

On October 18, 2006, SL reached over 1 million registered users. Many thanks to Gwyneth Llewelyn (http:// gwynethllewelyn.net/) for taking the screenshot shown in Figure 1-33 only 5,088 users after the moment. While this was not likely the number of unique human SL users, it was a tremendous milestone for LL and was really the point at which the "hockey stick" of SL growth began.

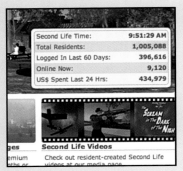

**Figure 1-33**
*One million of us.*

You may hear the term *Governor Linden* used to refer to Linden Lab and its role as the ultimate governmental authority. Governmental policy is determined and handed out in the form of the Terms of Service (TOS), Community Conduct standards, and software updates. You learn more about these in Chapter 12 and Chapter 5.

Gwyneth Llewelyn made this note in her post on SL government: *"Without even a representative form of government, it seems far-fetched to argue that Second Life boasts a participatory democracy. This world, in which what Linden Labs says goes, would be better classified as a benevolent dictatorship."*

To be fair, LL seems more to aspire to be the all observant but not present in daily life deity. LL has no desire to act as governor or king. It created the world, set up the basic laws of its universe, and every so often intervenes when circumstances warrant or RL legalities intrude. It is notably absent from the day-to-day dealings within the community itself.

At the end of the day, LL is running a business. In this, its primary function is to make sure the world exists tomorrow and remains attractive for the majority of its residents to spend their time and their money. My experience has been that LL has always taken pains to address and incorporate resident feedback every step of the way. You can contribute to the direction of SL by adding your voice to others and engaging LL on the topics that are of most concern to you. You can learn about the various communication venues

in the Linden Communication Venues Guide (http://secondlife.com/knowledgebase/article.php?id=357).

 For example, visit Linden Village, which houses the in-world offices of LL employee's: **http://slurl.com/secondlife/Kirkby/177/209/45.**

One blog to keep on top of is the Official Linden SL Blog (http://blog.secondlife.com/).

Other informative venues are the town hall meetings, which are usually held to gather feedback on some important topic or explain a decision LL has made.

There are also ample opportunities for you to volunteer your time in SL to help others get started in various capacities such as greeters, mentors, and instructors. You can find in-world locations for volunteers at http://wiki.secondlife.com/wiki/Inworld_Locations_for_Volunteers.

# AN INTERVIEW WITH CRAIG ALTMAN

Craig Altman (see Figure 1-34) is best known for his couples' animations, which can be found at his chain of stores called Bits and Bobs. I exchanged Q&A via notecards with Craig. Here is what he had to say about his initial SL experience:

**Figure 1-34**
*Craig Altman.*

***Ansel Gasparini:*** *How did you discover SL?*

**Craig Altman:** After playing games like Quake online and Ultima Online for 3 years, I was looking to try more friendly games, I tried the Sims online but found very few players, and those that were there were AFK [away from keyboard]. While looking on a Sims online forum to find out if anything happens there, I came across a post by someone talking of SL being better and the post had a link, so I signed up.

*AG: What was your initial experience like?*

CA: Confusing really, most of the precepts of other online games don't exist here, you don't need to eat, you can carry infinite things, you can just go anywhere in a split second, there are no NPCs (non player characters), and their seemed no actual way to play it.

I fell foul of the fact it's actually frowned upon to drop litter or rez objects wherever you want, a lot of old SL players seem to forget that in most other online games, the land is not owned by a player, and objects dropped just disappear after a short while, in fact it was actually a good thing to drop unwanted things on the ground in Ultima Online, that way other players could pick them up if they needed them.

I spent the first week here wandering aimlessly, chatting to people, building things on land that would let me (as I had seen some land say "you are not allowed to build here", I assumed if that didn't happen then I was!)

*AG: Why did you decide to stay? When did you decide to buy land?*

CA: At that time I was working a night shift, so I didn't spend a lot of time in SL, but when I did I mostly spent it at events at a club in the game who someone I had met took me to, it was there I met Jenny, we got on really well, she ran events at the club so I would help, yes many use the word "glorified chatroom", but to me it was nice and relaxing after those other types of games, nothing I needed to do if I did not want to.

It was about 3 months before I owned land, up until then the need for land in SL had confused me, you can carry infinite things and you have no actual need for a house, after a while I realized SL is not really about things you need, its more about making and having the things you could not in real life, rather like "if you could have anything you wanted, what would it be?"

*AG: What is the most annoying thing newbies do that they should not do?*

CA: That's a hard one really, as a lot of annoying things that happen are very often unintentional (like me littering others land), if the annoyance is intentional then it applies to all players, it's by no means only new players that do things like that.

Because SL is so different to other online worlds if a new player offends through not realizing a thing is not the done thing in SL, then how the mature player explains this to them is very important, to mute and ban or react in a hostile manner is likely to make the new player react in kind, he may then "shoot first and ask questions later" to the next player to approach him.

I guess the answer to the question is probably panhandling, often using the word need, do you ever need money in SL?

All online games do have people who ask for money, and often abuse you if you refuse, this I always found funny because in other games basically there is a set way to make money, you either go kill monsters/do quests etc., so any person asking for money in those games is basically saying "I can see you have gone out and spent ages doing what I know you need to do to get money, but I'm lazy so I'd rather you did that and give me it, than I do it myself".

In SL of course there is no set way to make money, so its more understandable, but in my first months here I never found I needed money really, I did work here as an event host for a short while, but it was more for fun than money, so it's not need its want, others should not be made to feel guilty about what someone else wants.

*AG: Any general advice for new residents?*

CA: If you came in because of tales of people making fortunes in SL expecting the streets to be paved with gold you are in for a disappointment, lately it seems the SL is marketed that way, if money is your motive you will find its very much like RL, its a lot of effort.

Also bear in mind that those are real people, don't act in a way you would not in RL if that person was stood in front of you, it amazes me how having anonymity changes people sometimes.

## SUMMARY

In this chapter, we started a journey together to learn about SL and discover your virtual artist, explorer, and entrepreneur! Now you may have a little better idea about what SL is, what you can do here, and how you might make friends and money as well.

But nothing compares to hands-on experience. In the next chapter we dive right in and start learning how to get around in SL, including how to fly and teleport.

If you have not already created your own SL avatar and gotten in-world, now is the time to do it! See you on the other side!

*One bit of advice I would give ANYONE.*
*Take the time, and spend a few days coming back;*
*SL is so vast it takes a while to sink in.*
*If you have trouble finding something you like,*
*it's because there is so much to find.*

**—Wise Clapsaddle**

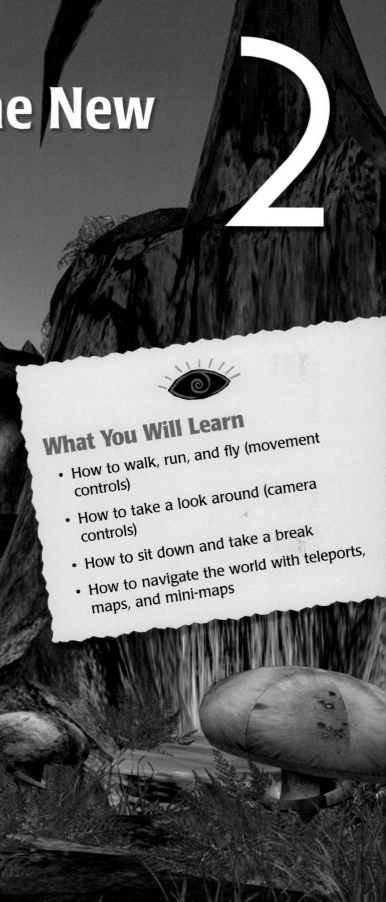

# Exploring the New Frontier

## 2

One of the lines used to describe Second Life is "It's like real life, only you can fly." This chapter shows you how to do just that. You learn how to look around you, walk, run, fly, teleport, and use SL maps. It's all about *how* to explore, not *what* to explore. The discoveries and all their surprises and thrills are left up to you.

Many people move too quickly through orientation and help islands, only to get frustrated trying to use SL controls. Some may be tempted to skip this chapter altogether and jump straight to the fun stuff, but trust me: Your ability to move around efficiently and manipulate your point of view (the camera) will greatly improve your enjoyment of SL. This chapter contains essential knowledge.

So, as Wise said, take your time, learn to look, move, and explore. Your investment in the basics will pay off. Let's begin by walking around.

## What You Will Learn

- How to walk, run, and fly (movement controls)
- How to take a look around (camera controls)
- How to sit down and take a break
- How to navigate the world with teleports, maps, and mini-maps

# GETTING AROUND: MOVEMENT CONTROLS

If you're not already familiar with moving around a 3D space on a computer, learning to walk, run, and fly in SL takes a little getting used to. However, getting started is easy, and with a little practice, moving around will become second nature to you. The following sections provide the basic movement controls for walking, running, and flying.

## WALKING AND RUNNING BASICS

There are several ways to move your avatar around in SL. Using the arrow keys seems to be the easiest method for most new residents to grasp (see Figure 2-1). The up arrow moves your avatar forward. The down arrow moves your avatar backward. The right and left arrow keys turn your avatar in either direction.

Yes, that's it! I suggest you log in right now and try it. Here are a few exercises that will help you stretch your legs:

- Pick something you see in the distance and walk over to it.
- Try walking in a circle or a figure eight.
- Find a road or sidewalk and try to follow it.
- Try to follow another avatar around.

You start out in SL walking, but you can also run. Figure 2-2 shows me walking on the left and running on the right. When running, your avatar moves more quickly and uses a different animation as well. You toggle run mode on/off by pressing Ctrl+R.

Movement Controls

**Figure 2-1**
*Use the arrow keys to move your avatar forward/backward and turn around.*

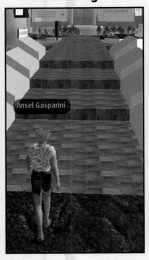

Walking   Running

**Figure 2-2**
*To switch between walking and running mode, use Ctrl+R.*

## LEARNING TO FLY

Flying is very useful in SL to move quickly from point to point, and it's easy to learn. While flying, your avatar moves even faster than when running. Flying has its own set of animations (taking off, landing, hovering, and flying). You use the Home key to toggle flight mode on/off. You can also use the Fly button at the bottom of your display to toggle flight mode (see Figure 2-3).

**Figure 2-3**
*Toggling flight mode on/off.*

When you enable flight mode, your avatar takes to the air and hovers there, waiting for your instructions. Just like when you are walking, you use the arrow keys to fly around (see Figure 2-4). The up arrow moves your avatar forward; the down arrow turns your avatar around and flies back toward you. The left and right arrow keys turn you around. In addition to the arrow keys, two other keys allow you to control your height. These are the Page Up and Page Dn keys. Page Up increases your altitude/height, and Page Dn decreases your altitude/height.

I suggest you try this out now! Hit the Home button to take off; then press and hold Page Up and watch yourself soar. Once you are up a good way, use the arrow keys and fly around.

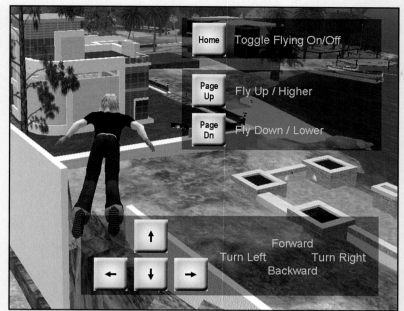

**Figure 2-4**
*Using the arrow keys and Page Up/Page Dn to fly.*

So, now you may want to know how to get down. Try falling! Once you are high up, toggle flight mode off by pressing the Home key. You should see your avatar start to plummet to the ground with a plummeting animation. Landing this way doesn't hurt you, but it is ungraceful and looks like new resident behavior.

You can land gracefully by pressing Page Dn until you are just above land and then disabling flight mode, but this takes two steps. An easier approach is to enable the auto-fly option. With auto-fly enabled, you automatically enter flight mode when pressing Page Up and automatically exit flight mode when pressing Page Dn and land on the ground or some other object. You enable auto-fly mode by editing your preferences (Ctrl+P or Edit->Preferences). On the Input & Camera tab, you can find the auto-fly option (see Figure 2-5).

Now try landing again. From walking on the ground, press and hold Page Up. You should automatically enter flight mode and start climbing. Now, by just pressing and holding Page Dn, you descend, land gracefully, and exit flight mode. Great job! Superman couldn't have done it any better!

There are two other things you should know about flying in SL before we move on. First, there is a maximum height you can fly under your own power. The ceiling is around 200m. Try this experiment: Press and hold Page Up. Keep holding it and, at some point, you stop going up. Now let go of Page Up. You slowly start to descend until you get to less than 100m, at which point you stop descending and hover. I call this your *maximum hover height*. That is a height where you can stop flight movement with the arrow keys and still remain at the same elevation, neither ascending nor descending.

The second and last thing to know about flying is that land/sim owners can dictate that their land is a no-fly zone. If you find yourself somewhere that you are unable to fly, this may be the case. A small glyph at the top of your display (it includes a red circle with a line through it) indicates whether the land/sim you are on is no-fly.

**Figure 2-5**
*The Input & Camera tab enables you to set auto-fly and other options.*

> **TIP**
>
> In SL, you can use jet packs, vehicles, and other scripted ways to go higher than this 200m limit. You might ask yourself: Why would I want to fly that high? Well, skydiving for one thing! The second thing is that you can build up above 200m, so there is much to be seen and explored up above, such as cloud castles and the like! Typically, builds located high up are there for privacy reasons, so be respectful of others during your explorations.

## ALTERNATIVE MOVEMENT CONTROLS

Besides using the arrow keys for movement, SL offers many other movement options. I've listed them here so that you can try them for yourself. Some may be easier for you to use than others. Keep what works and ignore the rest.

- **WASD keys:** If you've done any PC gaming in your life, you'll take to basic movement in SL quite quickly by using the WASD keys in place of the arrow keys. The only gotcha is that you can't use these keys to move around if the chat window is open.

- **Go Here menu:** You can right-click on any visible land (not an object or avatar) and select Go Here from the pie menu. Your avatar will automatically move to that point.

- **Page Up or E:** While not in flight mode, you can use these keys to jump.

- **Page Dn or C:** While not in flight mode, you can use these keys to crouch.

- **Onscreen movement controls:** You can enable a set of onscreen controls that allow you to move around by clicking on them with your mouse instead of using your keyboard keys. You do this under View->Movement Controls (see Figure 2-6).

**Figure 2-6**
*Onscreen movement controls.*

# TAKING A LOOK AROUND: CAMERA CONTROLS

Now that you know how to walk, run, and fly around, you need to learn the second most essential SL skill: controlling what you see. You learn in this section how to control exactly what you're looking at, all without moving your avatar! As with movement, looking around takes some getting used to, but with a bit of practice, you will be a natural in no time.

When you first arrive in SL, you see the world in *default* view. Your perspective is such that you look forward and slightly above your avatar, as you can see in Figure 2-7.

**Figure 2-7**
*The default view: looking forward over your avatar's head.*

The default view is like having a virtual cameraman hovering behind you filming you the whole time as you watch. You may have noticed that as you move around, the camera follows your avatar. You can also take control of this camera and move it around the world independently of your avatar. Learning how to control this camera enables you to

- Look at your own face while standing still.
- Look at what is behind you.
- Frame the perfect picture.
- Look at what you're building from different points of view.
- Zoom way out and see what's going on all around your avatar.
- Get a close-up view during a wedding even while you sit in the back row.
- Look deeply into the eyes of your dance partner.

There are two main perspectives in SL: the default view (which is what you have been using) and mouselook. In default view, you can see your avatar and the SL viewer interface (see Figure 2-8). In mouselook, it appears that you are looking through the eyes of your avatar, and much of the SL viewer interface is hidden (see Figure 2-9). In Figure 2-8 and Figure 2-9, my avatar is standing in exactly the same spot. Now let's see how to control the camera to look around in each of these perspectives.

**Figure 2-8**
*The default view near the top of Bliss Basin.*

**Figure 2-9**
*Mouselook view near the top of Bliss Basin.*

## CONTROLLING THE CAMERA IN DEFAULT VIEW

*I'm convinced one of the biggest reasons people leave SL too quickly is because they have trouble learning how to 'see' in it. After a few days, using the camera controls becomes as natural as turning your head, but in the beginning, it does take some getting used to.*

**—Chosen Few**

As you have seen, in default view you are looking at your avatar from above and behind, and while you move around, fly, or walk, your viewpoint automatically follows your avatar. This is great when you're moving. But what if you want to stop moving and take a look around? It would be inconvenient if you had to turn your avatar and walk up to everything that looked interesting just to get a closer look. Fortunately, using the camera controls, you can move your viewpoint independently of your avatar's location. Let's learn how, right now!

### Looking at an Object or Avatar (Focus Controls, Alt+Mouse)

One of the first things you will want to do after wandering around a bit is to look at yourself or take a close look at nearby objects. You can easily do this using focus mode. Focus mode points the camera at your avatar or any object you select. The focus object essentially becomes the centerpoint of your view.

To look at an object, first move your mouse pointer over the object you want to look at. Hold down the Alt key and press and hold the left mouse button. Now, by dragging your mouse forward/backward, you can zoom in/out on the object. By moving the mouse left/right, you can rotate around the object (see Figure 2-10).

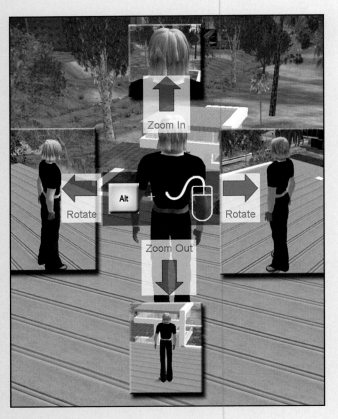

**Figure 2-10**
*Rotating and zooming the camera around an avatar or object using Alt+Mouse.*

Try it now! Hold down the Alt key and click/hold the left mouse button on the back of your avatar's head. Drag the mouse backward to get a bird's eye view of your avatar. Drag the mouse forward to get a close-up of your hair. Now, try moving the mouse to the right or left. You should see your viewpoint rotate around to the front of your avatar. Do you know what color eyes you have?

> ✋ **TIP**
> To return to the default camera position in default view, press the Esc key.

## 360° Rotation Around an Object or Avatar (Orbit Controls, Ctrl+Alt+Mouse)

Another keyboard/mouse combination allows you to orbit 360 degrees around any object or avatar. This is extremely useful when you're building so that you can look at an object from many angles because SL does not support multiple viewpoints.

To orbit an object, first move your mouse cursor over the object you want to see. Hold down the Alt and Ctrl keys and click/hold the left mouse button. At this point, you can rotate around the object just like in focus mode by dragging the mouse to the left/right. Dragging the mouse forward or backward rotates the view up over or down below the object in the center (see Figure 2-11).

Try it now! Hold down the Ctrl and Alt keys and click/hold the left mouse button on the back of your avatar's head. Drag the mouse backward to look at the top of your avatar's head. Drag the mouse forward to get a bug's eye view of your avatar. Now try moving the mouse to the right or left. You should see your viewpoint rotate just like it did in focus mode.

> ✋ **TIP**
> When in orbit mode, you can use your mouse scroll wheel to zoom in and out. Now you are in control of what you see!

You should now know how to rotate all around any object you see in SL and take a close-up or far-away view of that object. You should also know that you can get back to your default camera position by pressing the Esc key.

> 👁 **NOTE**
> You can use your camera controls while hovering as well. If you want to see what's directly below you before landing to avoid landing on someone, Ctrl+Alt+click on your avatar and rotate your view. You can see in Figure 2-12 that I have rotated my view and zoomed out to take this shot from 180m up.

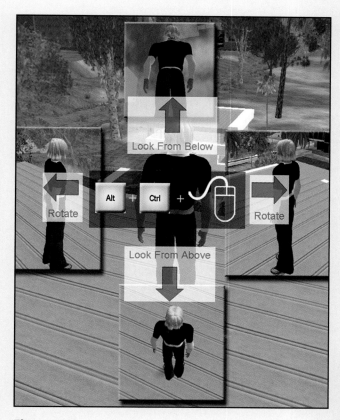

**Figure 2-11**
*Orbiting the camera around an avatar or object using Ctrl+Alt+Mouse.*

**Figure 2-12**
*You can use camera controls during flight to check for a clear landing.*

## Shifting Your View Right/Left and Up/Down (Pan Controls, Ctrl+Alt+Shift+Mouse)

The final camera control for default view allows you to fine-tune your view by moving the camera up, down, left, and right. This process is called *panning*. This type of control is most useful in SL photography or machinima when you are trying to fine-tune a camera location.

To pan, move your mouse cursor over an object you want to act as the anchor point for the pan. Hold down the Alt, Ctrl, and Shift keys and click/hold the left mouse button. At this point, you can pan the view. Dragging the mouse to the right moves the viewpoint to the left. Dragging the mouse to the left moves the viewpoint to the right. Dragging down moves the viewpoint upward; dragging up moves the viewpoint downward. If this movement seems counterintuitive to you, think of it as though you are selecting the screen itself and moving it around (see Figure 2-13).

Try it out!

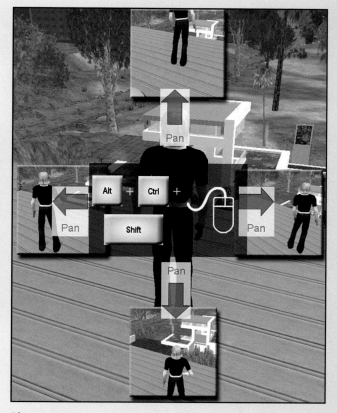

**Figure 2-13**
*Panning the camera using Ctrl+Alt+Shift+Mouse.*

## CONTROLLING THE CAMERA IN MOUSELOOK VIEW

The second perspective available in the SL viewer is called *mouselook*. As the name suggests, when you are in mouselook view, you look around by moving your mouse. Unlike the default perspective, when you are in mouselook, you are looking directly out of your avatar's eyes versus from a camera behind your avatar (see Figure 2-9).

 NOTE

In game design, the default SL view is called *third person view* because you are seeing yourself (your avatar) from the perspective of a third person. Mouselook view is called *first person view* because you are seeing the world from your own eyes.

While in default view, you enter mouselook by using the scroll wheel to zoom in or choose View->Mouselook. Try it out! Enter mouselook and then use your mouse to look around you. Dragging forward looks up; dragging backward looks down. Dragging right/left rotates your avatar around just as if you were using the arrow keys. You exit mouselook by pressing the Esc key or zooming back out.

Mouselook is good for the following situations:

- Looking at something up close (like a book)
- Reducing UI clutter if you want to take in a view
- Looking around at the same time as you move around
- Navigating tight spaces
- Using weapons in combat situations (this is incredibly useful)

Your ability to look around using the mouse while walking/flying is one of the greatest advantages of mouselook IMO. Use it if you like it; lose it if you don't.

 NOTE

Mouselook changes the behavior of the left/right arrow keys when you're walking/flying. In default view, the left/right arrow keys rotate your avatar. In mouselook, the left/right arrow keys move your avatar from side to side (commonly called *strafing* in gaming circles). Avatar rotation is accomplished by dragging your mouse left/right.

## ONSCREEN CAMERA CONTROLS

Like the onscreen movement controls, SL offers onscreen camera controls as well. Select View->Camera Controls and you see the controls shown in Figure 2-14. The disc on the left is rotate left/right and up/down. The disc on the right is pan left/right and up/down. The bar in the middle zooms in and out.

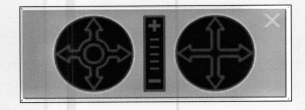

**Figure 2-14**
*Onscreen camera controls.*

# SITTING DOWN AND STANDING UP

After you have been flying a bit, you may start to feel fatigued. In SL, you can sit on almost any prim and therefore on almost anything you see. Simply right-click on something and select Sit Here. In Figure 2-15 I picked the nose of the space shuttle at the International Spaceflight Museum!

In Figure 2-16 I am sitting nicely. Can you say major flight delay, NASA!

To get up from a seated position, you use a button in the lower middle of your display that says Stand Up. Simply click this and you will stand.

**Figure 2-15**
*Right-clicking on an object gives you options including Sit Here.*

**Figure 2-16**
*Sitting on the nose of the space shuttle.*

**NOTE**

When you start sitting on things in SL, you will notice some quirks. For example, the default "sit" pose is what you see in Figure 2-16, and this works great for cubes and basic chairs. However, in this case, my feet are embedded in the nose of the shuttle. No big deal.

Some seats, couches, and chairs have different seated positions called *poses*. The pie menu may be named "Recline" or "Relax." When you sit on these objects, you may find yourself reclining or sitting with your legs crossed. These chairs contain a scripted item with a custom animation for the seated avatar. Some chairs have a *pose ball*, or an object near the chair itself that you sit on instead of the chair. By convention, pose balls are spheres, but they don't have to be. Often pose balls are blue or pink. Again, by convention, blue pose balls contain male animations and pink pose balls contain female animations.

For now, stand up. There is more exploring to do!

# TELEPORTING

SL is vast. It is so big that it is not possible for any one human to visit all of SL, expecially if you just walk. Fortunately, there is another way to travel in SL, called *teleporting*. When you teleport, you move immediately from one location to the next. As with real life, exploring by walking, driving, or teleporting gives you vastly different experiences. The fastest way to move between geographically separate regions is to teleport, but don't forget to try sailing, driving, or taking a train ride!

## FINDING AN EVENT, PLACE, OR PERSON

To start exploring SL is to spend some time on the Places tab in the Search dialog (see Figure 2-17). Click the Search button at the bottom of the screen to open the Search panel. Select the Places tab and type a key word (such as **spaceport**) in the Find box. Then press the Search button next to it (yes, another search button). The results are shown on the left listed by most traffic. Traffic is a rough indication based on the number of avatars and amount of time they spend in a location. Traffic rises and falls over time. Select an item to see more details. At the bottom left is the Teleport button. Clicking this button takes you to this location.

You also want to learn how to send your friends a teleport. This can be accomplished from your Friends list (accessed by selecting the Friends button at the bottom of the display). Select an online friend and click the Teleport button (see Figure 2-19). The fact that the button reads "Teleport" is somewhat confusing. It would be better if it read "Offer Teleport." You are really offering to teleport your friend. He must accept the teleport in order for it to happen.

Finally, if someone is not in your Friends list, you can locate him if you know his name by using the People tab on the Search dialog. Below the person's picture, you see a button labeled Offer Teleport (see Figure 2-20).

**Figure 2-17**
*The Places tab on the Search dialog.*

## NOTE

If you're interested in more details about searching, choose Help->Second Life Help (or press F1). Once you're in the help system, choose Home->Basic Help->Finding Your Way. There is a nice write-up here on how Traffic works.

**Figure 2-18**
*Click Teleport to accept the offer or Cancel to pass.*

**Figure 2-19**
*The Teleport button does not teleport you but instead offers a teleport to your friend.*

## ACCEPTING AND OFFERING A TELEPORT

You won't be in-world long before you meet someone who wants to show you something. Typically, the person teleports there ahead of you. Once she gets there, she offers you a teleport. You see a blue dialog pop up (see Figure 2-18), and you can either click Teleport or Cancel. If you select Teleport, you arrive at the same location as the person who offered you the teleport (assuming she's still there).

**Figure 2-20**
*The Offer Teleport button lets you offer a teleport to anyone.*

(see Figure 2-22). Landmarks show up in your Inventory under a folder called Landmarks, although you can move them anywhere. If you right-click on a landmark in your inventory, you can select Teleport. If you are big explorer, landmarks can quickly get out of control, so it helps to organize them in some way using subfolders. That way, you can quickly teleport to your favorite spots.

**Figure 2-22**
*Choose Create Landmark Here to record places you like.*

## NOTE

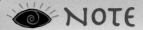

You may want to consider how well you know someone before accepting a teleport. Here is one resident's experience, *"When I was new, I accepted an invitation from someone I didn't know, without realizing of course that the sender had no interest in me in particular; he/she had just randomly spammed invites to as many people as he/she could find. When I arrived, I found myself right in the middle of a porn party! There were lots of less than tasteful RL pictures all over the walls. Lesson learned, don't accept random teleport offers."*

## ARRIVING VIA TELEPORT

When you teleport, you momentarily see a black screen (see Figure 2-21) as your avatar is moved from one simulator to another (or perhaps within a simulator) to the destination.

When you arrive, things start to appear around you. Typically, you should wait a bit before you start moving around. This is one aspect of *lag*, a word you will hear often in SL. Behind the scenes, SL is downloading all the information your client needs to show you what is going on in the new location.

## NOTE

You can give someone a landmark by bringing up her profile in the Search tool. You see a place that says, "Drop inventory item here." Open your Inventory and drag the landmark onto this spot. You are notified if that person accepts your offer. If she's offline, you are notified that the inventory item has been saved on her behalf.

**Figure 2-21**
*The black screen signaling that you are arriving.*

## SAVING A SPOT: LANDMARKS

The first time I entered SL, someone offered to show me a few things. He teleported me around to several spots, and when I logged on the next day, I realized I didn't know the names or locations of several interesting places I had visited.

So, a key thing to exploring SL is to record the places you like. You do this by creating *landmarks*. A landmark is basically a reference to a particular location. To create one, use the World menu and select Create Landmark Here

## TELEHUBS/ LANDING POINTS

On some land, you arrive at a defined entry spot (or telehub), regardless of the location you landmarked or are trying to reach. If this is the case, you may see a red beacon (see Figure 2-23) and a red arrow pointing to the spot you had attempted to teleport into. You can get rid of this beacon by clicking on the red arrow or by simply just walking to that spot.

**Figure 2-23**
*A red beacon after teleporting.*

## GETTING BACK HOME

You can pick one home spot by moving your avatar to the location you like and then selecting World->Set Home Here.

You cannot set your home to any old place. You can set your home only on your own land, within land deeded to a group of which you're a member, or to a mainland Infohub, which is a common area like the Watershed welcome area.

Once you have your home base set, you can always return there quickly by choosing World->Teleport Home or pressing Ctrl+Shift+H.

Figure 2-24 shows both the Set Home and Teleport Home options.

**Figure 2-24**
*You can set a home and, once it's set, return there quickly.*

# MAPS, MINI-MAPS, AND SLURLS

Do you use Google maps? Ever tried the satellite view? Well, SL has its own mapping features that would put Google maps to shame if they were available in RL. For explorers, knowing how to use SL maps is a must. Figure 2-25 is a screenshot of Google maps next to the SL world map (also shown in Chapter 1). Can you tell the difference?

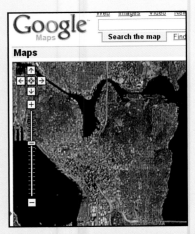

**Figure 2-25**
*Google and Second Life world maps.*

## WORLD MAP

To launch the SL world map, click the Map button at the bottom of your display or press Ctrl+M. Figure 2-26 shows a larger screenshot of the SL world map.

Your location is shown by a small white circle, outlined in yellow (as you can see in the key at the top-right in Figure 2-26). If your "home" location is on the part of the map you're looking at, it is indicated by a light blue house icon. You can enable many other icons, such as where other people are, land for sale, events going on, as shown in Figure 2-26. There is much you can do here, so play around a bit. Try zooming in/out for starters (if you zoom way out, you'll understand what people are talking about when they say something like "the northern continent"). You can also click and drag to move the map around.

**Figure 2-26**
*The SL world map.*

**Figure 2-27**
*You have many options for icons to mark various things.*

Among the many cool things about the world map, I really like two: teleporting and finding friends.

First, you can use the map to teleport anywhere you like in SL: Just double-click the location or left-click (which leaves a red marker) and select the Teleport button.

**NOTE**

You may not arrive at the exact point you picked because land owners can set up their land in such a way that all arrivals are to one or more specific locations. Land owners may also secure their land so you can't get there, but this is typically not the rule in SL.

You can zoom way in on the world map as well (see Figure 2-28). Everything shown has been created in SL. The world map is updated periodically (LL says every 24 hours, but there is evidence it takes longer), so essentially SL has a global satellite system that keeps you up to date on what is built/moved/removed and updates are free!

**NOTE**

Here are a few tidbits that you may care about at some point. Anything built up to 300m in the air shows up on the world map. Anything higher than 300m is not displayed on the map. The term *skybox* refers to an enclosed space in the air that is used for privacy; these areas are typically placed higher than 300m to keep them off the map, so they're less likely to be found by strangers. Island/estate owners can decide whether they want their land on the world map at all or if they want it hidden from the public.

**Figure 2-28**
*Zooming in on the world map.*

The second, really cool thing about the world map is the capability it provides to locate your friends. Friends must grant you permission to do this. Once permission is granted, you can select a friend from the drop-down menu, and the map will show where he is at that moment. Figure 2-29 shows the location of a friend of mine, Pannie Paperdoll, while she remained trapped at the Big Brother house in Kingdom of Media.

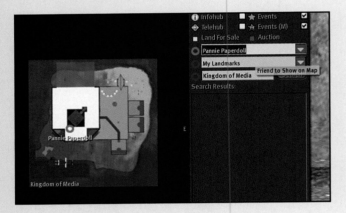

**Figure 2-29**
*Locating a friend on the world map.*

Once you find out where your friends are, you can teleport to this location and drop in on them unannounced. So, the lesson here is be careful whom you grant this permission to, particularly if you intend to do any virtual dating.

## MINI-MAP

The other map available is called the *mini-map* (see Figure 2-30). This is more of a "radar" screen showing what you are seeing in your general vicinity. Your avatar is at the center, and the direction you are facing is shown by a triangle with you at the apex. The size and shape of the triangle represent your field of view.

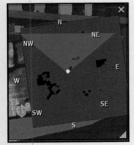

**Figure 2-30**
*The mini-map.*

When you turn your avatar, one of two things happens in the mini-map, depending on your preferences settings. Either the triangle rotates within the mini-map, or the mini-map itself rotates around the triangle. Which setting is best is entirely up to you and controlled by choosing Edit->Preferences, the General tab, and the Rotate Mini-map setting.

By right-clicking on the mini-map, you can set the zoom level. I find the default setting to be just fine. You can also select the mini-map and use your scroll wheel to zoom in/out.

The main purpose of the mini-map is to show you who and what are immediately around you. If you are in an area with other avatars, you see green circles, green Ts, and upside-down Ts (see Figure 2-31). The green circles represent avatars at the same altitude as yours. A T shape indicates someone above you, perhaps flying or standing on a mountaintop. An upside-down T indicates someone below you.

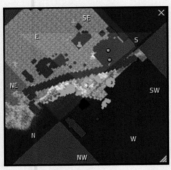

**Figure 2-31**
*The mini-map shows who is around you.*

## SLURLS

The final topic on maps covered here is Second Life URLs (SLURLs). URL stands for uniform resource locator, but it is basically a web link. So, http://www.secondlife.com is a URL, just like http://www.google.com. A SLURL is just like a URL except that it points to a location inside SL. SLURL is pronounced as one word (*slurl*), not as letters. When SLURLs were first introduced, the title of the Linden blog about them was the rhyme "Hurl a SLURL."

If you click on a SLURL in a browser, it takes you to a web page that shows the SLURL's location on the SL world map. From there, if you have the SL client installed, you can directly teleport to this location (see Figure 2-32).

SLURLs can be put on your website, on your MySpace page, in your blog, or in an email. The form of a SLURL is simple:

SLURL **http://slurl.com/secondlife/<Region>/
<X>/<Y>/<Z>/**

Replace <Region> with the name of the sim and <X>, <Y>, <Z> with the coordinates. You can see all this information at the top center of your SL client while you are in-world.

**Figure 2-32**
*Click on a SLURL and you are transported to this page.*

If you are creating SLURLs for business purposes, you can also pass additional information to display. You can get help creating a SLURL or learning more about them here:

 **http://slurl.com/build.php**.

As you have seen in Chapter 1, all SLURLs in this book use this icon to distinguish them from regular URLs.

# TUTORIAL: A VISIT TO SPACEPORT ALPHA

In this tutorial you discover how to explore SL using all the tools and techniques covered in this chapter. We visit the International Spaceflight Museum, located in the Spaceport Alpha sim, but feel free to pick any place you like.

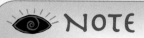 NOTE

If you are not at your home location, you may want to save a landmark at your current location so you can return there after this tutorial.

## STEP 1: SEARCH AND TELEPORT TO A LOCATION

At the bottom of your display, click the Search button or choose Edit->Search or press Ctrl+F. Select the Places tab and type **Spaceport Alpha**. You should see the International Spaceflight Museum (see Figure 2-33). I picked this place because it's fun to explore and is generally not very busy, so you may have the place to yourself. If you would rather try out your new skills in a social setting, try searching for an event on the Events tab.

At the bottom of the search panel is a button labeled Teleport. Click it, and you're off to your new location.

**Figure 2-33**
*Searching for the International Spaceflight Museum.*

## STEP 2: TAKE A LOOK AROUND

Take a look around; there is a lot of cool stuff here. Enter mouselook view by either zooming in with the mouse scroll wheel or choosing View->Mouselook. Drag your mouse around to look around a bit. You should see a walkway, several rockets, a satellite, and a planet over your right shoulder. Exit mouselook using the Esc key.

Note the plaque on the floor in front of you (see Figure 2-34). To see what it says, hold down Alt and left-click Hold on the panel. This locks the focus onto the panel. Now you can drag the mouse forward to zoom in.

If the plaque is not quite centered, try holding both the Ctrl and Alt keys and then click and hold the left mouse button and drag it around to fix the view.

**Figure 2-34**
*The arrival area at the International Spaceflight Museum.*

## STEP 3: VIEW THE VISITOR'S GUIDE

To your right, you see two books on a table. Use your view controls again to focus on a book, zoom in, or rotate your view. The left copy is the visitor's guide. Left-click on the visitor's guide to "touch" it.

You get a "notecard" that contains text about the International Spaceflight Museum. You can keep this, in which case it is put in your Inventory under Notecards, or you can discard it.

You could also right-click on the visitor's guide to get the pie menu. Notice the Touch menu option available here (see Figure 2-35).

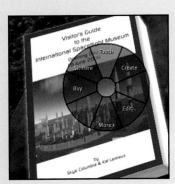

**Figure 2-35**
*Right-clicking on the visitor's guide to touch it.*

## STEP 4: TAKE A WALK OR RUN

Take a walk down the wide walkway in front of you (see Figure 2-36). Try pressing Ctrl+R to jog if you like.

After a bit, you come to an open amphitheater presentation location. On your left, you pass a map of the complex. This is also something great to take a look at and hone your camera controls.

Use your camera controls again to check out the map (see Figure 2-37).

**Figure 2-36**
*The map is ahead on your left.*

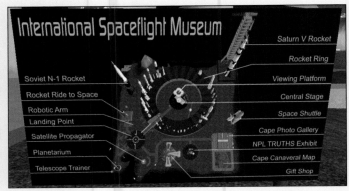

**Figure 2-37**
*The map of the museum.*

## STEP 5: TIME TO FLY

Have you really held off from flying so far! The museum has a space shuttle here, and I don't feel like walking. Press the Home key, or if you have auto-fly enabled, just press and hold Page Up to fly (see Figure 2-38).

Climb to about 75m (using Page Up/Page Dn). You can see how high you are by looking at the top of your screen. The three numbers there (see Figure 2-39) represent the x, y, and z coordinates of your avatar within the simulator (in this case, Spaceport Alpha).

The SLURL for this same location is the following:

 **http://slurl.com/ secondlife/Spaceport% 20Alpha/94/125/75/**

If you fly to the right, through the circle of rockets, you can find the space shuttle.

**Figure 2-38**
*You're flying!*

**Figure 2-40**
*Use the world map to get your bearings.*

Spaceport Alpha 94, 125, 75 (PG) - International Spaceflight Museum

**Figure 2-39**
*The x, y, and z coordinates of your avatar are displayed at the top of the screen.*

## STEP 6: GET YOUR BEARINGS

To get your bearings, bring up the world map and your mini-map using the buttons at the bottom of the screen. In the world map, zoom all the way in (using the mouse scroll wheel), and you see the Spaceport Alpha sim (see Figure 2-40). Check out the mini-map to see who else is around (count the green dots if there are any).

## STEP 7: TAKE A SEAT

As noted earlier, you can sit on almost anything in SL. Fly up close to the space shuttle, right-click the top of the big fuel tank, and pick Sit. You should see something that looks like Figure 2-41.

Use the Stand Up button when you're done taking in the view. Be ready, though, because you will no longer be flying after you stand up.

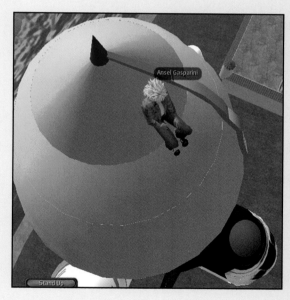

**Figure 2-41**
*Sitting on the space shuttle fuel tank.*

## STEP 8: GET A PICTURE

OK, the grand finale of the tour is to save a snapshot for your scrapbook. First, rotate the view around so you can see yourself. Remember, you press Alt, left-click, and drag left/right. Zoom to where you like the shot by dragging up/down. For finer orbital control, use Ctrl+Alt.

Click the Snapshot button at the bottom of your screen. You can select three options for what to do with your snapshot: Send a Postcard, Upload a Snapshot, or Save Snapshot to Hard Drive (see Figure 2-42). Select Save Snapshot to Hard Drive if you don't want to pay an upload fee, or if you want to use this picture in the picture frame tutorial coming up later, pay the L$10 upload fee.

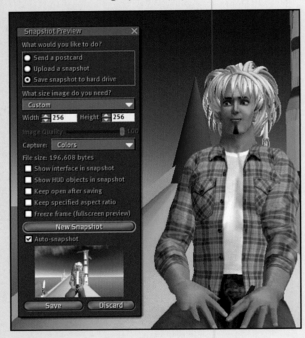

**Figure 2-42**
*You can choose from three options for what to do with your snapshot.*

## STEP 9: RETURN HOME OR PICK ANOTHER SPOT

Your final step is to return home or, better yet, pick another spot! To return home (assuming you have set a home location), select World->Teleport Home or press Ctrl+Shift+H (see Figure 2-43).

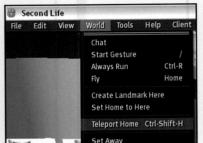

**Figure 2-43**
*It's easy to return home.*

# SUMMARY

In this chapter, you learned how to walk, run, and fly using SL movement controls. You also learned about the two perspectives, default and mouselook, and how to control the camera in each view. You learned how to find locations and teleport to them. And finally, you learned how to use the world map and mini-map to you get your bearings in the vast space of SL.

Now that you understand all this, you are almost ready to attend an event. Since events are generally loaded with other avatars, you need to learn how to communicate and interact with others in SL. That's what we cover in the next chapter.

*We mostly learn from each other in SL.*

**—Anika Davison**

# Communication and Social Networking

# 3

Second Life (SL) is a very social world. You communicate in SL via typed text. However, unlike real life (RL) chat and instant messaging, in SL you can see the people you're talking to. They may look beautiful, dangerous, furry, armed, or even naked. In any case, you can be more creative communicating not only using text, but also using gestures and other techniques you learn in this chapter.

Technologies such as IM, chat, Webex, teleconferences, and videoconferences do not offer the rich communication options that SL does for groups of people who are not co-located. I asked my friend Anika Davison about advice she had for new residents in SL.

## What You Will Learn

- The basics of communication in SL
- How to make your avatar gesture and express emotions
- Common pitfalls, mistakes, and privacy
- Tools for communicating and networking with groups in SL
- How objects communicate in SL
- Effective SL presentation skills

Here's what Anika had to say:

"We mostly learn from each other in SL. I know a lot of what I have learned socially was from some of my best friends in SL. I found it easier to talk with my friends and have them walk me through it and I do the same for them. There are people who are in the welcome area, who have been in SL for sometime willing to help newbies out."

To learn to communicate in SL you should make friends, ask questions, and, above all else, listen to what others have to say. You can read this chapter and learn about the mechanics of communication in SL, but the culture and social aspects of SL are constantly evolving, so get out there and talk to each other!

# SL COMMUNICATION BASICS

Communication between avatars in SL takes the form of a near real-time exchange of typed text. You do not audibly hear what someone types. When someone "says" something, that person is typing it into a chat window. When someone "hears" something, he is seeing the typed text in his own chat window. While these are the facts, you will quickly discover the immersive qualities of SL lead you to use terms such as *saying* and *hearing* versus *typing* and *seeing*. So, that's what I do in this chapter.

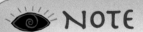 NOTE

As of this writing, an upgrade is planned that supports voice (that is, if you talk into a microphone plugged into your computer, others will hear what you say if their avatars are nearby). This will be a major cultural change in SL and is already sparking much debate about the pros and cons, with avatars lined up on both sides of the aisle.

There are two primary means of communication in SL: chat and instant messaging (IM). In general, chat is public and IM is private. Chat is used to communicate between you and whomever is around your avatar locally. IM is typically used to communicate between you and one other individual (although it is possible to establish IM with a group or selected set of individuals). Chat is a local; you

must be present to receive it. IM messages you receive no matter where you are in-world. Table 3-1 shows a quick comparison.

**Table 3-1    Chat and IM Comparison**

| CHAT | IM |
| --- | --- |
| Public | Private |
| Many to Many | One to One or Selected Groups |
| Broadcast Locally | Transmitted Anywhere In-World |

It is a big advantage if you are already familiar with IMing in RL. Typing speed and accuracy are also big pluses.

There are two reasons why knowing how to chat is advantageous: first, all the acronyms used, and second, the "culture of chat," as Kymber Schnook (see Figure 3-1) put it to me one evening. Here is an excerpt from our discussion.

**Figure 3-1**
*Kymber Schnook.*

**Ansel Gasparini**:
*Does someone need to know IM/chat to communicate in SL?*

**Kymber Schnook:** certainly makes it easier, but not essential, not so much the mechanics, but the culture of chat

*AG: What is the culture of chat?*

KS: hmmmmm, the language, the timing, the structure. There is etiquette to be followed and jargon to learn. It's easier for me to consider basic errors. ALL CAPS, FOR EXAMPLE means you are shouting or angry and is a common beginner mistake. The timing is a more subtle issue.

KS: I have a tendency to write in incomplete sentences, to clue someone in to the fact that...

KS: I'm still talking (finishing a thought). A lot of people do. Ellipses are handy for asking others to wait...

KS: giggle, The jargon's prolly the biggest hurdle and the acronyms

There is a culture to chat, as Kymber points out. It turns out that listening in SL is just as important as it is in RL, and it can be just as challenging. There are distractions. You may try to think/type ahead of the person you're talking to. Someone may "talk slowly" by typing more complete sentences than you feel you need to understand her point, or maybe she is just a slow typist.

It also helps a great deal to learn some lingo to communicate in SL, particularly if you haven't used chat/IM in RL. You can find a lot of resources on the Web that offer libraries of chat abbreviations and emoticons such as ;-) for winking. Take a look at the section "Slang and Acronyms" for a sampling to start. Learning to communicate in SL takes some getting used to, but if you practice, take it slow, pay attention, and listen, you'll do fine.

Let's jump into the mechanics and some of the fun tips and tricks of SL communication.

# CHAT: LOCAL AND PUBLIC COMMUNICATION

As mentioned, the two primary forms of text communication in SL are chat and IM. The following sections cover chat, which is a way of communicating publicly in a local area. What you say in chat will be seen by all avatars who are nearby, but not those far away or in another SL location altogether. Chat is public. That is, you can't decide which avatars can or cannot hear you. Let's get into how to do it.

## CHAT BASICS

Click the Chat button at the bottom of the SL user interface (UI), and a blank line appears, ready for you to type into. In Figure 3-2, someone has typed **hello there**. At this point, he has not hit the Return or Enter key, and no one has seen/heard what was typed. After he hits the Return or Enter key, *You: hello there* appears in his UI, as shown in Figure 3-2. Any avatar close by can see what has been said. However, instead of *You: hello there*, others see something like *Ansel Gasparini: hello there,* where Ansel Gasparini is the name of the avatar who spoke.

**Figure 3-2**
*Before and after typing "hello there" in the chat window.*

When you're communicating through chat, anyone (or anything) within 20 meters can hear what you say, just like in RL. So, picture this: You're talking to someone, and you see another avatar walk up. At this point, the RL person behind this avatar can hear what you're saying. By default, if you are farther away from a conversation, the text is in shades of gray instead of white, and eventually you will not see the text at all as you move beyond the 20m range.

On occasion, you might want to communicate more broadly to those around you, say, at an event or large wedding when you're the maid of honor or best man. To do this, you shout in SL. Shouting extends the radius where you can be heard from 20m to 100m.

When you shout, you see *You shout: <text>* in the chat window. You can see this in Figure 3-3.

**Figure 3-3**
*Shouting as it appears in the chat window.*

Your avatar also animates differently, showing that you are shouting. You can see me shouting in Figure 3-4! You can shout either by clicking the Shout button in the dialog (next to the Say button), or you can press and hold the Ctrl key and press Enter after you've typed your text.

**Figure 3-4**
*My avatar shouting.*

## CHAT HISTORY

Notice that the text of your conversations disappears from the screen after a few seconds. If you happen to fall behind in a conversation, or maybe if you just want to reread something, don't worry, you can. Simply click the History button (or press Ctrl+H), and you see the stream record of chat since you last logged in (see Figure 3-5 for an example).

In addition to the typed chat text from other avatars, SL provides more information in the chat stream, such as when a friend logs in or someone accepts an item you offered. Objects can also talk to you (which we discuss in a bit). Figure 3-5 shows a chat history. The first line (in green) is my Hug attachment telling me how to use it. The second line tells me a friend of mine, Pannie, is Online. The third line tells me another friend accepted an offer from me. Next, a group member has given me a note to read. Finally, (in white) you see what I (Ansel Gasparini) typed into the chat window.

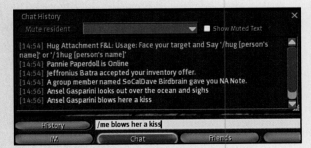

**Figure 3-5**
*Chat history.*

# IM: PRIVATE AVATAR-TO-AVATAR COMMUNICATION

Instant messaging (IM) is used to communicate privately and without regard for an avatar's location in-world or even her online status. IM is used for three primary purposes:

- Communicating privately with another avatar
- Communicating privately with someone whose avatar is not within chat/shout range
- Communicating privately within a group of individuals regardless of their location

## IM BASICS

To communicate via IM, you use the IM dialog. Open this dialog by selecting the IM button in the lower left of the SL client. A dialog like the one in Figure 3-6 appears, where you type messages. You may conduct several IM sessions at the same time; each one appears as a different tab. In Figure 3-6, you can see one tab labeled Heather Goodliffe; this is where I type IM messages to Heather and where I see her returned messages.

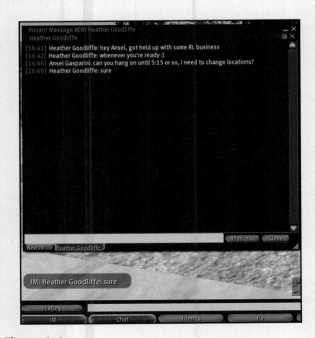

**Figure 3-6**
*The IM dialog box.*

You can start IMs by using several methods, such as from the New IM tab on the IM dialog, by right-clicking on a nearby avatar and choosing Send IM, or from any user's profile found using Search->People.

You may see IMs in the chat stream at the bottom of your display. IMs in the chat window are prefixed with *"IM:"*. You can see an IM from Heather in Figure 3-6: *"IM: Heather Goodliffe: sure"*. Even though they show up here, they are not visible to others around you as would normally occur with chat. If you find this confusing, you can disable this feature in your preferences by choosing Edit-> Preferences, Communication tab, and then disable Include IM in Chat History.

IMs are private and not seen by anyone else. In other words, an IM sent to an individual can be seen only by that individual, and one sent to a group can be seen only by members of the group. While you typically use IM to communicate with someone who is not physically (OK, virtually) in the same SL location as you, you can also use IM to carry on a side conversation with someone while involved in conversation with several avatars in the main chat stream.

This capability leads to an interesting social dynamic that is not possible in RL. For example, you can say *IM: Ansel Gasparini: That Boris Pendragon is so full of himself* to someone sitting next to you without having to lean over and whisper and without Boris ever knowing he is being discussed in real time.

A skilled SL resident can carry on multiple conversations via chat and IM. However, it is rude to keep someone waiting to hear back from you while you're talking to someone else. It's kind of like trying to talk to someone in RL while you carry on a conversation on several cell phones at once.

Just as you would if you were at dinner with someone and your cell phone rang, it is polite to say, "Sorry, I need to handle an IM for a sec" before breaking away from a conversation (see Figure 3-7).

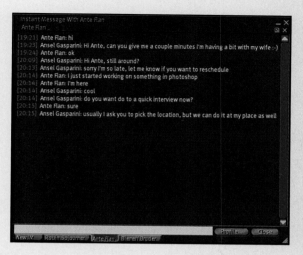

**Figure 3-7**
*You follow the rules of politeness in IM just as you would in real life.*

## IM AND EMAIL

When IMing someone, you may see a message indicating this person is not online and that your message will be saved until she logs in again. IMs are saved if you are not online, and this leads to an interesting challenge in SL: handling all the new IMs waiting for you when you log in. If you don't handle them before you log out, they are lost. If you find yourself frustrated and in this situation, you can change a few preferences under the Edit->Preferences ->Communication tab. Enable Log Instant Messages and Show End of Last IM Conversation. When you IM someone, you see the logged/past IMs.

### NOTE

There is an upper limit on the number of IMs a user may have stored. Very popular avatars or business owners may reach this cap.

You have the option to have IMs sent to an email account as well while you are not in-world. When someone sends you an IM, an email message with the text is sent. You can reply to this message within a short time window, and your reply text will come back as an IM to the person in

SL. I truly love this RL/SL cross-over feature, but it also has its downside if you get a lot of IMs.

You can enable or disable this feature through the Communications Preferences dialog in the SL client. You can also enable/disable it by logging into your account on the SL website, as shown in Figure 3-8.

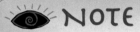

**Figure 3-8**
*You can change settings so that IMs go to an email account.*

> **NOTE**
>
> SL has an object called a *notecard* that is basically a text document which can be stored in your inventory and shared with others. It is often more appropriate to send someone a notecard if he is offline rather than a long set of IMs, which may generate separate emails.

# EXPRESSING YOURSELF VISUALLY: ANIMATING YOUR AVATAR

Now that you've learned how to type to communicate, you can begin to add some pizazz and motion to your avatar. Before 3D virtual worlds, chat was text only, so various ways were invented to express more emotion and action, such as emoticons like the classic smiley :-). SL gives you many tools to animate your avatar to express emotions and actions while chatting.

The following sections cover the various ways you can augment your chat to be more expressive.

## TEXTUAL "GESTURES" AND EMOTING

Two-dimensional chat systems supported methods for you to express emotions and actions in words to augment the "verbal" chat.

SL does this as well with the /me command.

In Figure 3-9 you can see I typed **/me blows her a kiss.** After I hit Return, SL reformats this message into an action. Perhaps I will get a kiss in return? Simple things like typing **/me nods** give your communications a more realistic feel than typing **yes**, **I understand**, **really**, and so on.

Even better than the /me command are SL gestures, which we cover next.

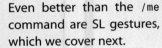

**Figure 3-9**
*Blowing a kiss textually.*

## GESTURES

What's the use of a 3D avatar if you can't make it do what you want? You learned earlier that when you walk, your avatar's animation changes to a walk animation, and when you're standing, your avatar is shown standing, and so on. But what if you're talking to someone and you want to laugh, cry, clap your hands, jump for joy, or pump your fist in the air? You can do all that and more with SL gestures.

The first step in using SL gestures is to activate (or enable) the ones you want. To do this, go to your inventory and look for a folder called Gestures, as you can see in Figure 3-10.

If you right-click on any gesture, you can select Activate, and

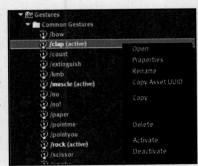

**Figure 3-10**
*The Gestures folder.*

you should see the gesture go bold with an (active) indicator. This gesture is now ready for use.

There are several ways to use a gesture. You can start one using the pull-down menu, keyboard shortcuts, or gesture menu, or you can simply type a gesture shortcut. Find the approach that works best for you.

In the example shown in Figure 3-11, I enabled a gesture called /clap. First, I type **Hey that was /clap great**! When I press Enter, the chat window displays *You: Hey that was great!* It does not display my typed gesture text /clap. However, you can see my avatar is performing the chat gesture at the same time the chat is displayed. Some gestures include an audible component as well, so others can hear you clapping or laughing, for example.

**Figure 3-11**
*A clapping gesture.*

It's that simple. I have met a few people who are very effective with gestures, and I wish more people used them in SL. They add a lot to face-to-face meetings. You can also buy new gestures from several stores in SL (use Search to find current locations), and once you've learned how, you can make your own!

## EMOTER HUDS

After you have spent some time in SL, you may notice that the faces of avatars are kind of wooden. Avatars have a kind of blank look all the time. To fill a need for better facial expressions, SL residents have created *Emoter HUDs* (see Figure 3-12). *HUD* stands for *Heads Up Display*, a term from a kind of display that does not block a user's view.

**Figure 3-12**
*An example of an Emoter HUD.*

In RL, HUD technology was first introduced in military aircraft to project vital information into the pilot's field of view so he would not have to look away from the action. In SL, HUDs are resident-created extensions of the SL interface that allow you to do various things.

Emoter HUDs extend your UI and enable you to pick from a variety of facial expressions. You learn more about HUDs in Chapter 4, "Your Avatar, Your Virtual Self."

Emoter HUDs are used often in SL photography work but also can enhance a chat greatly if you can afford to buy one. You can buy them at various stores throughout SL, and there are also several free Emoter HUDs available. Try Yandi's Junkyard to start. And as with everything else in SL, you can learn to make an Emoter HUD yourself, if you are so inclined. Figure 3-13 shows Kymber sticking her tongue out at me with an Emoter HUD active!

**Figure 3-13**
*Emoter HUDs help to create facial expressions.*

## ANIMATION OVERRIDES

Let me just add a quick note on the topic of animation overrides (AOs). We know that avatars have a set of default animations for when you walk, run, fly, land, fall, and even type (see Figure 3-14). The use of AOs is fairly mainstream (some might say essential). AOs allow you to add personalized flair/expression, by replacing the default walk animation with, say, a sexy, hip-swinging runway walk or a casual macho saunter. The downside of AO use is that they sometimes interfere with other animations and pose balls. In addition, in very large crowds or laggy areas, you may be asked to remove them to improve performance for everyone.

If you're interested in finding one, try searching for "animation overrider." Several freebies are available. Sometimes you will find AOs built into objects you wear, such as walk animations built into advanced shoes.

**Figure 3-14**
*The default animation: typing.*

# SOCIAL NETWORKING AND COMMUNICATION TOOLS

There are millions of residents in SL, and you may meet many once and never again, but there are those who become friends, those who are neighbors, and those you want to keep in touch with. You may also want to form groups around like interests or for business purposes.

Unless you have an incredible memory, you need some way to organize your friends and your interests.

SL offers several tools for social networking and organization. These are *calling cards*, a *Friends list*, and *groups*. Let's see how each is used.

## CALLING CARDS

Calling cards are like business cards in RL. They offer a quick way of cataloging the name and contact information for an avatar. You offer someone a calling card by using the right-click pie menu over her avatar and selecting More until you see Give Card, as shown in Figure 3-15.

**Figure 3-15**
*The Give Card option in the pie menu.*

Calling cards show up in your inventory under a folder by the same name. In your inventory, you can right-click on a calling card and either start an IM (Send Instant Message) or offer a teleport (TP), as shown in Figure 3-16.

It is polite to ask for a calling card from someone whom you would like to contact again in the future but whom you may not know well enough to add to your Friends list.

**Figure 3-16**
*Right-clicking a calling card yields several options.*

> **TIP**
>
> You can initiate a semiprivate group IM without creating a group, by creating a folder in your calling cards area (for example, Ansel's Conference Call). Drag the calling cards of the people you want into that folder. Right-click the folder and select IM All.

## FRIENDSHIP

To establish a more formal connection to someone, you can create a friendship relationship. You do this by right-clicking on the avatar whom you want to establish a friendship with and selecting the Add Friend option from the pie menu (see Figure 3-17). You can also add a friend by opening the Friends list (via the Friends button at the bottom of the screen) and following the prompts to add the person's name to your list. This capability is useful when the person you want to add is not in front of you at the moment.

**Figure 3-17**

*You can select the Add Friend option from the pie menu.*

**Figure 3-18**

*Three things to know about friendship.*

A common newbie mistake is to use Add Friend on someone without asking first! You are, in fact, establishing a joint relationship, not just adding this person to your own private Friends list. Read on before you do it!

Establishing a friendship with someone is a mutual decision. You both must agree to the friendship, and you will both have each other's names in your Friends list. When you select Add Friend, a window appears on the other person's screen stating that you are offering friendship. When someone offers you friendship, you see a similar window and can accept or reject the offer.

It is considered rude to offer friendship to someone without first asking. Be polite and ask first, and if that person agrees, then use Add Friend.

In addition to enabling you to quickly access someone's profile, start an IM, or TP someone, friendship also includes a few other permissions you should be aware of before you agree to be someone's friend. You can control these three friendship options by checking or unchecking them in the Friends dialog, as shown in Figure 3-18. Let's explore these three options further.

First, your friends receive notification when you log in and log out of SL. This feature is allowed by default when you create a friendship with someone.

Second, if you so choose, your friends will be able to determine your whereabouts in SL. This capability is referred to as *mapping* someone because it is done from the world map.

I still remember wondering why I kept running into a new friend of mine all the time. Because SL is so vast, I knew it was highly unlikely we would keep bumping into each other. It turned out she had been teleporting into my location. That behavior was a bit stalker-ish, and she stopped when I asked her to. By default, this capability is not granted to new friends.

Third is the capability of a friend to modify your objects and vice versa. This capability is also disabled by default, but it can be very useful when someone is helping you fix a build or manage some of your objects.

Friends are what make SL come alive, so go out and get some!

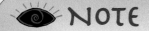

### NOTE

Honestly, you should **never** grant modify rights to anyone unless it is absolutely necessary. No matter how well you think you know the other individual, granting this power makes it possible for him to destroy everything you have ever built in a matter of minutes, purposely or accidentally.

# GROUPS

Groups in SL are a way for a set of residents to connect with each other based on a shared interest. There are groups for newbies on almost any topic; there are groups for activities such as live music, skydiving, and sailing; and there are groups formed around business partnerships and land ownership.

Groups are used for many reasons, including but not limited to

- Managing a list of residents outside your Friends list
- Sending in-world notifications and attachments to a list of residents
- Conducting private group IMs with a list of residents
- Managing joint ownership of land
- Restricting access to land to a list of residents (for events or other purposes)
- Managing a set of member roles and abilities
- Conducting voting on proposals or other topics
- Managing a shared Linden balance and sales distributions
- Sending notices about events or news
- Granting selective permissions for land use
- And last, but not least, setting up a cool title, charter, and insignia for your super-secret fan club (membership by invitation only)

## Finding and Joining a Group

There are many groups out there just waiting for you! Taking part is just a matter of finding one and joining it. To start, you can search for groups on the Group tab of the Search dialog. For example, in Figure 3-19 I typed **sky diving**, and you can see a group came up, along with the description and owners.

Before you join a group, I suggest reading the description to understand what the group is about and how long it has been around. Then take a look at the profiles of the group owners or officers, and ask yourself questions such as whether they sound like people you want to know or would be helpful to you.

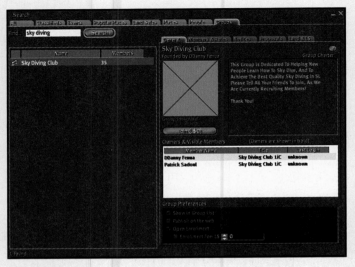

**Figure 3-19**
*Searching for groups interested in sky diving.*

Also, check whether the group has an enrollment fee. If a group has an enrollment fee, perhaps contact one or more members using their profile and IM to see what they think about the group before you spend your L$.

You may be invited by another avatar to join a group; if so, you'll see a dialog like that shown in Figure 3-20. You can join or decline.

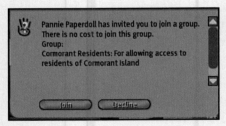

**Figure 3-20**
*To join or not to join?*

Finally, not all groups have open enrollment. For those that do not, you have to be invited by someone who has the authority to add members to the group. There are also groups that do not show up under Search.

## Managing Your Groups

You can see what groups you belong to and manage your active title from the Groups dialog. To access this dialog, right-click on your avatar and select Groups from the pie menu (see Figure 3-21). You can also get to this menu by choosing Edit->Groups.

**Figure 3-21**
*The Groups option appears in the pie menu.*

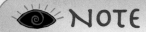

**NOTE**

Your group membership is available for all to see in your profile. You can learn quite a bit about someone by looking at her group membership. What do your groups say about you?

In the Groups dialog, you can select one group to be Active (see Figure 3-22), and the title for group members is then displayed above your avatar name for others to see if they like. You can also select None, which is usually what I have mine set to.

**Figure 3-22**
*The Groups dialog allows you to control display of your active group allegiance.*

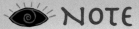

**NOTE**

Builders be aware that objects can have a group assignment. When you build, your avatar's currently active group is used as the default group to which new objects you create will be set. So, it's always best to make sure you activate the group to which you want your project to be set *before* you begin working.

Also, ownership of objects can be transferred from individuals to groups. Group ownership of objects may be important when you're building on group-owned land so that others in the group can edit the objects you are building as well.

**NOTE**

If you don't see group titles or avatar names, you may have this setting disabled. Enable it by choosing Edit->Properties.

## Communicating with a Group

You can communicate with members of a group by IMing the group. Bring up the IM dialog, and you see a tab labeled New IM. As you can see from Figure 3-23, your groups are also listed above your friends' names (which I've blanked out).

One annoyance about groups is that when you first join a group, it is automatically set as your group title. This title can be a bit embarrassing if you're not aware of it.

For example, say you're online at 3 a.m. and visit the XXX Nightclub. You decide to join the group. You then might have the tag XXX Nightclub VIP floating above your head for all to see. To fix this if it happens to you, bring up your Groups dialog, either select a different group or select None, and click Activate.

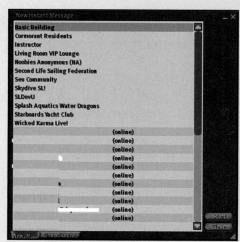

**Figure 3-23**
*Groups and friends are listed.*

Be aware that when you IM a group, the message goes out to all online residents in that group. Your IMs are added to the chat stream of all these residents, and it can sometimes be annoying if you start spamming a group with multiple IMs. Some groups welcome basic newbie questions, whereas others do not, so make sure you joined the right one!

Depending on the abilities granted to your membership level within a group, you may also communicate by broadcasting a group notice (including attachments) or initiating vote on a proposal.

### Creating a Group

You can create your own groups in SL for a mere L$100 (at least as of this writing). As you can see in Figure 3-24, a screenshot of the group's property panel, a lot of group features are available, many of which may not be applicable or useful to the type of group you're planning to create.

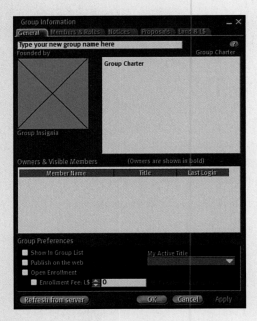

**Figure 3-24**
*The group properties panel includes many features.*

As with all great book projects, because of space constraints, some things are never covered as well as you would like, and so it goes with groups. For more information on creating and managing a group, see the online help. Help is just an F1 key away under the topic "Groups."

## OBJECTS AND COMMUNICATION CHANNELS

Objects in SL can also communicate via chat. They can also listen and respond to chat! For example, a sensor object may detect your presence at a store and send a greeting announcing today's sale items. Your SL infant may complain it needs to be held. Your SL dog may listen for the command "sit" and respond appropriately.

By default, if an object says something in SL, the message appears in a light green color rather than white, making it easier to distinguish the real from the robot.

All chat occurs on a main channel by default (channel 0). As we have seen, this chat shows up in the UI. However, other communication channels do not show up in the UI.

These alternate channels are the SL way of sending messages between objects. You can also privately communicate with one of your objects on another channel so that your messages do not appear in the main chat window.

For example, say you have a light that listens to on/off messages on channel 23. You can type the following: **/23 light on**. Any scripted object listening on channel 23 would hear "light on." A scripted light could then turn itself on or off.

You create objects that listen and respond to chat by using the Linden Scripting Language, which we cover later.

Finally, objects have access to a mode of chat called *whisper*. Whereas shout has a 100m radius and default chat has a 20m radius, whisper is heard only within 10m.

## COMMUNICATION PITFALLS AND MISTAKES

There are several common mistakes and pitfalls in SL communication, some of which mark you as a newbie and others that even long-time residents still fall into. This section outlines the most common pitfalls.

- **Speaking in all capitals:** When you TYPE IN ALL CAPITALS, you are considered to be yelling or expressing strong emotions. One common newbie mistake is to type with the Caps Lock key on. Use all capitals to express yourself like "This SUCKS!" or "WOW, I'm truly amazed," but don't keep it on all the time.

- **Carrying on two conversations:** You have to practice listening skills in SL and that means trying not to type ahead of a reply or response from the person you're talking to. I find myself doing this all the time. What happens is that two separate threads of conversation start up, and before too long, both of you get confused about a response someone made and whether it refers to topic one or topic two. It is better to slow down and try discussing one thing at a time.

- **Typing into the wrong channel:** Pannie Paperdoll had this to offer, *"The biggest struggle I see noobs having, is typing things meant for the main chat in IM ...or typing things meant for IM in main chat. Older residents do it too when they get a bit excited *grins*."*

This one has bitten me and many others. If you're having a side IM conversation with someone or IMing with multiple people, be sure you're typing into the right place. Typing a private IM into the main chat at a crowded place can be very embarrassing!

One trick that may help is to tear off tabs from the IM panel so you have separate windows for each conversation.

- **Spamming someone's email:** When you send IM to someone who is offline, you get a message in your IM window telling you that person is offline. For some people, the message you typed was sent to them in email. Once you know this person is offline (as you would if he is one of your friends), try to type your message all in one long line instead of many short lines as you would if you were talking to the person directly in SL.

- **Sending an offline IM with no context:** If you're going to IM someone and she is offline, make sure you establish some context. IMs from people that say nothing more than "I have a question for you." or "I was wondering about your group." will either be ignored or the person will kindly IM back "What is your question?" At this point, you may be offline or have forgotten what you were going to ask. So,

remember, if someone is offline, establish the context so that she can quickly answer your query when she logs in again.

- **Forgetting about the person in front of you:** You may get an IM while you're talking to someone. In fact, it may grab your attention, and you may start a conversation in IM with this other person while chatting. This is OK; it happens to everyone in SL. But one pitfall is when you start spending a lot of time in IM while the person in front of you is waiting for a reply. IM is for delayed chatter, but if your avatar is talking to another avatar directly, pay attention to this conversation, and if you need to take time out for IM, let that person know.

It is also polite to say, *"Hang on a sec; I need to handle a couple IMs."* It is also polite when you leave the keyboard to refill a drink or take a bio-break to simply say *"brb"* for "be right back." If you start talking to someone and he doesn't reply, others around you may indicate *"They are afk"* or "away from the keyboard."

# PRIVACY AND OTHER CONSIDERATIONS

You can easily capture the text of the chat stream and private IMs: A simple Ctrl+A (select all), Ctrl+C (copy), and you have it. With this ease of access come some important considerations about resident privacy. In general, this can all be summed up in one rule:

> Never capture or share an individual's or group's chat or IM text without that individual's or group's knowledge and permission.

When you joined SL, you agreed to the Terms of Service (TOS) and the community standards (CS), and in those, there is a basic code of conduct expected that we cover in Chapter 5, "Second Life Culture and Relationships."

Here are a few points to be aware of:

- Like email, what you type may come back to bite you, so just be sure you want to share something before you do.

- From the TOS: "Linden Labs generally does not regulate the content of communications between users or users' interactions with the Service." This means that by entering SL, you may be exposing yourself to things you would rather not see or hear. As in RL, just stay away from those locations or individuals.

- A number of in-world devices can be used to capture chat, with or without the speakers' permission. These can be planted on or carried by an individual or planted within the environment.

- Devices may also "chat" for their owner. For example, an event organizer may have a device that issues basic details so she doesn't have to type them in over and over again.

# TUTORIAL: GO MEET SOMEONE!

OK, if you've been wandering around SL silently avoiding everyone, now you are armed with all the information you need. So, it's time to meet someone new.

## STEP 1: FIND A GOOD LOCATION

Welcome areas are great places to meet new friends. People who are new are easily recognizable by their default avatars, so walk up and introduce yourself if you just want to share the learning curve with someone. People with more advanced avatars tend to hang out at welcome areas to help new residents, so you can talk to them as well. Another way to meet people is to search for events and pick one that interests you.

## STEP 2: GO UP AND SAY HELLO

Walk up to someone and type in your chat window **"Hello, <INSERT AVATAR NAME HERE>, How are you today?"** Trust me, 9 times out of 10 you'll initiate a dialogue with this person. If he ignores you, just try it with someone else.

You'll find most SL residents willing to help out, and you may be surprised about a new place they show you, a group they tell you about, or even some object they give you!

Remember to ask before you try to add them as friends!

# VOCAL COMMUNICATION IN SL

I felt I should add a quick note to this chapter about vocal communication or voice in SL. At the time of this writing, a 3D spacial voice chat capability for SL is in public beta. It is likely to be available by the time this book shows up in print. Voice allows individuals with a microphone-equipped computer to actually talk to each other instead of just typing text. The 3D spacial nature of the implementation is really cool. For example, avatars closer to your avatar sound louder than those farther away, and avatars on your left sound like they are on your left.

An alternative to SL voice chat that was used before this capability became available and I predict will continue to be used is Skype (http://www.skype.com). Skype is basically a Voice over IP (VoIP) technology through which, given a microphone and speakers, you can talk and hear others on a single or shared "line" just like a phone call or teleconference.

Vocal communication in SL is an extremely useful tool for people who collaborate closely on projects in SL or who have gotten to know each other at a deeper level. You can communicate faster and with more emotional detail if you can hear someone's voice!

It is important to understand that the addition of voice to SL will have profound social impacts on the SL community, the results of which remain uncertain at this point. If you are new to SL, you may be asking yourself why?

The answer is complicated, but let me provide a few examples. SL provides for some pseudo-anonymity, and many people take advantage of that. You can be a 55-year-old grandmother and role-play as a 20-something man. Some people would rather not "talk" because the human voice reveals a lot about age, sex, and even ethnic background. Their own voice gives away too much information about their RL self. The choice is entirely yours.

Another aspect is that voice is particularly challenging if most of your SL time is spent at home in a shared family room or at a local wireless spot (that is, unless you don't mind funny looks as you talk to your computer). It is likely that individual communities that favor voice and non-voice communication may develop.

As we have discussed, you get very good at carrying on many conversations at once using chat and IM in SL. SL residents almost expect others to be carrying on multiple conversations at once. Adding voice will certainly affect this aspect of SL communication.

Finally, let me offer you this. It is a lot easier to break up with your SL partner avatar if all you get back is text chat and perhaps some creative gestures. Imagine if you could hear the other human being crying? More positively, the roar of a live enthusiastic crowd cannot be compared to listening to a few canned clap sound clips.

For a particularly interesting perspective of the topic, see Gwyneth Llewelyn's post here: http://gwynethllewelyn.net/article147visual1layout1.html. It is fairly long, so consider skipping ahead to the section titled "Multicasting vs. Broadcasting in a Collaborative Environment."

# EFFECTIVE SL PRESENTATIONS BY JEFFRONIUS BATRA

A good RL friend of mine spends time doing a lot of presentations, and now he is doing them in SL. Doing an effective presentation in SL requires a few different skills than doing one in RL and exercises all the communication abilities we've covered in this section, so I thought his blog post (http://www.jeff-barr.com/?p=707) on this topic was particularly informative. My thanks to Jeff for sharing his wisdom here. Take it away, Jeff (see Figure 3-25).

**Figure 3-25**
*Jeffronius Batra.*

In the weeks since I've done my first two Amazon Web Services presentations in Second Life, I've spoken to lots of people about what it is like to do a presentation in Second Life. First off, they are generally amazed that is it possible to do a presentation at all. After I tell them about it, the next thing that they want to know is how to do it and how to be effective.

## SPEND TIME IN-WORLD

This may be the most important piece of advice that I can give. Experienced residents can detect an outsider or a newbie at a glance. Don't show up in Second Life as a generically dressed outsider, don't marvel at what you see onscreen during your presentation (making it obvious to everyone that you are seeing it all for the first time), and don't treat long-time residents like geeks or freaks. If your corporate PR department has asked you to show up in Second Life as part of some effort to show that your company is hip to the latest trends, be extra careful. Attempts to look cool when you are not usually backfire.

Spend a serious amount of time in Second Life before you are scheduled to present. Make sure that you feel at home and that you know some of the jargon. If you don't know the terms *lag* or *rezzing*, you aren't ready to present. You'd better know what a *furry* is too.

## ATTEND SOME EVENTS

There are hundreds of events taking place in Second Life every day. You can log in and visit the Events tab of the Find dialog to locate them, or you can visit the Events Page on the Second Life site. Watch how the presenters interact with the audience, and make sure that you are confident that you can do much of what they do—movements, gestures, chatting, IMing, and so forth.

## MASTER THE BASICS OF SECOND LIFE

Before you even think about presenting, you must be able to move your avatar, spend money, find locations and teleport to them, sit and stand up, invoke gestures, get yourself dressed (and undressed, actually), chat, IM, and move the camera. Apparently, some corporate presenters don't actually manipulate their own avatars and instead employ a puppeteer.

To each his own, but this seems a bit lame and detached to me. Part of the experience of being in Second Life is to actually be there at the keyboard. If you are not at the keyboard, you are not truly in the world. I have found that the most interesting part of any presentation is actually interacting with the audience—listening to their questions and concerns, watching their body language (are they captivated, bored, excited, or even asleep) and responding appropriately. Anything less and you are simply broadcasting to them.

## DRESS THE PART

Don't even think about showing up looking like a newbie, dressed in one of the default generic outfits and with nonprim hair. Putting on and taking off clothing is definitely a fundamental Second Life skill, and if you can't be trusted to get dressed, can you be trusted to present good content?

There are plenty of good Second Life fashion blogs and magazines. For you dudes, I can recommend *Men's Second Style*. For you gals, there are plenty of places to look including *Fashion World of SL* and *PXP*. If you are in a hurry, you might want to consider hiring a personal shopper and spending a few thousand Lindens on some attractive clothes. Last month I actually worked with SL resident Pannie Paperdoll to improve my avatar's image. In short order we acquired a fresh new skin, a suit, some good shoes, and some prim hair. I still need to blog about this virtual makeover, but it was easy and fun.

## GET YOUR GESTURES READY

Gestures are short animations (with optional sounds) that mimic the gestural body movements of RL (see Figure 3-26). The gestures are invoked via function keys or by double-clicking them in the Gestures window (press Control-G to open it). I have found that using gestures such as "Yes", "No", "Laugh", "Shrug," and so forth add a lot of realism to my presentations. Avatars start out with a fairly extensive set of default gestures, but you can buy more at a number of locations in-world including Ludd's Gestures and Mr. P's Animation Superstore. I actually created a little "cheat sheet" listing my 5 or 6 favorite gestures before my first presentation. Using these gestures as part of your

presentation will take some presence of mind, but they will add realism to what you do, and will also make clear to the audience that you truly understand what makes Second Life special.

**Figure 3-26**
*Your avatar can gesture.*

Somewhat related to this, don't be afraid to show up a bit overdressed (an overcoat and a hat) and to make yourself a bit more comfortable part-way through. Once again, these are some real-world cues that add realism and intimacy. You probably don't want to turn your presentation into a strip-tease, though!

## PRACTICE

Doing a run-through in advance isn't a bad idea at all. If you are presenting in someone else's space, pay it a visit and get the lay of the land. See what you will see as a presenter and as an audience member. Try out the presentation device and your gestures and make sure that everything you'll need to do your job is close at hand.

## PREPARE BIOLOGICALLY

A good presentation is going to take you one or two hours and you are not going to have the opportunity to take a break in mid-presentation. You will probably want to have your favorite work-safe beverage close at hand, and you'll want to pay a visit to the bathroom before you start.

## WATCH YOURSELF

If you have two computers, you can create a so-called "Alt" account and log in twice—once with your primary identity and once with your alternate identity. You can then park your avatar out in the audience and see how you look as you present (see Figure 3-27). Doing this will require even more presence of mind, but I have found that it can be very helpful. During my second presentation I saw that at least one person was sitting on top of the presentation screen, and I never would have seen him but for the eyes of my alt. I know that I can move the camera around, but this was easier.

**Figure 3-27**
*You can see how you look as you present.*

## MAKE A GRAND ENTRANCE

In the interest of adding realism to your presentation, consider making some sort of grand entrance. You could appear from within an explosion, rappel down a rope, or fly in on a dragon. I showed up in my Toyota Scion for my first event, and in my Argolas Hovercraft for my second.

## PRESENT

When the big day arrives, give yourself enough time to deal with an unexpected issue or two. Make sure that you are not suddenly faced with the need to download a fresh Second Life client. Follow the Official Linden Blog and be aware of planned outages.

For my second presentation, I asked my audience to express their questions, concerns, and thoughts in the chat window as I presented. I did this to get immediate feedback and to feel more connected with my audience. Tracking all of this real-time input and incorporating it into my presentation was tricky but worthwhile. I also entertained private questions via IM as I was chatting out my presentation to the whole group. Once again tricky, but also worthwhile—I had 8 or 9 simultaneous private threads going at one point.

## SLANG AND ACRONYMS

What follows is a brief introduction to common slang and acronyms you are likely to encounter in SL. Knowing and using them greatly enhances your street cred (credibility) and moves you past appearing like a newbie! These may appear in upper, lower, or mixed case.

| | |
|---|---|
| afk | Away From the Keyboard |
| ao | Animation Override |
| av or avie | Avatar |
| cya | See Ya |
| brb | Be Right Back |
| degt | Don't Even Go There |
| fwiw | For What It's Worth |
| g2g | Got to Go |
| gmta | Great Minds Think Alike |
| LM | Landmark |
| HUD | Heads Up Display |
| imo or imho | In My (Humble) Opinion |
| in-world | Existing within the SL world |
| jk | Just Kidding |
| k or kk | OK |
| Lindens (L$) | The Linden Dollar, currency of SL |
| A Linden or Lindens | Employees of Linden Lab, creators of SL |
| lag or laggy | Sluggish SL performance |
| ll | Linden Lab (The Company Behind SL) |
| ltr | Later |
| lmao | Laughing My Ass Off |

| | |
|---|---|
| lol | Laughing Out Loud |
| mwah or muah | The sound a friendly kiss makes |
| newb, newbie, noob | A new resident/newcomer to SL |
| np | No Problem |
| OMG | Oh My Gosh! |
| resident | A common name for an SL player |
| rez | To bring an object into existence |
| rl | Real Life |
| rofl | Rolling On Floor, Laughing |
| sl | Second Life |
| tmi | Too Much Information |
| tp | Teleport |
| ttyl | Talk To You Later |
| ty | Thank You |
| tyt | Take Your Time |
| wb | Welcome Back |
| wtf | What the F***? |
| wtg | Way To Go |
| yw | You're Welcome |

Here are a couple URLs for more information on chat acronyms and slang:

http://www.city-net.com/~ched/help/lingo/chatslang.html

http://www.netlingo.com/emailsh.cfm

# SUMMARY

In this chapter, you learned the basics of communication in SL and how to chat and shout at other avatars nearby. You learned how to communicate one on one with avatars at a distance or privately even if they are standing next to you. You also learned how to animate your avatar and avoid common mistakes. You even had a glimpse at what it's like presenting to a crowd in SL.

So the next step is obviously to go out there and start talking. You'll be amazed at what you find.

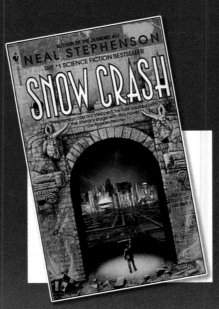

*Your avatar can look any way you want it to. ...*
*If you're ugly, you can make your avatar beautiful.*
*If you've just gotten out of bed, your avatar can still be*
*wearing beautiful clothes and professionally applied*
*makeup. You can look like a gorilla or a dragon or*
*a giant talking penis.*

**—Neal Stephenson from Snow Crash**

# Your Avatar—Your Virtual Self

# 4

Who do you want to be? How do you want to look? In Second Life, you can look like whatever you want, and you can change your mind minute by minute. You have a three-dimensional representation of your-self called an *avatar*, also referred to as *AV* or *avie*. You are your avatar in SL. Others see your avatar, not you. A friend of mine says, "The best thing about SL is you don't have to wear any pants." One of the things that I love about SL is that everyone looks very different! SL has many wild and varied avatars.

When you first arrive in-world, you get a default avatar. To everyone else, you look like a newbie; this has both advantages and disadvantages. Some people are very helpful to new arrivals, and others are not. At some point, you will want to add your own character to your avatar. This chapter tells you what you need to know to take the first steps.

## What You Will Learn

- What makes up an avatar and how you can change it
- How to change your shape, hair, eyes, and skin
- What clothes your avatar wears and how they layer
- How to create your own basic clothes
- How to find free or nearly free avatar accessories
- How to go shopping to improve your avatar look

# WHAT IS AN AVATAR?

Let's start with what the term *avatar* means before we get into how it's used in the context of SL. This is what Wikipedia has to say on the subject of avatars:

> The term 'avatar' derives from the Sanskrit word Avatara, meaning 'descent' and usually implying a deliberate descent into mortal realms for special purposes.... As used for a computer representation of a user, the term dates at least as far back as 1985, when it was used as the name for the player character in the Ultima series of computer games. The Ultima games started out in 1981, but it was in Ultima IV (1985), that the term 'avatar' was introduced. ... The use of Avatar to mean online virtual bodies was popularized by Neal Stephenson in his cyberpunk novel *Snow Crash* (1992).

So, an avatar represents your "visual" self in SL. Note that I did not say your "virtual" self. Your avatar provides only what others see of you or your visual self. Your virtual self has as much to do with what you do, say, create, and how you interact. At the most basic level, your avatar represents how you look to others in SL. So, also, when you're looking at someone, you see her avatar.

Just like in RL, how you look conveys the first signs of what you are all about to those you interact with. Will it be love at first sight, or should you duck and run? You can decide and, even better, you can change looks as you see fit for different occasions.

If you're wondering how to start with all this, think about creating an "altered" ego (for example, if you're short, do you want to be tall?) or trying to reproduce how you look in real life. Let's start with the first choice you need to make when sculpting your avatar.

# YOUR FIRST AVATAR

When you entered SL, you picked one avatar to start with. But you have access to all the Linden avatars in your Library. Go to your Inventory (the blue button at the bottom of your screen), and open the Library->Clothing folder (see Figure 4-1). Here, you see all the default avatars available.

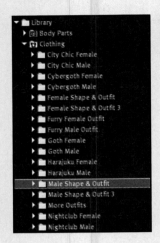

**Figure 4-1**
*Default avatars in the Clothing folder.*

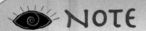

**NOTE**

You can change from one default avatar to another by simply right-clicking on the folder containing a default avatar and selecting Replace Outfit. Be aware, however, that if you have customized your avatar in any way, the changes will be lost. You learn how to save and modify your avatar later in this chapter.

As of this writing, you can select from a total of 12 avatars. They are organized as male/female, but they also represent some subcultures in SL. The most basic of these are Girl and Boy Next Door. You shouldn't stick with any of these defaults for more than a few minutes!

A basic description of each default avatar style follows:

- **Girl and Boy Next Door:** Nice but boring; get yourself another avatar!

- **City Chic Male and Female:** You're hip, your So-CAL/LA. Relax on the beach and hang.

- **Night Club Male and Female:** It's time to go out. 'Nuff said.

- **Harajuku Male and Female:** From Tokyo, Japan, *Harajuku* is the name for an area around Harajuku Station. Wikipedia says, "Harajuku became famous in the 1980s due to the large numbers of street performers and wildly dressed teens who gathered there on Sundays when Omotesando was closed to traffic. A Japanese clothing style that combines otherwise incompatible fashions in a jumble of colour and clothing."

- **Cyber Goth Male and Female:** From Wikipedia, "The goth subculture is a contemporary subculture prevalent in many countries. It began in the United Kingdom during the late 1970s to early 1980s in the gothic rock scene, an offshoot of the post-punk genre. … Styles of dress within the subculture range from death rock, punk, Victorian, androgynous, some Renaissance style clothes, or combinations of the above, most often with black attire, makeup and hair."

- **Furry Male and Female:** From Wikipedia, "The term 'furry' dates back to a specific genre of fantasy art and literature from the 1980s. By 1987 enough interest had been generated for the first furry convention, and as the Internet became more accessible, it became the most popular means for furry fans to keep in touch and share their artistic efforts."

If you think this list of default avatars represents the wild diversity of SL avatars, you would be horribly mistaken. There are child avatars, very large avatars, dragon avatars, elderly avatars, micro-mini avatars, animal avatars, dragon avatars, alien avatars, robot avatars, vampire avatars, cartoon avatars, and even inanimate object avatars (such as a table lamp, which is great for going unnoticed). There are also ugly avatars and fat avatars, although you don't see too many of them.

Whatever you do, don't stick with your first avatar for long. It's like walking around with an "I'm new here" billboard over your head. The rest of this chapter should help you make changes to your newbie look.

# MANAGING YOUR APPEARANCE

Most of this chapter focuses on changing aspects of your avatar and assumes you have a base avatar from which to start. However, in SL it is possible to totally change your look by switching from avatar to avatar. The following sections cover that topic up front because you're likely to

move between avatars for a while until you settle on a look you like.

## SAVING YOUR AVATAR

To begin, let's start with a quick overview of saving everything about your avatar. If you are about to try a brand new avatar, take it from me and save your current look. It took me several hours to reconstruct what I had put together when I tried a freebie avatar for the first time and didn't like the result.

First, right-click on your avatar to open the pie menu. Select the Appearance segment, as shown in Figure 4-2. Once your appearance panel opens, find a button labeled Make Outfit near the bottom. The short story on this button is that it creates a folder containing everything you're currently wearing, including your shape, skin, eyes, and so on. It copies items that can be copied but moves items that cannot, so be aware that things may shift around in your Inventory.

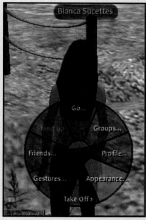

**Figure 4-2**
*Right-click Appearance pie menu.*

Simply select everything (my recommendation until you get the hang of it) and name your outfit (see Figure 4-3).

Now a folder is available with the name of your outfit under Inventory->Clothing. You can return to this outfit by simply dragging the entire folder from your Inventory onto your avatar (see the section "Outfits and Managing Your Inventory" for more information).

Now you're ready to make some changes.

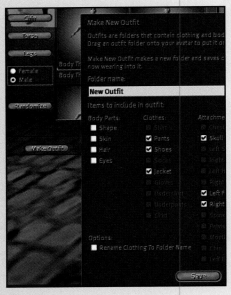

**Figure 4-3**
*Select everything and name your outfit.*

## CHANGING YOUR AVATAR

The quickest way to change from one avatar to another is to right-click on a folder that contains a complete outfit and select Replace Outfit from the pop-up menu. Figure 4-4 shows me trying out the Cybergoth avie!

**Figure 4-4**
*I'm trying the default Cybergoth avatar.*

## BUYING AVATARS AND FINDING FREE AVATARS

Before we get into what makes up an avatar and how to modify its various components, it's worth noting that you can easily find complete avatars in SL, some of them free.

Start by searching for "avatars" in the Places dialog, and you get quite a long list. Two places to look that have been around a long time are YadNi's Junkyard and Luskwood.

### YadNi's Junkyard

YadNi's Junkyard (see Figure 4-5) has been around a long time, and you can find almost anything there free or for L$1.

**Figure 4-5**
*YadNi's Junkyard.*

**SLURL** YadNi's Junkyard can be found at **http://slurl.com/ secondlife/leda/210/28/54/**.

Once you arrive, head toward the back, where you will see many boxes. Get close to the boxes, and you will see text above them showing what they contain. Figure 4-6 shows a box with four free avatars.

**Figure 4-6**
*A box containing four free avatars.*

### Luskwood

Another great place to find avatars is Luskwood. Plus, it's a great place to just hang out. But if you want a furry avatar, this is the first place to check out. Luskwood is one of the oldest mainland communities in SL.

**SLURL** You can find Luskwood at **http://slurl.com/ secondlife/lusk/193/101/52/**.

Once there (see Figure 4-7), you can use its avatar construction kit to design your own avatar. Of course, you have to pay for the kit, so maybe you should check out YadNi's first.

**Figure 4-7**
*Luskwood.*

# YOUR SEX: PICK ANY MESH

The shape of your avatar is determined by what is referred to in 3D modeling realms as a *mesh*. You can safely not care about this issue if you prefer, but a mesh is basically a set of points in 3D space that are connected by lines or "edges" to form a grid of triangular faces called *polygons*.

The two meshes to choose from are named Male and Female (see Figure 4-8). You can see both of them here.

Now, don't be too worried. In SL you can change your avatar from male to female and back again just like changing a shirt. This changes the mesh underneath. You cannot, however, change the mesh directly in SL.

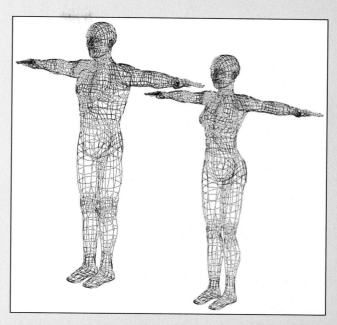

**Figure 4-8**
*Meshes for male and female avatars.*

The fact that these meshes are labeled Male and Female doesn't mean you can't be a robot, fox, dragon, or block of wood.

The choice of mesh does influence what controls you have on your shape, which we get into next. For example, the female mesh has several controls for breast size that the male mesh does not have. The male mesh has several controls for facial hair that the female mesh does not have. How sexist is that?

When you arrive in-world, you select a default male or female avatar and have the associated mesh assigned to you, but as I said, you can change this any time you wish.

# YOUR BODY: SCULPTING SHAPE, SKIN, HAIR, AND EYES

Avatars in SL require four features: shape, skin, hair, and eyes (you are not required to have any clothes in SL, and some residents take full advantage of this). You can create and own multiple shapes, skin, hair, and eyes, but you always wear one of each of these features. Let's take a look at these features and how they affect your avatar's appearance.

# MODIFYING YOUR APPEARANCE

The scene in Figure 4-9, from Orientation Island, shows a new avatar. If you stick around here long enough, you'll see a lot of similar AVs arriving; the hairstyle looks different, but the shirts, pants, and so on are pretty much the same.

**Figure 4-9**
*New avatars arriving at Orientation Island.*

You modify your avatar by right-clicking and selecting Appearance from the pie menu.

Your avatar turns around, and it moves to a neutral position, which is standing with arms straight out to the side. Be aware that others still see you in this mode, so they know you're editing your appearance.

Also notice a submenu called Take Off (see Figure 4-10). This submenu enables you to remove clothing without having to go into edit appearance mode. Because shape, skin, hair, and eyes are required, you cannot find them in the Take Off submenu. You can also right-click to select attachments (for example, sunglasses) and then click Detach to remove them.

**Figure 4-10**
*The Take Off submenu can be used to remove clothing.*

You can see the main appearance dialog in Figure 4-11. This dialog is divided into Body Parts and Clothes. Body parts are all the required elements. On the right side are subcategories that contain individual settings you can change.

**Figure 4-11**
*The Appearance dialog.*

There are 150+ settings/characteristics about your body you can change. The number differs depending on your choice of male/female mesh. I don't go into each of them here because half the fun of sculpting your avatar is playing with all these settings. Let's start with sculpting your shape.

## SAVING YOUR CHANGES

When you're altering any of the four essential wearables (shape, skin, hair, eyes), you are modifying the currently "worn" element. After completing modification, you can overwrite the worn item wherever it is stored in your Inventory by using the Save button. Alternatively, you can use the Save As button to store your modifications as a new Inventory item. If you choose the latter, what is now worn is the newly created Inventory item.

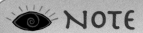

A bug affects Make Outfit and Save As. If you start with a newbie shape and then save it as something else, the new shape lists the creator either as "newbie template" or as "nobody." The only way to have any body part shown as made by you is to make a brand new one from Inventory. You do this by right-clicking a folder in your Inventory and selecting New Body Parts ->New Shape, for example. Being identified as the creator really becomes important if you want to sell your creations.

## YOUR SHAPE

To sculpt your shape, you choose Body Parts->Shape. Shape subcategories include Body, Head, Eyes, Ears, Nose, Mouth, Chin, Torso, and Legs. You start by picking Female or Male. Female is shown in Figure 4-11.

Under the Body subcategory, you can see the first setting of the Body is your Height. You see two examples of how you would look with the Height setting. These sample pictures are adjusted based on your other avatar settings, so they change as you make changes. You use the slider under these pictures to adjust your Height. All the way to the left, and your body will be as short as possible; all the way to the right, and your body will be as tall as possible.

You can make precise changes by filling in a number. Numbers go from 0 to 100—in this case, 0 being the shortest and 100 being the tallest. The next setting is Body Thickness, and if you scroll down, you see additional settings for your body.

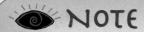

If you're involved in 3D modeling or game development, these settings are essentially morph targets applied to the underlying meshes. The actual male and female meshes that make up SL avatars are available from Linden Lab at http://www.secondlife.com/. However, at the time of this writing, they do not come with the morph targets.

What you're doing here is making changes to the shape associated with your avatar. As you modify your shape, you see the Save, Save As, and Revert buttons at the bottom of the dialog. If you click Save, you save the shape that is on your avatar right now! You can also choose Save As, which saves the shape to your Inventory. If you don't like the changes, you can revert your avatar back to the last time you saved by clicking Revert; it's basically a Cancel function.

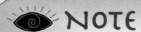

You should use Save As on your shape before you start playing so you can always get back to it. Do Save As and name it **My Original Shape**.

Work your way through all the subcategories and settings and play around until your avatar looks the way you want it. Then click Save. Don't worry about it too much; you'll come back here over time and evolve your shape.

Once you have your shape defined, you need to cover that shape with something, and that's where skin comes in.

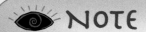

All the subcategories under Shape are about the, well, "shape" of your avatar. Shape->Eyes refers to the shape of the eyes around the eyeball (lids, lashes, bags). The Body Part->Eyes is about the eyeball coloration.

## YOUR SKIN

Your skin is what covers your shape (or mesh); you are required to have a skin for a basic avatar in SL. Skins can also be created and saved in your Inventory. A skin is basically a texture (a two-dimensional image such as a digital photograph) applied across your body. In fact, it's made up of three textures: head, upper body, and lower body. You can modify how your skin looks by using the Skin category.

The subcategories available are Skin Color, Face Detail, Makeup, and Body Detail. Notice your viewpoint moves to your face when you're working with a skin (see Figure 4-12).

**Figure 4-13**
*The anatomically incorrect, default, male shape.*

**Figure 4-12**
*Your viewpoint changes when you're working with skin.*

Under skin there are three gray squares with black X's through them labeled Head Tattoo, Upper Tattoo, and Lower Tattoo. These options correspond to additional textures that can be applied, as the name implies, as tattoos to your skin. They essentially are layered on top of the skin texture. Creating tattoos requires the capability to create textures with transparency, which is an advanced topic, but say you wanted a dragon tattoo on your left ankle. You can buy one in SL.

Figure 4-13 shows a full-on, default, male shape and default skin with no clothes. Yes, he is naked, and it's not a pretty sight. The default male avatar is not anatomically correct. Can you say Ken doll? We'll clothe Ken after we cover the final required body parts: hair and eyes.

## YOUR HAIR

The next required part of an avatar is your hair. Figure 4-14 shows the Hair section of the Appearance dialog. Hair is a wild thing that's not easily tamed. It is essentially made up of two things: a mesh that is placed on top of your avatar's head and a texture applied to the mesh to give it the appearance of hair. You control the shape of your hair under the Style subcategory. You can control the color of your hair under Color. You control how your eyebrows look under Eyebrows, and if you're using the male mesh, you can also control facial hair using the settings under Facial Hair.

**Figure 4-14**
*The Hair section of the Appearance dialog.*

**Figure 4-20**
*Default undershirt for female avatar.*

You can take off clothes here using an option called Take Off. You can also remove clothing directly from the pie menu using the Take Off submenu.

The following sections cover the various articles of clothing and their relationships to each other. I do not show all the dialogs here because most are similar.

## UNDERWEAR: UNDERPANTS AND UNDERSHIRT

The bottom layer of clothing is your underpants and undershirt. In Figure 4-21 the underpants and undershirt are shown in red. Note that the undershirt is beneath the blue shirt.

Also note that the shirt and underpants align perfectly at the waist of your avatar. If you go swimming, surfing, or sailing a lot in SL, you may want to have a nice pair of swim trunks for your underpants. This makes it really easy to get ready by simply taking off your pants!

**Figure 4-21**
*Underpants and undershirt in red, shirt in blue.*

However, if you're on a date, you may want to put on something a little bit more, ah, comfortable.

> ## TIP
>
> Because of the layering order, some designers have used the undershirt layer on which to paint (non-prim) necklaces using a lot of transparency in the texture.

## PANTS AND SHIRTS

On top of your underwear and underpants come pants and shirts. They are both shown in blue in Figure 4-22.

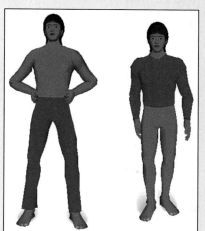

**Figure 4-22**
*Blue pants and blue shirt.*

Pants and shirts meet exactly at the waist, so if you want to have a superman jumpsuit, for example, you must use a solid color or be careful when aligning textures (more on that in Chapter 7).

You can use multiple layers of clothing and clothing adjustments to get RL looks. For example, if you adjust the collar of your shirt lower than the collar of the undershirt, you can see the undershirt beneath, as in the example shown in Figure 4-23 with a blue shirt and red undershirt.

**Figure 4-23**
*The blue shirt layers on top of the red undershirt.*

## SHOES AND SOCKS

Basic avatar shoes and socks are also textures. You can see in Figure 4-24, with green shoes and red socks, that the shoes sit on top of the socks.

There is a relationship between shoes, socks, and underpants. In Figure 4-25, I have a pair of shoes (green), socks (red, as well as my shirt), and underpants (blue). Underpants sit on the top, then socks, and then shoes. You can see here that shoes can get really high! This allows you to create very high-legged boots, for example.

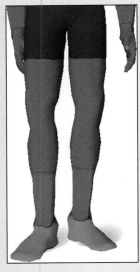

**Figure 4-24**
*Green shoes over red socks.*

**Figure 4-25**
*Shoes, socks, pants, and underpants showing the layering relationship among them.*

## JACKETS

Jackets are the only basic clothing texture that combines both upper and lower body textures. When done seamlessly, the texture looks like a jacket, as seen in greenish-blue in Figure 4-26. Jackets can be used to create, well, jackets, but also robes, capes, and shirts that are not tucked in. Other than the skirt, jackets layer on top of all other clothing.

As you can see in Figure 4-27, upper and lower fabrics are defined for a jacket in addition to the color tint.

**Figure 4-26**
*A greenish-blue jacket.*

**Figure 4-27**
*Upper and lower fabrics are defined for jackets.*

## GLOVES

Next up are gloves. The glove texture covers the hand, as you can see in Figure 4-28, where the glove is red. Gloves can be short or long, and you can make them fingerless if you're going for that bum look.

**Figure 4-28**
*Gloves are also available.*

In the layering diagram in Figure 4-29, you see a jacket in greenish-blue, a shirt in red, and gloves in yellow. I have shortened the sleeves way down on the jacket and shirt and then moved the gloves to their maximum length.

So, you can see that you can make gloves pretty long by adjusting their settings.

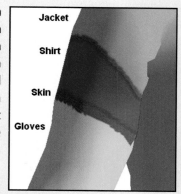

**Figure 4-29**

*A layering diagram of gloves, skin, shirt, and jacket.*

## SKIRTS

The final piece of clothing you can create is a skirt. Unlike all the other basic clothing, the skirt is actually another mesh. That is, there is another object (the skirt) associated with your avatar mesh. Remember, all the other clothing is simply made up of textures layered on top of each other.

The skirt, therefore, trumps all other clothing. As you can see in Figure 4-30, the skirt (purple) covers any jacket (cyan) you may be wearing.

Skirts make great kilts as well!

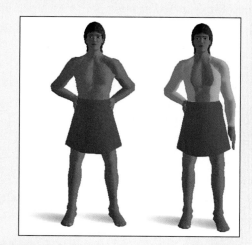

**Figure 4-30**
*Skirts are mesh objects.*

# TEXTURES: MAKING CLOTHING LOOK REAL

In all the previous examples, clothing didn't look too realistic; that is, it was just a plain, flat color. What makes basic clothing look real in SL are the textures. For example, Figure 4-31 shows a texture of a pair of light blue jeans. It is essentially a flat picture that is painted onto your avatar's legs.

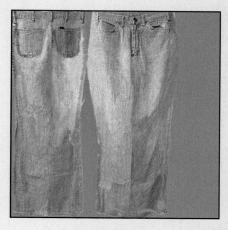

**Figure 4-31**

*Blue jeans texture.*

You can see what, if any, texture has been applied to a piece of clothing by looking at the fabric swatch in the Appearance dialog. For example, a different blue jean texture is applied to a pair of pants in Figure 4-32.

**Figure 4-32**
*Blue jean texture applied to pants.*

You use textures that have been designed for specific clothing articles by dragging them from your Inventory onto this Fabric swatch.

Now, you may be asking, "Where do I find these textures?" or "How can I create them?" You can find examples in your Library. Creating these textures requires some advanced techniques that are described in Chapter 7.

You can find free clothing or buy clothing with the textures already built in. Using a texture on a new shirt is covered in the tutorial "Creating a New Shirt by Alina Mikadze." Shopping for a new skin with texture included is covered in the tutorial "Applying a New Skin by Alina Mikadze."

# ADVANCED AVATARS

One of the coolest things that happens in SL is how your avatar evolves. You will learn more, see things you like on other avatars, and decide to make changes to your avatar's appearance.

Pannie Paperdoll, shown in Figure 4-33, a good SL friend of mine, agreed to try on several of her old avatars for me. I photographed them and composited the image in Photoshop (see Figure 4-34). This figure shows a great example of the evolution of an avatar.

**Figure 4-33**
*Pannie Paperdoll.*

On the far left is one of Pannie's earliest avatars. Notice the plain hair and textures and flat skin. The second one has more interesting skin and hair, and then some subsequent avatars had darker skin and changes to various body shapes, including what might appear to be breast augmentation. Pannie has also played around with a couple of other avatars like the tiger and child and has settled into a more sophisticated look as of late.

**Figure 4-34**
*Evolution of an individual's avatar.*

You may be looking at this picture and saying, "Her hair looks pretty advanced, and what is up with that tiger avatar?" Well, avatars can become pretty interesting when you move beyond the basic controls available in the Appearance dialog. The following sections just scratch the surface describing where you can take your avatars in SL.

## ACCESSORIES: SHOES, SHADES, STONES, AND FLEXI-SKIRTS

Once you get the hang of avatar basics, you'll soon discover you can attach additional objects to your avatars that move with you. For example, let's take a pair of sunglasses. There are no sunglass clothing items! So, how can I go from no sunglasses to sunglasses, as shown in Figure 4-35?

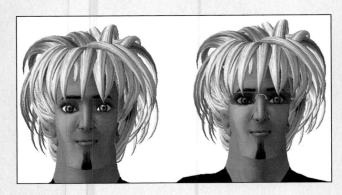

**Figure 4-35**
*No sunglasses to sunglasses.*

The answer is you can create additional objects in SL and attach them to your avatar. These objects are made up of prims (or primitives), which you learn more about in Chapter 6, "Building Basics."

As the title of this section implies, you can also attach things like advanced shoes, which have much more detail than is possible with basic shoes. Take Herb Greenspan's shoes shown in Figure 4-36. I'd hate to be kicked by those!

**Figure 4-36**
*Attaching some items to shoes.*

You can also attach necklaces, earrings, nose rings, and so on. You are limited only by your imagination.

Figure 4-37 shows Alina Mikadze with a very nice set of earrings and necklace attached.

**Figure 4-37**
*Alina Mikadze wearing nice earrings and a necklace.*

Finally, you will find a lot of attachments that move in SL. They are made up of *flexi-prims* (creating these is covered under "Building Flexible Primitives (Feature Tab)" in Chapter 6). A great example showing how flexi-prims are used is in the creation of wings and more realistic skirts

that move when you walk. Figure 4-38 is an example of a flexible skirt (modeled by Attim Hokkagai). On the left, the skirt is resting while Attim is standing still.

She then jumped up and landed, and as you can see, the flexi-prims on the skirt rise and fall with gravity as you would expect. Flexi-prims are also used for hair, which I cover next.

**Figure 4-38**
*A flexible skirt.*

## PRIM-HAIR

One of the cooler things that can be attached to avatars is *prim-hair*. Prim-hair is basically hair that has been built out of primitives and attached to your head. Prim-hair can be styled in ways that normal hair cannot. It also looks more realistic than SL hair.

With prim-hair, you often need to "hide" your basic hair. You do this by first wearing hair that makes you look bald. Then you put on the prim-hair. Figure 4-39 shows how this is done. On the left of the figure is my avatar with his basic hair, in the center we see it with the bald basic applied, and then on the right it appears with the prim-hair applied.

You can edit prim-hair as well, but that's an advanced operation that requires you to be familiar with SL building tools. If you haven't done any building, learn a few building basics or have someone help you adjust your prim-hair before you try because it's easy to mess up.

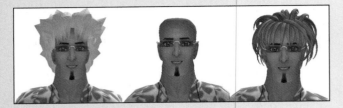

**Figure 4-39**
*Basic hair to bald basic to prim-hair.*

Flexi-prim hair moves as you do. Having prim-hair is one of those things that I think separates basic avatars from advanced avatars. In fact, it is often a good indicator of how new someone is to SL. So, if you want to look like a local, go shopping for some prim-hair.

## OTHER ATTACHMENTS (HUDS, COLLARS, AO'S, OH MY)

You can attach anything you can build to your avatar. You are really limited only by your imagination. Wings are a popular attachment. Figure 4-40 shows one of my favorites—a fish that swims in circles around your head. This behavior requires some scripting, which is covered in Chapter 8, "Making the Magic: Scripting Basics."

**Figure 4-40**
*Fish attachment swimming around my head.*

Figure 4-41 presents several other sample attachments from friends who graciously volunteered to have their avies photographed. Notice things like a working cigarette, more prim-hair, neckties, and attachments that make you look semi-human. Now things are starting to get interesting!

You also can add another type of attachment to your avatar called a Heads Up Display (HUD). These attachments are not seen by other avatars, and they essentially appear as additional controls or UI elements. These HUDs can influence the way you see the world or provide additional data.

**Figure 4-41**
*Avatars with various attachments.*

The HUD in Figure 4-42 contains controls and information about the wind when I am sailing.

**Figure 4-42**
*Heads Up Display.*

## NO MODIFY CLOTHING

Once you move out of freebie land, you will find most items you buy are *no copy, no modify*. That is, you cannot make any changes to the item, and/or you cannot create additional copies.

In Figure 4-43, you can see that a set of eyes I bought came with no modify permissions. I cannot make changes to them in my Appearance dialog.

**Figure 4-43**
*Eyes with permissions set to no modify.*

For most things in SL, you have them in your Inventory, and when you rez them, there is a copy in the world. For no-copy objects, be careful when giving them away or dropping items because you may lose them altogether.

## OUTFITS AND MANAGING YOUR INVENTORY

Once you get your shape, eyes, clothing, and the rest the way you like it, it is a good idea to save all these settings in an Outfit. To do this, select Appearance from the pie menu.

At the bottom of the dialog that comes up is a button labeled Make Outfit, like the one shown in Figure 4-44.

 **Figure 4-44**
*The Make Outfit button.*

When you click this button, the dialog in Figure 4-45 shows up.

When you create a new outfit, you create a folder in your Inventory under a top-level folder called Clothing. In the Make New Outfit dialog, you can select the things you

want to include and do not want to include. For example, if you want to save everything about your avatar, check all the boxes in the dialog. If all you want to save is your clothes, just check those.

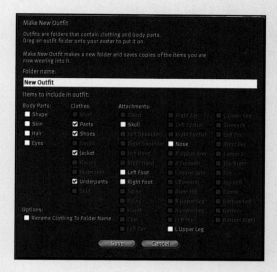

**Figure 4-45**
*The Make Outfit dialog.*

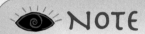 NOTE

If you have purchased something with No Copy permission, the Make Outfit function *moves* the item from wherever it was stored in your Inventory into the folder containing your new outfit. This capability can be handy, but I have found it does the wrong thing about 50% of the time.

The Rename Clothing To Folder Name check box renames the objects. So, say you created a new outfit called Gothic Clubbing and you're wearing a new shirt you created called My New Shirt; it would be renamed to Gothic Clubbing Shirt.

Using Outfits, you can manage several different clothing options or several different avatars. To change from one outfit to another without tedious undressing and redressing, just drag the Outfit folder from your Inventory onto your avatar.

I have one other note on this subject. If you save multiple items in one folder—say two shirts—the first shirt is worn, and the other is ignored.

## ADVANCED AVATAR TOPICS

Working with avatars just gets better, so I have to share a bit here. The simple capability to attach objects to avatars has led to extremely large and small avatars. It has also enabled very nonhuman-looking avatars. In fact, I'm sure that SL residents have taken avatars way beyond any original concepts that Linden Lab put into the design.

In the very large case, it is possible to attach large primitives that surround your human-shaped avatar to create, for example, a massive dragon or some other fantastic shape. You can also attach primitives that can make parts of your avatar mesh invisible, such as your legs. Figure 4-46 shows a small selection of the variety of avatars possible in SL.

**Figure 4-47**
*Crunch pose and avatars by Joshua Nightshade.*

I wanted to introduce you to these concepts so that you can think outside the box if you want a truly creative avatar. All the fun details of how to create such avatars are left for you to discover or to await a second edition of this book.

**Figure 4-46**
*Variety in avatars.*

Finally, and this capability is really advanced, you can get your avatar to adopt a "crunch" pose. In a crunch pose, the mesh is folded as tight as possible and then you surround yourself with primitives.

In Figure 4-47, you can see Joshua Nightshade (the human avatar) in a crunch pose and then how he looks surrounded by three different robot avatars he created. While "flying," the robot avatars appear to hover and fly around.

# TUTORIAL: CREATING A NEW SHIRT BY ALINA MIKADZE

First, I want to thank Alina Mikadze (shown in Figure 4-48) for her work on these tutorials. We met at the first Second Life in Seattle Meetup, and she was quick to join the cause of educating new residents. In this tutorial, she shows you how to create a new shirt from scratch, name it, and save it to your Inventory.

**Figure 4-48**
*Alina Mikadze.*

## STEP 1: FIND A PRIVATE PLACE TO WORK

Since clothes may be coming on and off, you should find a place where you can work undisturbed. A friend's place or a sandbox is fine; however, make sure the sandbox is rated mature and not PG, or rez a hollow cube around yourself just in case. In these photos, I'm in the restroom downstairs at The Shelter; this is a good place to go if you don't have your own house.

The Shelter is a great place for new residents to go and hang out with others in their same shoes.

 You can find The Shelter at **http://slurl.com/secondlife/isabel/44/244/79/**.

**Figure 4-49**
*You can create a new shirt.*

## STEP 2: SAVE YOUR CURRENT LOOK

Before you start, it's a good idea to save your current look so you can get back to it.

Right-click on yourself to open the pie menu, and then select Appearance to open your Appearance dialog. Choose Make Outfit (see Figure 4-44) at the bottom. A window opens with check boxes for all the items you're wearing. Check all the boxes. Label the outfit something like **Default** or **Default (***date***)** so that you can start from scratch if you tinker something beyond repair.

## STEP 3: CREATE A NEW SHIRT

Take a look at your Appearance dialog again. The clothing tabs on the left allow you to edit the item you're wearing (if you're allowed) or create a new one if you aren't wearing anything on that layer. As you can see in Figure 4-49, I don't have a shirt on (!), so there is a button named Create New Shirt that does just that. Click the button. If you have a shirt on, click Take Off; then you can create a new one.

Take off your shirt if you already have one on.

## STEP 4: EDIT YOUR SHIRT SETTINGS

Like in other parts of the Appearance dialog, there are quite a few different parts you can customize here (see Figure 4-50). Scroll down and use the slider bars to set your sleeve length, collar, fit, and so on.

**Figure 4-50**
*You can customize a number of different parts of the shirt.*

## STEP 5: CHANGE THE TEXTURE AND COLOR

To change the fabric, click the Fabric box to the left of the sliders (see Figure 4-51) to open a texture window. The dialog accesses fabric textures from your Library and also from your Inventory if you have any there. I picked a marbled green one to use. Check the Apply Immediately box to see the texture change right away. Choose Select when you're done.

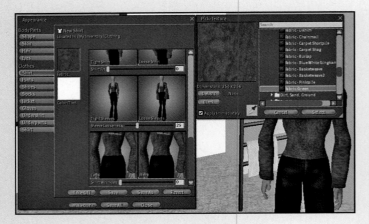

**Figure 4-51**
*Changing fabric is easy.*

Next, you can edit your shirt color using the Color/Tint box. Click on the white square to open the color picker (see Figure 4-52) and try some different shades. Your shirt texture is tinted with the color you choose here; if you leave it white, it remains the default color of the texture. If you leave the Texture box blank, your shirt is tinted the basic color only.

**Figure 4-52**
*Clicking on the color/tint square opens the color picker.*

The color change applies immediately. In the photo, tinting the green texture with light purple turned my new shirt a nice dark teal; you can experiment here to get something interesting. When you're done, click the Select button.

Figure 4-53 shows my shirt before and after the tint change.

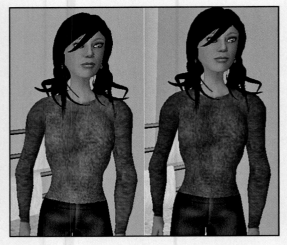

**Figure 4-53**
*Before and after the tint change.*

## STEP 6: SAVE AND NAME YOUR NEW SHIRT

When you're ready, click the Save button to save your new shirt. Open your Inventory, and there it is! But since you don't want all your handmade shirts to be New Shirts, right-click your new shirt and select Rename to give it a different name (see Figure 4-54). Voila!

Notice that the names of items you're currently wearing are indicated as worn.

**Figure 4-54**
*Rename your new shirt.*

# TUTORIAL: A SHOPPING EXPERIENCE BY ALINA MIKADZE

In this tutorial, we go to a great store for new residents where you can find a lot of free or nearly free stuff. You find something you like and buy it.

Sometimes things you buy unpack themselves nicely in your Inventory. Other times, you have to extract the items manually. This tutorial shows you how to extract items from an unscripted box/package.

## STEP 1: FIND A STORE AND BUY AN ITEM

Pick any store and any wearable item you like! Use all the navigational knowledge you've already gained. Many things you purchase and many things you receive free come in a box, even if it doesn't tell you that specifically.

## STEP 2: FIND THE ITEM IN YOUR INVENTORY

Locate the item in your Inventory; if you just got it, it is probably in the Objects folder. If you just bought something, try the Recent Items tab.

In this case, I got a Talk Like a Pirate kit (see Figure 4-55).

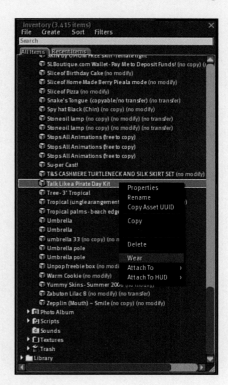

**Figure 4-55**
*I select the Talk Like a Pirate kit.*

If you right-click and select Wear Out of Habit, you'll probably end up looking like what is shown in Figure 4-56. You are, in fact, wearing the packaging! Don't do that.

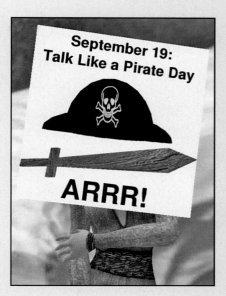

**Figure 4-56**
*You don't want to wear the packaging.*

## STEP 3: REZ THE BOX

Click on the box in your Inventory and drag it right out of the window onto the ground in front of you. You end up with something like Figure 4-57, where you can see a box (or sometimes a bag).

**Figure 4-57**
*A box!*

## STEP 4: OPEN THE BOX/OBJECT

Now right-click the box. Then click Open on the right of the pie menu, as shown in Figure 4-58.

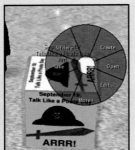

**Figure 4-58**
*Open is on the right side of the pie menu.*

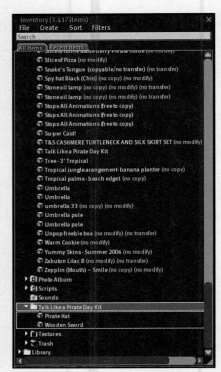

**Figure 4-60**
*The new folder is somewhere in the top level of your Inventory.*

You get a window showing you the contents of the box. Click Copy To Inventory to, well, copy it to your Inventory (see Figure 4-59).

At this point, you may get a pop-up box warning you that some of the items are no copy. This means you cannot create a copy of the object, so if you continue, the item moves from the box into your Inventory. Continue.

**Figure 4-59**
*Click Copy To Inventory.*

## STEP 5: LOCATE THE NEW FOLDER IN YOUR INVENTORY

The new folder should be somewhere in the top level of your Inventory (see Figure 4-60). Now you can drag it anywhere you want to store it. If the folder has a generic name, you might want to rename it to make it easier to find later.

## STEP 6: USE YOUR NEW LOOT!

Select the items and "wear" them (see Figure 4-61). Nice!

**Figure 4-61**
*I'm sporting my pirate kit clothing.*

# TUTORIAL: APPLYING A NEW SKIN BY ALINA MIKADZE

In this tutorial, you find, purchase, and apply a new skin to your avatar. You can search for "Skins" to find all kinds of skin providers in SL. You can also find freebies as well. One great thing to do when you arrive is to get a free skin. Tete a Pied offers one free if you are younger than 30 days old. That's what we use here.

## STEP 1: SEARCHING FOR AND TELEPORTING TO TETE A PIED'S STORE

**SLURL** You can find Tete a Pied's store at **http://slurl.com/secondlife/isabel/44/244/79/.**

## STEP 2: GET YOUR NEW SKIN

You can create your a new skin using the creation tools in the Appearance dialog, or you can get a ready-made one to put on your avatar. In this tutorial, we use Tete a Pied's free newbie skin pack (see Figure 4-62).

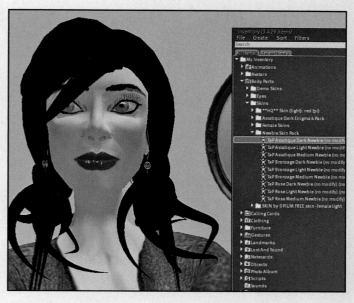

**Figure 4-63**
*My default skin.*

**Figure 4-62**
*The free newbie skins from Tete a Pied.*

## STEP 3: UNPACK AND FIND YOUR NEW SKINS

If you purchased or received a ready-made skin, unpack the box and find the new skin in your Inventory. In Figure 4-63, I have my default skin on (boy, was that a long time ago!) and have selected the skin I want to change into.

## STEP 4: WEAR YOUR NEW SKIN

Right-click the new skin and select Wear to put it on, as shown in Figure 4-64. It will probably take a bit for the face to rez. Don't worry; this is normal.

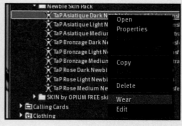

**Figure 4-64**
*Right-click the new skin and select Wear.*

## STEP 5: SMILE!

That's it! You're now wearing your new skin. I'm shown in my new skin in Figure 4-65. Notice, though, that you can't simply right-click and "take off" your skin. Like eyes and other body parts, your skin needs to be replaced by another skin to change; otherwise, you'd be skinless in between. Not healthy.

**Figure 4-65**
*My new skin.*

You can edit settings for homemade skins or the occasional ready-to-wear one in the Appearance dialog. However, most purchased skins are no modify, so what you see is what you get. Remember that the same skin can look dramatically different on avatars with different shapes.

## SUMMARY

You learned in this chapter about your avatar, your virtual self. You now know how to change your shape, hair, eyes, and skin—the basic components of an avatar. You also know how to dress yourself and create your own basic clothing. Finally, you were exposed to the ways to find freebies and shop in SL.

To this point, you've learned how to walk, how to talk, and now how to make yourself look the way you'd like! Avatar tuning is a pastime for some and an obsession for others. The knowledge you have now should allow you to get out there and make your avatar your own.

It's now time to move beyond basic controls and learn how to create your own objects.

*There are REAL PEOPLE behind these avatars*
*and no MATTER what we say, we FEEL things that*
*happen to our avatars in here.*

**—Circe Broom**

# Second Life Culture and Relationships

# 5

The more time I spend in Second Life, the more I realize the SL experience is about the people. Most of those I have met in SL are adventurous, creative, and infectious to be around. There are, of course, the bad seeds, those full of drama, the needy, the desperate, and the depressed. I'm glad they're here, for a perfect world would be, well...dull.

The difference between real-life (RL) and Second Life relationships is a lot like the difference between skiing and snowboarding. The basic concept is the same—strap something slippery to your feet and plummet down a snow-packed mountain—but they have fundamental differences.

## What You Will Learn

- The ground rules and guidelines for SL relationships

- What your profile says about you

- The pace of SL relationships and how to manage it

- Partnering in SL and how it can enhance or destroy your SL experience

- Virtual sex—what you should know about it

- SL culture and the community standards

Understanding SL relationships and how they are different from RL relationships will improve your enjoyment of SL. SL can change your RL relationships in very positive ways and potentially negative ways as well. For some, SL offers opportunities some people would never have in RL (for example, consider someone who is housebound). SL offers opportunities to interact with other people such as RL educators and professionals to whom you might not have access otherwise. Finally, SL is already an international group. You can interact with people from around the globe without leaving your hometown.

This chapter introduces you to the social side of SL and helps you avoid pitfalls, emotional traumas, and potential RL catastrophes. Unlike other chapters that have definitive answers like "How do I resize a prim?" or "How do I teleport from A to B?" this chapter is a collective opinion, sorted and distilled down from more than 70+ interviews and group discussions.

Please take what you can use and leave what you can't. I understand that learning from experience is sometimes the best way to go.

Read on or skip ahead; the choice is up to you.

# GROUND RULES AND GUIDELINES

The term *relationship*, as it's used here, applies to both romantic as well friendship types of relationships. The following sections cover the five main ground rules or guiding principles you should know about SL relationships:

- There are real human beings behind each avatar in SL. You and they have real emotions.

- You do not know for certain anything about the other person you're interacting with.

- Take your time getting to know others in SL before committing to deeper relationships or partnerships.

- There are bad people in SL as well as good; not everyone plays well with others.

- SL will impact your RL in good and bad ways. The impact may be quite profound.

## VIRTUAL WORLD, REAL EMOTIONS

There are real human beings behind each avatar in SL. You and they have real emotions. This is the #1 thing to keep in mind! Whether by LL design or accident, avatars in SL are obvious and extremely hard to fake or turn into *bots* (automated beings) as you can in other multiplayer online role-playing games (MMORPGs). You will not encounter a bot or scripted person in SL without knowing it! If it looks like an avatar, it is, and avatars are driven by humans.

I have read so many bad articles on SL where claims are made such as "you can do whatever you want" and "it is a dream world without constraint," but this is not really true. Our human emotions are as real in SL as they are in RL. I cannot stress this enough: There is NO difference.

Be aware of this point and sensitive to the fact that there is another human on the other side of that avatar you're chatting with. That person is not miles away from you, only milliseconds.

## THE ANONYMITY OF AVATARS

You do not know for certain anything about the other person you're interacting with. Who are these other humans? You can learn quite a bit about them in the first few minutes of chat. You can learn even more by looking at their profiles (as you will see in the section "What Are You Revealing About Yourself?").

You may not care too much about who the person really is if this is just a casual acquaintance, but trust me, you do care if you are about to get emotionally attached or enter into a business partnership with another SL resident.

One resident shared this story: *"I once dated a guy [in SL] who turned out to be a woman who, I think, was maybe really a guy the whole time pretending to be a woman for a while, now you figure out the reasons for that."*

I don't want to say you should be paranoid and ask for all kinds of RL proof before you get involved, but simply be aware that the person you're interacting with may be any age, any gender, any ethnicity; may be located anywhere; and may have any motivation to be in SL and talking to you.

Gina Marchionne had the following lines from Bob Dylan's song "Gotta Serve Somebody" in her profile, and I thought they were quite appropriate:

> You may like to gamble, You might like to dance, You may be the heavyweight champion of the world, You may be a socialite with a long string of pearls, You may be rich or poor, You may be blind or lame, You may be living in another country under another name.
>
> —Bob Dylan

A friend had this to share: *"I have recently come to suspect that one of my oldest friends in here is not my girlfriend, as I'd thought. Rather, I am beginning to put a lot of things together and I think my friend might be male but hey she/he is still my friend, right!?"*

## TAKE YOUR TIME; THERE'S NO HURRY

Take your time getting to know others in SL before committing to deeper relationships or partnerships. Relationships (both romantic and friendship) form quickly here (see the section "The Pace of SL Relationships"). Take your time and get to know why the person you are involved with is here in SL. Understanding why you're both here and whether these two things are compatible will go a long way to avoiding a lot of emotional strife. So, take your time; there's no hurry.

**Pannie Paperdoll:** This is one bit of advice no one will listen to, and everyone should.

## THERE ARE SOME BAD PEOPLE HERE

As I noted previously, there are bad people in SL as well as good; not everyone plays well with others. Some have their fun at the expense of other residents. This can occur in obvious ways, but it can also take the form of emotional abuse. Here are a couple of relevant samples:

**Circe Broom:** I watched a musician be heckled worse than anyone would ever do in RL, last night and I felt like crying at how absolutely EVIL some people think they can get away with being, just because they are in here ANONYMOUSLY as an avatar.

**Ayla Holt:** I was going to quit SL, but I ended up only leaving for 3 days. My [RL] husband wanted me to quit, because he said that it made me sad too much of the time. But then he said I should come back and just made me promise to try and get the unhealthy people out of my SL.

AH: I have a theory. It's that everyone is here to fill voids in their RL and everyone has different voids. Maybe they just don't have enough fun, or sex, or love, or a place to be creative. Anyway, when I came back I logged in and didn't have anyone on my friends list because I had taken them all off and I decided that the people caused the drama for me so I would design and open a store and not talk to anyone. That worked for about a day, LOL!

You have a lot of control over your SL experience, including the option to leave it altogether for a night or permanently. Be aware of what is happening and how you're feeling. Take a deep breath and then figure out what you want to do about it. We'll cover a lot more on griefers and strategies to combat them in Chapter 12, "Practical Matters: Under the Hood of the Metaverse."

## WHAT YOU DO IN SL WILL IMPACT YOU IN RL

SL will impact your RL in good and bad ways. The impact may be quite profound. Remembering this will help you in many ways. Say you have always wanted to open your own business; it's easy and certainly less expensive to try your hand at this in SL. The lessons you learn in marketing, customer support, and sales can carry through to your RL.

Imagine you play guitar but aren't comfortable playing to an RL audience. You may find playing to SL audiences easier, and it may build your RL confidence to the point you take the leap.

Perhaps you are very introverted and uncomfortable in RL relationships. Try being more bold and open in SL relationships; the confidence you gain may help you in RL.

**Julia Hathor:** It needs to be mentioned that SL has the power to impact your RL, in a way that can be good or bad. What other 'games' or 'platforms' do that so thoroughly as this one? To me that is what makes this world so unique—it gets under your skin very quickly, very completely.

**Pannie Paperdoll:** You can get dragged into things you don't want to be dragged into. You could fall into things you never dreamed of but love.

For some, SL allows them to do things they would never be capable of in RL. One SL friend of mine is agoraphobic, housebound, and an RL recluse. SL has allowed her to develop deep friendships and an active social life, which would not otherwise be possible. Honestly, I would never have guessed this, even months into our friendship; she is so energetic and alive in SL.

There are many of these extremely positive examples, but let me just give you one scenario to consider. Say Johnny is unhappy with his marriage in RL. He gets into SL for fun and a bit of escape, nothing serious. But he ends up meeting Suzie and starts spending more and more time in SL. His RL marriage starts to suffer. At some point he realizes he is falling in love with this person and decides he wants to meet in RL. Perhaps he even starts considering leaving his RL marriage.

When Johnny reveals his desire to meet in RL, Suzie pulls back sharply. Johnny finds out Suzie is married in RL and has no intention of ever leaving her spouse. Suzie spends time in SL just for fun. She just wants to be friends. Johnny is emotionally crushed and is left with issues to deal with both in RL and in SL.

Does falling in love in SL sound far-fetched? Trust me; it's not. And if love moves forward, the next logical step is to move an SL relationship to RL. This move is an extremely challenging process. It's not impossible, but very few couples bridge the gap.

Reiterating the main point, what you do in SL will impact your RL in good and bad ways. I hope now you understand why I say that the impact may be quite profound.

# WHAT ARE YOU REVEALING ABOUT YOURSELF?

Your avatar's profile is available to everyone in SL. When you encounter someone new for the first time, you

should expect that person is pulling up your profile at the same time she is typing "hello there" in the chat window. To access the profile of someone that's nearby, right-click on her Av and chose Profile from the pie menu. You can also search for any person and look at her profile.

Your SL profile can tell a lot or a little. Most of the information in your profile you control, but some of it you cannot. Understanding what your profile says to other SL residents is very important, as well as understanding how to interpret others' profiles.

Rather than subjecting any of my SL friends to this level of scrutiny, let's walk through the rather mundane profile of my own avatar, Ansel Gasparini. We'll see what we can and cannot change and what I might want to improve.

## BASIC SECOND LIFE INFORMATION

The first tab, 2nd Life, can be seen in Figure 5-1. On this tab, you see the basic information about Ansel. First, there is his name and a picture. I cannot change my name, but I can change my picture. The one shown here is an old one, so perhaps I should update it (you can do this by clicking on the picture in your profile and selecting a replacement from the Texture Picker). To the right and just above the Born date, you may see whether another person is online. Your ability to see this information depends on whether the other person allows this.

You will also see a Born field that contains a date. The date the avatar was created gives you an idea of how long someone has been in SL. You may be tempted to use this date to judge someone's SL experience, but beware, some residents have more than one avatar (or alts). The person behind a "young" avatar may be more experienced than you expect.

It is common for people to celebrate their SL birthdays in-world, and a nice practice is to send close SL friends a birthday present or just a friendly happy birthday IM on the SL birthday.

Below the born date is something called Account. This tells you whether the resident has a credit card on file and whether that credit card has been used to make a payment or buy L$.

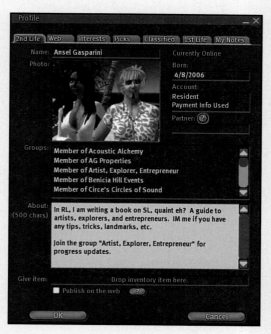

**Figure 5-1**
*Avatar Profile, 2nd Life tab.*

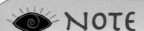

At the time of this writing, rumor has it that LL is phasing out the payment information. A person's profile will no longer show whether he or she has payment info on file. Instead, it will show whether he or she has verified his or her age and identity with LL. LL will be contracting a third-party ID-specialty company to do the verifications, and then only verified adults will have access to areas flagged as containing adult content. Landowners will have the option to allow/disallow ID-verified accounts onto their land, just as they have the option to do so with payment-verified accounts now.

Next is Partner. This field may list another avatar name. In this case, you can see Ansel doesn't have an SL partner. You can be a partner of one and only one avatar in SL. We'll talk more about partnering in the section "Partnering in SL."

The next section is Groups. I find it very interesting that LL decided to make the groups to which you are subscribed public knowledge. You can learn about people by quickly browsing the groups they belong to. The reverse is also true; think about what you're saying about yourself whenever you request or accept membership in a group.

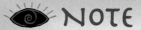

You can double-click on a group in the profile to look at details about the group. If you find a group you want to join, you can join directly if the group owner has allowed open enrollment; otherwise, you will have to request membership and be invited to join.

Beneath Groups, you will find an area, About, where you can describe yourself or make any statement you like about yourself.

Beneath About is a field called Give Item, and in that field is the text *Drop Inventory Item Here.* This is very important to know, so listen up! If you want to give something to someone and that person is not around, do the following: Open his profile and open your Inventory. Drag the item you want to give him from your Inventory over this field and let go. The item will be sent to the other person. Why this critical capability is presented in this way I'm not sure, but that's how you do it.

Finally, in your profile, there is a check box where you can choose whether your information will be published to the Web. Think about whether you want your SL information shared outside SL. That's the decision you're making here.

## LINKS TO RL WEBSITES

The second tab, Web, can be seen in Figure 5-2. Here, you can specify a website people can visit. This is a great way to link to a business website if you're an SL seller and want to have more storefront than you can get in your profile or classified, or you might use this to link into your MySpace page if you're going for more full disclosure. When you look at someone's profile on this tab, you can either load the page or open the page. Loading the page opens the web page in the same window as the Web profile tab, as you can see in Figure 5-2. Open launches a browser window outside the SL viewer.

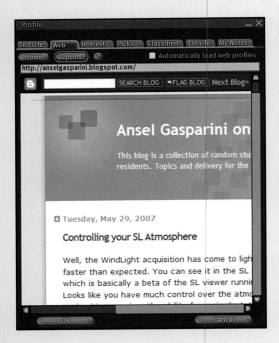

**Figure 5-2**
*Avatar Profile, Web tab.*

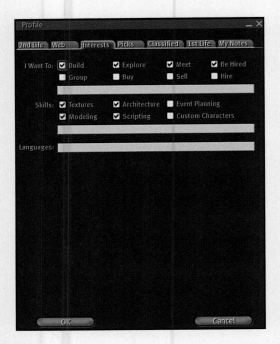

**Figure 5-3**
*Avatar Profile, Interests tab.*

**Palemoon Twilight:** If you don't have a business or personal site of your own to promote, why not promote a charity or some other favored site on your Web Profile page?

## YOUR SL INTERESTS, SKILLS, AND LANGUAGES

The third tab, Interests, can be seen in Figure 5-3. The third tab allows you to identify your SL interests such as the things you like to do and the skills you have. There is a line where you can write in your own comment. These lines are sometimes quite interesting/informative. The Languages bar is intended for your use if you're multilingual or just want to communicate what languages you can speak or read in SL.

## YOUR SL PICKS

Ansel Gasparini has not created any entries on the Picks tab—unbelievable really, and an area of my profile I should improve. To highlight this tab, I have asked Pannie

Paperdoll if it's OK for me to share her Picks, Profile page. The fourth tab, Picks, can be seen in Figure 5-4. The purpose of Picks is to specify locations in SL that others might find interesting and teleport directly to by using the Teleport or Show On Map buttons.

To create a pick, you go to the location and click New from your own profile at the top of the Picks tab. You can add a picture, specify a title, and give a description. Often, SL residents use picks as kind of a personal photo album or a place to declare their affection for friends and partners. Pannie has several picks. Figure 5-4 shows a pick that is essentially an endorsement of her friend's store Splash Aquatics.

**Kymber Schnook:** The Picks tab gets widespread use. And it's not used merely as a revolving gallery; it has utility—as a free spot for advertising goods/service, for example. I've heard many times, "TP to the 2nd pick in my profile, I'll meet you there!" Not everyone has cause to post a Classified ad. "Picks" is the tab that people heavily populate. You can create up to 10 entries, after all.

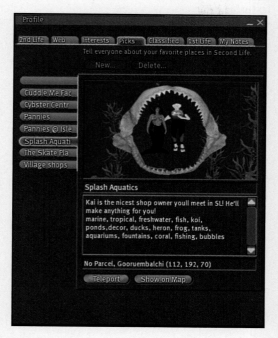

**Figure 5-4**
*Avatar Profile, Picks tab.*

## YOUR SL CLASSIFIEDS

The fifth tab, Classifieds, can be seen in Figure 5-5. Here, you can see other avatars' classified ads, but this is also the place where you create/manage your own classified ads. Classified ads can also be found via Search-> Classifieds and are kind of like newspaper classifieds.

There are several important decisions to consider when placing your first ad. First, each ad is associated with the posting avatar. A link to your profile will be included in the search result. Each ad is also associated with a location, which is the place you are when you create the ad. This is important, for example, if you want people to teleport into your store or, alternatively, if you're posting a personal ad, you may want to consider where potential suitors will show up.

You can set a location to your store, specify an image, and choose the category under which it should be listed. You must also decide whether your item is mature content. This is left up to you (at least as of this writing), and you should know that Search, by default, excludes mature content.

Finally, you pay a price in L$ for your listing. Paying more will get your item listed higher in the search priority in SL, just like Google Ads work on the Web. Ads run for one week and can be set to automatically renew on that schedule. If you want to stop an ad that is automatically renewed from running, simply uncheck the renewal box.

When creating an ad, you can select a check box to have the ad be automatically renewed each week. To stop running the ad, uncheck the box.

**Figure 5-5**
*Avatar Profile, Classified tab.*

## YOUR 1ST LIFE OR RL INFORMATION

The sixth tab, 1st Life, can be seen in Figure 5-6. On this tab you can list any RL information you want to share, including a picture. Some people share quite a bit; many share nothing. At first I didn't list anything, but I decided to add *Married with Kids* to cut down on any relationship confusion. I also used this spot to advertise the SL meet-up group I run in the Seattle area.

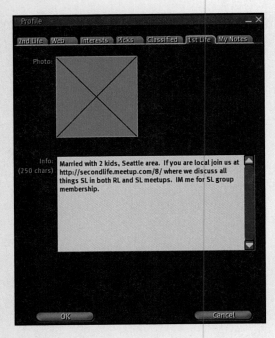

**Figure 5-6**
*Avatar Profile, 1st Life tab.*

**Figure 5-7**
*Avatar Profile, Notes tab.*

## YOUR NOTES ON OTHER AVATARS

The seventh and final tab, My Notes, can be seen in Figure 5-7. This is a place for you to add notes about others you meet. Unlike the other tabs, the notes on this tab are your notes about the other person. Even though this is a tab on the other person's profile, these notes are **not** visible to anyone else, including that person. This tab is useful if you want to keep track of customers, business associates, or acquaintances. I use it, for example, to note who originally introduced me to this person. Figure 5-7 is Pannie Paperdoll's profile, where I noted I met her when interviewing Xavior Nicholas. There is a limit to the amount of text you can place in this box (about 1,000 characters).

## TIPS AND ADVICE ON PROFILES

And that's about it for profiles. Remember that this information is publicly available to anyone in SL, so don't be afraid to look at other people's profiles to learn more about them. My final word of advice is to revisit your profile every couple of months. I've often found bits I put there that were no longer relevant.

I'll let Julia Hathor and Jade Steele have the last words on profiles:

**Julia Hathor:** Don't make an unfriendly profile, especially one that issues threats to strangers that you have never met—it just labels you as a jerk. Leave out your extreme nudity or obscenities, your profile is the picture you will leave in someone's mind—do you really want to paint an ugly picture?

**Jade Steele:** Profiles are essentially a public expression of what you are all about…the groups you are in, what you say about yourself, the picks you choose. Lots of people are "profile stalkers", an affectionate term used to describe those who like to browse through profiles of friends and people they know…hehe I'm a self admitted profile stalker :) But its a great way to let people get to know you more, a great way to advertise a business you may have, express your love for your SL partner and on an on…

In fact, profiles are not allowed to contain any mature photos, content, or language.

# THE PACE OF SL RELATIONSHIPS

One of the most interesting differences between SL and RL relationships is the speed at which they form and dissolve. I'm talking not just about romantic relationships, but friendships as well. I have had many SL friends share very personal RL joys, struggles, and tragedies. Most shockingly, I found myself sharing my own right back.

> **Jade Steele:** It surprises me, and I sometimes stand back in shock, at how easily it is to get emotionally attached here.

Don't say I didn't warn you. The real question I had was "Why?" Why are SL relationships so accelerated? Trust me; it would make a great master's or doctoral thesis for someone. The answer, even after my many interviews and conversations concerning the topic, remains unclear. However, I can share several themes, theories, and ideas with you.

## THE TRUE SELF THEORY

The true self theory goes something like this: In SL, we are stripped of many biases and prejudices that we have in RL based on someone's physical appearance. The biggest examples are race, gender, ethnicity, social status, and age (to some degree). Because of this, we get to know the real or true person more quickly and/or easily.

> **Attim Hokkigai:** Honestly, in real life I'm somewhat reclusive, and I find it enjoyable to come on here and be around people who don't judge me by looks/sexual preference/beliefs as much.

It is true that prejudices are reduced in SL, and this brings together individuals who would be unlikely to have a close RL encounter. It is hard for me, however, to believe that stripped of the rich RL communication information like facial expressions and body language, you can really get to the true nature of a person.

However, evidence suggests people are willing to share personal data in SL faster than they would normally in RL. It is also true that basic things like manners, listening skills, and other social graces are easily seen or obviously forgotten in the context of chat.

> **Krix Zaughn:** There is a huge amount of literature in the social psych and interpersonal communication fields concerning self-disclosure and its role in the development of relationships. The amount and level of self-disclosure are said to be positively correlated with relationship development. Also, there is literature suggesting that self-disclosure is easier for many people to do in situations where they feel safe in doing it—i.e., they won't ever see that person again like the person next to you on the plane. This data supports the evidence that people are more willing to share personal information in SL.

## THE SELF-DECEPTION THEORY

The self-deception theory goes something like this: In SL, we believe more easily that other people are both who and what we want them to be. There are none of the realities of RL dating to distract us such as bad breath, cigar smoking, type of car they drive, or the annoying way they eat their peas. It is, therefore, easier to dream up the perfect relationship.

Ironically, the self-deception theory can also be argued using the same principles as the true self theory (the reduction of RL prejudices). If the avatar I'm with in SL looks HOT, she is HOT to me, regardless of whether she is in RL a beer-bellied, tobacco-chewing trucker sitting at an Internet-connected freeway truck stop.

> **Pannie Paperdoll:** There's also something that I never expected and is very important! Poseballs [objects that cause avatars to animate/move] cause feelings. They are so realistic. I can't tell you how many times I've fallen in love on slow dance 3. You cuddle each other and lay your heads on each others shoulders. When you combine a good animation with good conversation it's a strong lure.

> **Kymber Schnook:** I think the evocative backdrops (ideal surroundings, tender poses, etc)…facilitates the advancement of emotions…like being swept away in some fairy tale imagery.

This is an important point: *"combining a good animation with good conversation."* I would argue the true self theory and the self-deception theory are all parts of the same hearty stew that bubbles on the SL stove of relationships.

## THE LACK OF CONSEQUENCES THEORY

The lack of consequences theory states that it is easy to form relationships because there is no real commitment, and little or no consequences are involved. In SL, there is an extremely low level of commitment required to form relationships. If something goes wrong, the consequences are also extremely low to nonexistent. In general, this leads some people to be more cavalier in their SL relationships.

That is, to many, SL is just a game, so they are not emotionally committed; they are just playing. But to others, they are emotionally engaged. When these people encounter each other, it can be very fun at first, but the fallout is usually disastrous for the emotionally involved and has ruined many SL experiences.

> **Jade Steele**: I think there is often times a much different level of commitment here, then that of what you find in RL. And I'm sure you are aware that SL in and of itself is so many things to so many people … a game to some, a platform to others, and educational business tool to another. I think there is likely the same varying outlooks on relationships in the degree of seriousness they take from one person to another.

## THE LEARNING TO BE LOVED THEORY

The final theory, and one of my favorites, is the learning to be loved theory. Kymber put it best, so here it is in her words:

> **Kymber Schnook:** My basic theory on people is that we hold back what we consider to be unloveable. And as long as we do that, we don't find out that to be fully disclosed and THEN be loved, is to truly be loved… intimately be loved, for all that we are, and all our weaknesses, etc. Here [in SL] we can practice.

OK, I'm stretching my existential wings here, but I interpret this to mean that, at a very basic level, we yearn to be loved along with all our imperfections. The SL community (at least today) is an extremely accepting one. Coupled with the lack of consequences already discussed, this environment may allow people to bravely divulge more about themselves more quickly. If we receive positive results for this disclosure, we will go deeper more quickly. Perhaps the safety, acceptance, and ease of escape the SL community provides allows for more open, deeper, and faster relationships to develop.

Can we practice being loved and loving in SL? I think so.

## SUMMARIZING THE PACE OF SL RELATIONSHIPS

If you're coming off your latest SL breakup, I hope you are shouting, "AMEN, BROTHER!" If you're a reclusive LSL scripter, I've probably lost you by now, so feel free to jump ahead to Chapter 6, "Building Basics."

Everyone agrees that SL relationships move quickly. The inside joke is one month of SL dating is the same as one year of RL dating. As you have seen in the previous sections, there is no single reason why relationships move so quickly. SL relationships, just like RL relationships, are complicated, exciting, exasperating, energizing, and often emotional. As my friend Pannie puts it: *"All of it hinges on the fact that we are all human."*

Kymber Schnook had this to say on the topic—a more serious, perhaps more thoughtful analysis:

> **Kymber Schnook:** I find it interesting that, in SL, folks focus discussion around the "rate" of relatedness…but don't ponder longevity/sustainability. Which do you perceive to be a better measure of relationship quality/health? A lot of people try to create a dog-years (type) calculation to describe the accelerated pace of SL coupling. Very few of these partnerships last a year. If they do, it's considered somewhat extraordinary. If 'recalibrated' into dog-years…maybe one can feel better about the surprising brevity of SL relationships. That, to me, is the deception.

Time isn't compressed in SL. Sure, relationships progress more rapidly if you give more of yourself, more quickly. But these intense SL relationships often fail—short-lived by RL standards. They can't hold up to the less impulsive (more realistic) pace that settles in. We are human, on the other side of our Avs. No amount of ideal scenery can hold together an SL relationship that wouldn't hold up in RL. That folks have many throw-away relationships in SL…full of intensity for, say 3-6 months…means, to me, they weren't much of a relationship to begin with.

I will say that for me it is very satisfying to share SL with others, but you should consider your relationships there very much as you would any other RL relationship.

Let's move on to how to take a relationship further by making the commitment between avatars public through SL partnering.

# PARTNERING IN SL

You can publicly declare a relationship with another SL avatar by *partnering*. LL marketing says, "Can't be married in real life? Try Second Life!" Ironically, you must request an SL partnership outside SL by going to this URL: http://secondlife.com/community/partners.php.

As of this writing, each partner pays L$10 to form a partnership. The only real thing that happens is that your avatar names will appear in each other's profiles.

Typically, partnering means something of a virtual marriage and exclusive dating. But reasons for SL partnering vary, from simple role-play fun to seriously looking to move from SL into RL. Some people use partnerships to represent SL business partners, but most are romantic. It is important to discuss with your potential partner the reasons for partnering and to set each other's expectations.

**Stroker Serpentine**: I think everyone should partner…SL can be a vaccuum…its best shared with someone who enjoys all the things that SL has to offer.

If one partner decides to end a partnership, that person must pay L$25. There is no recourse, no waiting period, and no splitting of collective assets, as partnering does not mean any shared land usage or special permissions.

**Charla Vellhi:** Why last week baby you were riding around naked on Help Island, and now you want HALF?!?

The following interviews with Jacqueline Trudeau and Jade Steele shed some light on how partnerships evolve and dissolve and other things to consider.

## AN INTERVIEW WITH JACQUELINE TRUDEAU

Jacqueline Trudeau (see Figure 5-8) is a builder of SL classic sailing yachts. She fell into yacht building based on an SL friendship. Here are a few bits about SL partnering extracted from several hours of conversation. Thanks, Jacqueline.

**Figure 5-8**
*Jacqueline Trudeau.*

*Ansel Gasparini: So, tell me about sailing in SL.*

**Jacqueline Trudeau:** well… it starts back in my first land….I became friendly with my neighbor… We had ended up getting adjoining land… up to about 2K of land by then and for Christmas, I wanted to get him a sailboat for a present, a sort of traditional looking one.

I thought, there was everything in SL, this shouldn't be too hard to find. Well, it wasn't out there. So, I thought, ok, I've learned a little building, combined with my building knowledge from worlds, how hard could this be and not only that there were these sailboat scripts on the scripting wiki.

So… i put together my first boat…. sliced and dimpled and few spheres and tori together, textured it, dropped the Kanker's scripts into it, and it promptly capsized. [smiles]

JT: I don't want to give the impression that SL sailing started with me and my first boat. Kanker Greenacre's flying tako sailboat really started the SL sailing revolution. Before Kanker's scripts, as another SL sailor has said, SL sailboats were like "driving cars on water".

*AG: How do you think partnering in SL is different than in RL?*

JT: the differences to RL… well i think there are more pressures in RL partnering…living up to what society, friends , family want you to do. Here… you can partner with a bisexual robot … or a furrie… or whatever and no one gives another thought to it. In RL … it's the hunt for the *right* partner

And as much as I love [my SL partner] and my life in SL … first life is just that, my first priority

*AG: Care to comment on sex in SL?*

JT: I'd say the fascination wears off the longer you are here ;) Speaking for myself of course ;)

*AG: What advice would you have for new residents who want to experience SL sex or make money as a dancer/ escort?*

JT: SL sex… be careful! and i don't mean condoms…. I know of many a RL relationship that was torn apart by VR "adultry" not only here… but in the VR world i came from - worlds.com

It should be discussed with your RL partner if you are in a serious relationship… or well hidden, preferably the first. But thats the thing also… alot of people use something like SL as a dating service for transitioning into a RL relationship, and I'd say… very few make it to that point

If you have a RL relationship and you are here [in SL] primarily for the sex, well, obviously something is not going right for you in RL and it's unlikely that a great guy you meet here is going to come to RL rescue and sweep you out of a dissatisfied marriage

*AG: How does partnering add or detract from your SL experience?*

JT: oh! partnering with the right person adds immensely! lari inspires me… we collaborate on projects. We are able to help each other with RL issues we both go through. Like i said.. the *right* partner… otherwise it can also be a lot of drama and agita :))

*AG: I have been hearing a lot about that, drama and agita that is.*

JT: another partnership i had… one that wasn't *right* ..i spent many consecutive sleepless nights over that. I've never done that in RL! lol.

*AG: Any closing thoughts on the whole relationship/ social/sexual topic?*

JT: My philosophy is partnering here is like partnering in RL, opposites may attract, but finding a compatible partner and one, most important IMO, that shares similar reasons for being in SL as you. Someone who's here for gor RP is not going to be the most likely candidate for me… or vice versa :))

With that we headed off for a sail:

**Figure 5-9**
*Sailing aboard Trucordia.*

```
[Trudeau Yawl HUD whispers: HUD
Channel set to: 234991812

Trudeau Trucordia Yawl (Rez and Sit)
whispers: Raising sails, prepare to
get underway…

Trudeau Trucordia Yawl (Rez and Sit)
whispers: Helpsail setting Off

Trudeau Trucordia Yawl (Rez and Sit)
whispers: Using skipper wind speed
and direction settings - speed 8,
direction 0]

Ansel Gasparini: WHHHHHOOOOOOOOOOO!
```

## AN INTERVIEW WITH JADE STEELE

Jade Steele (see Figure 5-10) is a long-time SL resident, former club owner, and currently the owner/operator of Midian City in SL (see Figure 5-11). Midian City is a role-playing area that is inspired by a combination of the movies *Sin City* and *Blade Runner*. "A futuristic dystopia," as she puts it. We sat down for a discussion on SL relationships one night at my home in Viciae. What follows is a summary of that conversation.

**Figure 5-10**
*Jade Steele.*

**Ansel Gasparini:** *hello*

**Jade Steele:** hi!

*AG: You have a music preference?*

JS: i like anything … this is a great place!

*AG: TY, Shall we dig in?*

**Figure 5-11**
*Jade in Midian City Lights.*

JS: Sure! Let me grab a glass of wine, have to have a nice glass of wine with music like this!

*AG: Why do SL relationships seem to evolve/dissolve so quickly relative to RL relationships? Do you think that is the case? Do you have any thoughts as to why?*

JS: definitely think that is the case. They seem to run at enhanced speed, compared to RL … from start to finish. I'm not really sure why. I have some ideas, but I don't know that I can put my finger on it. I think there is often times a much different level of commitment here, then that of what you find in RL.

SL in and of itself is so many things to so many people … a game to some, a platform to others, and educational business tool to another. I think there is likely the same varying outlooks on relationships in the degree of seriousness they are take from one person to another. As irony would have it, my ex just IMed me ;)

*AG: Happy to have him/her over if you like*

JS: Hmm, no that's okay :) I've only been in one SL relationship in my two and a half years here, though a new one seems to be on the horizon.

*AG: I recall from a past conversation that you were surprised that a SL partnership evolved for you.*

JS: Yes I was … and really I shouldn't have been, as I had seen it time and time again with friends. Experiencing it for myself was another story … the fact is that no matter how much one tries to separate RL from SL, there is a point where RL emotions become involved.

*AG: So, what do you think new residents need/want to know about SL relationships?*

JS: I would suggest that a new resident take an SL relationship slowly … it's fun to meet people and a wonderful thing to get swept off your feet in SL just as it is in RL. But I have seen sooo many people go through this, with such haste and intensity … and inevitably, that same person ends up burned, upset and ready to leave SL over it.

So many approach their SL relationships with the idea that its just SL … RL is RL and SL is SL .. but as I said, inevitably RL emotions will come into play with one or both parties. That was essentially the downfall of mine. It became so intense, so real … that the next step would be to take it RL.

*AG: I would expect that taking the relationship from SL to RL would present a serious problem if the other person turned out to be married, role playing, etc.*

JS: Exactly … which is part of what I meant earlier in that SL is so many things to so many people … likewise with SL relationships. To some it is role play, to others its more of a close friendship and I know of many here in SL relationships who are in them because they are in an unhappy RL relationship that they feel trapped in.

Other things someone new to SL might want to know … that the outlook and motivations for being in a relationship can be quite different. Its crucial to know up front that the two of you are on the same page.

Be sure that you and your potential partner are on the same page, because here we are stripped of many of the RL biases and such in this virtual world. Its is all very new territory for humankind, and I'm not sure that

some quite know how to take that, how to act, how to be …

Really it depends on what one is looking for. You have to be realistic about it in that it is virtual reality and its likely that your relationship will only be in this world. But despite my cautions and such, they truly can be a wonderful fullfilling thing. SL is about community, not matter what your outlook on it. Yes, even amongst the 'platform/creating/technology' crowd. What makes Second Life is finding someone you have something in common with … that one person you connect with … its a wonderful thing and I believe why the majority of people stay in SL

*AG: How did partnering add to your SL experience, if you don't mind me asking?*

JS: Well to me it started out as just an SL thing … almost a roleplay if you will, though I hesitate to use that word as it sounds like I approached it with carelessness. It did mean a lot to me and added a lot to my SL experience. He is a wonderful, funny, caring person and it meant a lot to me to be able to share my time and experiences here with him … someone to explore the vasts sights with, someone to go to clubs with, someone I trusted enough to run a business with …as I said, SL is about community. It is a social world and spending it in the company of someone you enjoy greatly enhances it.

*AG: Anything else you think I should cover on partnering before we leave the topic?*

JS: Its far more that paying your L$10 to partner and have someone's name in your profile. Finding someone you connect and can share SL with is the core the SL experience. But just like a RL relationship, it requires openness and honesty with one another, as well as an understanding of the level of commitment that can be devoted to one another in this virtual world.

While we were speaking I received an IM from a person I'm slowly getting into my second relationship with, I was told to pass this on … and it is true:

"You can tell him that meters feel like miles, first kisses are just as good as RL, we are free from the preconceptions of RL visuality, and able to explore who we really are. =) OH… and I hope a month from now you can say… "Humm.. I was wrong… SL relationships can be good!"

*AG: Well, again thank you for your time, I hope our paths cross again sooner*

JS: I hope I was able to add a little insight.

## SUMMARIZING SL PARTNERSHIPS

You will have the most success in SL partnering if you discuss your expectations with potential partners beforehand and remember that people enter into SL partnerships for many reasons. Having an extremely close friend to share your SL experience can add significantly to your SL experience, while a bad partner can significantly detract from it.

Let me close the discussion on partnering by sharing the two SL wedding experiences that I have been part of. The second wedding I was invited to in SL was between SunshineBlonde Fairymeadow and Osiris Acropolis. Osiris is an SL artist, and the two met when SunshineBlonde asked to have a portrait done. They are perhaps the most loving couple I have met in SL. Sunshine and I chatted briefly a day or so before her wedding:

**Ansel Gasparini:** *Mind me being nosy?*

**SunshineBlonde Fairymeadow:** Go for it

*AG: Are you married in RL?*

SF: Divorced right now, but in RL relationship, 7 yrs now, living together

*AG: How did you meet your SL wedding partner? Do you know them in RL?*

SF: We met when I asked to have a [SL] portrait done. He is artist here. I didn't know him at all in RL or SL. My RL relationship is not good… was planning to leave RL man soon… possibly meeting SL hubby RL someday. I guess SL was a good place to go when I felt alone.

A month or so after their SL marriage, I chatted with SunshineBlonde and Osiris about SL married life. Osiris shared something that is really an SL-only kind of thing that was extremely touching. When Osiris met Sunshine, he wore an animal avatar—"the beast." The beast was an

emotional shield of sorts as he described it. He "took on human form," for Sunshine as an expression of his commitment to her. Only in SL. Figure 5-12 shows the before and after shots.

**Figure 5-12**
*SunshineBlonde and Osiris before and after.*

And before we leave the topic of partnering, I should let you know that you can have virtual kids in SL as well! You can see Sunshine and baby in Figure 5-13.

**Figure 5-13**
*SunshineBlonde and baby.*

The first SL wedding I attended was between Anika Davison and MagnAxiom Epsilon, two friends from Worlds of Warcraft role-playing a married couple in SL and no longer together. Anika had this to share with me on SL relationships and having an SL child:

**Anika Davison:** It's always good to talk to your partner about where the line is…and what you are…or are not looking for in RL and SL. The line is differently for everyone. Some want to take it more into RL….and others never want to say anything about themselves in RL

With me and Mag…we are very different in RL, but we both want the same thing in SL. I am not looking to start a RL relationship in SL, and he isn't either but we love to roleplay as a married couple and family, we have a new baby

***Ansel Gasparini:*** *So, I have to ask, how is the baby? How does that work in SL?*

AD: well before we decided to have kids Mag and I talked it over. We talked over the SL Options. We decided we wanted to experience pregnancy in SL. The options are 1. Adoption (jumping straight to a roleplay child), 2. SL pregnancy and birth with SL scripted baby at first until toddler age, then a roleplay child (basically someone who comes to SL wanting to roleplay a child character).

Well, one great thing about SL is you can safely have sex as much as you want without the risk of pregnancy, so let's move on from SL partnering to the topic of virtual sex in SL.

# VIRTUAL SEX AND AVIEROTICA

***Ansel Gasparini:*** *My wife is worried about SL sex, what should I tell her?*

**Julian Dibbell:** oh, tell your wife: be afraid. be very afraid.

Sex sells and it should be no surprise that SL has heavily erotic components. The first place someone took me in SL was to the Barbie Club (at the time the hottest strip club in SL). The following sections discuss the basics of virtual sex and how it is done in SL.

## WHAT IS VIRTUAL SEX?

I think Jade Steele described virtual sex best during one of our conversations:

**Jade Steele:** Virtual sex in SL essentially entails writing out and describing your sexual feelings, your fantasies, your actions and how you are reacting or would be reacting physically and emotionally if it were a RL encounter. It is essentially a form of roleplay really, but one that often leaves one or both partners a bit … um, what's the word … excited :).

Virtual or cyber sex has been around for a while in multiplayer text-based worlds, chat rooms, and through the use of webcams and phone calls. Like other VR sex, SL sex offers a way for people to experiment sexually in a physically safe environment. For example, you can have a one-night stand without worrying about getting infected.

Perhaps more adventurously, you can try your hand at bondage, without worrying about being tied up in someone's RL basement.

Unlike other text-based venues like chat rooms, SL offers a rich 3D environment in which to explore these sexual activities, including customizable animations that take two (or more) avatars through a series of sexual actions/poses.

However, always remember you're dealing with another real person, and there are real emotions involved. Here is what Julia Hathor had to say on the subject:

> **Julia Hathor:** Never forget that there is a real person behind the Avie. Even if you don't believe that sex is a serious matter in a virtual reality, they might! Experts will tell you that the mind is the most important organ in Sexual encounters and it is. If you are in a serious relationship in RL , you run the risk of ending it, or at the very least creating difficulties with your RL partner. If you aren't in a serious RL relationship it may be a good way to meet people, but always keep in mind that you have no way of knowing what a person tells you is true. Relationships in a virtual world should be taken very slowly and with a generous amount of caution.

## HOW DO YOU DO IT?

To be good at virtual sex, you need to learn the art of typing great sexual chatter, while driving your SL avatar through a series of animations, and at the same time perhaps trying to satisfy your RL self. Let's just say it's very different from RL sex.

All you really need is a willing partner and some privacy, but SL also offers many toys and trinkets to enhance your SL sexual experience. The most notable one is a functioning virtual penis. If you're using a male avatar, you're like a Ken doll or eunuch when you enter SL. Yes, that's right; you have no parts!

While having a penis is not necessary, strictly speaking, you will want one if you get into all the SL animations. An impressive amount of scripting has gone into these devices, allowing your partner to touch them and get reactions out of them. As to animations, you can buy

them separately and use them when and where you like. There are also highly scripted beds available that allow you to control the action between two or more avatars.

There is fierce competition in this field, so just search classifieds to see what's available.

Figure 5-14 shows a PG version of an animation in action modeled by RL husband and wife Pannie Paperdoll and SCOTTis Stradling. You'll have to use your imagination for the animated part (it shouldn't require much imagination).

**Figure 5-14**
*Pannie Paperdoll and SCOTTis Stradling demonstrate an SL animation.*

You are about to be disappointed if you were expecting me to break out the step-by-step in-depth tutorial with accompanying video at this point.

Extracted from the following interview with Stroker Serpentine:

> **Stroker Serpentine:** Personally…if avierotica appeals to you…then I would seek out an experienced escort. It's like the old frathouse cliche. Get a hooker!

Regina Lynn discussed the topic of cybersex at the 2006 Second Life Community Conference (SLCC). For broader information on the subject of virtual sex, check out

Regina's book *Sex Rev 2.0* (see Figure 5-15), available at http://www.amazon.com/gp/product/1569754772 or go to her website at http://www.reginalynn.com.

**Figure 5-15**
*Regina's book.*

# AN INTERVIEW WITH STROKER SERPENTINE

*"Stroker came here with a mind full of wicked ideas."*

**—Obscuro Valkyrie**

Stroker Serpentine is an SL businessman who makes his virtual living from virtual sex or, as he puts it, *avierotica*. His opening remarks at the 2006 Second Life Community Conference say it all: *"My name is Stroker and I am a Pervert!"* He is responsible for Stroker Toyz and the Eros sims, most notably Amsterdam (see Figure 5-16), "Everything you would expect from Second Life's favorite Adult Playground."

SLURL 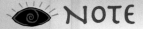 You can get to Amsterdam by going to **http://slurl.com/secondlife/Amsterdam/136/233/25/**.

If anyone has cracked the code on SL relationships and virtual sex, I figured he might have a clue. What follows is an extract from our conversation:

> 👁 NOTE
>
> As of this writing, Stroker has reportedly sold the Amsterdam Sim for a considerable amount of real-world dollars.

```
[You arrive in the as yet unfinished
Bangkok Island sim]

Ansel Gasparini: Hey man, thanks for
taking the time

Stroker Serpentine: No worries
```

**Ansel Gasparini:** *so, maybe a quick background on yourself*

**Stroker Serpentine:** heh... Hmmm...lurker for decades, entrepreneur IRL for many years...Hallmark...Event Planning... Contractor...CLub Owner. I have been in Moove.com...Seducity....here

*AG: So, any questions before I start firing at you?*

SS: Do me!

*AG: How did you discover SL? You said you came kicking and screaming?*

**Figure 5-16**
*Amsterdam, an Eros sim.*

**Figure 5-17**
*Stroker Serpentine.*

SS: Yes…I was doing very well in Seducity…I had several shops and
many friends…they began migrated
here one by one

*AG: Was there a defining moment, when you knew you were switching over?*

SS: Well its rather mundane…but I made a simple pair of sunglasses…A friend allowed me to sell them on her popular sim…I made L$10K in one week

He has displayed in his club several pics of avierotica coincidentally…at the same time I was taken to the most popular club in SL at the time…CLub Elite…ran by BigJohn Jade. We were all dumbstruck and the lightbulb went on

*AG: Now at the time SL was every more primitive (pardon the pun)*

SS: yes about three or four thousand members I believe. I began to explore the sexual aspects and found rudimentary devices to accomplish sexual animations

*AG: What do you think a new resident needs to understand about SL relationships and how are they different from RL relationships?*

SS: Well…I believe that any relationship is only as healthy as the two people in it. There is an underlying factor to MMORPG's that tend to attract people with addictive personalities. I have found (for me) that those who do not have successful RL relationships find it very difficult to develop and nurture virtual ones. I could go on for hours on this subject…so let me know what is applicable

Many SL relationships blossom at the speed of fiber optics…only to fizzle in a few weeks. I'm sure that it has to do with the "Kid in a candy store" principle. Why be monogamous…or committed if there is such a plethora of attractive and available potential partners.

*AG: The speed at which SL relationships develop and the honesty and sharing was extremely surprising to me, I am still trying to really understand why things move so fast here.*

SS: Its the Metaverse Ansel! We move at the speed of byte :-). You hear a lot about "Oh, she is a drama queen"…or "He is nothing BUT drama"… Drama is as integral to Second Life as it is in real.

*AG: There does seem to be almost a thirst for drama among some people*

SS: I have a theory on that… many of us (myself included) have very short attention spans…virtual worlds tend to attract a good portion of society that are looking for an escape from their real lives. Be it an abusive relationship…a dysfunctional upbringing or an isolated existence.

We come to an environment such as this for a fresh start…a paradigm shift… yet, because of the skillset we bring and emotional baggage, it becomes evident to many that they cannot be someone other than themselves…even in a virtual environment. Because no matter how far you go…there you are. Sounds cliche, but as you mentioned, when you "peel the onion" there you are…warts and all. SL is a vegetable peeler…LOL

*AG: How should a new resident approach partnering? Does it enhance the SL experience?*

SS: Partnering… Being somewhat of an event planner I officiate many weddings here. Some how I attained the mantle of relationship guru…dont ask me how…I generally just listen. I think everyone should partner… SL can be a vaccuum…its best shared with someone who enjoys all the things that SL has to offer. I find it interesting that a good majority of the "oldbies" have had long-term partners

*AG: Do you think there is some shared idea of what it means to partner here? Or is it really just decided by the individuals involved?*

SS: I think a good portion of it is societal conception…marriage being the predominant definiton…but if you remove the moral restrictions it forces you to define your partnership

*AG: Hmm, I think that is a very good point. What advice do you have for new residents on forming relationships/partnerships?*

SS: Take the time to get to know your perspective partner. Make a concerted effort to be "present" in their SL. There is no hurry…a disastrous partnering could jade one's opinion of SL as a whole. I've seen many people leave SL because of a broken heart…only to return as an alt

*AG: A fresh fresh start*

SS: True that…but you also lose friendships…not to mention that 40K item inventory!

*AG: I'm sure you are asking a million times. How do I get laid here?*

SS: You go to an Eros sim :-) (unabashed plug)

*AG: Walk me through it? I'd ask you to do a tutorial for me but that would be asking too much :-)*

SS: Well…as irl there is a visual appeal involved. One has the ability to portray themselves as anything from a porn star to a Victorian maiden. So…grab someone you find attractive of the opposite sex…be polite…ask them what they find attractive in an avatar. This does two things…it sparks a repoire…as well gives you some insight as to their likes/dislikes

The conversation will undoubtedly turn to clothing and skins…and popular places. I have yet to meet anyone who will tell you to "Get Lost". We all identify with being a "newb" and are happy to expedite that uncomfortable situation into a sense of belonging. So…you "tweak" your avie first…

*AG: ok, we chat, she says you need to get some prim hair :-) (kinda like you need to go brush your teeth)*

SS: exactly :) I believe honesty and humility go a long way…dont be afraid to ask for help

*AG: so, do I need equipment to have sex in SL?*

SS: There are differing styles of "sex" in my opinion. I can find a well detailed and intelligent "cyber session" as erotic and fufilling as hopping on a poseball. Be explicit yet not too pornographic…it's an artform. Text teasing can be foreplay. Pick-up lines are passe…all we have is text to express ourselves…be imaginative

*AG: So, is this one style of sex? text-only?*

SS: Yes. There are those who have perfected and refined it over many years of chatrooms and bulletin boards (I'm dating myself). Just as in real life there should be some time spent on enticing and sensual expression. "Hey baby…nice shoes…wanna screw" will only get you a rate card from an escort. Unless of course you are at an orgy ;P

*AG: LMAO! Now that would be an experience to be had! What other styles of sex are there here?*

SS: We are all human on the other side of the modem. Well there is of course avatar sex…that is where one uses a scripted device to animate their avatars into provocative positions. Second Life is full of them…some more creative than others…but then just watching your character do the "horizontal mamba" on your monitor can be as boring as Tolstoy.

Personally…if avierotica appeals to you…then I would seek out an experienced escort. It's like the old frathouse cliche. Get a hooker! You can jumpstart your lovemaking skills considerably by employing a professional.

# SL CULTURE AND COMMUNITY STANDARDS

While it may seem so at first, SL is not all about sex. This section provides a few words on the SL culture and LL's published community standards. The culture of SL continues to evolve as the population grows from 5 individuals to 5 million to 10 million. SL culture has and will continue to change in significant ways. However, there are some general characteristics you will find in most SL residents today. Most are creative, adventurous, tolerant, helpful, friendly, sharing, and above all else resilient to change—and for the most part patient with the architects of this world.

**Julia Hathor:** It needs to be stressed that this is an unfinished world, one that is often in turmoil. It is going to best appeal to those of an adventurous spirit, the ones that can roll with the punches, or who have the creativity to make a mark on it. Don't look for something that works flawlessly or predictably or you will be disappointed.

The best place to start when learning about SL culture is to read the community standards. It gives you a very good overview of what is most important in SL culture. If you disagree or feel like you cannot live by these standards, perhaps SL is not the right place for you.

The community standards also give you a strong view of what type of society LL hopes SL will have. While the community standards are enforced, they are enforced in a way similar to how speed limits or stop signs are enforced in RL. There is not a policeman on every street corner waiting to write you a ticket if you blow through a red light at night. But if you ignore traffic lights altogether, you will eventually get caught. The community standards are cultural norms with commonly agreed-upon social enforcement.

Residents are encouraged to report abuse of these standards. To take the traffic light analogy way too far, imagine Granny Smith who has lived on a street corner her whole life. Whenever she sees someone run a red light, she calls the cops. This can be done in SL by filing an abuse report. The community standards have this to say on reporting abuse:

> Residents should report violations of the Community Standards using the Abuse Reporter tool located under the Help menu in the in-world tool bar. Every Abuse Report is individually investigated, and the identity of the reporter is kept strictly confidential.

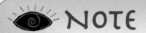

## NOTE

Not all TOS reports are handled by LL. To avoid becoming the world's police force, sim owners/managers may have the abuse reports automatically directed to them. Within those regions you *cannot* report to LL directly, and you'll get a message informing you that LL isn't in the loop.

You can look at the 25 most recent violations and actions taken by the SL abuse team in the police blotter located here: http://secondlife.com/community/blotter.php.

I'll not republish the whole community standard here but will reprint the "Big 6." You can find the latest and full version of the community standards at http://secondlife.com/corporate/cs.php.

## THE BIG SIX: COMMUNITY STANDARDS

The material here is taken directly from http://secondlife.com/corporate/cs.php:

> The goals of the Community Standards are simple: treat each other with respect and without harassment, adhere to local standards as indicated by simulator ratings, and refrain from any hate activity which slurs a real-world individual or real-world community.
>
> The Community Standards sets out six behaviors, the "Big Six", that will result in suspension or, with repeated violations, expulsion from the Second Life Community. All Second Life Community Standards apply to all areas of Second Life, the Second Life Forums, and the Second Life Website.

- Intolerance

   Combating intolerance is a cornerstone of Second Life's Community Standards. Actions that marginalize, belittle, or defame individuals or groups inhibit the satisfying exchange of ideas and diminish the Second Life community as whole. The use of derogatory or demeaning language or images in reference to another Resident's race, ethnicity, gender, religion, or sexual orientation is never allowed in Second Life.

- Harassment

   Given the myriad capabilities of Second Life, harassment can take many forms. Communicating or behaving in a manner which is offensively coarse, intimidating or threatening, constitutes unwelcome sexual advances or requests for sexual favors, or is otherwise likely to cause annoyance or alarm is Harassment.

- Assault

   Most areas in Second Life are identified as Safe. Assault in Second Life means: shooting, pushing, or shoving another Resident in a Safe Area; creating or using scripted objects which singularly or persistently target another Resident in a manner which prevents their enjoyment of Second Life.

- Disclosure

  Residents are entitled to a reasonable level of privacy with regard to their Second Lives. Sharing personal information about a fellow Resident—including gender, religion, age, marital status, race, sexual preference, and real-world location beyond what is provided by the Resident in the First Life page of their Resident profile is a violation of that Resident's privacy. Remotely monitoring conversations, posting conversation logs, or sharing conversation logs without consent are all prohibited in Second Life and on the Second Life Forums.

- Indecency

  Second Life is an adult community, but Mature material is not necessarily appropriate in all areas. Content, communication, or behavior which involves intense language or expletives, nudity or sexual content, the depiction of sex or violence, or anything else broadly offensive must be contained within private land in areas rated Mature (M). Names of Residents, objects, places and groups are broadly viewable in Second Life directories and on the Second Life website, and must adhere to PG guidelines.

- Disturbing the Peace

  Every Resident has a right to live their Second Life. Disrupting scheduled events, repeated transmission of undesired advertising content, the use of repetitive sounds, following or self-spawning items, or other objects that intentionally slow server performance or inhibit another Resident's ability to enjoy Second Life are examples of Disturbing the Peace.

# AN INTELLECTUAL TAKE ON AN EMOTIONAL TOPIC

I am a software engineer by training, not a psychologist or sociologist. So, I hope you will forgive me that I cannot leave the topic of SL relationships without some attempt to organize things a bit more…logically. Feel free to skip ahead if you'd rather; I'll never know.

Richard Bartle, one of the true pioneers of the multiplayer computer game industry, wrote the book *Designing Virtual Worlds* in 2003. In it, he reported on research he had done on the motivations of people for playing multiplayer games. His first work categorized users as socializers, killers, achievers, and explorers along two dimensions. I have reused these two dimensions from Bartle's work and have added my own SL take on motivations and types of SL play.

The dimensions can be seen in Figure 5-18. On one end are those who are mainly motivated to spend time in SL because of all the other residents. The world is essentially less interesting to them than the people. On the other end are those mostly motivated to spend time in SL due to the platform, build tools, scripting, texturing, and so on. The people in SL are essentially less interesting to them than the platform itself. This resident/world split is the first dimension.

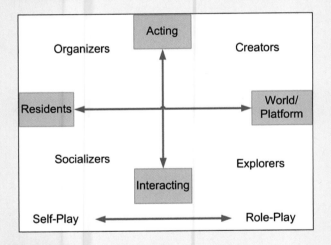

**Figure 5-18**
*Resident focus types matrix.*

The second dimension describes a certain preference for a style of play. On one end are people who prefer to take direct action upon residents or the world. They are motivated to influence or change the world or other residents. On the other end of this dimension are those who prefer interacting with other residents or the world. They are motivated to play with and be involved with the world and other residents.

These two dimensions give us four categories or types of SL residents:

- **Socializers:** These residents enjoy interacting and playing with other residents. You'll find them in clubs dancing, listening to live music, or hanging out together.

- **Explorers:** These residents enjoy interacting with the world itself. You'll find them traveling around looking for new things to see and experience.

- **Creators:** These residents enjoy acting on the world itself. You'll find them building, scripting, texturing, and attending classes to learn how to improve their skills.

- **Organizers:** These residents enjoy acting on or influencing other residents. They are the people who draw crowds, organize events, run nonprofits, and the like. Organizers may be more like politicians if they want to get their point across.

A couple of additional categories or types are in SL, and I fit them in thusly:

- **Griefers:** These residents are like organizers in that they enjoy acting on other residents, but unlike organizers who are trying to bring groups together or politicians who are trying to influences other's opinions, griefers are there for the fun of making trouble for others.

- **Businesspersons:** There are a lot of aspiring businesspeople in SL. I put them on the top-middle of the graph. They are definitely interested in acting on the environment, but they want to create and then influence others to buy their stuff.

As you know or will come to find out, people move all around this chart as their SL experience matures. You are not locked into one role. These are not personality types. Most of us will spend some time as an explorer early on as we learn about the world of SL. We'll then most likely drift toward socializing or creating.

**Pannie Paperdoll:** I think everyone…goes through stages. It's like growing up. When I was new. I was all focused on exploring. It's all I cared about, finding new things. Then within two weeks I met someone and that changed everything.

Finally, there is a 3rd dimension I'll call roleself play. On one end, people in SL are playing themselves, perhaps an idealized version of themselves, but they are there as themselves. I call this self-play. On the other end are people who are specifically role-playing someone or something entirely different. The classic example is RL males playing female avatars.

So, who are you right now: a socializer, creator, organizer, or explorer? And who are you hanging out with? Ask them. Feel free to IM me and tell me I'm full of it, or suggest improvements to this model.

# SUMMARY

In this chapter we covered five key points you should understand about SL culture and relationships. We discussed how your profile says a lot to others about who you are. We also talked about the accelerated pace of SL relationships and the need to take your time. In addition, we discussed SL partnerships and virtual sex. Finally, we covered the SL community standards and discussed different styles of play.

I hope the words of caution contained in this chapter do not scare you away or overshadow the great emotional joys, personal growth, and friendships you will find in SL.

**Pannie Paperdoll:** When I've fallen for someone, I've been in heaven and the true friendships I've made here are priceless.

Most people agreed that the excitement and love they discovered in SL was no less real to them than any RL relationship, and as one put it: *"I've expanded my definition of love. I realize that the human heart is capable of much more than I would have previously given credit for. This comes from my having loving relationships in both lives—simultaneously—and deciding that is neither a contradiction or a hypocrisy."*

SL allows you to experience and do things in ways you would never be able to in RL. You will meet and befriend people outside your normal age group of friends, outside your normal ethnicity of friends, and outside your normal social class. You will have access to people you would not normally be exposed to, such as educators and other

**Chapter 5**  *Second Life Culture and Relationships*

professionals. This exposure to different people and different ways of thinking will change you for the better.

You might be wondering what I take away from SL relationships. For me, it's thrilling to share this nascent moment of an emerging 3D Internet with all these wild, wacky, and creative people.

I'll leave Cubey Terra (see Figure 5-19) to close out this chapter.

**Cubey Terra:** The biggest mistake someone can make is to arrive on Orientation Island asking, "How do I make money?" That's not what SL is about. SL is about people. The builds, the economy—all of that is a by-product of people interacting with each other. Behind every avatar is a real flesh-and-blood person. We should focus on that, rather than the pursuit of L$.

**Figure 5-19**
*Cubey Terra.*

*I like to make things that people can enjoy and look at and
I've always been fascinated by architecture.*

**—Attim Hokkigai**

# Building Basics 6

Building in Second Life is an act of pure creation limited only by your imagination. Truly, it is heady stuff. In SL, you build in-world. You can watch and learn while others build, others can watch you build, and you have the capability to collaboratively create works. Getting good at building takes time, effort, and practice; however, it's easy to get started, as you will soon see.

Another builder, Julia Hathor, has been in SL for quite a while and is a phenomenal artist. When you see her work in SL, you'll realize she has attained a magician status with her textures, homes, and garden creations. Yet, Julia confided in me the difficulties of trying to learn to build in SL when she got started.

## What You Will Learn

- Where to build even if you don't own land
- How to create new primitives and objects
- How to edit, move, rotate, and size objects
- How to link objects into groups
- How to use basic texturing to make your objects look good
- How to set basic object permissions
- How to create flexprims and lighting
- How to create a deck, rock, room, picture frame, and avatar tail

*"I explored around the world for about 4 months without even thinking of building. To me, the creators seemed like magicians, I thought I could never do it. Then one person showed me how simple it was to create a waterfall. OMG I was hooked after that!"*

You too can create a waterfall or whatever you like. Be patient with yourself, practice, and you'll be surprised how quickly you improve. This chapter introduces you to the brick, mortar, and basic mechanics of building in SL. So, put on your work gloves and let's get started.

# WHERE DO I BUILD?

Building in SL occurs in-world. Therefore, to start building, you must find a place to build—your workshop, if you will! If you already own land, this is a great place to start practicing your building techniques. If you don't own land, no worries; you're looking for a place called a *sandbox*.

It is possible to build anywhere that you have permissions (and by default you have permissions even on someone else's land). It's not neighborly, however, to start erecting your next masterpiece in a public place or on your neighbor's land, so it is best to find a sandbox.

Sandboxes are open spaces set aside for the purpose of building and are even used by long-term residents when they're working on something for a client that their own land does not easily accommodate.

To find a sandbox, search under Places for "sandbox." When you find one that you like, teleport there and find a nice quiet corner with enough space for what you have in mind. Sandboxes with high traffic may offer more people who could help you if you get in a bind. Sandboxes with low traffic may be smaller but offer you more privacy.

Sandboxes get scrubbed or cleaned at different intervals, so it's a good idea to be aware of the rules and regulations of the sandbox you choose (they are usually posted on a sign). It's also a good idea to keep a copy of your work in your Inventory. I never really started trying to build until I figured out I could keep things by *taking them into my Inventory*. That is, you can build an object, select it, and choose Take or Take Copy from the pie menu. If you select Take, the object is moved from in-world to your Inventory. If you select Take Copy, you leave the object in-world but also place a copy of it into your Inventory.

Be aware that sandboxes can sometimes present problems. Julia Hathor notes, *"Each sandbox is different, they all have different rules, and to tell you the truth I hate building in them, they are very laggy, and it is hard to concentrate, LOL."* Suffice it to say, some love 'em, some hate 'em, and others fall in between.

Most people building in sandboxes are trying to get something done, so if you need help, ask nicely and be respectful. You'll find most people will be willing to help you, but if someone is busy, respect his need to go about what he's building. You can learn a lot just by observing. The first tutorial shows you how to find a sandbox.

# THE BASIC BUILDING BLOCKS: PRIMITIVES OR PRIMS

Building in SL starts with the basic building blocks called primitives or *prims*. You can "link" multiple prims together to create "objects" in the world. To be precise, an object can be one prim or several linked prims. SL Help defines primitives in the following way: "Primitives are basic 3D shapes, like cubes, cones and cylinders. Primitives can be resized, reshaped, hollowed out and otherwise modified, then combined and connected to make more complex shapes and objects. All building starts with primitives."

Unlike most real-life 3D modeling tools, you do not work with triangles, quads, vertices, or meshes to form an object; rather, you model and link primitives to sculpt your creations. In fact, you cannot import a 3D mesh into SL at all (well at least not as you might think).

## CREATING A PRIM

You do not need to have any prior modeling experience to get started building in SL. To create a prim, click the Build button at the bottom of the screen. Alternatively, right-click anywhere you are allowed to build to get the pie menu and select Create (see Figure 6-1).

Three things will happen:

- Your viewpoint will change to get closer to the action (unless you have disabled this setting in your properties).

- Your cursor will change to a magic wand.
- The basic creation dialog will appear, as shown in Figure 6-2.

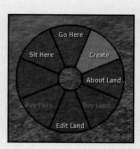

**Figure 6-1**
*Select Create.*

**Figure 6-2**
*The basic creation dialog.*

Wow! Very cool. Each icon represents a primitive you can create. This chapter covers all but the last two, which create trees, bushes, and grasses. Those are covered in Chapter 9, "Land Ownership, Terraforming, and Landscaping."

Select the cube, which is the first shape in the top row, and then click your magic wand somewhere. Voilà, you have built your first cube (see Figure 6-3). Easy, right?

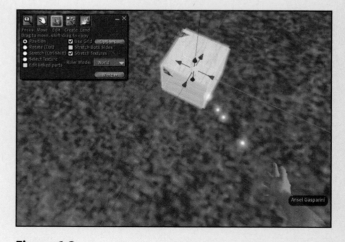

**Figure 6-3**
*Your first cube!*

You will also notice that you are now in edit mode on your cube. That is, the creation dialog is now on the edit panel instead of the creation panel. We'll get back to that one in a moment. For now, click on the Create button again, select another shape, and create it.

If you want to create multiple prims without going back and forth between edit and create modes, simply check the Keep Tool Selected box. Then each time you click, you create a new prim of that type.

There are a couple things to notice. If you click on the land, your prim will be placed on the land. If you click on a wall or other vertical surface, your prim will be placed against that surface, defying gravity. If you click on top of another prim, your new prim will be placed, well, on top of the other prim. So, for example, if you check Keep Tool Selected, you can quickly create a stack of boxes. Try it.

There are, at the time of this writing, eight types of primitives you can create (see Figure 6-4). They are the Box, Cylinder, Prism, Sphere, Torus, Tube, Ring, and Sculpted. You might wonder why there are 13 icons in the creation menu (excluding the tree/bush). The other shapes are simply shortcuts to commonly used modifications of the eight basic prims. We'll talk more about how to apply modifications to prims later in the chapter.

For example, the second shape from the top left of the create dialog (refer to Figure 6-2) is a ramp or wedge. Figure 6-5 shows how the box prim type can be transformed into a ramp. You start with a box, taper the top to a point, and then use Top Shear to move the top edge over to the side. Voilà, you have a ramp!

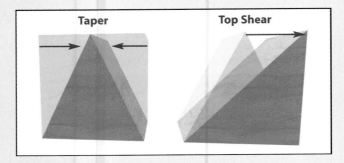

**Figure 6-5**
*Transforming a box into a wedge/ramp using Taper and Top Shear.*

Other variants include a pyramid (a box whose top is tapered down to one point), a half sphere (or hemisphere), a cone (a cylinder with its top tapered down to one point), a half cone, and a half cylinder.

## PRIM SELECTION AND VIEWPOINT

After you've created a few prims, you may want to change their position, size (stretch), orientation (rotate), and other properties that affect how the prim looks. To do any of these things to a prim, you must first select the prim by clicking on it while in build mode.

Figure 6-6 illustrates a prim box that is unselected (on the left) and another that is selected (on the right). A prim that is selected is surrounded by light yellow lines/glow. If you select an object composed of multiple linked prims, the root prim will glow yellow, while the rest of the prims are outlined in light blue (more on linked prims later).

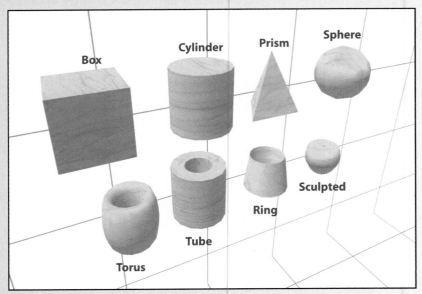

**Figure 6-4**
*The basic building block types of prims.*

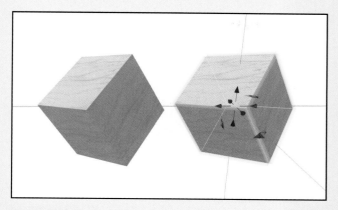

**Figure 6-6**
*An unselected prim box and a selected box.*

Before you start manipulating your prims, you often want to have a different vantage point, either closer for small objects or further away for bigger objects. You may also want to look at the opposite side. In fact, as you build, you will constantly be shifting your perspective. The techniques you learned to control your camera in Chapter 2 are essential if you are to become a serious builder.

Recall that you can hold down the Alt key and select an object with the left mouse button. Moving your mouse up and down zooms your view; moving it left and right rotates your view around the object. You can also use Ctrl+Alt or Ctrl+Alt+Shift as well. If you skipped over Chapter 2, now is a good time to go back and refresh your knowledge of camera controls.

When using these keys, you may notice that the build window switches to the Focus dialog (see Figure 6-7) with the appropriate zoom, orbit, or pan controls selected.

**Figure 6-7**
*Changing the camera viewpoint using the focus controls.*

## PRIM MOVEMENT

Now you're ready to learn how to move or reposition your prims. The move controls are automatically enabled when you select an object. The move controls are the red, green, and blue arrows going through the center of your prim.

The red arrow represents the x-axis and runs east to west. The green arrow represents the y-axis and runs north and south. The blue arrow represents the z-axis and runs up and down. It takes awhile to get used to this axis if you're like me and typically think of the y-axis as up/down. To move a prim, simply click and drag the arrow representing the direction you want to move the prim.

In Figure 6-8, I selected the green arrow and dragged the box prim from left to right. The transparency in this image is used to show where the box was. You will also find a move dialog in the build window, but using this is an extremely inefficient way to work.

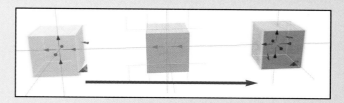

**Figure 6-8**
*Selecting the green arrow move control and moving a prim from left to right.*

## PRIM SIZE: STRETCHING AND SCALING

When you create a prim box, the sides measure 1/2 meter. You can resize any prim by stretching. This procedure is often called *scaling* or *resizing* in other applications. To do this, select the prim and hold down the Ctrl and Shift keys (or select the Stretch option in the edit dialog). When you enter stretch mode, you will see a semiconfusing array of colored handles (see Figure 6-9). Here's where the fun begins.

**Figure 6-9**
*Entering stretch mode on a box prim.*

If you select and drag the gray handles at the corners, you will proportionally scale the prim along that axis. You will also notice blue, red, and green handles centered at the sides of the prim. If you select and drag one of these, you will stretch the prim on that end. To stretch the prim symmetrically (equally on both ends), select the Stretch Both Sides box in the edit dialog. Resizing prims is just that simple.

Prims can be only as large as 10 meters or as small as 0.010 meters. The 10m limit is based on some scalability and infrastructure design decisions related to how SL works. A Linden post to the forums says this: "llSetPos has a 10m limit because of how sim-sim transfers work—basically, a sim knows about objects in its neighboring sims for a 10m border, so if you move an object from one sim to another, it is easier when both sims know about it, so we have a 10m limit. This is also the reason behind why prims can't get any bigger than 10m."

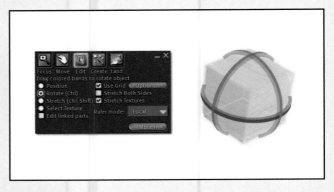

**Figure 6-10**
*Rotating your prim.*

> ## PRO TIP
>
> Objects may appear much smaller than the 0.010m prim limits. An object's size is listed in meters on the object's tab. This is the prim size, but not necessarily the visual size of the object. For example, create a sphere that is 1m in diameter. Then use the Path Cut tool to make it into a half sphere. The object appears smaller, but its prim dimensions remain the same. Using this technique, you can create objects that appear smaller than 0.010m. This technique is often used in very fine jewelry work.
>
> There are also some artifact objects from the early days of SL that are larger than 10m and called *mega-prims*. It is no longer possible to create these mega-prims, but you can find them typically free or sold in packs for around L$200–500. Although they are sold with full permissions, they typically cannot be scaled. There is some controversy surrounding their use and their impact on sim stability, but they clearly save on prim count for large builds.

## PRIM RULER MODE AND COORDINATE SYSTEMS

This section introduces you to ruler mode and coordinate systems. You will need to understand ruler modes when you want to move a prim along some coordinate system other than the world coordinate system. Before we go much further, let's talk about the world coordinate system.

SL uses an x, y, z coordinate system to identify any point in the SL world. Typically, coordinates are specified within a region. When you want to identify a point within a given region of the world, the region precedes the coordinates. Regions measure 256×256m, and points can be determined one per meter. The y-axis represents world compass coordinates north-south. The x-axis represents world compass coordinates west-east. The z-axis indicates elevation. The south-west point in a region is (0,0). This coordinate system is called the *world coordinate system* (see Figure 6-11). When you first rez a prim, it is aligned with the world coordinate system.

To understand coordinates better, rez a box and rotate it. The box is no longer aligned with the world coordinate system.

## PRIM ROTATION

When you have your prim located in the right spot and properly sized, you may want to rotate it into the appropriate orientation. You do this with the rotation tools accessed by selecting a prim and holding down the Ctrl key. A red, green, and blue ring will appear (see Figure 6-10). Selecting and dragging any ring will rotate the prim along that axis.

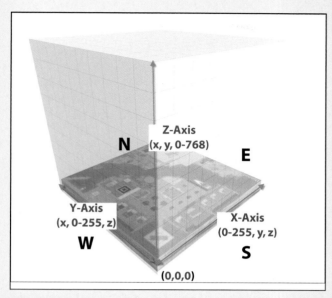

**Figure 6-11**
*World x, y, z coordinates.*

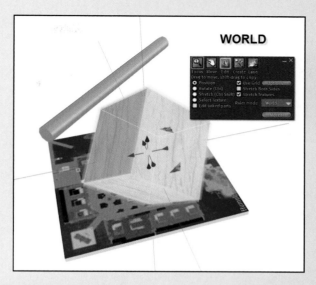

**Figure 6-12**
*World ruler mode.*

To move a prim along its own coordinate system, select Local ruler mode, as in Figure 6-13. If you look at the red, blue, and green lines, you'll see they come out of the exact center of the box. The red arrow makes it the most obvious. In this case, when you move the box, it will move up/down and left/right based on the local orientation of the box. The final ruler mode is reference mode.

> **NOTE**
>
> Zero on the z-axis does not necessarily represent ground level. In most sims, 20m is sea level, so Z=0 is actually 20m under water. The maximum height at which you can build (at least as of this writing is Z=768m).

Figure 6-12 shows a box, a silver cylinder, and a base map that represents the world. The box and tube have both been rotated and do not align precisely with the world coordinate system. In the edit dialog, you can see that the ruler mode selected is World. If you look carefully, you will also notice that the green, red, and blue arrows line up with the world, not the box prim itself. It's easiest to see this if you look at the green arrow. If you move the prim around, it will move exactly north, south, east, west, up, and down relative to the world. What if you wanted to move the box relative to itself?

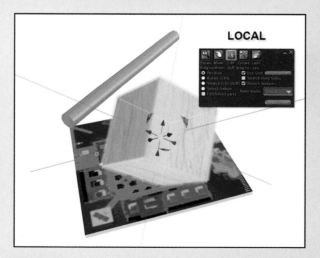

**Figure 6-13**
*Local ruler mode.*

Sometimes you want to move an object relative to another object. You do this using reference ruler mode. You select the object you want to move relative to. In Figure 6-14, I started by selecting the silver cylinder. You press Shift+G or select Tools->Use Selection for Grid. Now select the object you want to move. Again, in Figure 6-14, I selected the box. This time you'll notice the red, green, and blue arrows align with the silver cylinder. The blue arrow is the most obvious. Now, no matter the orientation of the box or the world, you will be able to move the box precisely along the cylinder's coordinate system.

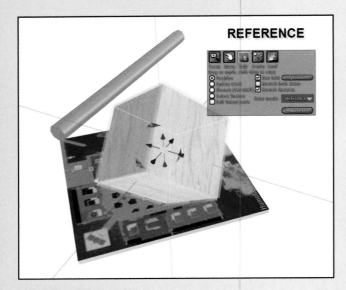

**Figure 6-14**
*Reference ruler mode.*

## PRO TIP

If you select a linked object, it should be oriented relative to its root prim; however, there is a long-standing bug that affects local rotation of linked objects. Local rotation for linked objects is not consistently handled as of this writing.

# PRIM PROPERTIES (GENERAL AND OBJECT TABS)

If you click the More>> button in the edit dialog, you will reveal several additional tabs that let you take prim editing to another level. The first is the General tab.

## THE GENERAL TAB

The General tab (see Figure 6-15) provides basic information about an object. At the top is the name and description of the object. Here, I named the box **My Cube** and added a description **Oh Look At My Cube**. Below that, you can see who created the object and who owns it. What's the difference you might ask? Well, in SL, you can create something and then sell it to someone else, who may (if permissions allow) give it to all her friends. So, many people may own different copies (instances) of an object, but it will always be clear who originally created it.

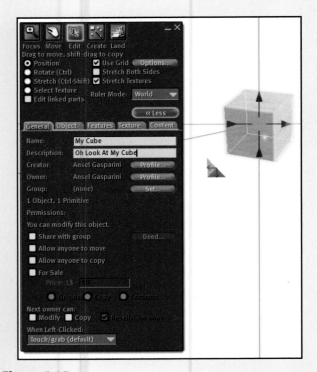

**Figure 6-15**
*The General tab.*

Next is the Set group, which defaults to (none) if it has not been set. Objects may be owned by a group so that they can be edited by multiple individuals. After the group, you can see how many primitives an object is made up of, and following this, the tab lists the object's permissions, which we cover later.

At the bottom of the tab is a drop-down box called When Left-Clicked; by default, it is set to Touch/Grab, which means when someone left-clicks on an object, it acts as if it has been touched. Other options include Sit on Object, Buy Object, Pay Object, and Open. For example, if you want to create a couch that, when clicked, someone sits on, you could set the left-click setting to Sit on Object.

The main point you should remember about the General tab is that you go to it to name your objects so that they will have distinct names in your Inventory. When you create a new prim, it is given the default name Object. Say you create four table legs, a table top, a drawer, and a basket of fruit. All of these items will be called Object unless you rename them. To keep things straight and make them easier to find in your Inventory, you should get in the habit of naming your objects as soon as you create them.

## THE OBJECT TAB (BY THE NUMBERS)

The next edit details tab is labeled Object (see Figure 6-16). If you really want to become a serious builder, understanding this tab is critical. First, notice the following four object properties:

- **Locked:** This property prevents you from accidentally modifying something. Say you build a great house and set it up just right. You may want to lock the floor, walls, ceiling, or whatever so that you don't accidentally select them and make a change or delete the object while you work on some interior door or furniture.

- **Physical:** Objects that are physical react to and can be acted on by the SL physics engine. Physical objects could be dominos or vehicles. We discuss these objects more in Chapter 10.

- **Temporary:** Temporary objects are prims that, when rezzed, exist for only a short period of time (less than a minute or two). This property is useful for objects that should be short-lived—bullets, for example.

- **Phantom:** Phantom objects exist in the world as solids. However, they do not collide with avatars, so someone could walk right through them. For example, you could walk right through a phantom wall or plant.

On the Object tab, you directly control the placement, size, and rotation of your objects by entering these properties as specific numbers. This process is sometimes referred to as "building by the numbers." For example, you can take four boxes that you have sized to 10×10×0.1m and precisely place them together forming a 40×40×0.1m seamless floor, ceiling, or whatever.

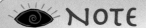

### NOTE

If you were to try to place objects together by eye, there may be an overlap that is visible as a flickering line as you move about. Precise placement of objects will avoid this visual side effect.

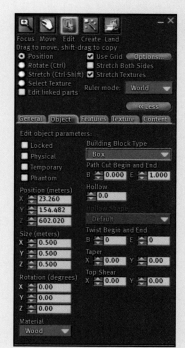

**Figure 6-16**
*The Object tab.*

Let's say you want to place several tubes end to end to form a tunnel, or you want to have eight spokes coming out of the hub of a wheel at the exact rotation/location. For any of these, hand editing using the controls previously discussed can be difficult. Using the numbers on the Objects tab can increase your precision and speed for many tasks. Another way to increase precision without using the numbers is to use the grid, which we cover later in this chapter.

The Object tab also contains many other interesting modifiers and properties for primitives. By learning how they work and then applying them creatively, the basic builder can become a master. Truly, the ability to take real-world shapes and imagine how they could be realized with a variety of modified prims is something you will acquire only through practice, but I offer the following bits of information for each modifier and prim to help get you started.

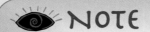

> ## NOTE
>
> The Ivory Tower Library of Primitives offers a wealth of information in-world for new builders and treats each property/modifier separately with in-world prims that highlight each effect quite nicely. A trip here is a must (see the SLURL later in this chapter).

All primitive types share some object properties on the Object tab. These properties are Position, Size, Rotation, Material, and Building Block Type (see Figure 6-16). Position, Size, and Rotation are the "by the numbers" settings for objects. Other object properties are available on some but not all prim types (for example, Dimple is available only for the sphere). We'll cover all of these properties next.

## Position (All Types)

Position indicates where in the world space coordinates (x,y,z) the prim's center is located, as we discussed earlier in the section on coordinate systems and prim movement.

## Size (All Types)

Size indicates how large in meters the prim's bounding box is in each of the x, y, and z dimensions, as we discussed earlier in the section on prim size and stretching.

## Rotation (All Types)

Rotation indicates by how many degrees in (x,y,z) space the prim is rotated relative to the world, as we discussed earlier in the section on prim rotation.

## Material (All Types)

Below Rotation is a drop-down for Material type; by default, the material is Wood. As of this writing, your choices are Stone, Metal, Glass, Wood, Flesh, Plastic, and Rubber. This setting is useful when you're creating physical objects (which we cover later) and defines how an object acts, not how it looks. For example, you can have a glass-looking prim that has its material set to flesh. Material settings define the sound an object makes when it collides with something and the amount of bounce during the collision or when the object is dropped.

## Building Block Type (All Types)

At the top of the second column in the Object's tab, you'll find the Building Block Type drop-down. You can use this drop-down to change from one prim type to another without disturbing its size or position. This is the only way (as of this writing) to create a sculpted prim (more on this in a minute).

## Path Cut (All Types but Sculpted)

The Path Cut modifier cuts away part of the prim. Create a box and try using just this setting. You'll quickly see it cuts away a portion of the box. If you cut away half the box, you create a ramp or wedge object. You'll find there are often multiple ways of doing the same thing in SL building.

## Hollow (All Types but Sculpted)

Hollow does exactly what its name suggests—it hollows out the primitive. This setting works for all prim types with the exception of the sculpted prim. The Hollow setting can be between 0% (solid) and 95%. Hollowing out a box is extremely useful when you're building rooms, as you'll see in "Tutorial: Creating a Room."

Here are a couple of interesting things to know when using the Hollow property. Hollow works on the z-axis, which means you may need to rotate the object before sizing it. The other thing that we cover again later is that the hollowed portion of the prim can have only one texture, so, for example, the inside of a hollowed box has only one face versus the four you would expect.

Figure 6-17 shows all the prim types hollowed to 90%. The sphere, torus, tube, and ring have been cut using Path Cut, so the hollow is on the inside of these prim types. That is, you cannot see the hollowed area unless you cut into the shape. I added a slight green tint to the inside surface of these prims so it's easier to see the hollow.

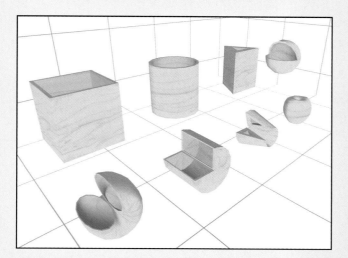

**Figure 6-17**
*Prims hollowed to 90% with tinted interior.*

## Hollow Shape (All Types but Sculpted)

The next prim parameter is Hollow Shape. This setting becomes available if you set Hollow above 0. You can set the shape of the hollow to Default, Square, Circle, or Triangle. Looking again at Figure 6-17, you can see the default hollow shapes. The box and tube use Square. The cylinder, sphere, and torus use Circle. Finally, the prism and tube use Triangle.

By experimenting with all these settings, you'll discover some very interesting shapes. The hollowed tube in Figure 6-17 looks like a great start on a BBQ grill to me.

The sculpted prim type does not support Hollow Shape.

## Twist (All Types but Sculpted)

Twist takes the prim and twists it along the z-axis. B (or Begin) twists one face; E (or End) twists the other. This effect is obvious for boxes and prisms, but less so with cylinders where you see only texture distortion (see Figure 6-18). The twist range for a box, prism, or cylinder is +/– 180 degrees.

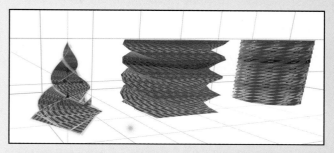

**Figure 6-18**
*Maximum twist applied to a box, prism, and cylinder with texture pattern applied.*

Sphere, torus, tube, and ring prim types have a twist range of +/– 360 degrees and are quite a bit different. Think of a torus like a doughnut and cut a slice into it. Then take the two ends and twist one or both, depending on your B or E setting. To really understand this setting best, you need to use it, but see Figure 6-19 for an example.

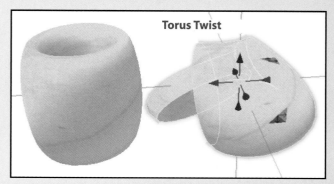

**Figure 6-19**
*A torus and twisted torus.*

## Taper (Not Sculpted, Not Sphere)

Taper takes the size of the top and makes it smaller than the size of the bottom or vice versa if you use negative taper. The x and y values are basically values between 0 and 1 and represent a percentage of the size to reduce the top. Create a new box and taper both x and y to 1 or 100%. Congratulations, you've created a pyramid, a derivative of the box shape. You have essentially tapered the x and y sides down to nothing. See Figure 6-5 for an example. Taper is not available for spheres or sculpted prims.

## Top Shear (Not Sculpted, Not Sphere)

Top Shear moves the end faces of a primitive relative to the center of the prim. For example, when you create a box, the top and bottom are directly aligned over each other (on the z-axis). That is, their centers on the x,y-axes are completely aligned. When you use Top Shear, the top is moved in one or both x or y directions. Top Shear values range from –0.50 to +0.50. Zero is no shear, and 0.50 moves the center of the top one-half of the prim dimension to one side, placing the face center over the edge of the opposite face. See Figure 6-5 for an example. Top Shear is not available for spheres or sculpted prims.

## Dimple Begin/End (Sphere Only)

Dimple is a parameter only for the sphere primitive. A Dimple creates a conical hole or depression with its point at the center of the sphere, in one or both sides of a sphere. As you increase the Dimple setting, you increase the angle of the cone, which at 0.5 is 90 degrees. The B range is 0–0.95, and the E range is 0.05–1. See the spheres shown in Figure 6-20. For the first three, I adjusted only the E setting. For the final sphere, I adjusted both to create an interesting shape, perhaps the roof of a gazebo.

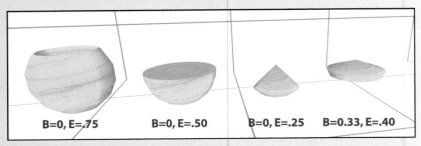

B=0, E=.75    B=0, E=.50    B=0, E=.25    B=0.33, E=.40

**Figure 6-20**
*A dimpled sphere.*

## Skew (Torus, Tube, Ring)

Skew is a valid parameter for the torus, tube, and ring. To understand Skew, think of a torus like a doughnut. Take a knife and cut the doughnut, and then pull the two pieces at the cut in different directions. This is basically skew, as you can see in Figure 6-21.

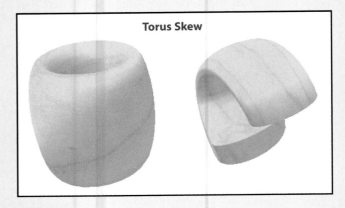

Torus Skew

**Figure 6-21**
*A torus and skewed torus.*

## Hole Size (Torus, Tube, Ring)

Hole Size can be used on the torus, tube, and ring. Hole Size is different from Hollow. In Figure 6-22, I used Path Cut to allow you to see inside the torus. Hollow provides room in the doughnut for the cream filling. Hole Size is really a bad name. It implies the parameter is about the size of the hole in the middle of the doughnut. However, the adjustment really adjusts the profile of the solid (circle for torus) and in doing so indirectly affects the size of the hole. You can adjust the x and y settings. In Figure 6-22, I adjusted the x setting between the first and second hole size example. Notice how the circular profile becomes more oval and the size of the hole increases.

## Profile Cut (Torus, Tube, Ring)

The Profile Cut parameter is available for torus, tube, and ring prims. The Profile Cut property cuts the profile of the prim (a rectangle for the tube), unlike Path Cut, which cuts a whole piece out of the prim. In Figure 6-23, I first used Path Cut to cut away most of the tube. Then, using Profile Cut, I created this circular bench-like shape or perhaps the exhaust pipe for a space ship. The profile of both tubes is highlighted in yellow.

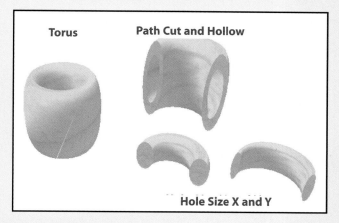

**Figure 6-22**
*Torus with Path Cut and Hole Size adjustments applied.*

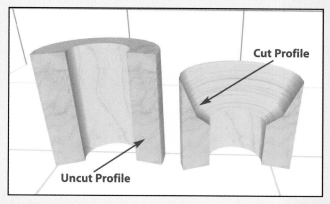

**Figure 6-23**
*A tube with Profile Cut.*

## Revolutions (Torus, Tube, Ring)

The Revolutions parameter is available for the torus, tube, and ring prims. Revolutions rotates the prim profile around while keeping the same general size of the prim. This setting is great for creating springs or similar objects. You can do from –4 to 4 revolutions with this parameter. Figure 6-24 shows a torus with 4 revolutions applied.

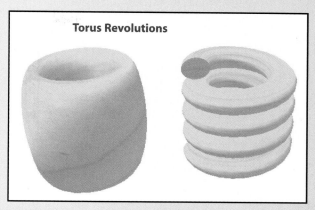

**Figure 6-24**
*Torus and torus with revolutions applied.*

## Radius Delta (Torus, Tube, Ring)

The Radius Delta parameter is available for torus, tube, and ring prims. Radius Delta works in conjunction with revolutions and allows you to control the radius of revolutions. In Figure 6-25, the left prim is a default torus, the next prim over is a stretched torus, the third uses the maximum revolutions with no Radius Delta, and the final prim has the Radius Delta adjusted to form the final shape.

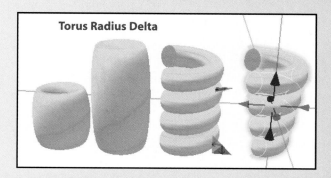

**Figure 6-25**
*Radius Delta allows you to vary the radius of revolutions.*

## Sculpt Texture (Sculpted Only)

The Sculpt Texture parameter is available only for the sculpted prim type. Sculpt Texture controls the physical shape of the sculpted prim. Creating sculpt textures is an advanced topic that is covered in Chapter 10. It is possible to find free or reasonably priced sculpt textures to use in your builds. Figure 6-26 shows a sculpt texture on the object page and the default sculpt shape of an apple.

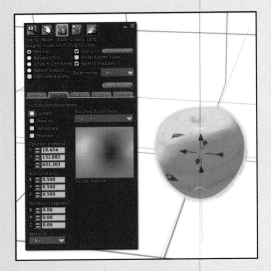

**Figure 6-26**
*The Sculpt Texture parameter and a default sculpt texture.*

## Sample Shapes Using Random Parameters

When you're getting started, and even if you're a regular builder, it is often helpful to take some time playing with prim settings. You'll be surprised what you might come up with. Figure 6-27 shows a box, cylinder, prism, sphere, torus, tube, and ring, respectively, with various parameters settings. The ones I like the most are the sphere, which could be used as kind of a 1960s chair; the prism, which looks like some great crown molding; and the ring, which is basically a nice wine goblet. Experiment and see what you come up with; you can create pretty complex shapes that require only one prim.

### TIP

Objects are streamed over the Internet to SL clients. Because objects are completely dynamic; you cannot preload the client with a set of data. It has to arrive in real-time. For that reason, it is not practical to stream traditional 3D mesh information. Instead, prims are basically simplified mathematical descriptions of the 3D shapes they are intended to represent. They are all (with the exception of sculpted prims) essentially 2D shapes (called *profiles*) extruded or revolved around a path in 3D space:

- A box is created by revolving a rectangular plane around a rectangular path.
- A cylinder is formed with a rectangular plane around a circular path.
- A prism is a tapered rectangle around a triangular path.
- A sphere is a semicircle around a circular path.
- A torus is a full circle around a circular path.
- A tube is a rectangular plane around a circular path.
- A ring is a triangle around a circular path.

Play with the Path Cut property a bit more and you'll get the picture. By cutting the path, you prevent the 3D shape from fully completing, and you expose the profile shape.

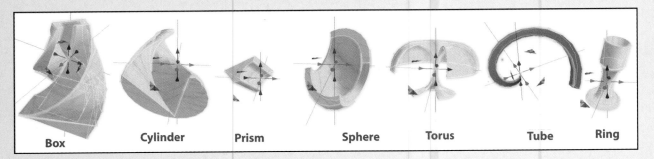

**Figure 6-27**
*Sample shapes using random parameters.*

# WHY DO YOU CARE ABOUT ALL THESE OBJECT PARAMETERS?

You might be wondering why we spent so much time on using object parameters to coerce a single prim into a complex shape. The reason is that prims are a limited resource in SL, related closely to land. A parcel of land supports a limited number of prims, unlike your Inventory, which can (as of this writing) contain an unlimited number. Because of this, prim count in an object becomes important.

If you have only so many prims, you need to decide how to spend them. For example, in a standard dwelling, you need to decide how many prims are necessary to make the house, furniture, windows, doors, and don't forget the landscaping and backyard pool.

In general, an object with fewer prims will be more desirable if both objects are visually similar. Learning how to achieve the same effect using fewer prims is what it's all about. In Figure 6-28, I've created two chairs; the first with pink handles uses 4 prims. The back is one prim (blue) and the seat (yellow) is a second prim. The pink arm/leg combo is made up of one box prim for the left side and one for the right side. I used Hollow and Path Cut to achieve this shape. So, imagine I have a dining room table with eight chairs. Eight chairs will use 32 prims of my allowed limit.

Now look at the chair next to it on the right. This chair requires 10 prims. The back and seat are identical to the first chair. This chair, however, uses 4 prims for legs, 2 for arm rests, and 2 for arm supports. Using eight of these chairs at my dining room table will cost me 80 prims.

I should be clear that high-prim-count objects do not necessarily mean bad. Maybe I have plenty of prims, and I want fancy chairs. Maybe the dining room table is the centerpiece of my build, and this is the place where I want all the detail. I might even use these high-prim-count objects near my house and the low-prim-count objects in the garden, which gets less traffic.

Anyway, I hope you get the idea that learning how to use prim parameters will allow you to build more intricate objects using fewer prims. It's all up to your imagination.

The use of textures helps objects appear more detailed without your adding prims as well. In Figure 6-29, I applied some wacky textures to the same chairs. We cover the basics of texturing a prim next.

**Figure 6-29**
*Adding texture to prims increases detail without adding prims.*

# PRIM TEXTURING BASICS (THE TEXTURE TAB)

Sometimes it seems that everything in SL is made of plywood, but you can change that! Textures in SL change the way an object looks. Does it look like glass, metal, wood,

**Figure 6-28**
*High and low prim chairs.*

or fire? The default texture for all prims looks like plywood. However, it is important to understand that there are two different uses of the term *texture* in SL. The first use refers to a flat 2D image that you will find in your Inventory (Robin Sojourner calls this the *texture image*). The second use of the term refers to all the other attributes an object may have that affect its appearance, including color, transparency, luminosity, bumpiness, and shininess. SL Help defines texture as follows: "Textures are the visual patterns applied to sides, or faces of primitives or objects."

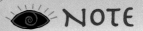

# NOTE

For those of you who are deep into 3D texturing in RL, SLers wish there were bump maps, specularity maps, translucency, reflection, refraction, diffusion, and more ambient light controls, but alas these features have not yet arrived. There is a default set of bump maps and you can use the darkness/lightness of your texture as bump, but that's about it. We will cover more about texturing in Chapter 7.

You edit an object's texture on the Texture tab of the edit dialog, as shown in Figure 6-30.

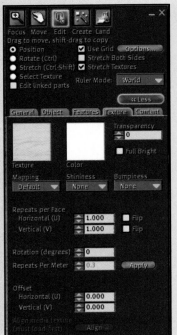

**Figure 6-30**
*The Texture tab.*

You see two squares in this dialog: one labeled Texture; and the other, Color. The texture here is the 2D texture image. When you apply a texture image to an object, it is painted onto that object in a specific way. This painting on of a texture is called *mapping*. For a square texture and square box, it may be obvious what happens, but what about a square texture and a torus? You can think of mapping as kind of taking the texture image and wrapping it around the object, stretching it here, pulling it there, and smoothing it out to get it to fit.

You apply textures to objects by going into the edit dialog, selecting the Texture tab, and clicking on the texture image (bricks in this case) to launch the texture picker (see Figure 6-31).

On the left is the texture you selected. On the right is your Inventory and the standard library where you can pick other texture images. If you check Apply Immediately, when you select different textures, they will appear on your object as you click on them. This capability is extremely handy for getting an initial impression of how this texture image looks on your object.

**Figure 6-31**
*The texture picker dialog.*

You can always get back to the default texture by selecting Default, and you can assign no texture, if you want just a plain color, by selecting Blank. The eye dropper can be used to select a texture image from any object in-world, which you can modify. Once you have the texture image you like, click Select to choose it.

The next basic setting you can use is the Color setting. This is the square on the Texture tab next to the Texture image square (see Figure 6-32).

**Figure 6-32**
*The texture Color setting.*

**The Color square on the Texture tab**

If you select a Blank texture, the object will be colored exactly the color you chose. However—and this is cool— if you select a texture **and** a color, the color acts as a tint. Try it out. Figure 6-33 shows a basic plywood cube and another one that has been tinted light green.

**Figure 6-33**
*Selecting a texture and a color results in a tint.*

That's it for basic texturing! Of course, there is a lot more to textures if you want the most visually appealing objects in SL. Some of the tutorials cover additional steps you can take to improve your textures, but much more is covered in Chapter 7, "Advanced Textures and Clothing," where you learn how to create and upload your own textures.

So, get in-world now and texture something! If you want to glimpse the potential of textures or just want an SL WOW moment, find your way to Julia Hathor's Serenity Falls here:

**SLURL** **http://slurl.com/secondlife/serenity%20falls/ 168/105/25/**

Next, let's build a couple of things.

# TUTORIAL: CREATING A DECK

In this tutorial, you create and texture a one prim deck ready to hold a barbecue grill or a swimming pool. As this is the first build tutorial, I'm going to assume you don't know how to get to a build site and that you do not own any land.

## STEP 1: LOCATE A SANDBOX

The first step to starting a build is to locate a suitable building site. To do this, follow these steps:

1. Select Search from the main window.
2. Select the Places tab.
3. Type **sandbox** in the Find box (see Figure 6-34).
4. Click the Search button.

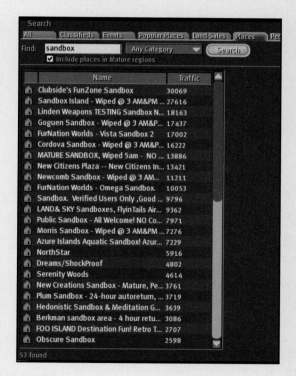

**Figure 6-34**
*Type **sandbox**.*

You will see a list of sandboxes and perhaps some commercial sites posing as sandboxes. You will also see the amount of traffic these sites get. High-traffic sites may offer a great location, help from others who are around, and other amenities. They also may not give you much peace and quiet, and you may get disrupted or distracted from your building task. The choice is really up to you.

## STEP 2: SELECT A SITE AND TELEPORT THERE

You can see a preview of the area in the search window. In Figure 6-35, I chose a low-traffic site. Click the Teleport button.

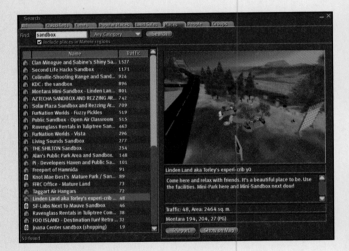

**Figure 6-35**
*Once you've found a site you like, click the Teleport button to be taken there.*

## STEP 3: OPEN THE EDIT WINDOW

In Figure 6-36 I have arrived at Montara (223, 201, 26), a nice minisandbox on Linden-owned land.

Get the lay of the land and find a nice spot to start building! It's not uncommon for the TP landing point to be in a no-build section (kind of a welcome area), so you may need to move around a bit to find a buildable spot. Select the Build button, or right-click on the ground where you want to create your cube and select Create from the pie menu (see Figure 6-37).

**Figure 6-36**
*The Montara minisandbox.*

**Figure 6-37**
*Select Create.*

## STEP 4: REZ A CUBE

*Rezzing a cube* is often the start of something new and an expression you will hear a lot in classes. Selecting Create brings up the edit dialog with Create and Box already selected (see Figure 6-38).

Click somewhere with the magic wand cursor that appears, and you should see a nice plywood cube appear (see Figure 6-39).

**Figure 6-38**
*Create and Box are already selected.*

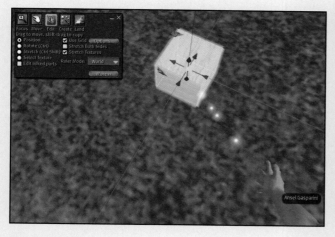

**Figure 6-39**
*A plywood cube appears.*

The white moving dots (you can change the color in your preferences) show which object you're editing, and other people can see them. This feature is helpful when you're building something collaboratively.

## STEP 5: CONTROL YOUR VIEWPOINT

One of the hardest things to get used to when you first start building is how to adjust your view. The initial view when you start editing is pretty close up (unless you disabled the preference for Automatic Edit Camera View). You can adjust your view in several ways, but when you're just starting, try selecting the Alt key and clicking on the object. You will zoom in/out and around the object using the mouse. You should expect to be changing your viewpoint all the time while you're building. All of the camera controls you learned in Chapter 2 should be paying off now! If you skipped Chapter 2, get yourself back there.

## STEP 6: NAME YOUR OBJECT

After you create objects, it is good practice to name them so that they're easier to identify when you place them into your Inventory. And if you, shall I say it…, sell them, well, the person who buys them knows you are no newbie!

You name objects on the General tab (see Figure 6-40). You may need to select the More>> button to see these tabs.

**Figure 6-40**
*Back to the General tab.*

I called the object **Deck** and added a description: **My First Build**.

## STEP 7: SIZE THE DECK (STRETCH)

The next step is to size your deck. You can do this using the manual size controls, but if you're doing precise work, you will want to do it by the numbers. Go to the Object tab and create a deck that is 3m on the x-axis, 5m on the y-axis, and 0.25m thick on the z-axis (see Figure 6-41).

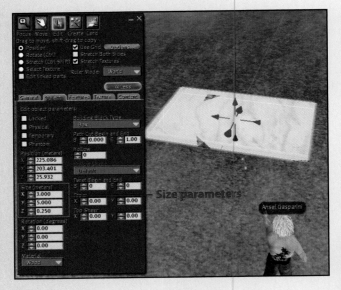

**Figure 6-41**
*Sizing your deck using the Object tab.*

I recommend, for this tutorial, using the same size deck as I did, so when you texture it, you will get the same effect.

## STEP 8: TEXTURE THE DECK

Go to the Texture tab and click on the plywood texture. (Plywood doesn't make such a good deck.) You should see the basic texture picker dialog appear (see Figure 6-42).

**Figure 6-42**
*The texture picker dialog appears.*

You can find some cool textures available in SL. Some are free, and some cost money to buy. You may also want to upload your own textures. But for now, let's use one of the textures available in the library. Open the Library folder; then under Textures folder, open the Wood folder and look for a texture named Redwood.

Alternatively, you can enter **Redwood** in the search window to get to it more quickly. Make sure you check Apply Immediately so that you can see the texture on your object. I usually adjust my view so I can see both my object and the texture picker dialog (see Figure 6-43). When it looks good, click Select.

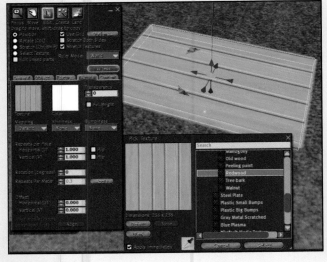

**Figure 6-43**
*Adjust your view so you can see both the object and the texture picker dialog.*

## STEP 9: ADJUST THE TEXTURE

You may notice that for a 3×5m deck, we must be using some high-quality, old-growth, really BIG boards. To do really nice builds in SL, you need to learn how to adjust the textures to fit the objects they're on. We're going to do two things to this texture. First, the boards should run across versus lengthwise. To do this, we must rotate the texture, which we do on the Texture tab. In Figure 6-44, notice that I rotated the texture 90 degrees.

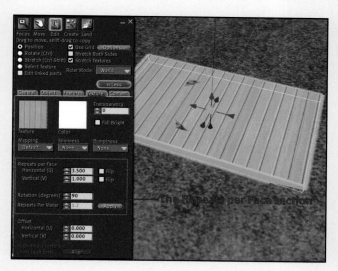

**Figure 6-44**
*The texture is rotated 90 degrees.*

**Figure 6-45**
*The finished deck.*

Notice the section called Repeats per Face. This is set to 1 horizontal and 1 vertical by default. That means that just one version of the texture is placed on or stretched across the object. If we still had our 1×1 cube, this would probably be fine, but we have a large construction here. I changed the horizontal repeats to 3.5. That is, the texture is duplicated and repeated 3.5 times across the horizontal plane. It's pretty cool to watch this happen in real-time as you adjust it.

You should now have a cool, basic deck. There are more ways to fine-tune the texture on the sides of the deck, which we will cover in Chapter 7 on advanced texturing.

**Figure 6-46**
*A shot from above.*

## STEP 10: TRY IT OUT

I built this deck near a hillside, so I slid it into the side of the hill a bit and climbed on top for a first snapshot, as shown in Figure 6-45.

The second shot is taken from high above the sandbox (see Figure 6-46); notice someone else nearby working on a fountain or pond project.

## STEP 11: TAKE IT WITH YOU

Finally, you'll want to keep this deck. Maybe you'll use it later with a bunch of friends. It's always good practice to clean up after yourself, particularly in a public sandbox. To do this, select your deck (not in edit mode) and right-click to open the pie menu. Select Take. This will place your new deck in your Inventory. If you named it as I suggested, you should be able to easily find it under the Inventory->Objects folder.

# TUTORIAL: CREATING A ROCK

In this tutorial, you learn how to build and texture a one-prim rock for use in your garden or home.

## STEP 1: REZ A CUBE

First, rez a cube and then name the object **Rock** with the description **My First Rock** (see Figure 6-47).

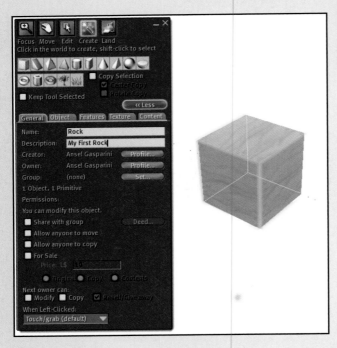

**Figure 6-47**
*My first rock.*

## STEP 2: RESIZE THE CUBE

This rock needs to be a bit bigger. The default cube (or box) size is half a meter on each side, but we want our rock to be about 1m on each side and 1.5m high.

To do this, go to the Object tab and modify the values under Size. Or just adjust the cube by eye using the stretch controls. Set X to 1m, Y to 1m, and Z to 1.5m. You should see a much larger plywood cube (see Figure 6-48).

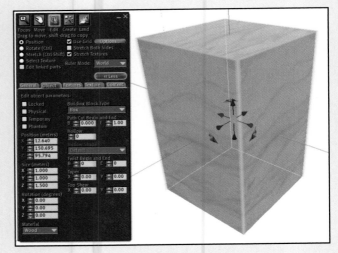

**Figure 6-48**
*A much larger version.*

## STEP 3: TAPER AND CUT THE CUBE

OK, this thing needs to look more like a rock. Let's start on that by first tapering the cube.

On the Object tab, modify the taper settings. The base of the cube stays the same 1×1m, but the top is made smaller depending on the values you enter for X and Y taper. I used 0.45 for X and 0.75 for Y (see Figure 6-49), but feel free to pick values you like. This basically means that the top of the cube in the X direction is 45% of the bottom, or in this case 0.45m. The top of the cube in the Y direction is 75% of the bottom, or in this case 0.75m. Now that's more like it.

Let's add some more interest by cutting into the cube a bit. You do this with the Path Cut Begin and End options. I just want a small sliver out of the cube, so I set the Begin to 0.049 and left the End at 1. Basically, a prim goes from 0 to 1 in a circle around the object. If I set both of these options to 0.5, we wouldn't see any object because it would be totally cut away. The same would happen if I set the start to 1 or the end to 0.

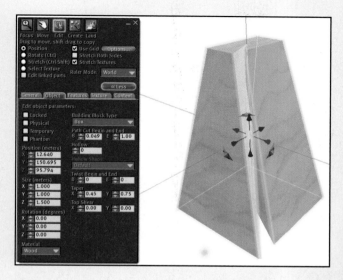

**Figure 6-49**
*Tapering and cutting the rock.*

## STEP 4: TWIST THE ROCK

Rocks are generally not as uniform as we have created so far. We need to add some more interest to our rock by twisting it a bit. We do this by modifying the twist parameters. I set the beginning of the twist to 27 and the end to −18 (see Figure 6-50). This is the degree of twist being introduced.

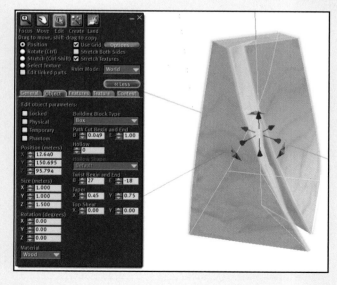

**Figure 6-50**
*Twisting the rock.*

## STEP 5: ADD SOME TOP SHEAR

OK, one more thing to deform the rock a bit more—using Top Shear. Basically, when you create a cube, the top and bottom are aligned; that is, the center of the top is the same as the center of the bottom. Top Shear moves the top along the x- and y-axes. For Top Shear, I entered 0.05 for X and 0.45 for Y (see Figure 6-51). These figures represent percentages of X/Y in both positive and negative directions.

Now this is more like it.

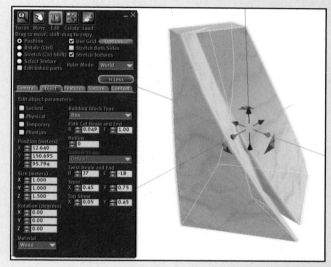

**Figure 6-51**
*Top shearing.*

## STEP 6: CHANGE THE MATERIAL PROPERTY TO STONE

At the bottom of the Object tab is a drop-down menu called Material. It's set to Wood, as the default cube/box has a plywood texture. Even though I have no plans to make this rock physical, for good housekeeping, we can change it to Stone.

## STEP 7: TEXTURE THE ROCK

OK, now that we're happy with the shape of the new rock, let's make it look like a rock rather than some strange plywood sculpture. To do this, go to the Texture tab and click on the plywood texture.

What you're really doing here is applying an image that wraps around and covers your shape.

You'll learn how to find more textures and create and upload your own textures in later chapters. For now, let's work with the set of textures that Linden Labs has bestowed upon you. They're located under the Library folder. Open it now.

## STEP 8: APPLY A ROCK TEXTURE

Navigate to the Texture folder and then down to the Rock folder (see Figure 6-52).

**Figure 6-52**
*Navigate to Textures, Rock.*

Man, textures are cool! I could spend a lot of time clicking around this folder tree finding interesting textures that I can put on my prims.

If you click on a texture, you'll see a preview of the texture, but you can also see how it looks on your object if you move the texture window out of the way. Click and drag on the top of the window just like you would do normally.

Here, I selected Heavy Moss. You can pick one you like, but I suggest you pick Heavy Moss so that you can see the same things I'm describing.

## STEP 9: FIX UP THE TEXTURE

Often you have to tinker with textures to get them just right. Notice the texture looks a little squirrelly on each side, particularly the x-axis (see Figure 6-53). You can fix this by changing the texture mapping from default to planar. Click Select and choose the Rock - Heavy Moss texture.

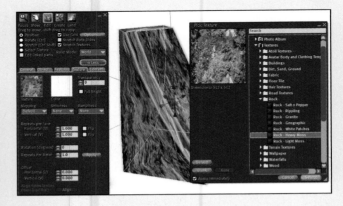

**Figure 6-53**
*The texture looks a little squirrelly on the sides.*

Then go to the Mapping drop-down menu and select Planar (see Figure 6-54). Don't worry about what this is right now because I cover it later, but notice how your rock texture improves.

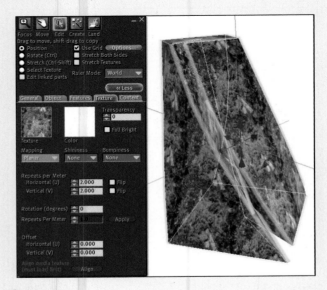

**Figure 6-54**
*Applying Planar texture mapping.*

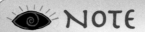 
## STEP 10: TINT THE TEXTURE

I think the texture looks a little bright. However, you may be perfectly happy with it. Let's assume it needs work. To darken it and make it a bit mossier, let's add some tint. Click on the Color box (see Figure 6-55). I know it's called Color, but as we've discussed, it is really the tinting of the texture. I picked a light green. If you drag the color chooser off to the side, you can see the effect you're having on your object.

If you want exactly the color I picked, you can enter the numbers as Red 208, Green 231, Blue 207. As discussed previously, this is called *RGB color*, and each value ranges from 0 to 255. The number 255 represents all color and 0 represents no color. So, 0,0,0 is pure black and 255,255,255 is pure white.

**Figure 6-55**
*Click on the Color box.*

## STEP 11: PLANT YOUR ROCK SOMEWHERE

Your rock is done! You now need to find a good spot for it. Rocks may have fallen down a cliff, but mostly they're embedded in the ground. Experiment with moving your rock around. You do this by dragging on the arrows and using the Ctrl key to switch into rotate mode. Figure 6-56 shows my finished rock on the bank of a pond I have on my land.

**Figure 6-56**
*The finished rock.*

That was a great start to building. Now let's get into some of the more advanced topics.

# CREATING OBJECTS/ LINKING PRIMS

Pretty quickly, once you get into building you will be creating objects that are composed of multiple prims. What if you want to move them around? It would be painful to have to move each prim one at a time. To solve this problem, SL allows you to create a single object by linking (or grouping) multiple prims.

There are several things you need to understand about linking:

- There are limits to the number of prims you can link together.
- There is a one-level hierarchy to linked objects. That is, each linkset has one prim, which is the parent or root prim.
- You cannot nest linksets. That is, there is no multi-level hierarchy other than the single parent/root prim and a flat list of children.
- The order in which you select prims for linking is important. The last prim selected will be the parent/root prim.
- Distance between prims (as measured from their centers) can impact your ability to link them.
- The name of a linked object is defined by the name of its parent/root prim. For example, if you change the name of a linkset and then unlink the object, the root prim will retain the linkset name.
- It is possible to edit subparts of a linked object without unlinking.
- You can't link to prims for which you do not have modification rights.

To link objects, you must be in edit mode. You select one object and then hold down the Shift key and select another. If you're familiar with the basic multiselect functionality on your PC, it is similar. As just mentioned, the last prim you select will be the root/parent prim. You can also click-drag and select several objects and then press Shift to unselect and reselect the object you want for your root prim.

When you have multiple prims selected, go to the Tools menu and select Link, or use the keyboard shortcut Ctrl+L. To unlink objects, you select Tools->Unlink or press Ctrl+Shift+L.

> ✋ TIP
>
> You can also unlink one item by selecting the linkset, choosing Edit Linked Parts from the object menu, selecting the part you want to remove, and using Unlink.

What follows is a great thread on linking from the Second Life Forum, where linking topics are summarized quite nicely by Ceera Murakami (see Figure 6-57); you'll hear more about Ceera when we get into estates and islands. Here is what Ceera says about linking (the full thread is available at http://forums.secondlife.com/showthread.php?t=105708):

**Figure 6-57**
*Ceera Murakami.*

The limits on linking objects are no more than 256 objects in one linkset, and a maximum center to center distance of 30 M between any two parts. That maximum can end up being less, if some of the prims involved are small. It's difficult to predict exactly how far apart the farthest pieces will be, except by trying in-world.

There is no hierarchical way to link multiple linksets. For example, if you make a bed as a linkset, and a dresser as a linkset, and a chair, you can't link them into one linkset without losing the connections that made them individual objects. If the total prims and maximum distances would fit in a single linkset, and you link them, you get a single linkset, with only one root prim, and you can't split it neatly back into the separate items again without unlinking all the parts and re-selecting and linking just the parts for one item. Hierarchical linking is a feature that has been requested many times, and would be very welcome!

What you can do is to multi-select linksets! For example, I routinely make a house, using multiple linksets as required to conform to the limits stated above, I put furnishings in it, each piece as a single linkset, and then I select all of those at once, by either shift-clicking on each set, or by selecting one and then drag-selecting across the others—hold down shift, point to the ground, left-click and drag to make a rectangle that will select all items it crosses. (Make sure you have "select only my objects" checked in the Tools menu, so you don't get other people's stuff!)

Multi-selected linksets can, with care, be moved, rotated, and even scaled as a single unit. If you take a multi-selected group of linksets into inventory, it becomes a single item in inventory, named as the last selected item was. But when you rez that object, it rezzes as the multi-selected group was. To keep the multi-selected group highlighted when you rez it, be in edit mode BEFORE you rez the multi-selected group.

If necessary, you can have a linked object and edit one of its pieces without unlinking. In the edit dialog, check the Edit Linked Parts box (see Figure 6-58). You will then be able to select each individual piece of the linked object and edit that piece. You can also use this technique to unlink a subpart without unlinking the whole.

**Figure 6-58**
*Check the box Edit Linked Parts.*

The last point to make (or remake) about linking is that order matters. The last prim you select will become the root prim for the new object. The root prim acts as main prim for the whole object. As you will see in future chapters, the root prim matters a great deal for vehicles, avatar attachments, and scripted objects.

# OWNERSHIP AND PERMISSIONS (OBJECT TAB)

Every object in SL has a set of permissions. You can examine them and make changes to them on the Object tab while in build mode. You need to understand permissions if you want to buy, sell, give away, or copy objects.

**Kymber Schnook:** For anything I own, I want to understand its permission settings. Without the basics, I'll not know whether I can modify, copy, or sell/transfer the items in my inventory. Likewise, before I acquire a new item, it behooves me to know its permission states. If I go to a cutting garden in SL and find a freebie plant to 'take,' but that item has no copy rights attached, I may need to "take a copy" 10 times to get the number of originals I'll need. If I am debating a purchase of a new sofa but don't like the upholstery and wish to change it, it is essential that I determine whether I have such modification rights, before I spend my Lindens. If I give a snapshot to a friend, but don't want them to share it with others, I'll need to understand permissions to prevent that image from being passed around. If I buy a birthday present for my partner, but the item comes to me without transfer rights…I can't give him the gift.

I think this quote drives home the point why you need to understand basic permissions. Let's dig in. Rez a cube and go to the Objects tab. Below the name and description are all the permissions settings (see Figure 6-59).

**Figure 6-59**
*The Object's Permissions dialog.*

Each object has a creator and an owner. The **creator** is the original person who, using the build tools, brought this object to life. The **owner** is the current owner of the object or copy (instance) of the original object. When you buy something in SL or someone gives you something, that person **transfers ownership** of that object to you. The creator always remains the same. This is done to protect the intellectual property of the creator.

Optionally, objects may be members of a **group** or even owned by a group. Objects also may have **next owner** permissions. That is, if I resell or give away this object, what permissions will the next owner have?

Any object you own you can move or delete. These are considered fair use rights and are built into the system, so they are implicit permissions. The key explicit permissions you will encounter are Modify, Copy, and Transfer (the user interface calls Transfer, *resell/give away*). With **Modify** permissions, you can change the properties of an object such as the scale, texture, and name. Using Kymber's example, if you buy a couch in SL, you need Modify permissions to be able to resize it to your house or change it from leather to faux fur.

**Copy** permissions allow you to make multiple copies of an object. For example, if I buy a candle with no Copy permissions, then I have bought only one candle. However, if I buy a candle with Copy permissions, I can fill a room with candle copies.

Finally, **Transfer** permission means I am able to sell or give away an object. To use Kymber's example, let's say I have a snapshot I want to share with someone, but I don't want that person giving it away. I can disable next owner transfer. Similarly, if you are buying someone a gift, you had better make sure you have Transfer permissions so you can give it to that person.

If a group is set, you can share an item with the group such that group members can make changes to it. You can also **deed** it to the group, in which case the group becomes the owner. This capability is particularly important if you're building a group business because any payments made to a deeded group object are shared evenly among group members.

You can also set broad permissions for everyone on an object by selecting Allow Anyone to Move and Allow Anyone to Copy. As Kymber noted, there are some plant/flower cutting gardens in SL, where the plants and flowers are set to allow anyone to copy them. You can right-click Take Copy of these objects freely.

Finally, this is the place where you indicate that an object is for sale and identify its price. You can sell the specific object, a copy of the object, or if someone buys the object, he can, in fact, buy the contents of the object itself.

For a more in-depth look at permissions, including some great sample scenarios, see the forum post by Phoenix Linden at http://forums.secondlife.com/showthread.php?t=6729.

# ALIGNING PRIMS

One of the first SL builder frustrations you will encounter is trying to line up a bunch of prims. If you're used to 3D modeling and having access to orthographic views, then this may be a particularly hard transition for you! Basic alignment is possible, and there are several ways you can do it without doing it "by eye." I know of four primary ways to do this, and I expect there are other tricks still lurking in the minds of SL builders. The ones I know about are by the numbers, using the grid, using Copy Previous while building, and using builders tools. The following sections cover each briefly.

## ALIGNMENT BY THE NUMBERS

Every object in SL has an X, Y, and Z position found on the Object tab. If you've been dragging/or building away, you will probably have positions that are down to the third decimal place in terms of precision, such as X=116.192, as shown in Figure 6-60.

**Figure 6-60**
*Accurate to three decimal places.*

The first thing to do if you're going to use the alignment by the numbers method is to clean up these numbers so that you have some nicer numbers to work with (of course, this is not necessary, but it does make things easier). Don't worry; if this moves your object into the wrong place, you can always reposition it later. The second thing that makes it easier is if your objects are of whole number sizes. In Figure 6-61, I changed my position and sizes to "friendly" values.

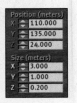

**Figure 6-61**
*Position and sizes changed to "friendly" values.*

Figure 6-62 shows three identical prims that I created by Shift-dragging them. To do this, in edit mode with Position selected, hold down the Shift key, click on one of the arrows, and drag. An identical copy will be created and stay aligned on the other two axes. After Shift-dragging these three, I want to line them up to make a walkway, railroad, or some such. The position values indicate the center of the object. Here, my object is 3m long; the centers, therefore, should be 3m apart. So, if I simply add 3m to the 110m position, I get 113m. Figure 6-63 shows the first segment nicely lined up after I changed the X position to 113m.

**Figure 6-62**
*Three identical prims.*

**Figure 6-63**
*The first segment lined up.*

Again, in this case, we are already aligned on the y- and z-axes because I used the Shift-drag creation method. If you didn't do this, use the same technique to line up the y- or z-axes.

Although the alignment by the numbers method requires a small bit of math, it is an essential technique for the serious builder.

## ALIGNMENT WITH THE GRID

The "grid" in SL is like grids in other applications and effectively allows you to "snap" objects to specific points in the grid. This capability really helps in alignment and can be used quickly to Shift-drag out a series of aligned prims.

At the top of your edit controls, select the check box called Use Grid (see Figure 6-64). Selecting the Options button

brings up the Grid objects. The first setting (Grid Unit) is the space between each grid line, while the second setting (Grid Extents) is the length of the grid display (longer is better for large builds, shorter for small builds). Grid Opacity controls how visible the grid is when building.

**Figure 6-64**
*The Use Grid check box.*

Figure 6-65 shows the grid enabled. Now, when I Shift-drag the object, a grid appears above and below the axis I'm dragging on. I can drag the object normally as long as my mouse is between the two grid lines.

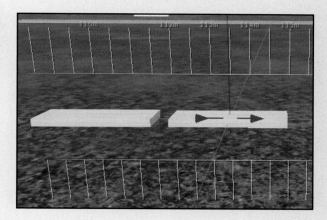

**Figure 6-65**
*The grid enabled.*

If you want to use the grid itself, drag your mouse pointer up into the grid (while you continue to drag the object). In Figure 6-66, a white line and double-headed arrow appear. The arrow shows where exactly on the grid the object is, and you will "feel" how it snaps from grid line to grid line. The figure shows that I have Shift-dragged a copy of the object to the 113m point (as measured at its center). They are now aligned with no number crunching!

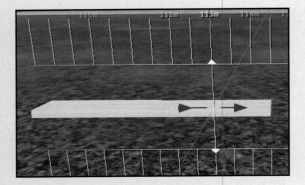

**Figure 6-66**
*I Shift-dragged a copy to the 113m point.*

## ALIGNMENT WITH COPY PREVIOUS

The third trick came to me from Pannie Paperdoll. I'm not sure who passed it on to her, but this is great way to quickly build a series of walls, sidewalks, roads, and so on. To use it, create a box and resize it to the shape you like (in Figure 6-67 I highlighted one edge red, just to show you where to click).

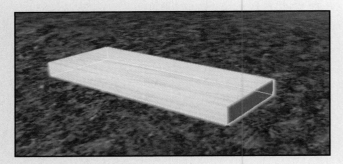

**Figure 6-67**
*You click on the edge that's highlighted.*

Go to the Create tab (by selecting Create at the top of the edit dialog) and check the boxes for Copy Selection and Center Copy (see Figure 6-67).

**Figure 6-68**
*Click Create and check Copy Selection and Center Copy.*

Now back in the world, simply click on the side or face you want to extend (the red face in this example). You can see in Figure 6-69 I created a three-prim-long board with three simple clicks, all totally aligned. Make sure to uncheck the Copy Selection box when you're ready to move on.

**Figure 6-69**
*A three-prim-long board created in three clicks.*

## PRO TIP

When you're using Copy Selected, the next prim you create is a copy of the currently selected prim. Typically, you click on the same prim as the one you have selected, like in the preceding sample, but you can click on any other prim. Selecting the Center Copy check box centers the new prim relative to the prim you clicked on (not the selected prim). Rotate Copy, if checked, will rotate the new prim relative to the prim you clicked on. If Rotate Copy is unselected, the new prim will have the same rotation as the selected prim.

## BUILDING TOOLS

Finally, there are several building tools in-world that you can use to align objects and do many other things. These are extremely creative scripts and HUDs that help builders do difficult things like aligning objects or even building spiral staircases. Check out www.slexchange. com and www.slboutique.com to find the latest tools out there.

# LET THERE BE LIGHT (FEATURE TAB)

SL would be pretty dull if it was always dark, and this is where SL lighting comes into play. There are two lighting modes in SL. The first is the Sun (or Moon at night) only, which simulates reflected light from the sun/moon. The second mode enables local lights in addition to the sun and moon. It is also possible to fake the "look" of lighting using texturing effects. Since there is always the sun/moon, let's consider how to add fake and real local lighting to your scenes.

## FAKED LIGHTS WITH FULL BRIGHT

First, if you want something to look like it's lit, you can simply check the Full Bright box on the Texture tab. When Full Bright is checked, the texture of the object ignores the lighting of the sun/moon. The texture you have chosen displays as the pure texture you have assigned. So, when it gets dark, a "full bright" object will appear lit. It will not, however, cast light onto surrounding objects (because it's not a light source; it's a texture option).

The screenshots shown in Figure 6-70 illustrate the differences between a sphere at midnight. The first has no lighting, the second has full bright turned on, and the third is a real light (enabled on the Features tab). Notice how the fully bright object casts no light on the ground or the wall.

So, you may ask, Why would I ever use full bright objects instead of real lights? The answer is that there are limitations with SL lighting that make fake lights an attractive addition to a well-lit space.

## CREATING "LOCAL" LIGHTS

Creating a light in SL is easy and satisfying. Simply rez a prim (any prim), go to the Features tab, and select the Light check box (see Figure 6-71).

**Figure 6-71**
*To create a light, simply select Light.*

To see lights, you need to have local lighting enabled. This is done under the Edit->Preferences->Graphics Detail tab (see Figure 6-72). You might want to set the sun/moon to midnight via World->Force Sun->Midnight.

You can set the color of the light as well as its intensity, radius, and "falloff." Whoa! Wait a minute. What does "falling off" have to do with lights? Well, read on, where we cover each of these properties:

- **Color:** Color determines the color of the light that's cast. Setting the color to black essentially turns off the light.

- **Intensity:** Intensity determines the strength of the light. It is kind of like the difference between a 300-watt halogen bulb and a 60-watt bulb. A value of 1.000 is full intensity/brightness. Smaller values dial

| No Light | Full Bright | Local Light |
|---|---|---|
|  |  |  |

**Figure 6-70**
*Faked lighting using Full Bright compared to Local Lighting.*

the lighting back. Setting the intensity to 0 essentially turns off the light.

- **Radius:** Light is emitted from the center point of a prim (not its surface, as you might intuitively think). Lighting in SL also radiates out in a 360-degree sphere from that center point (regardless of the shape of the prim). The radius determines how far out (in meters) from the center the light goes. The maximum radius for a light is 20m. Setting the radius to 0 essentially turns off the light.

- **Falloff:** In RL, a light is more intense (bright) closer to its source than further away. Falloff determines how quickly a light goes from full intensity to shedding no light whatsoever. The Falloff property goes from 0 to 2. At 0, there will be very little falloff (the SL Knowledgebase says the minimum is actually .001), so the light will be mostly uniform through the entire radius. At 2, the light will fall off very quickly. The SL Knowledgebase on lighting indicates that the falloff function used to calculate light falloff is as follows:

Intensity = (1.0 – (distance/light radius)) ^ Falloff

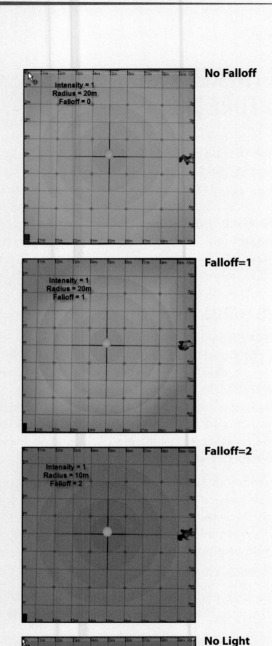

No Falloff

Falloff=1

Falloff=2

No Light

**Figure 6-73**
*Sample local lighting settings.*

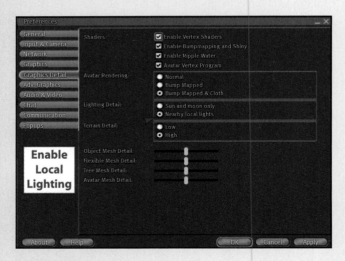

**Figure 6-72**
*Enable local lighting by selecting Nearby Local Lights.*

Figure 6-73 shows some sample settings, taken from a bird's eye view at my workshop. The green circle in the center is a sphere with lighting turned on. You are seeing a 10m×10m grid (the weird shape to the mid-right is me standing there).

So, that's about it for the simplicity of lighting. However, there are several tips, tricks, and considerations you should be aware of before you run out and create a strand of 80 Chinese lanterns for your back deck.

## LIGHTING CONSIDERATIONS

Following is a collection of tips, tricks, and details about lighting in SL.

### Not Everyone Sees Local Lighting

The work to produce a lighting effect is done on the client side (your desktop/laptop), and the heavy lifting is done by your graphics card or graphics processing unit (GPU). Not everyone will have local lighting enabled. Chosen Few had this to say on a forum post, *"Turning [local lighting] on causes a performance hit, which not every computer can handle. If you've got a low end video card or CPU, you may be out of luck."*

This means, as a builder, you need to consider how important lighting is to all the avatars who will see your work. The good news is most GPUs today can handle this basic lighting. Graphics cards that are compatible with SL can be found at http://secondlife.com/corporate/sysreqs.php.

### Only Six Lights Are Visible at Any Point

SL as an OpenGL application allows rendering of up to eight light sources at a time. Two of them are always reserved for the sun/moon and an ambient light (backlight, which simulates the reflected light from the sun/moon), which leaves six available for your use as local lights. If an avatar is surrounded by more than six local lights, SL will perform a calculation to determine what six lights to show. As an avatar moves away from some lights and toward others, there is the effect of lights going off and on.

Remember, which lights are on is determined per individual avatar. So, if there are several avatars in the same area with a lot of lights, they are all likely to be seeing different lights as on and off. So, it is best, for example, not to use local lighting for a game system.

### Light Is Cast from the Center of a Prim

Light is cast from the center of a prim. To see how this works, create a 10m cube, enable lighting, but make the light radius 1m. You will not see the light unless you hollow out the cube. The surface of the whole cube will take on the tint of the color of the light, but light will not be cast beyond the radius setting.

### SL Lights Do Not Cast Shadows

There are no simulated shadows in SL (at least as of this writing). So, if you have a light and put a prim underneath, the light will essentially shine through the prim. Likewise, the light from a wall sconce will shine through the other side of the wall. In Figure 6-74 a red rectangle is set to red light. You can see the red cast of light on the wood and ground all around it.

Below the red rectangle light, I placed a cube. It's directly between the light and the wood floor, but as you can see in Figure 6-74, there is no shadow.

**Figure 6-74**
*No shadow from local lighting.*

> ## ✋ TIP
>
> Some texture artists who are going for a realistic look will "bake" a shadow onto the wood floor texture where they know a shadow should be. While creating this effect is time consuming, it is a very nice and noticeable effect for objects that never move. It is also possible with some scripting to have these baked-in lighting effects change with the time of day.

## There Is No Directional Lighting in SL

Lights in SL are omnidirectional; that is, they cast light from the center point of a prim in all directions at the same time. In 3D applications, these are typically referred to as *point* lights. There are no directional, spot, or box lights that cast lighting in one direction or across a surface. That doesn't mean you can't be creative in simulating directional lighting. Many have done so with great success; just visit an SL disco one night.

## Static Versus Dynamic Lights

Lighting is treated slightly differently depending on whether lights are moving or not. Lights are considered to be static (nonmoving) or dynamic (moving). For example, moving lights may be attached to vehicles (headlights) or avatars (carrying a candle). Lights that move place a heavier load on the graphics processor than static lights. Only nonmoving, nonflexible, and unattached primitives use static lighting. Here are some key points from the SL Knowledgebase:

- **Hardware Versus Software Lighting:** The sun, moon, and moving lights are calculated in hardware, while static lights are calculated in software. There may be an initial delay before the effects of static lights become visible, as the software lighting is done as a background task.

- **Lighting Performance:** Static lighting performance is better with many small lights. Dynamic lighting performance is better with a few large lights.

- **Lighting Calculations:** A list of nearby lights is generated. This list is calculated once per frame. Six lights are chosen from the list. Priority is based on the effective intensity of each light at the viewer's avatar. Dynamic lights are given slightly higher priority.

## LIGHTING SUMMARY

We've completed our brief overview of SL lighting. Creative use of textures, full bright, and lights can add significantly to a place's ambiance, especially at night. Now, on to another really cool building feature: flexprims.

# BUILDING FLEXIBLE PRIMITIVES (FEATURE TAB)

One of the really cool building features in SL is the capability to make prims flexible, the so-called **flexiprims** or **flexprims**. When you first create a prim, it is rigid and does not respond to any environmental forces such as wind or gravity. Flexprims do! Flexprims can be used to make flags, sails, realistic skirts, prim-hair, wagging tails, curtains, or bushes that sway in the breeze and all sorts of other things (see Figure 6-75).

**Figure 6-75**
*Flexprims add a degree of realism.*

As of this writing, only certain basic primitive types can be made flexible. They are the box, cylinder, and prism. To enable flexibility, you use the Features tab in the edit dialog. Simply check the Flexible Path box (see Figure 6-76).

Figure 6-77 shows all of the flexprim properties. Here, you can see a cone (a cylinder that tapers to a point) that has been made flexible.

There are several settings that are great fun to play with. The settings are a mix between the "composition" of the flexprim and the "forces" acting on it.

Rather than consider them in the order of the UI, let's look at these properties in the order in which I think makes it easier to set up a flexprim. That means first setting the basic flexprim composition and then determining the forces to apply to the flexprim.

**Figure 6-76**
*Check the Flexible Path box.*

**Figure 6-77**
*Playing with flexprims.*

# FLEXPRIM COMPOSITION PROPERTIES

Flexprim composition is set using three settings: Softness, Tension, and Drag. Here is a bit more on each of the settings:

- **Softness:** Softness determines the number of joints in the prim and has nothing to do with forces acting on the prim itself. It has a range of 0 to 3. What's really happening is the object is being divided into a number of segments (2 raised to the power of the softness value). At the maximum softness (3), your object will have eight sections.

  Turning off softness is not the same as disabling flex. It simply removes any segments from your prim, so the flex is along the whole length.

Figure 6-78 shows a few samples of a 5m long pole with various softness settings.

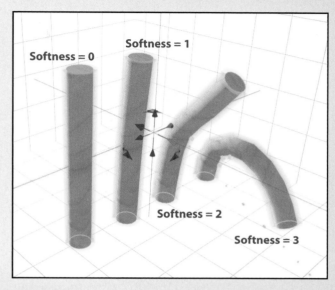

**Figure 6-78**
*Poles at various softness settings.*

- **Tension:** Tension determines how easily the segments of your prim flex bends or how rigid the object is. Setting tension to its maximum of 10 will give you a very rigid object, even if it has a maximum softness. Think about a straw that has eight sections; trying to bend it is pretty hard. A straw is tense. Now what if you had a piece of rope? Rope is not tense at all; it's very flexible.

- **Drag:** Drag determines how easily a prim can move through the air. This setting relates to the properties of the prim, not a force being applied. A low drag setting means an object can move easily or quickly through the air, which is great for wiggling or flapping motions. A high drag setting means the object moves slowly through the air, which is great for swaying motions. Drag has a range of 0 to 10.

# FLEXPRIM FORCE PROPERTIES

If no force acts on a flexprim, it will not move at all, which may be just what you're looking for, like a piece of rope lying on a dock, for example. However, to make things more dynamic in SL, you can control how existing forces like wind affect your flexprim, and you can also apply your own forces to the flexprim. Let's look at the options:

- **Gravity:** The Gravity setting applies a force to your object, the force of gravity. Gravity is a downward force applied to the object relative to the world. In SL, you can defy gravity, with forces applied upward on the object relative to the world. You can control how much gravity or antigravity your object experiences by tuning this between 10 (maximum gravity) and –10 (maximum antigravity).

- **Wind:** Did you know there is wind in SL? Well, there is! It's hard to see unless you have a flexiflag, flexicurtains, or you sail. The wind direction and force change and are different across each sim. This setting determines how much or how little the flexprim is affected by this wind force. It does not actually set the wind force. This is done by the simulator. If you're building something that should react to the wind (like a flag), then this setting is for you. It ranges from 0 to 10.

- **Force X, Force Y, Force Z:** Finally, you can apply a specific constant force in any x, y, and z direction. These forces follow the world axis settings (+/–X = East/West, +/–Y = North/South, +/–Z = up/down).

## BUILDING TIPS FOR FLEXPRIM OBJECTS

Here are some tips and steps for building with flexprims that have worked well for me.

First, position and size your prim. Since the number of joints and segments is set by softness, the scale of your object is important to its flexible behavior.

Second, rotate the prim properly. One of the key tips to building with flexprims is understanding that a portion of the flexprim is anchored and unmoving. The unanchored part of the prim moves. The anchored part is the bottom face of each prim type when it is first rezzed. For boxes, the bottom face is a square; for cylinders, a circle; and for prisms, a triangle. So, when you're building a curtain, make sure the anchor point is at the top by rotating the prim 180 degrees.

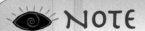

**NOTE**

You cannot link together a set of flexprims and have them behave as though they are one big flexprim. The anchor faces are still there even when linked.

Next, think about the material or composition of the prim. Determine what the right softness, tension, and drag should be. Don't stress; just take a stab at these settings. It's fun and you'll get a better feel for how they work over time.

After you've guessed at these settings, think about what forces should interact with your object. If it is to be a realistic in-world object, you probably want to have a bit of wind and/or gravity.

At this point, finding the right settings is a matter of playing around. If a prim is not bending well, you could try reducing the tension, increasing the softness, or just adding more wind. There are many ways to achieve the same effect. If you want complete control over the forces applied to an object, set the wind to 0 because wind is random in both direction and force.

When you have it close, you can do some fine-tuning by applying a little static force to the prim by setting the Force X, Y, and Z properties.

Whether your flexprim will be moving (attached to a vehicle, robot, or avatar) or static (sitting on the ground, attached to a building) makes a big difference. If your flexprim is going to be moving, you need to test the settings you've chosen under the same movement conditions. The quickest way to do this is to use the Positioning controls while editing the prim. Simply drag the object around and see how the flex works. I also use a little script that jiggers a flexprim about so I can see how it's working. I use a timer event and llSetPos(llGetPos() + <x,y,z>) function, which you will learn about later under scripting.

## HOW DO FLEXPRIMS WORK?

There are a couple important points to understand about flexprims. First, they do not interact with the world. That is, they do not collide with other prims, and they cannot be made physical. Curtains blowing in the wind will blow right through a wall, window, chair, or even an avatar. These effects are disconcerting but can be taken into account if you build carefully.

Second, all the work going into flexible prims is happening on the client (that is, your laptop or desktop machine). While all avatars will see something as flexible, they will not all see exactly the same thing because the flex-simulation is happening on each client, not centrally on the server. This is similar to the way local lights are handled.

This feature is great because it does not slow down the server, but it may make your client slow. If necessary, you can turn off flexprims on your client by unchecking Flexible Objects under the Client->Rendering->Features menu or by pressing Ctrl+Alt+9.

Now, get out there and flex your prim muscle!

> The client and server menus (originally called Debug) may not be displayed. You can show or hide them by pressing Ctrl+Alt+D.

# BUILDING TIPS AND TRICKS

Following is a collection of building tips and tricks that did not find their way into previous sections and yet are important to know.

## LOCKING PRIMS AND OBJECTS

As you start to edit more and more complex things or you get your house placed just as you like it, you don't want to mess around with it. You will soon discover that when you're in editing mode, you might click on something and accidentally select your floor or a wall. If you also accidentally move this, things can get pretty frustrating pretty quickly if you try getting all the pieces back in place.

To avoid this problem, you can lock an object. Lock is the first check box on the Object tab. When it's checked, all aspects of this object will be fixed such that you cannot

resize, move, change texture, and so on. So, when you're done with anything that will be a semipermanent fixture on your land, lock it. You can always unlock something by simply unchecking the Lock box.

## BACKING UP YOUR WORK

The safest place for your creations is in your Inventory. To be honest, I'm uncomfortable that everything I make in SL is kind of "somewhere" that I do not own and have very little control over. But, as of this writing, there is no way to stream your objects or your Inventory out of or into SL. Perhaps this discomfort is similar to the feeling I have when I think too hard about the fact that we all live on a small ball in the middle of an asteroid-strewn universe.

Either way, if you're working on a complex object or about to do something that may screw up an as-yet-great project, it's a good idea to take a backup copy. Just link up your object and select Take Copy. You may want to rename the object in your Inventory to identify the copy with either a running version like Spaceship V1, Spaceship V2, and Spaceship V3 or a date.

## GETTING AT ENVELOPED OBJECTS

At least once, you will create a great object, and then as you're moving it, you will accidentally move it inside another object and let go. When you try to select it again, you select only the enveloping object. How do you retrieve your object? There are several options:

- **Undo (Ctrl+Z):** If the object you erroneously positioned is still selected (or can be selected), you can undo your mistake.

- **Move the enveloping object:** Move the containing object away so that you can access your object. This is the most obvious solution and, if you're lucky, the easiest recovery mechanism. However, often the thing you need to move is your elaborate house that was precisely placed on a tiny parcel. So, what other options are available?

- **Drag-select a selection box around the object:** You can left-click and drag a marque/lasso around where you think the object is inside to select it. This approach works if there are no other objects inside the selection or behind the selection. If you get it, you will see the yellow outline of your object, and you should be able to move it back. This technique works only when you're in edit mode, so you may want to select Tools->Select Only My Objects.

- **Set debug rendering mode to hide selection:** This is a little more advanced approach, but you can use a debug setting to hide prims when you select them. First, you have to add the Client/Server menu to your window. Do this by pressing Ctrl+Alt+D. You should see a new menu at the top of your window called Client. Under this menu, find Client->Rendering->Hide Selected. Next, select the object that is obscuring the one you want. You should now see your object. Select it (it will disappear). Then uncheck Hide Selected. You should now have your object selected and can move it back to where you can see it.

- **Set debug rendering mode to hide surface patches:** If you have accidentally embedded something in the ground, you can turn off ground rendering from the Client menu as well so that you can see and select the object.

- **Adjust camera position to inside the containing object:** In SL, you can move your point of view (your camera) right through solid objects. This technique takes some maneuvering, but it can be an effective way to find an object that's hidden inside another. Alt+click on the ground (or any other surface) near the object you want to look inside and then drag the mouse to swing the camera around until it goes right through the outside of the object. With a little practice, you should be able to find the second object hidden inside.

## PRO TIP

When the camera is seeing things from inside a prim, that prim will become temporarily invisible to you. The reason is that objects in SL are visible only from the outside. In 3D graphics terms, it's called *backface culling*.

## LEARNING FROM OTHERS' WORK

OK, this is an essential tip, so listen up! You can learn from the masters very easily in SL. If you're a traditional painter, you may try to reproduce a master's work to learn more about her techniques and methods. In SL, this is easy to do (too easy, some may say). You can select any object in SL and select Edit. If you don't own the object, you, of course, cannot modify it, but when you do this, the object will be highlighted in such a way that you can see each of the prims involved.

This was one of the first ways I learned about waterfalls. Find one you like and select it. You will see rotating cubes, tori, spheres, and so on. I found a great treehouse with a giant tree made from prims that I spent hours trying to reproduce after I figured out how it was constructed.

You should know that when you do this, it is obvious to others that you are looking at the object, but don't be afraid to check out others' work. However, avoid trying to examine someone else's work while he's in the process of editing it himself! This can cause problems for the builder.

Remember also that objects are the intellectual property of the creator. Just as with art, you may try to copy a masterpiece to learn how it was done and use the reproduction for your own purposes. However, don't try to pass off your reproduction as the original or sell it for profit. This is considered theft by many people who are trying to build their own businesses in SL and it is illegal.

One last point: Be aware that when people are building an object, they may be completely unaware of your presence or that you are talking to them. Building may well cover their screen with edit, texture, and Inventory windows, so they can't see incoming chat or IM messages. If they don't reply, wait patiently until they seem less active in their building efforts.

## BUILDING FOR AVATAR SIZE AND CAMERA CONTROLS

In SL, avatars tend to be created a bit larger than in RL. On average, avatars are 6 to 6.5 feet tall. Also, rather than looking through your eyes (with mouse look), typically people navigate with the camera behind them. This means that if you were to build an SL house or staircase to RL proportions, it would be hard for people to navigate your creations without the camera ending up inside the wall or ceiling.

A great discussion on building for avatar size and camera controls exists on the Build Forum:

http://forums.secondlife.com/showthread.php?threadid=149215

## CREATING TINY PRIMS

In SL, the minimum prim size is .01×.01×.01 meters, but using cutting, slicing, and hollowing tools, you can get prims to appear even smaller. This capability is particularly nice for fine jewelry work. See this Build Forum post:

http://forums.secondlife.com/showthread.php?t=27520

# TUTORIAL: CREATING A ROOM

In this tutorial you build your first house. Yes, you can build a complete house with only two prims! I remember a question that came up on the SL Build Forum: "How do I build a house?" It was funny in a way, because it would be almost the same as asking that question in RL. Figure 6-79 shows what Renee Roundfield had to say about it in a forum post on How to Build a House:

The more you get into SL building, the funnier this gets in a kind of "planes, trains, and automobiles" way! However, it's not too hard to build your first house, so you're going to do it now.

## STEP 1: FIND A SANDBOX

First, find a nice sandbox with a bit of space you can work in (see Figure 6-80).

Here we go!

---

**How to Build a House**

!. Muck around with building things in general.
2. Get an idea.
3. Start building.
4. End up accidentally wearing part of your house on your head.
5. Learn camera controls.
6. Have trouble lining things up.
7. Review camera controls.
8. Take ASL classes.
9. Revisit Ivory Tower.
10. Start over, much inspired.
11. Real Life interferes.
12. Everything looks like crap.
13. Start over.
14. Obtain Freebie textures.
15. Purchase expensive textures.
16. Learn GIMP, pay 450L to upload.
17. Learn to apply textures.
18. Everything looks like crap.
19. Vist Robin Sojourner's texture tutorials.
20. Reinspired, start over.
21. Carefully apply textures.
22. Near adequacy.
23. Accident in land makes returning everything to self necessary.
24. Learn to name objects and link.
25. Start over, because reassembling too daunting.
26. Again, near adequacy.
27. Accidentally remove textures from entire house.
28. Consider the "I did that on purpose" strategy.
29. For a long time.
30. Reapply textures.

There are more steps, but I haven't done them yet.

Renee Roundfield

**Figure 6-79**
*Renee Roundfield on building houses.*

**Figure 6-80**
*A sandbox.*

# STEP 2: CREATE AND RESIZE A CUBE

I've chosen to build the maximum size for one prim of 10×10×0.5m (see Figure 6-81).

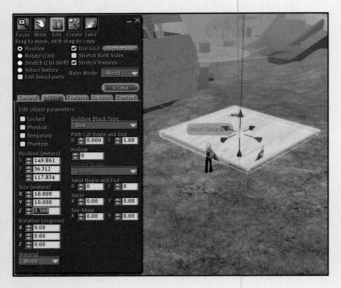

**Figure 6-81**
*A 10×10×0.5m cube.*

# STEP 3: HOLLOW THE CUBE

Hollow the cube as much as possible, which is 95% hollow (see Figure 6-82). Note that using these techniques is an important part of building. By using the Hollow capability, you can create a room that will soon have walls using just one prim instead of four separate prims! This is not typically done because the inside of a single prim allows only one texture. This is not typically done because the inside of a single prim allows only one texture, and you typically want a different texture on each inside wall.

**Figure 6-82**
*Hollow the cube as much as possible.*

# STEP 4: CREATE THE ROOM

To create the room, you need to give it some walls. I adjusted the z-axis to 4m. You will also need to lift the cube out of the ground because 2m of your house will be underground. Now, we need a doorway, so use the Path Cut tools to open one.

Unfortunately, it's not possible to adjust the split point of the object, so to center a door on a wall, you end up needing to use more than one prim. However, for this tutorial, we will consider the door location all right. You should now see something like Figure 6-83. Wow, your first room with only one prim!

**Figure 6-83**
*Your first room and it took only one prim.*

# STEP 5: REMOVE THE PLYWOOD TEXTURE

The next step is to texture your house. We could get into windows and so on, but for simplicity's sake, let's just make the whole house glass! The first step is to remove the plywood. Go to the Texture tab, click on the plywood texture image, and choose Blank (see Figure 6-84).

**Figure 6-84**
*Choose Blank.*

## STEP 6: PICK A WALL COLOR

Next, let's pick a color for the soon-to-be glass walls. Do this by selecting the color box on the Texture tab. I picked the nice shade of blue shown in Figure 6-85.

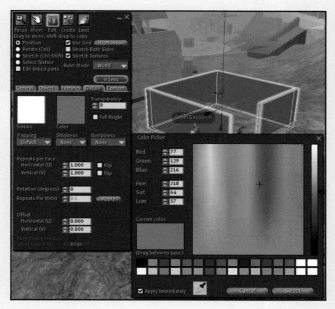

**Figure 6-85**
*I like this blue.*

## STEP 7: PUT ON A ROOF

The next step is to create the roof. You could rez another cube and resize it and then try to position it directly over your room, but that would be doing it the hard way. Part of becoming a great builder is to learn how to work efficiently. Try this.

In edit mode, select your room. Hold down the Shift key, then left-click on the blue arrow, and drag upward along the z-axis. What you're doing here is duplicating your room exactly over the top of the previous room. You could even use this technique to make a second story. Now you should see something like Figure 6-86.

## STEP 8: MAKE YOUR ROOF

You need to make several changes to get the second room to look like a roof. First, change the color to black or brown or whatever!

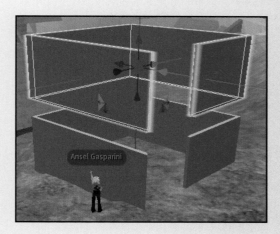

**Figure 6-86**
*A second story or a roof.*

Then remove the doorway by resetting Path Cut Begin to 0 and End to 1.

Remove the hollow so no rain will come in (that is, unless you're going for an interior courtyard). Set Hollow to 0. Finally, resize the roof. I changed the z-axis to 0.5m.

Voilà! You have a roof (see Figure 6-87). Next, lower your roof onto your one-room house (see Figure 6-88).

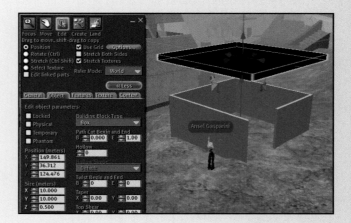

**Figure 6-87**
*Change the color to a roof color.*

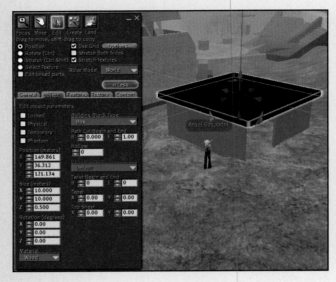

**Figure 6-88**
*Lower the roof.*

## STEP 9: MAKE THE WALLS TRANSPARENT

If you walk into your house, it's pretty cool. Maybe it needs some furniture, but it's really neat to have the basics created at least. However, it is kind of claustrophobic (see Figure 6-89). Let's open it up a bit by turning our walls into glass.

**Figure 6-89**
*The walls have only one opening.*

Select the walls and set the transparency to 60% or so (see Figure 6-90). Adjust the setting to suit your taste of privacy versus view. See the difference!

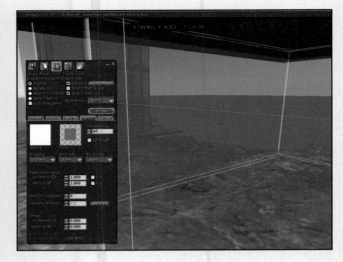

**Figure 6-90**
*Wall transparency.*

## STEP 10: LINK THE PRIMITIVES AND CLEAN UP

The next step in the process is to link the primitives, name your house, and take the house into your Inventory. First, select the roof and then, while holding the Shift key, select the walls. The last primitive you select, as you may recall, is your root primitive. Both walls and roof should be selected.

Link the two by pressing Ctrl+L. You now have a new object. If you go to the General tab, you will notice it has the generic name **Object**. Rename it to **My First House**.

Finally, clean up your work, select your house while not in edit mode, right-click to open the pie menu, and select Take. You now have your house in your Inventory. Big Inventory, eh? Rez it for a friend sometime or get yourself some land to put it on.

## STEP 11: LEARN FROM NEW FRIENDS

While I was doing this tutorial, I met Justy Reymont. He told me that he thought he could do better with two prims and proceeded to construct a circular house with a nice dome (see Figure 6-91)!

**Figure 6-91**
*A circular house with a dome built with two prims.*

What a great idea. As you now know, all of the basic building tutorials have used boxes, and this would have been a great way to introduce a cylinder and a half sphere.

You should try this yourself. Can you build Justy's two-prim round house?

While this two-prim house is not even close to the elaborate constructions you will find in SL, I hope it gets your juices started. If you had trouble building this house, don't fret; there are many freebie starter homes available in SL.

# TUTORIAL: FRAMING A PICTURE

For this final tutorial, we bring together everything you've learned with a smaller project, a basic picture frame where you can hang your SL snapshots for friends and family. This project uses three prims, which for a picture frame would be considered "prim heavy." It is possible to achieve a similar effect that would pass with the casual observer by creating your own textures, but that's for a later chapter.

I cover the steps here with a bit less detail assuming you have already worked through a few of the earlier tutorials.

## STEP 1: CREATE A CUBE

Start as usual by creating a cube and resizing it. I chose a 1×1m frame and reduced the z-axis to 0.1m.

Duplicate the frame three times by holding down the Shift key and left-click, dragging the z-axis up arrow. You should have something like the three perfectly aligned, identical shapes shown in Figure 6-92.

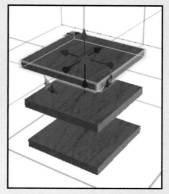

**Figure 6-92**
*Three perfectly aligned, identical shapes.*

## STEP 2: CREATE THE FRAME

Move two of the prims out of the way for a bit (that is, move them upward so they remain exactly centered with those below them). Edit the basic frame. Name it **Frame** (get in the habit of just naming your objects). As shown in Figure 6-93, hollow it out to 60%, "blank" the plywood texture, and color it a really dark gray.

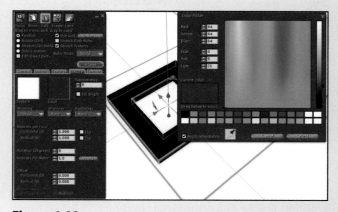

**Figure 6-93**
*Hollow and blank the texture; then color it dark gray.*

## STEP 3: CREATE THE MAT

Grab the next section and move it down so that it's above the frame. This will be your mat; name it **Mat**. Adjust its size so it is smaller than the frame on x,y and thinner than the frame on the z-axis. Move it down into the frame, as shown in Figure 6-94.

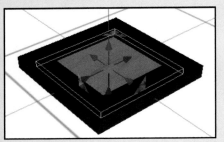

**Figure 6-94**
*Creating the mat.*

## STEP 4: COLOR THE MAT AND ADJUST THE FRAME

Remove the plywood texture image and pick a nice color for the mat; I chose a light blue. At this point I thought the frame was too thick, so I hollowed it out even more. Figure 6-95 shows the result.

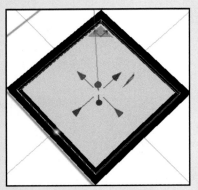

**Figure 6-95**
*The thinner frame with a blue mat.*

## STEP 5: ADJUST THE MAT AND RESIZE THE PICTURE

The next step is to hollow out the mat and bring down the picture and then resize it so that it just overlaps a bit with the hollow in the mat (see Figure 6-96). Again, make it thinner than the mat as well.

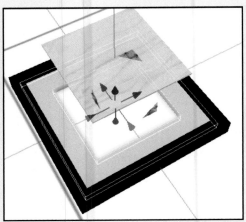

**Figure 6-96**
*Hollow out the mat and resize the picture.*

## STEP 6: APPLY THE PICTURE

Now you need a picture. If you don't have one already, read about taking a snapshot in Chapter 2 and get yourself one. Alternatively, grab a snapshot or texture from the Library. I used one of the earliest pictures I have of my newbie self here. Select your snapshot as the texture image you want to use to replace the plywood. Then move it into place (see Figure 6-97).

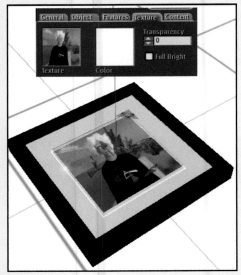

**Figure 6-97**
*Move your snapshot into place.*

## STEP 7: LINK THE FRAME, MAT, AND PICTURE

Select all three prims by holding down the Shift key as you select each prim or click-drag to select all three (see Figure 6-98). Then you can link them into one object by pressing Ctrl+L or selecting Tools->Link.

**Figure 6-98**
*Select all three prims.*

After you select the object, you can see the children prims in blue and the parent (or root) prim highlighted in yellow. The parent (root) prim is the last prim you select when you create the linked object.

## STEP 8: HANG YOUR PICTURE

Name your framed picture and take a copy into your Inventory for safe keeping (by selecting the picture not in edit mode and using the pie menu option Take Copy). Now rotate it 90 degrees on the x-axis and hang it on your wall somewhere.

In Figure 6-99, the new picture is right next to my skydiving picture and above the button that teleports me upstairs.

**Figure 6-99**
*The picture is up.*

# TUTORIAL: CREATING A FLEXIBLE TAIL WITH PANNIE PAPERDOLL

Hi there! Remember me? I'm Pannie Paperdoll (see Figure 6-100). Ansel asked me to show you how easy flexprims are to work with, and I'll give you a fun fashion accessory at the same time. Ready? Good! Here come baby step-by-step instructions for making a flexible tail that wags on its own.

**Figure 6-100**
*Pannie Paperdoll.*

## STEP 1: CREATE A CONE

Click the Build button at the bottom of your screen, or right-click on the ground and choose Create from the pie menu. An object editor box will appear on your screen. On the top of this box is a series of shapes to choose from. Left-click on the cone shape; then left-click the ground in front of you. This should make the cone appear on the ground in front of you (see Figure 6-101). This cone is going to become your flexible tail.

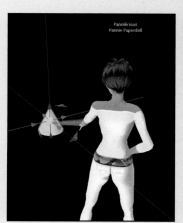

**Figure 6-101**
*The cone should appear in front of you.*

## STEP 2: DEFINE THE LENGTH AND THICKNESS

Hold down your Ctrl and Shift keys. You should see colored boxes appear around your cone. Grab the top blue one and drag it upward till you're happy with the length of your tail (see Figure 6-102).

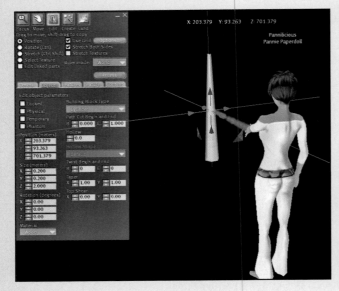

**Figure 6-102**
*Get the tail length you want.*

Now, adjust the thickness of your tail. Here, I changed the numbers in the Size (meters) section of the edit box. I changed x and y to 0.200 (see Figure 6-103).

**Figure 6-103**
*Changing the Size settings.*

## STEP 3: MAKE THE TAIL FLEXIBLE

Click the Features tab of your object editor. Select the Flexible Path check box and edit the numbers until you like the movement of your tail (see Figure 6-104).

You can experiment with this setting by dragging the tail around.

I changed Softness to 3.00, left Gravity alone, reduced Drag to 1.00, and increased Wind to 1.00.

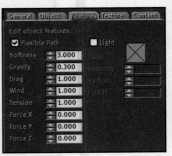

**Figure 6-104**
*Getting flex in the tail.*

## STEP 4: ATTACH THE TAIL TO YOUR BODY

Now, attach the tail to your body. Right-click on it again and choose More->Attach->Torso->Pelvis (see Figure 6-105). Do not try to attach it to your spine because it will move from one butt cheek to the other when you walk!

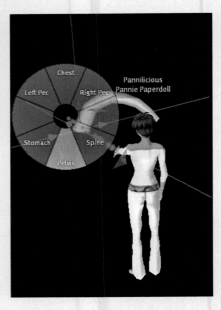

**Figure 6-105**
*Attach the tail to your pelvis.*

## STEP 5: POSITION AND ROTATE YOUR TAIL

Now your tail is attached, but it looks more like it's following you. To fix this, you simply use the arrows to move the tail up to your lower back. Then you will need to rotate it properly.

There are two ways to rotate your tail so that it's facing the proper direction. You can put a check mark in the Rotate box as shown, or you can simply hold your Ctrl button to make the colored lines (officially called *alignment rings*, but known to everyone who builds as "the colored rings you rotate things with") appear. Either way, once you have the colored rings, grab one and move it one way or the other to rotate the tail. Keep playing with the rotation until you're happy with how your tail is positioned (see Figure 6-106).

**Before**

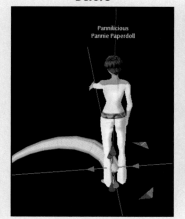

**In Between**

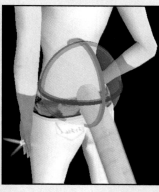

**After**

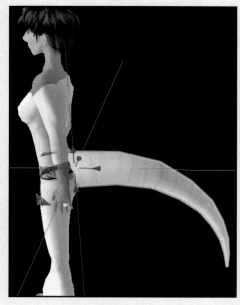

**Figure 6-106**
*Rotate the tail until you're happy with it.*

## STEP 6: ADJUST LENGTH AND THICKNESS AGAIN

The tail may look too big or too small now that it's on you. You can edit prims even though they are already attached to your body. I decided that my tail is still too fat, so I changed the size of x and y to 0.100.

## STEP 7: APPLY A TEXTURE

Next, we'll add a texture. First, choose the Texture tab; then click the plywood square. This brings up your Inventory of textures. If you know the name of the texture you want, just type it in the Search box. If you don't know what you want, scroll through your folders. As you click on each texture, it will show in the preview box, and if you have Apply Immediately checked, it will also show on your tail. I've chosen a leopard skin texture that I found in the Library (see Figure 6-107).

**Figure 6-107**
*Leopard skin!.*

## STEP 8: ADMIRE YOURSELF!

You're now wearing a tail that twitches, wags, and generally looks alive (see Figure 6-108)! WTG!

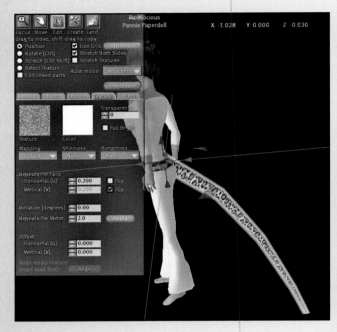

**Figure 6-108**
*Your finished tail!*

# THE IVORY TOWER LIBRARY OF PRIMITIVES

No chapter on building basics would be complete without mentioning the Ivory Tower Library of Primitives (see Figure 6-109). The Ivory Tower is an in-world, self-paced way to learn all about building. If this chapter has sparked your interest and creativity, you owe yourself a visit to this place.

SLURL You can find the Ivory Tower Library of Primitives at **http://slurl.com/secondlife/natoma/207/170/25/**.

## A VISIT WITH THE IVORY TOWER'S CREATOR

*"I like to show what can be done with prims…rather than what is being done with prims."*

*–Lumiere Noir*

I sat down for a brief chat with the Ivory Tower's creator and long-time SL resident Lumiere Noir (see Figure 6-110). What follows is a snapshot of our conversation:

**Figure 6-109**
*The Ivory Tower Library of Primitives.*

**Figure 6-110**
*Lumiere Noir.*

```
[Ansel arrives on a flat piece of
land outside the entrance to the
Ivory Tower of Primitives. A cliff is
nearby. A giant tiki headed avatar is
building something.]
```

**Ansel Gasparini:** *hi!*

**Lumiere Noir:** nice to meet you, this is sort of a work area for me…bit cluttered and this is how I usually work. I don't get picked on as much in what I was just wearing ;-)but I typically look like this

```
[Lumiere switches to a black MAD
comic book spy vs. spy avatar. He
rezzes a couple rocking chairs. Ansel
struggles to sit in them properly.]
```

LN: humm…I need to fiddle with the camera views on these, lol. these are actually severely limited airplanes, found an interesting use to adapt them to

*AG: So, you have been in SL a while and how did you find out about SL?*

LN: yes…but off and on…I've tried a lot of MMORPGS and while in there.com some people told me that the things I was wanting to do were not really likely to happen in that world, but I'd have a better shot at it here. I came here in early beta and didn't really like the place, so I went back to There for a while, peeking in here from time to time after I got the hang of things here I moved…and haven't looked back much.

*AG: You are something of an icon amongst newbie builders, when did you conceive of the ivory tower project?*

LN: lol…I wouldn't know really…I'm usually pretty busy and just work on projects. but I do seem to be known. Well…I was self taught in building and I had a friend who started at the same time I did and he was (and is) excellent. Starax Statosky. We had something of a rivalry…probably still do in some ways but we built together a lot showed each other our work and so on and it was a good, way to bounce ideas off each other…and we spurred each other on. I'd say (and this is a pet subject of mine) that if any real art is produced in here he'll be the one to make it….who knows if

great art is possible in this world but he's the best of us in my opinion. Let me show you something of his.

```
[Lumiere produces a small magic wand]
```

LN: wand on

*AG: wow*

```
[A large statue several times life
size rezzes on the ground. A devil
figure firmly rooted on the ground
grasps a second figure by the ankles,
a brilliant angel with translucent
wings.]
```

*AG: So, back to the ivory tower, how did it come about*

LN: well…I just built a ton and started to find a lot of tricks

LN: wand off

LN: then I had some questions that I couldn't really figure out and eventually I went to a class and was disappointed to learn the instructors knew less than me. I'm a teacher in real life…so I don't want to hold classes in here really so I started making a tutorial thinking I could use the building system itself to teach the building system the tower is a sort of interface that describes another interface.

*AG: I have to think it takes a lot of prims*

LN: yes it does….I tend to build pretty extravagantly but I like to show what can be done with prims…rather than what is being done with prims. learn to make it, then build using what you're learning on the spot

*AG: So, do you have any advice to offer newbies on building, texturing, scripting?*

LN: well…yes, a lot really. But it can be summed up with the thought that the more you know about what is available to you, the more creative you can be. if you're always having to look things up you won't internalize them and you won't really be able to find the new connections between different things that is the mark of creativity and there's a lot to master in here.

*AG: well, thank you for your time, a real pleasure to meet one of the originals*

LN: I've enjoyed it Ansel

With that, we boarded an experimental rocket for the snapshot (see Figure 6-111) taken above the Ivory Tower of Primitives.

**Figure 6-111**
*Aboard an experimental rocket above the Ivory Tower of Primitives.*

# SUMMARY

In this chapter you learned where to build even if you don't own land and how to create, edit, move, rotate, size, and link new primitives and objects. You learned about basic permissions, flexprims, and local lighting. You may have also followed and learned from the various tutorials in this chapter. To learn more about building, you might want to check out a few additional resources:

- **The SL Build Forum**

  http://forums.secondlife.com/forumdisplay.php?f=8

- **Let There Be Lights**

  http://secondlife.com/knowledgebase/
  article.php?id=069

- **Forums Thread on Lighting**

  http://forums.secondlife.com/showthread.
  php?threadid=155415

- **Flexi-Prim Knowledge Base Article**

  http://secondlife.com/knowledgebase/
  article.php?id=068

- **Next Owner Permissions FAQ**

  http://secondlife.com/knowledgebase/
  article.php?id=336

- **Builder Groups**

  - Builders of Second Life
  - Basic Building

- **In-World Training**

  For the latest in SL training, bring up Search for Places, select Educational, and search for "building." If you're just looking to catch a quick class, select Events and Educational and search for the same.

*Don't be afraid of dirt; it makes things real. For a building to look real it should looked lived in. Try to think of what would make your creation special for others. It has to have the 'WOW' factor.*

**—Julia Hathor**

# Advanced Textures and Clothing

# 7

WITH CHOSEN FEW, JULIA HATHOR, AND ROBIN SOJOURNER

In Second Life, we all learn from those who have gone before us. I am deeply indebted to Chosen Few, Julia Hathor, and Robin Sojourner for sharing all their hard-won knowledge in this chapter.

A texture in SL defines to our eyes whether something is wood, metal, fire, water, cloth, or lace; it also defines something as soft, rough, porous, glowing, pitted, smooth, cyan, magenta, or yellow. Because textures are so important to the beauty of creations in SL, this chapter goes into textures perhaps a bit more than you might expect for an introduction—perhaps a bit more than I had originally planned.

## What You Will Learn

- How to add textures to primitives and objects
- How to apply different textures to different sides or faces of primitives
- How to utilize advanced texture properties such as mapping types, bumpiness, shininess, repeating textures, and texture offsets
- How to create and upload your own textures
- How to use transparency or alpha in your textures
- How textures are used to create avatar skins, eyes, and clothing
- How to create a brick patio, blackberry plant, and custom T-shirt

First, and perhaps most important, while the SL interface contains tools to apply textures to surfaces, it possesses none to actually create or edit them. So, to work seriously with textures, you need to know the basics of some image editing software such as Adobe Photoshop, Corel Paintshop Pro, or the GNU Image Manipulation Program (GIMP). This chapter assumes you know the basics of one of these programs.

If you don't know anything about digital image editing and you want to create textures, then spend some time learning a software package before you tackle this material.

If you just want good textures for your builds but aren't really interested in making them yourself, there are several sources of freebie textures and textures you can purchase in SL. You may also be able to find or hire a texture artist who can create custom textures for you.

# TEXTURES AND SL

In the following sections, we start with the basics and explain SL textures and why they are so important.

## WHAT ARE SL TEXTURES?

The word *texture* shows up in SL in a couple of places and can mean a few different things, depending on the context. First, *texture* is used to refer to the surface properties of a primitive. It may also refer to the *Texture* folder in the Library and your Inventory. This folder contains *textures* or, as Robin Sojourner calls them, *texture images*.

Texture images are basically pictures intended to be applied to the surfaces of objects, similar to how a map is applied to the surface of a globe or a painting is applied to the surface of a canvas. A texture image can be used to impact a surface's color, bumpiness, and/or transparency.

All the texture images you own in SL are stored and listed in your Inventory. Beside their names you'll see either of two possible icons, depending on the image type. Images you've uploaded from your own computer are defined by the Inventory as *textures* and are indicated as such by a rainbow-colored checkerboard icon. Photographs you've taken in-world with the snapshot tool are defined as *snapshots* and are indicated by a blue and yellow sunset icon (see Figure 7-1).

The two designations exist just to differentiate from where images have originated (inside SL or outside) and have no functional impact. Both types of texture images behave exactly the same way for texturing surfaces.

Texture images can be applied en masse to whole objects or separately to individual surfaces (or faces). For avatars, they are applied to create the look of skin, hair, clothing, eyeballs, and tattoos.

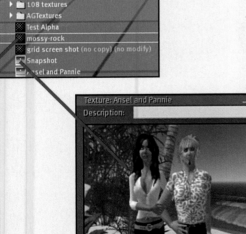

**Figure 7-1**
*Textures and snapshots are given different icons.*

## WHY ARE TEXTURES IMPORTANT?

In SL, textures make the difference between an okay build and a great build, just as in RL a great paint job can mean the difference between an ordinary object and a masterpiece. The ceiling of the Sistine Chapel, after all, was nothing but ordinary plaster until Michelangelo painted it.

Textures can also help you save on prims. For example, if you were to build a set of louvered mini blinds entirely out of prims, you'd have to use so many of them that you could quickly exhaust your prim limit. You might be able to have only one window in your house! However, with texturing, you could make a highly detailed set of mini blinds out of just a single prim, allowing you to have dozens of windows.

Take a look at the image shown in Figure 7-2 captured from SL.

**Figure 7-2**
*Textures make a difference.*

On the left is the default plywood texture applied to three box prims. In fact, they are the exact same primitive in size, just rotated and moved. Not too interesting.

However, on the right side, we have a wooden walkway, with metal grated railing and a wood door. It looks like

something, and it's kinda gritty. They are three identical prims, but WOW, what a difference textures make.

We will cover quite a bit of ground in this chapter, so let's get going!

## TEXTURE EDITING AND THE TEXTURE TAB

As was mentioned earlier, textures cannot be created or edited directly inside SL; that is done with external third-party tools. In this section, we discuss how to apply textures to prims, not how to create or edit the textures themselves. We talk a bit about texture creation later in the chapter.

To apply a texture to a prim, right-click on the prim and choose Edit from the pie menu (see Figure 7-3). The editor window will appear. Click More to expand the editor and then click on the Texture tab.

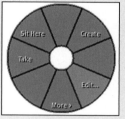

**Figure 7-3**
*Right-click the prim and choose Edit.*

Figure 7-4 shows all the various texturing settings for your selected prim's surface(s). You'll use these settings to apply texture images to surfaces and to control various texturing properties, which we now cover in detail.

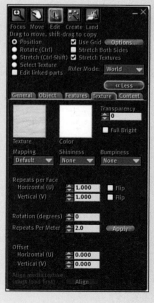

**Figure 7-4**
*All the texture settings are available to you.*

## THE TEXTURE IMAGE

The fundamental component of a prim's texture is the texture image used. A small "swatch," or thumbnail, of the current texture image is shown on the Texture tab. In Figure 7-5, it is the default plywood texture.

**Figure 7-5**
*The default texture is plywood.*

Click on the texture thumbnail to open the Pick Texture dialog, also known as the Texture Picker.

In the Texture Picker, you will see a larger version of the texture image thumbnail on the left and an Explorer-style window on the right; using it, you can browse through your Inventory and the library (see Figure 7-6). As you're browsing, the thumbnail will update to display any image file you select.

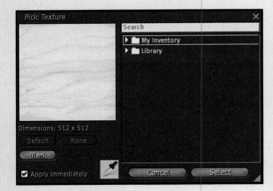

**Figure 7-6**
*The Texture Picker.*

**TIP**

You can type partial names in the Search field to filter the list of textures displayed.

If the Apply Immediately box is checked, then any texture you pick will automatically be applied to the prim you're editing.

**NOTE**

Apply Immediately does exactly what it says. While you can always click Cancel to undo the texture change, if you like how a prim looks and you're just experimenting with other textures, make sure to save a copy of the original prim or have a copy of the texture so you can reapply it if you want to get back to the original.

There are a few buttons below the texture thumbnail on the Texture Picker. The Blank button removes the texture image and replaces it with full white (the prim will get its color from the color swatch). Selecting the Default button will return a prim to its default texture (plywood, white, or none). The None button is not enabled for prims but will work for clothing or skins.

You can use the eyedropper to pick a texture off objects in the world around you. This capability can be helpful if you want to duplicate a texture from a scene you're creating. You cannot use the eyedropper on objects you can't modify because that would essentially be stealing the texture.

## THE COLOR TINT

The next item on the Texture tab is a swatch called Color (see Figure 7-7). When you select this, the color picker comes up (see Figure 7-8), enabling you to pick a color (either the SL color picker or the operating system color picker, depending on your preference setting).

The fact that this setting is called Color can seem a little misleading at first because it doesn't actually allow you to selectively color a prim. Again, SL has no image editing tools built in. What the color setting does is apply an overlying tint to the prim surface, which will combine with the applied texture image to produce the final result. Think of it kind of like looking at a painting through colored glass in the real world. The painting itself doesn't change, but the way you're seeing it does. If you want just a pure color, simply set the texture to blank.

In Figure 7-9 you can see we have an all-white texture image with red (255,0,0), blue (0,0,255), and green

(0,255,0) squares. We apply a full yellow "color." Yellow is full red and full green (255,255,0), so you can see that where the texture image is white, we get the pure yellow color. Where the texture image is red or green, it remains unchanged. However, where the texture image is blue, combined with the yellow tint, you get a final color of black (0,0,0).

**Figure 7-7**
*The Color swatch.*

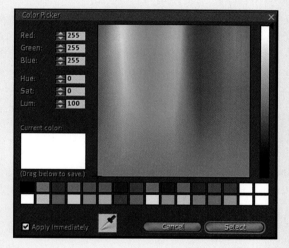

**Figure 7-8**
*The color picker.*

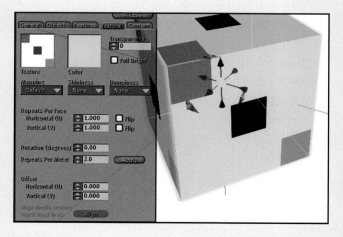

**Figure 7-9**
*How color is used in combination with the texture image.*

## FULL BRIGHT

The appearance of objects in SL, by default, is affected by the ambient light from the sun or moon. The light enables needed realism because objects should and do look different in bright sunlight than they do in the middle of the night. Sometimes, however, this behavior is undesirable or inappropriate for certain objects.

For instance, if you have a neon sign that's supposed to glow at night, you wouldn't want it to appear as dim as everything else in the faint of the moonlight. For this reason, SL provides you the option to disable ambient light rendering for any prim surface.

The setting that controls this behavior is called Full Bright (see Figure 7-10). When Full Bright is turned on for a surface, ambient light has no effect, and the surface is always displayed at its maximum brightness. When it's turned off (the default), normal lighting conditions apply.

**Figure 7-10**
*Full Bright texture setting.*

I have a Full Bright studio that I used for taking the screenshots for this book. By turning on Full Bright on the white walls, floor, and ceiling, I was able to eliminate in-world shading, giving me a pure white background in the photos, which would not have been possible under normal lighting conditions.

## THE TRANSPARENCY CONTROL

Transparency is very cool. It allows you to achieve things with textures that would not otherwise be possible. Simple transparency can also be set as a property of a surface, much in the same way as Full Bright and Color. This is done using the Transparency setting (see Figure 7-11) on the Texture tab, which has a range from 0 (default, full opacity) to 90 (very near full transparency).

**Figure 7-11**
*Transparency texture setting.*

In Figure 7-12 you can see a set of windows with no transparency on the far left, 40% transparent next, 90% transparent in the third window, and the final window has no glass pane at all.

**Figure 7-12**
*Various levels of transparency.*

## SHININESS

Shininess in SL is an effect that simulates luster on prim surfaces. SL cannot display true reflections or specularity, so the effect is limited to sort of a filtering of reflected light from the sun or moon.

Shininess can look quite nice, although it does come with a side effect. Shinier objects tend to have darker tint than less shiny ones.

The Shininess setting on the Texture tab (see Figure 7-13) has four settings: None (default), Low, Medium, and High. In Figure 7-14 there are two rows of four spheres each, set against a black background, demonstrating the four settings in order from left to right.

**Figure 7-13**
*Shininess setting.*

**Figure 7-14**
*Two examples of the four shininess settings on at noon (top), the other at sunset (bottom).*

To show how the shininess reflects ambient light, the top row was photographed at noon and the bottom row at sunset.

One drawback to using shininess in SL is that not everyone can see it. It's a somewhat resource-intensive process that can cause a performance hit on some computers, so there's a toggle in your preferences to turn shininess visibility on or off (Edit-> Preferences, Graphic Detail tab, Enable Bumpmapping and Shiny check box). Those with older or underpowered graphics cards may keep it turned off to improve performance.

## BUMPINESS

The Bumpiness setting (see Figure 7-15) adds the appearance of bumps or tactile patterns to surfaces. Its implementation in SL is rather limited at the time of this writing, but the available patterns can add a nice finishing touch to certain models.

**Figure 7-15**
*Bumpiness settings.*

Bumpiness is available in the following settings:

- **Brightness:** Raises the light areas of the applied texture image
- **Darkness:** Raises the dark areas of the applied texture image
- **Woodgrain:** Raises bumps on the surface in a pattern resembling wood
- **Bark:** Raises bumps on the surface in a pattern resembling tree bark
- **Bricks:** Raises rectangular bumps on the surface in a brick-wall-type pattern
- **Checker:** Creates the appearance of a rough surface resembling concrete or sandstone
- **Crusty:** Raises rectangular bumps in a beveled tile pattern
- **Cutstone:** Raises irregular rectangular bumps in sort of an Incan stonework pattern
- **Discs:** Creates the appearance of circular depressions
- **Gravel:** Raises small gravel-like bumps

- **Petridish:** Raises bumps in an organic pattern reminiscent of amoebae or bacterial formations
- **Siding:** Creates the appearance of textured vinyl siding, like one might find on a manufactured home
- **Stonetile:** Raises bumps in a pattern reminiscent of a stone walkway, with octagonal tiles
- **Stucco:** Creates the appearance of a rough stucco surface
- **Suction:** Creates circular depressions, reminiscent of suction cups
- **Weave:** Gives the surface a basket-woven appearance

Figure 7-16 shows a sample of four identical cubes with an identical texture image of a stone path (I shot this one in Italy). The first has no bumpiness and appears nice, but a bit flat. The second is set to Lightness. It raises the light values, so in this case it looks like the mortar is protruding out of the pavers. The third is set to Darkness. It raises the darker portions of the image, so in this case, it makes the mortar sink. The fourth shows the Petridish texture, and you can see the bumpiness is not related at all to the pavers underneath.

**Figure 7-16**
*Stone path material with various bumpiness settings.*

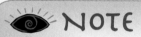 NOTE

Just like shininess, bumpiness can be disabled by any user, so do not rely on it for your textures. Another point to note is that the bump scale is impacted by texture settings like repeats and offset.

# DEFAULT (UV) AND PLANAR MAPPING

Texture mapping in SL can be simply defined as the way in which texture images are painted onto, or projected onto, prim surfaces. As we've discussed, texture images are two-dimensional rectangular pictures, like paintings. The objects they are applied to in SL are three-dimensional shapes, which the texture images wrap around.

Think of texture mapping kind of like how gift paper wraps around a birthday present. The paper itself is a flat rectangle, but the present is not. Therefore, the paper has to be bent and folded and twisted to wrap around it properly. In 3D modeling terms, the specific manner in which that wrapping happens is called *mapping*.

In SL, mapping comes in two flavors: default (see Figure 7-17) and planar. The default mapping acts as if the texture is painted onto the surface; i.e., if you change the shape of the surface, you likewise change the shape of the texture. Planar mapping acts more like a slide projector on a screen. Changing the shape of the screen has no effect on the shape of the image. We'll cover both mapping types in some detail in this section.

 **Figure 7-17**
*The Default mapping setting*

For much of this section, I will use a texture test pattern (shown in Figure 7-18) created by Robin Sojourner. This image helps make it easier to see what the mapping is doing to the 2D texture. If you're having a texturing problem, it is often helpful to apply this test pattern to the object to see what's going on.

The test pattern texture image is available at the Texture Lab in SL (SLURL provided later in this chapter) or on Robin's website at http://www.robinwood.com/Catalog/Technical/SL-Tuts/Test-Pattern.jpg.

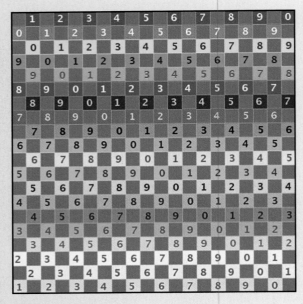

**Figure 7-18**
*Texture test pattern.*

## Default (or UV) Mapping

Each basic primitive shape in SL has a UV or default map. The example in Figure 7-19 shows how the four corners of the test pattern are tacked to the four corners of the cube. Even though the cube is tapered at the top, the texture's image is squeezed onto it.

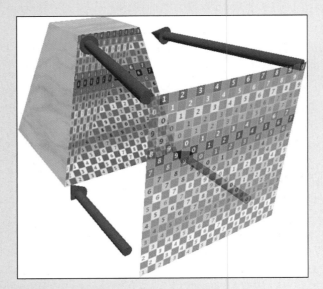

**Figure 7-19**
*The test pattern mapped to the shape.*

Figure 7-20 shows all the SL primitive shapes with the test pattern applied using the default mapping. The box looks normal, but you will note a few things, such as the squares in the top row on the sphere are all squished into red lines and that much of the pattern cannot even be seen on the top of a cylinder. This may or may not be important to a texture you're trying to apply.

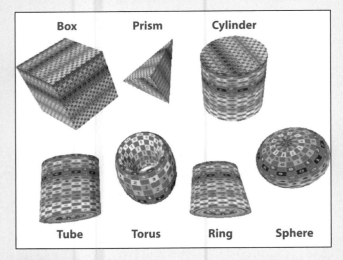

**Figure 7-20**
*All the SL primitive shapes with the test pattern applied using default mapping.*

## Planar Mapping by Chosen Few

Planar texture mapping rocks! It took a long time to get this particular mapping facility added to SL, so thanks, Linden Lab, for implementing it. Gone are the days of the evil squishies. No more having to precorrect for counter-distortion in Photoshop. Hooray!

The planar system can be a little confusing at first, but there are just a few things you need to know about it to use it effectively.

The first major concept to understand when exploring planar mapping is the way in which it differs from the default mapping described in the previous section. To quickly review, with default mapping, you can think of the image as being physically stuck onto the surface it's texturing, in the same way that a painting is stuck onto its canvas. Since textures are always square, the "painting" will display normally as long as the canvas is square. Change the shape of the canvas, though, and the painting will become distorted (and because computer graphics construct everything from triangles, not rectangles, the distortion can look really weird to the untrained eye).

Planar mapping, on the other hand, does not "paint" the image onto the surface at all. Instead, it "projects" the image like a film slide. The surface ends up acting like a movie screen, displaying the image, but not physically attaching to it (see Figure 7-21). This way, you can stretch and distort the surface all you want, and the shape of the image won't be affected.

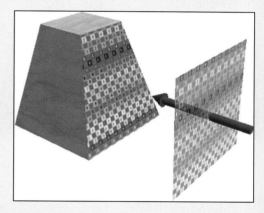

**Figure 7-21**
*Planar mapping works like film projected on a screen.*

With planar mapping, the size and shape of the "screen" (the object surface) are irrelevant (as long as we're talking flat surfaces) to the size and shape of the texture.

Whether we're projecting onto a triangle, square, rectangle, trapezoid, or whatever, the shape of the projection will not change. It will always be the same square of our texture. In places where the edge of the surface "cuts off" the square, that part of the projection will simply disappear over the edge. The surface won't try to cram the whole projection onto itself like it does in the default mapping. Therefore, there will be none of the warping we're used to seeing on irregularly shaped surfaces. The texture will always remain square.

Just as the shape of the surface does not affect the projection, neither does its size. To go back to the slide projector analogy, whether you're projecting onto a small slide screen or a full-size movie screen doesn't matter. The projection will always be the same size unless you adjust the projector.

This is why repeats per face can't work with planar mapping (notice that option is not available when planar mapping is turned on). The projector doesn't know or care how big or small the screen is. It only cares how big it's supposed to make the projection. If the screen is big enough, it'll pick up the whole thing. If it's too small, it'll display only part of it. Either way, the projection itself stays the same.

This inability to automate repeats per face can make aligning textures on multiple surfaces into a bit of a brain teaser at first. It's not as simple as just saying "repeat X times on each face" and then having it all line up. You have to account for the actual size of each face to determine the correct repeats per meter to make things line up on each one.

You can do this mathematically or by eyeballing it through trial and error. The latter approach can be a bit maddening if you don't understand the math. You don't necessarily have to do precise calculations, but you do have to understand the concept of what is going on in order to make it work.

The next thing to note is that projections in SL are always sourced inline with the surface normal. In other words, the "projector" is always oriented perpendicularly to the "screen," so it projects straight on. As a result, you can't skew a projection in SL like you can in other 3D packages.

For most people, this won't be a problem. Usually, you wouldn't have reason to skew a projection anyway. In most cases, the whole point of projecting in the first place is to avoid distortion, not to create it.

Projections always originate from the center of the surface. When you use offsets, you're offsetting from the center. This is pretty much the same as how it works with default mapping, but it can look confusing at first due to the Repeats per Face/Repeats per Meter changeover. Rotations and flips work the same in both modes.

There are, of course, advantages and disadvantages to both mapping schemes. Planar mapping is best suited to objects with flat surfaces. It is not a good match for surfaces that curve in 3D space, like the insides and outsides of spheres and tori or the sides of cylinders, rings, and tubes. Try projecting a slide onto a coffee can or a soccer ball some time. It doesn't work too well. Projecting onto curved surfaces is complicated and produces weird results in SL, as can be seen in Figure 7-22. Since we don't have much control over the "projector," it's not recommended to try to use planar mapping on curved surfaces.

For best results, use default mapping on curved surfaces and planar mapping on flat surfaces.

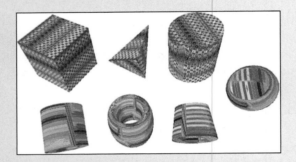

**Figure 7-22**
*Planar mapping on flat and curved surfaces.*

## DEFAULT MAPPING AND TEXTURE DISTORTION

Thanks to Chosen for that great description of planar mapping. I should mention one more thing: Default mapping works great as long as the prims have not been substantially altered using controls like taper.

Figure 7-23 presents a comparison of default and planar mappings of a tapered cube. You can see planar mapping holds up well, while the default mapping is distorted.

It is possible for an advanced texture artist to correct the texture for the planned distortion. Figure 7-24 shows an example of a texture that looks very wrong. If you apply it to an unmodified cube, it still looks wrong. But if you taper the prim, you'll see the texture lines up perfectly as a grid. How to do this is beyond the scope of this book, but you can find details and help at Robin Sojourner's Texture Lab in-world.

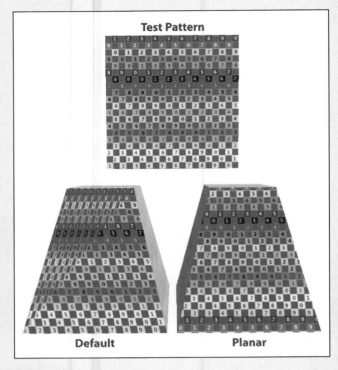

**Test Pattern**

**Default**       **Planar**

**Figure 7-23**
*Default and planar mapping applied to a tapered cube.*

**2d Grid**

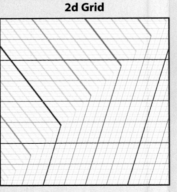

**3d Cubes**

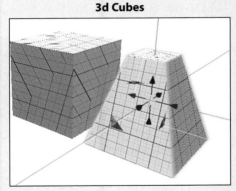

**Figure 7-24**
*Texture image corrected for planned distortion.*

## TEXTURING INDIVIDUAL FACES (OR SURFACES)

So far, we have been applying one texture to an entire prim. Prims have several faces, and you can apply different textures to different faces of the same prim. For example, a cube has six faces: top, bottom, left, right, front, and back. Well, not so fast—if you cut into a cube, there are two additional faces on each part of the cut (see Figure 7-25, faces 7 and 8). And if you cut a hole into it (called *hollowing* in SL), the inside surface of the hole is one more face (face 5 in Figure 7-25). Due to a peculiarity of SL, insides of holes are treated as one surface, even if the hole is square or triangular.

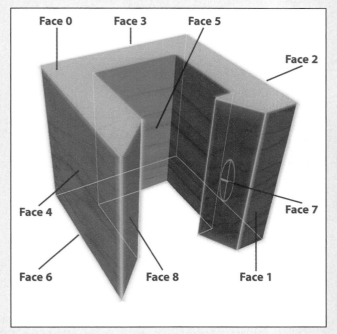

**Figure 7-25**
*A cube has nine faces when cut and hollowed out.*

To select one face to apply a texture, you need to change your build tool over to Select Texture. Figure 7-26 shows the edit controls and highlights the radio button labeled Select Texture. Once you've selected this button, you can click on any face in the prim. You can tell which face is selected by a light white crosshair target that you can see on Face 7 in Figure 7-25 or more clearly on the cube in Figure 7-27.

**Figure 7-26**
*The Select Texture build control lets you texture individual faces of a prim.*

> ## TIP
>
> Each face has a number that can be accessed in an LSL script. You'll learn about scripting in the next chapter. What number a face has depends on whether the prim has been cut and/or hollowed. See the following link for more information: http://www.lslwiki.net/lslwiki/wakka.php?wakka=side.
>
> If you want to know what number a face has, select the texture and then press Ctrl+Alt+Shift+T, and SL will whisper the answer to you.

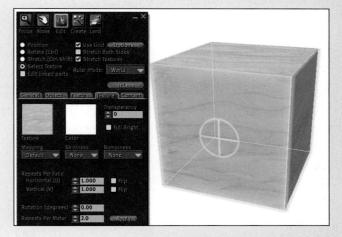

**Figure 7-27**
*A single face selected on a default cube with a plywood texture.*

> ## NOTE
>
> To apply a texture to one face quickly, you can simply drag and drop a texture from your Inventory or library onto the face of a prim.

You can now apply specific textures, tints, and so on to that face of the prim. The crosshair and texture outline are very helpful when you start using Repeats per Face/Meter, offset, and rotations (coming up next). Typically, you texture each face to create the right texture proportions on each side, but you can use texturing for other creative purposes as well. For example, you can build a window in SL that is transparent on one side and solid on the other side. You can see out, but no one else can see in!

## REPEATS PER FACE/METER

The rest of the Texture tab controls the repeats/tiling, placement, and scale of a texture image on any given face of a prim. The Repeats per Face (see Figure 7-28) and Repeats per Meter settings are used to control how many times the texture image is repeated across the face of a prim. If you check Flip, you will essentially flip the texture 180 degrees either vertically, horizontally, or both.

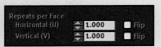

**Figure 7-28**
*Repeats per Face and flip texture controls.*

With default mapping, you can use Repeats per Face or Repeats per Meter. With Repeats per Face, you are controlling how many times the texture image is laid out like a pattern across the surface of a prim. The Repeats per Meter setting works a little differently. With default mapping, you can set Repeats per Meter, and when you click Apply, SL will calculate the right Repeats per Face based on the size of your primitive.

Planar mapping supports only Repeats per Meter, not Repeats per Face, because as was mentioned earlier, planar mapping works like a slide projector on a screen. The size of the screen (the prim face) cannot affect the size of the projection. The Repeats per Meter setting controls the size of the projection. The projector has no way of knowing how big the screen (prim face) is, so the Repeats per Face setting is not relevant to planar mapping.

To demonstrate how these features work, I've created the texture test pattern shown in Figure 7-29, which originated as a 256×256 TGA file. Here, the pattern is applied to a 1m cube, default mapping, with one horizontal and one vertical repeat per face. This is what you would expect.

Now, in the series shown in Figure 7-30, we have Repeats per Face set as follows: 0.25×0.25, 1×1, 2×1, 1×2, and 4×4.

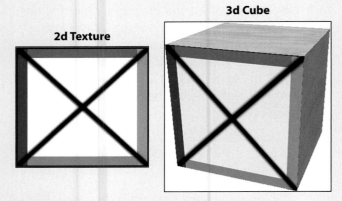

**Figure 7-29**
*The test pattern and a simple application of it.*

**Figure 7-30**
*The test pattern applied at various Repeats per Face.*

The figure shows a couple of interesting things. First, you can have less than one full repeat per face; in the 0.25×0.25 case, you can see that we selected only the middle quarter of the image. In the 2×1, 1×2, and 4×4 cases, you can see that the initial texture is centered so that part of the texture repeats across to the other face.

## OFFSET

The center of the texture image is aligned with a particular point on a prim. For example, a cube aligns with the center. Offset (see Figure 7-31) basically allows you to move the texture's center. As you learned while texturing a single face, you can visibly see where this center is as you adjust the offset if you're in Select Texture mode.

**Figure 7-31**
*The Offset control.*

In the samples shown in Figure 7-32 I have adjusted the offsets from the default (0,0) for the same five cubes used in Figure 7-30, so we are applying both Repeats per Face/Meter as well as offsets. The following offset values were used: 0.35, 0.35, 0.5, 0, 0.5, 0, 0, 0.5, 0.5, 0.5.

**Figure 7-32**
*The five cubes after Repeats per Face/Meter and offset adjustments.*

The first one is interesting because it now shows the upper-right corner of the texture. This extremely useful feature allows you to improve performance and save on L$ for uploads by creating one texture image that contains several textures. For example, a 512×512 pixel texture image may contain eight smaller 64×64 pixel texture images. Then using repeats and offset, you can select parts of a texture image.

The second sample is, in fact, the four corners of our texture moved to the center of the cube. The others just show how you can use offset to align the texture to the prim.

## ROTATION

Our final texture control is Rotation (see Figure 7-33). As the name implies, this control rotates the texture image around the texture center. The first cube in Figure 7-34 is adjusted 45 degrees with repeats and offset adjustments. The second cube is also adjusted 45 degrees with default Repeats per Meter and offset. The third cube has no rotation at all.

Now that you know all the controls, it's time for a practical tutorial on applying a simple texture to a custom prim.

**Figure 7-33**
*The Rotation control.*

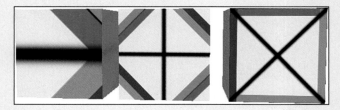

**Figure 7-34**
*Texture rotation used on three identical cubes.*

# TUTORIAL: CREATING A BRICK STEP

In SL, you don't need to stack individual prims one per brick to make a brick wall. Instead, you can use a brick texture applied to one prim and get roughly the same effect. In this tutorial, you will create a one-prim brick porch, wall, walkway, fireplace mantel, or whatever. You will modify the texture settings on each face of the prim for a better look. Using textures like this is the way you go from a basic texture job to one that holds up under inspection.

## STEP 1: REZ A CUBE

Rez a cube and resize it to the shape you're planning to create (see Figure 7-35).

If you want to be more RL accurate, measure the size of an RL brick. Then multiply the measurement by the number of bricks you want to use.

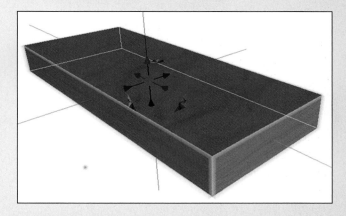

**Figure 7-35**
*The resized cube.*

## STEP 2: FIND A BRICK TEXTURE

You can find a nice default brick texture in the library (see Figure 7-36), you can make one yourself in Photoshop, or perhaps you already have some freebie textures you want to use.

Take a look at the texture once it has been applied. Your actual results may be different from those shown in Figure 7-37, depending on the size of the object you're creating.

**Figure 7-36**
*Brick texture in your library under Buildings folder.*

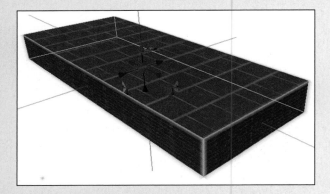

**Figure 7-37**
*The texture needs some correcting.*

If you've created a large and thin rectangular object, you'll notice the bricks on top look pretty unbricklike. But even more unbricklike are the sides where the bricks are quite small and thin. Let's start to correct this look.

## STEP 3: ADJUST THE REPEATS PER FACE

In Figure 7-38 I have changed the values of the Horizontal and Vertical Repeats per Face to 2 and 1, respectively. This adjustment may differ for you based on the size of your prim. If your bricks are too large with the default repeat of 1, by setting it to 2 you will get twice as many bricks.

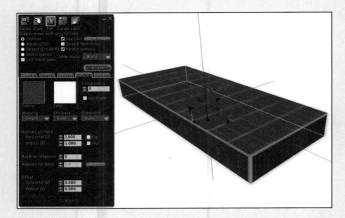

**Figure 7-38**
*The adjusted texture Repeats per Face.*

## STEP 4: SELECT A FACE

To work on a specific face of the primitive, you select the radio button labeled Select Texture in the upper-left corner of the Edit menu. When you first activate this control, all faces show the circle/crosshairs. Once you click on the face you want to work with, the crosshairs will appear only on that face (see Figure 7-39).

We set every face in the previous step to two repeats horizontal and one repeat vertical. You can see there is half a texture on the left, then a whole, then another half, for a total of two repeats. There are no white lines going vertically because we have one full repeat of the texture.

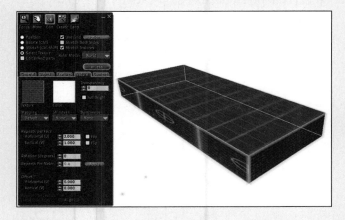

**Figure 7-39**
*Select the face you want to work on.*

## STEP 5: ADJUST THE TEXTURE REPEATS PER FACE

In this case, we have too many small bricks, so we need to use less than one repeat. For example, a repeat of 0.5 will have half the number of bricks. I adjusted the vertical repeats to 0.3 (see Figure 7-40). This essentially means I am using just one-third of the texture on this face. See how the bricks widen when you do this. I also adjusted the horizontal to 1.7, basically to get some full bricks to line up with the edges as they would in real-life masonry.

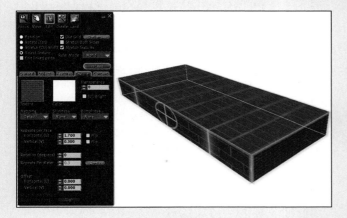

**Figure 7-40**
*The bricks widen using less than one repeat.*

## STEP 6: ADJUST THE REMAINING FACES

Select the end and adjust it as well. In Figure 7-41, I ended up with the same settings that aligned the bricks on the other face. Repeat this procedure for all faces, and now you have a brick prim ready for use at home or on a street corner.

> ### ✋ TIP
>
> Once you establish the desired scale of bricks on one face, you can calculate the relationship between horizontal and vertical repeats with the size of the prim face. Using this information, you can mathematically calculate the exact repeats needed for each face to obtain exactly the same size bricks on all sides. If you use regular-sized prims (like 1m × 2m), this is fairly easy; otherwise, break out your calculator.

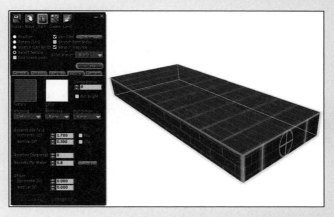

**Figure 7-41**
*Adjust the other faces.*

## STEP 7: MAKE IT LOOK REAL

If you want your bricks to look real and not like they're painted onto a cube, you need to make sure the bricks align on each face. Using an illustration makes it easier to see (see Figure 7-42). The bricks on the left are not aligned to the cube or each other. For example, some rows are very thin. The bricks on the right are aligned and look much more like real bricks. You adjust the alignment of the bricks using the Offset control. You can eyeball this or use a little math to get it exactly right.

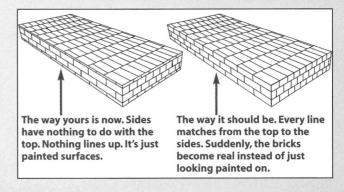

The way yours is now. Sides have nothing to do with the top. Nothing lines up. It's just painted surfaces.

The way it should be. Every line matches from the top to the sides. Suddenly, the bricks become real instead of just looking painted on.

**Figure 7-42**
*Use Offset to align the bricks for more realism.*

# TUTORIAL: CREATING AND UPLOADING A SIMPLE TEXTURE

Now that you've learned how to apply an existing texture image to a prim, it's time to go through a basic tutorial on how to create and upload your own texture image. The creation and upload process is almost identical for small textures, large textures, and even advanced textures, so you can apply everything you learn here to more complex textures as well.

A really common thing you may want to create in SL is a sign. You can use a sign to welcome people, explain something, provide directions, and, of course, advertise your store. A sign is a good texture to start with because we don't need to address issues such as texture tiling or transparency (which we discuss later). For this tutorial, let's say you have a store called Positively Primitives, and you need a new sign out front.

## STEP 1: PICK YOUR IMAGE EDITING SOFTWARE

To create a texture, you need some external image editing software. The software most widely used by texture artists today is Adobe Photoshop. If you know how to use Photoshop or some other similar image editing software, I recommend using the one you know for this tutorial. If you don't have any image editing software, you don't want to buy one, but you still want advanced features, I recommend learning the freely available GNU Image Manipulation Program (GIMP) at http://www.gimp.org/.

This tutorial shows you how to create a texture image using one of the most basic and ubiquitous editing tools, Microsoft Paint. This is done with tongue in cheek, as Microsoft Paint is not going to take you very far if you get serious about textures. If you're on a Mac, please forgive me! In parallel, I will note basic instructions if you're using Photoshop or some other image editing software.

## STEP 2: CREATE A NEW IMAGE IN YOUR IMAGE EDITING SOFTWARE OF CHOICE

Launch your image editor. For Microsoft Paint, select Start->All Programs->Accessories->Paint. In most image editors you use File->New to create a new image, and Paint is no different.

## STEP 3: SIZE YOUR IMAGE

The first thing you must be aware of when creating new images for use in SL is that size and dimensions matter. SL favors images that are square and less than 1024 pixels in either width or height. Further, it wants dimensions that are powers of 2 in number of pixels.

Image sizes that avoid any upload distortion issues are (in pixels) 16×16, 32×32, 64×64, 128×128, 256×256, 512×512, and 1024×1024. Images larger than 1024×1024 do not really improve quality, and they slow things down for everyone, so stick to 256×256 where possible.

If you want to create rectangular images, combine width/height values such as 64×128, 256×512, or 256×128. You'll have to just trust me for now (the definitive list of SL image sizes is covered later in this chapter).

When you create a new image in Microsoft Paint, it does not ask you what size you want! Rather, it creates a new image from the last size you used (which could be anything). There is no property or other menu option to size your image. You must manually resize it by selecting the small black dot located in the lower-right corner of the image and dragging it around. While you're dragging it, you'll see the dimensions in pixels shown in the bottom status bar on the far right, as you can see in Figure 7-43. Drag the image until you have 256×128 pixels.

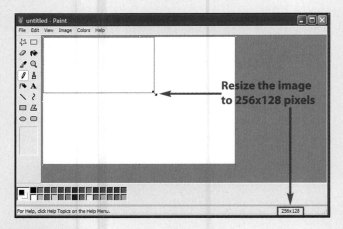

**Figure 7-43**
*Creating a new image 256×128 pixels in dimension in Microsoft Paint.*

Most image editors ask you to set the width and height of the image when you create a new image. If you're using Photoshop, you'll see a dialog like the one in Figure 7-44. Remember to use pixels for your measurements.

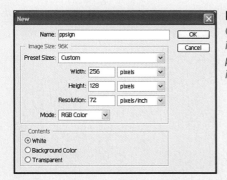

**Figure 7-44**
*Creating a new image 256×128 pixels in dimension in Photoshop.*

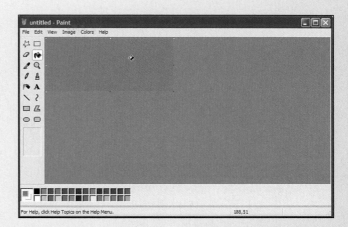

**Figure 7-46**
*A goldish color background in Microsoft Paint.*

## STEP 4: CREATE A NICE BACKGROUND

Now that we have a new image, let's create a nice background for our sign. To do this, select a color in the toolbar along the bottom (see Figure 7-45). If you don't see this toolbar, it may be turned off. Make sure View->Color Box is selected. The current foreground and background colors are displayed in the lower left of the color toolbar in two overlapping squares.

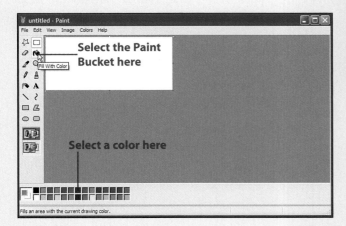

**Figure 7-45**
*Selecting a fill color for the background.*

After you've selected the color, fill your image with this color by selecting the Paint Bucket, as seen in Figure 7-45. Drag the Paint Bucket over to your image and click once. It should fill with the color you picked (see Figure 7-46).

For Photoshop, I decided to try for a brushed metal sign. First, I started with a star gradient background and then applied some Filter->Noise and Filter->Blur->Motion Blur. Finally, I added a bit of yellow using Image->Adjustments ->Color Balance to arrive at the color shown in Figure 7-47.

**Figure 7-47**
*A nice brushed metal background in Photoshop.*

## STEP 5: ADD SOME TEXT AND EFFECTS

Now that we have a background, let's add the words to our sign. First, we need to set the background color to the same as the background you just created. Do this by right-clicking on the color you used for your background in the color toolbar at the bottom of the image. Next, pick the color for your letters by left-clicking on the color you want. I selected a light blue. If you want to pick your own color, try choosing Color->Edit Colors and selecting the Define Custom Colors button to pick exactly the color you want.

Next, select the Text tool (the letter A on the left panel) and position your cursor in the top left of your image. Type **Positively Primitives**. You should now see something like Figure 7-48. Either your text is too big, or you simply can't see everything you typed.

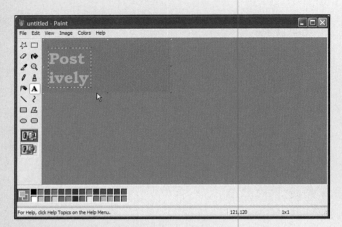

**Figure 7-48**
*Colored text on background in Microsoft Paint.*

Grab the lower-right handle of the selected text and resize the text box to fit properly. You can right-click on the text and select Text Toolbar to pick a different font or make the font larger or smaller to fit. To move the text around, you need to use the resize controls. If you want to center the text, you need to add spaces. Yes, Microsoft Paint is primitive.

For a final effect, select black as your main color (left-click on the black color square at the bottom of the display). Add a thick line along the bottom and right side of your sign by selecting the line tool (the straight line below the can of spray paint) and pick a wide width. The lines along the bottom and right make the sign appear to have some depth. I ended up with the sign shown in Figure 7-49.

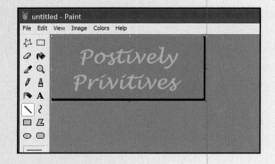

**Figure 7-49**
*My Positively Primitives sign made using Microsoft Paint.*

For Photoshop, you also use the Text tool. For both the background and text layers, I applied some blending options to achieve the effect in Figure 7-50. To add an

effect, select the layer, right-click, and select Blending Options. To get this sign, I used bevel and drop shadow.

**Figure 7-50**
*My Positively Primitives sign made using Photoshop.*

## STEP 6: SAVE YOUR IMAGE

Now that you've created your sign, the next thing you need to consider when working with textures and SL is image file formats. You can upload bitmap (.bmp), JPEG (.jpg or .jpeg), or TARGA (.tga) files into SL. The best option is TARGA (.tga), so if possible, store images in this format. Of course, Microsoft Paint doesn't support TARGA, so save your image in bitmap (.bmp) format. Do this by choosing File->Save As. Name your file something you will remember like **positive-sign.bmp**.

For Photoshop, when you save in TARGA format, you will be offered the option of 24-bit or 32-bit. If your image has no transparency, the best choice is to save it in 24-bit format. Our sign has no transparency, so save in 24-bit TARGA.

## STEP 7: LOG IN TO SL AND UPLOAD YOUR IMAGE

After you've saved your image, log in to SL and select File->Upload Image (or press Ctrl+U). You will see a file chooser dialog. Navigate to your image file and select it. Next, you will see the upload preview dialog (see Figure 7-51). Make sure you have Preview As Image selected and that you're looking at the right image. Once the image is uploaded, you cannot make any further modifications to it without uploading again.

You may notice that the image preview seems distorted. In fact, the image preview shows the texture as a square.

Because we picked an image size SL likes, we don't need to worry about this too much. Rename your texture so that you can find it in your Inventory and select Upload (of course, you need to pay L$10 to do this).

**Figure 7-51**
*Texture upload preview dialog before uploading.*

After uploading the image, SL will display it. Here are a couple of things to note: First, you will see the image in its proper size. Second, you will see the image dimensions directly below the image. In this case, they are 256×128, the same dimensions as the image we created in MS Paint or Photoshop. You will also see a blue dialog indicating you have paid for this upload (see Figure 7-52).

**Figure 7-52**
*Texture dialog after uploading.*

## STEP 8: APPLY YOUR TEXTURES TO A PRIMITIVE

The final step is to apply your texture to a primitive. If you want to avoid any distortion, the size of the primitive must be proportional to the size of your texture. The texture is 256×128, so the ratio is 2 to 1. So if we create a primitive that is twice as long as it is high, then we will not need to make any offset or scaling adjustments to it to avoid distortion.

For Figure 7-53, I created two signs, each 2 meters by 1 meter, and applied my MS Paint and Photoshop textures. I then positioned these signs above the door of my fictitious store. I'm open and ready for business.

**Figure 7-53**
*Sign primitives with textures applied and in place.*

Now that you've learned how to apply textures and create a basic texture, it's time to learn about more advanced texture techniques—specifically, textures that have transparent components. For answers to your questions about transparency, we will turn to Chosen Few.

# FREQUENTLY ASKED QUESTIONS ABOUT TRANSPARENCY ANSWERED BY CHOSEN FEW

The most frequently asked question in the SL texturing forum is "How do I create transparency with alpha channels?" So, if you're wondering, you're certainly not alone. I've answered the question for people hundreds, if not thousands, of times over the past several years (see Figure 7-54).

I've tried to make the following sections as layman-friendly as possible while still providing a lot of useful information. They should be the definitive resource for anyone with a question on how channels work, what they do, and more specifically, how to create and use alpha channels for transparency.

The following sections contain frequently asked questions about channels in general, nonspecific to any particular software but common to them all. The FAQ section discusses governing principles of color screen imagery, and thus is applicable as general knowledge that will be beneficial to anyone using any graphics software for any purpose.

**Figure 7-54**
*Chosen Few.*

## HOW DO I GIVE MY IMAGE A TRANSPARENT BACKGROUND?

Transparency in SL textures is defined by an image element called an *alpha channel*. For transparency to exist in an image, it must contain this element. The following sections are loaded with information on what alpha channels are, how they work, and how to create them. Read on.

## WHAT ARE ALPHA CHANNELS?

Simply put, an alpha channel is a data map embedded into an image that contains information about a certain aspect of the image other than color. For SL purposes, an alpha channel can be defined even more simply as a transparency map. Strictly speaking, alpha channels can contain information about all kinds of image aspects besides just transparency, but transparency is the only one SL can use.

## WHY DO THE TRANSPARENT AREAS OF MY IMAGE APPEAR WHITE IN SL INSTEAD OF TRANSPARENT?

If this is happening, your image contains no alpha channel. Without the alpha channel present, SL has no way of determining which pixels are supposed to be transparent, since the alpha channel is what contains all the transparency data. Without it, the only data present in the image is color data. Since the "transparent" pixels have no color, SL interprets them as white. To solve the problem, make sure your image contains an alpha channel and that you've saved your image as 32-bit TGA.

## COLOR SPACE AND CHANNELS: WHAT ARE THEY?

Images designed to be shown on a color screen exist in what is known as *RGB color space*. That means they are composed of the three primary colors: red, green, and blue. The relative brightness of each of these primary colors in each pixel determines each pixel's actual color. For example, a pixel composed of equal values of red and blue without any green would appear to be purple. A pixel composed of maximum values of all 3 colors would appear to be white.

Under the RGB color space model, there are 256 available shades for each of the 3 primary colors. These shades are calculated as numerical values ranging from 0 to 255. Since there are 3 colors in use, and 256 possible values for each, the total number of colors available in RGB color space comes to about 16.7 million ($256 \times 256 \times 256 = 16,777,216$).

The image shown in Figure 7-55 is a snapshot of the SL Color Picker window. You can see Current Color is a nice shade of blue. This particular shade demonstrates a mix of all three color channels: a large amount of blue with just a little bit of red and green mixed in to soften the tone a bit.

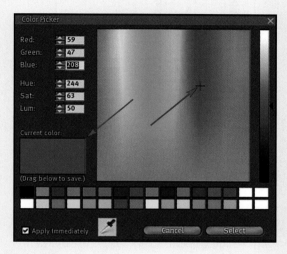

**Figure 7-55**
*The Color Picker window.*

As you can see in the top-left section of the color picker, the red channel is set to 59, the green channel to 47, and the blue channel to 208. Notice the amount of blue in this shade is almost double the amount of red and green combined, which is why the overall tone of the shade is blue. Were we to increase the amount of red and green to make the three color values equal, we'd be looking at a shade of gray. Were we to remove the blue value (set it to 0), we'd be seeing just red and green, which would multiply to a shade of yellow.

Now, before you go thinking you need a math degree to figure all this out, don't worry; all this number information is really just for informational purposes, for your own understanding. It's not something you need to deal with at all as you're actually working. Art should be art, after all, not math. To choose a color, you just need to identify one you like from that big rainbow-colored field in the middle of the picker and click on it. The picker will, of course, show you the RGB values, and you can edit the numbers if you want, but it's much more intuitive just to pick the color visually.

OK, so that's color space in a nutshell. So what are these "channels" we keep talking about?

Basically, they are visual representations of the math, or to put it another way, they are data maps that illustrate physically where all the various amounts of red, green, and blue are in the image. I'll explain how they work.

When taken separately, the individual mathematical values for red, green, or blue in each pixel are represented by specific shades of gray, ranging from black, which represents 0, to white, which represents 255. Under this system, all the representative pixels together form a grayscale image called a *channel*. Each channel, again, is basically a data map which governs, pixel by pixel, the amount of its representative color that is present in the image.

Every RGB image has a channel that governs red, a channel that governs green, and a channel that governs blue. In each individual channel, white represents the maximum possible concentration of color, and black represents the absence of color. Shades of gray represent amounts of color that are less than the maximum. The darker the gray, the lesser the concentration of color. The lighter the gray, the more color is present.

## CHANNELS AND TRANSPARENCY: WHAT DO ALPHA CHANNELS DO?

Images that support SL transparency start with the three primary color channels (red, green, blue), but also have a fourth channel, called *alpha*, that represents opacity. They therefore exist in what is called *RGBA color space*, an obvious extension of RGB. For RGBA images, white in the alpha channel represents complete opacity (no transparency), and black represents the absence of opacity (fully transparent). Shades of gray represent semitransparency: The darker the gray, the more transparent; and the lighter the gray, the more opaque.

So, for example, if you're making a bikini top for your avatar, the alpha channel would be white in the shape of the bikini top and black everywhere else. The white part makes the bikini top 100% opaque so that you won't be able to see through it when it's on the AV, and the black part makes the rest of the image invisible so that there appears to be nothing on the AV's arms, stomach, etc.

## HOW DO I MAKE ALPHA CHANNELS?

Look at this forum thread: http://forums.secondlife.com/ showthread.php?t=80851. Make sure to scroll down to the tutorial section with specific instructions for creating alpha channels in Photoshop, Photoshop Elements, and Paint Shop Pro. For a quick tutorial using Photoshop, see the section "Tutorial: Creating an Alpha Channel in Photoshop with Chosen Few."

## HOW DO I MAKE PART OR ALL OF AN IMAGE TRANSLUCENT AS OPPOSED TO FULLY TRANSPARENT?

Areas of an image that are semitransparent should be gray in the alpha channel. As described previously, the darker the gray you use in the alpha channel, the more see-through the corresponding part of the image will be. The lighter the gray you use in the alpha channel, the more opaque the image will be.

For example, a piece of frosted glass would require a very light gray in the alpha channel. Frosted glass is almost opaque, so the alpha should be almost white.

Something like a pair of nylon stockings would be in the medium gray range. Stockings are generally transparent enough that you can see the skin underneath them, but not so transparent that the stocking material itself isn't readily noticeable. They're about halfway between transparent and opaque, so their gray value on the alpha channel would be about halfway between black and white, medium gray.

Water would fall into the dark gray range. Water is very see-through, but not completely invisible. It's mostly transparent, so its gray value on the alpha channel would be almost black.

Just as a reminder, note that none of the grays in any of these examples affect the color of the image in any way. Alpha channels govern only transparency, not color.

Figure 7-56 shows a sample shoji screen type image I whipped up really quickly and an example of what its alpha should look like (note the alpha would have no black border; this was added just so you could see the image on white paper). The image itself is a little rough

since I made it in all of about 60 seconds, but it should be enough, I hope, to help you complete your understanding of how alphas work.

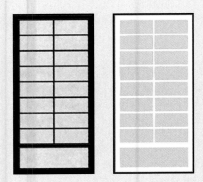

**Figure 7-56**
*Sample shoji screen image and alpha.*

Notice that the area constituting the framework in the image is white on the alpha, so it will be completely opaque. The area that makes up the screening is gray on the alpha, which will make that part if the image translucent. It's a fairly light gray, so it will be more toward the opaque side of the transparency scale, but since these screens are made of paper in RL, which isn't incredibly see-through, you might want to go even lighter with it. The lighter you go (on the alpha channel), the less you'll be able to see through it.

## WHY DO SECTIONS OF IMAGES SOMETIMES DISAPPEAR OR SEEM TO CHANGE POSITION IN SL?

This phenomenon has to do with a glitch common to nearly all 3D applications in what's known as *alpha sorting*. It happens in almost all video games and even in high-end 3D modeling packages costing thousands of dollars. What happens is that when two or more 32-bit images are placed so that they intersect or overlap in close proximity, the renderer has trouble determining which one to draw first. As a result, the images can appear to flip-flop their positions in 3D space, to cancel each other out, or to otherwise behave strangely.

The way to cut down on this is to make sure that 32-bit images are used only when absolutely necessary. Images that do not need transparency should always be saved as 24-bit.

Beyond that, there are certain building techniques in SL that can minimize the effect and others that actually take advantage of it.

## WHY DO I SEE A WHITE HALO AROUND MY PARTIALLY TRANSPARENT IMAGES IN SL?

The appearance of a white or lightly colored haloing effect in partially transparent images is a common phenomenon that can be easily corrected. First, let's talk about what causes it, and then we'll cover how to prevent it.

The halo effect is caused in the alpha channel by antialiasing, the method by which computers smooth the appearance of diagonal edges and curves. In the areas of the alpha channel canvas where black meets white, some of the pixels on the border between the two colors are blended into gray. This blending is necessary to keep edges from looking jagged or pixelated, but it comes with a side effect. Since gray in the alpha channel means translucency, the antialiased pixels end up becoming translucent.

How this results in a white halo is pretty simple. If there's whitespace (or blank space) surrounding the opaque parts of your image, those antialiased, semitransparent edge pixels end up combining their coloring with the white around them. They become so lightened by the process that they appear to form a white halo.

The ways to avoid the halo ranges from very, very simple to slightly complicated. The simplest thing to do is just to give your images a dark background. Technically this gives you a dark halo instead of a light one, but dark halos are usually undetectable in SL. Most of my tutorials include this method, since it's the easiest to explain, and the most universally applicable for all situations.

Other methods include bleeding the coloring of the opaque areas into the transparent areas. This approach is visually superior to the dark background method, but a little more complicated to do. Photoshop users may wish to view Robin Sojourner's wonderful tutorial "Making a Perfect Alpha Channel, with No White Halo " on her

website at http://www.robinwood.com/Catalog/Technical/SL-Tuts/SLTutSet.html, showing how she eliminates the halo by using a Flaming Pear's Solidify filter.

Of all the third-party plug-ins for Photoshop that can be useful for de-haloing, my favorite is a filter from Flaming Pear called Solidify. At the time of this publication, Solidify is available free on Flaming Pear's website, http://www.flamingpear.com/goodies.html, in the Free Plugins package. It's a nice one-step solution to bleed coloring all over the transparent areas, completely eliminating any chance of a halo.

# TUTORIAL: CREATING AN ALPHA CHANNEL IN PHOTOSHOP WITH CHOSEN FEW

Here is a quick experiment using alpha channels in Photoshop, but you can find instructions for other applications in this forum post at http://forums.secondlife.com/showthread.php?t=80851. Make sure to scroll below the FAQ section to find instructions for Photoshop, Photoshop Elements, and Paint Shop Pro.

## STEP 1: CREATE A NEW IMAGE

Create a new 256×256 image in Photoshop (see Figure 7-57).

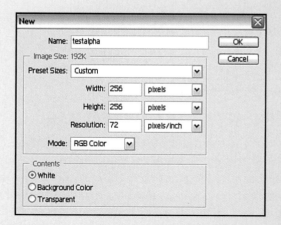

**Figure 7-57**
*Create a 256×256 image.*

## STEP 2: FILL THE BACKGROUND LAYER

Fill the background layer with any solid color you like. Anything bright and easy to recognize will work well, like bright red (see Figure 7-58) or bright blue.

**Figure 7-58**
*Fill the background layer with a solid color.*

## STEP 3: CREATE A NEW ALPHA CHANNEL

As shown in Figure 7-59, go to the Channels palette and create a new channel named Alpha 1 (Photoshop should pick this name automatically by default).

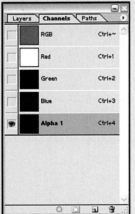

**Figure 7-59**
*On the Channels palette, create a new channel named Alpha 1.*

## STEP 4: GET A TEST ALPHA PATTERN

To start, you need an interesting grayscale image. You can find the one I made for this tutorial here: http://anselgasparini.blogspot.com/2007/01/alpha-channel-test-pattern.html. You can also obtain this texture without upload fees at the in-world companion site in Humuli here:

SLURL http://slurl.com/secondlife/humuli/222/123/29

It looks something like Figure 7-60.

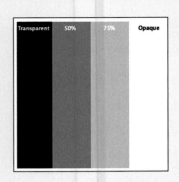

**Figure 7-60**
*My grayscale test image.*

Copy this image, go back into Photoshop, and paste the image you just copied directly onto the Alpha 1 channel.

Do this by selecting Alpha 1 on the Channels palette and then pressing Ctrl+V.

Alternatively, you can make a similar pattern yourself simply by painting directly onto the alpha channel with any of Photoshop's painting tools. Notice Photoshop's color gamut will automatically switch to grayscale whenever you're working directly on a channel.

## STEP 5: SAVE THE IMAGE

Make sure you save the image as 32-bit TGA (see Figure 7-61). If you save it as 24-bit, you will not be saving the alpha channel.

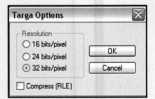

**Figure 7-61**
*Save the image as 32-bit TGA.*

## STEP 6: UPLOAD THE IMAGE TO SL

To upload the image to SL, use the File menu; it will cost you L$10. After you pick the file, you will see a preview something like that in Figure 7-62.

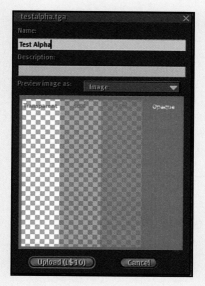

**Figure 7-62**
*The preview of a texture with transparency.*

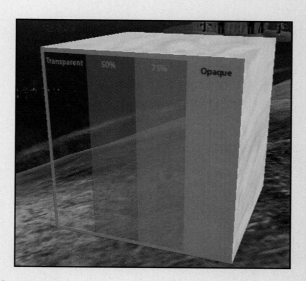

**Figure 7-63**
*The texture provides four different degrees of transparency.*

## STEP 7: APPLY THE TEXTURE

Apply the texture to a prim. Assuming you do everything correctly, what you should see on the prim is a square image with a solid colored border around it, and four vertical sections of varying transparency.

The section on the left should be completely transparent, with the word *Transparent* printed opaquely and appearing to float in mid-air near the top. The section immediately to the right should look partially transparent, with 50% written opaquely near the top. The next one should look mostly opaque but still a bit see-through, with 75% written opaquely near the top. The section all the way to the right should be totally opaque, except it should have the letters of the word *Opaque* appear to have been punched out of it so you can see through them.

Figure 7-63 shows the uploaded texture applied to one side of a standard cube.

Notice the variance in transparency, created entirely by the different gray values on the alpha channel.

# TUTORIAL: CREATING A PLANT TEXTURE WITH JULIA HATHOR

My deepest thanks to Julia Hathor for providing this wonderful tutorial in which you will create your own SL plant. Think about a garden or a park nearby. What piece of RL can you bring into SL using this technique? Take it away, Julia.

Plant textures often involve a lot of tedious work. You can make it easier on yourself by trying to isolate your plant from similar colors or shadows when you take your photograph. I find that noon (when shadows are at a minimum) is the best time to take your photo. Even better is to take your picture on an overcast day. If the plant is small, you can place a backdrop of black or white poster board to keep surrounding objects out of the picture. (If you cannot do that, you will have to isolate your desired plant by working on the photo in Photoshop. With the Erase tool—or better a channel mask—you must separate your background from around your plant, and needless to say, this can be difficult if many colors are similar in shade to your plant colors.

## STEP 1: TAKE A PICTURE

For this tutorial, I took a picture of a blackberry vine against white poster board and some white paper on an overcast day (see Figure 7-64). I worked in Photoshop CS and am assuming that you know a little about working in Photoshop.

**Figure 7-64**
*A blackberry vine.*

## STEP 2: QUICKLY SEPARATE THE BACKGROUND

To separate some of the obvious unneeded background, click on your Paint tool; then use the color picker and click on your white background (see Figure 7-65). Paint out the background that shows and some of the shadows that are close in color to your plant. Don't spend a lot of time trying to paint out everything; this is just something done quickly to help later in your selection of the plant.

**Figure 7-65**
*Use the color picker to click on the white background.*

## STEP 3: CAREFULLY SEPARATE FROM THE BACKGROUND

With the magic wand set to a tolerance of 33, click on the white background. Holding down the Shift key, keep clicking on as much of the background as you can (see Figure 7-66). You may have to magnify your picture (click the zoom symbol in the Toolbox) to get at small areas in between the plant parts.

**Figure 7-66**
*Select the white background.*

If you accidentally click on a plant color and select more than you want, just go to the Edit menu and click on Step Backward, trying again. If you find that it's difficult not selecting some of the plant with the background, you may have to lower the tolerance level of the magic wand. If you're having a hard time selecting all the background in a section, you may have to raise the tolerance level. I found that a tolerance of 33 worked well for me.

Take your time with this step; it's critical to your plant's looking as realistic as possible. When you're sure that you have as much background selected as you can, choose Select->Inverse. You will see the "crawling ant" selection lines change to envelop your plant.

## STEP 4: CREATE A NEW FILE

Select File->New. A new window will pop up. Name your project **Blackberryvine2** and then be sure that Width= 1024 pixels, Height=512, Resolution=72, Color=RGB, and the background is listed as Transparent. Click OK and reduce the size of the window so that you can see both this and your Blackberryvine1 window at the same time.

## STEP 5: TRANSFER YOUR BLACKBERRY VINE

Click on your Blackberryvine1 project to bring it to the foreground in Photoshop. Click on the Move tool. Grab your selected plant and slide it over to Blackberryvine2. At the top of your screen, click on Edit, and then in the drop-down menu, choose Transform and then Scale. Using the anchor points, adjust the size of your vine. Go back to Transform and choose Rotate to angle the vine section like you want. When you have it sized and placed where you want it, click the Move tool. When the next tiny window pops up (see Figure 7-67), click Apply.

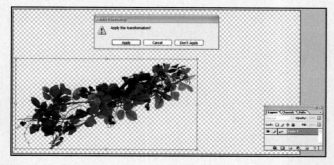

**Figure 7-67**
*Choose Apply.*

## STEP 6: BUILD UP YOUR PLANT

Click on the Layers palette to bring it to the forefront. Right-click on Layer 1 and choose Duplicate Layer.

With the Move tool active, click and drag your vine selection until you see the duplicate. Then select Transform, Scale, Rotate, and Flip Vertical. Next, place this new section as you want it (see Figure 7-68). Repeat for a third vine section to be added to the picture, also changing the look of your vine even more by playing with Skew until you get the look you want.

**Figure 7-68**
*Add another vine.*

## STEP 7: MERGE VISIBLE AND SELECT OPAQUE

Go to the top of your screen, click on Layer, and then choose Merge Visible. All of your layers will now be joined as one.

Select your opaque areas: On your Layers palette, hold down the Ctrl key and click on what is now called Layer 1 copy 2. All of the opaque areas of Blackberryvine2 should now be selected.

## STEP 8: CREATE AN ALPHA CHANNEL

Click on the Channels palette to bring it to the forefront. At the bottom of the palette, click on the symbol with the shaded rectangle and white circle (see Figure 7-69). If you hover your mouse pointer over it, you'll see Save Selection As Channel.

Once you click on this symbol, Photoshop will save your selection (your plant) as an alpha channel. This will tell what will be visible and what will be hidden. Scroll down the Channels palette and make sure to check the box on the alpha channel so that the eye symbol appears.

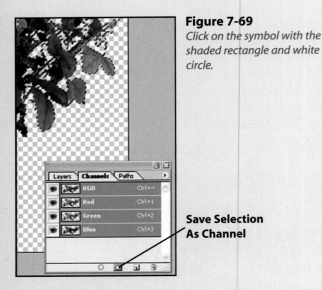

**Figure 7-69**
*Click on the symbol with the shaded rectangle and white circle.*

**Save Selection As Channel**

You will see a red tint appear over the areas that will be invisible in SL, the background areas. If you uncheck the RGB channel and view only this alpha channel, you will see that it's mostly black and white. Black will become invisible when the texture is uploaded into SL. White will be seen. Any gray will be semitransparent. If you've done everything correctly up till now, you'll see a white silhouette of your plant on a black background.

## STEP 9: DO QUALITY CHECK

With the eye on the RGB Channel unchecked, you will see your white-and-black alpha channel only. Look for white or gray specks that may be where you don't want them (see Figure 7-70).

Remember, whatever is black won't be seen, but anything white or gray will. You don't want to upload your texture to SL and see tiny specks appearing in it. So click on your alpha channel and, using your paint brush, paint black wherever you see white or gray where it shouldn't be. When you're done, recheck the RGB channel so the eye symbol appears. In fact, before proceeding to the next step, double-check that all your layers have an eye symbol, showing that they are visible.

## STEP 10: ADD A BACKGROUND COLOR LAYER

Why are we adding this color background? If you used your texture the way it is now, it would have a white halo around everything. To lessen the chance of that, we need a background color.

Create a new layer. Then go to the Paint Bucket Fill tool and select it. Click on Color Picker and then click on a medium value green color in your plant picture. Fill your new layer with this color (see Figure 7-71). Things will look quite different with this sudden splash! Don't worry, though; it's just the way the color layer is reacting to the alpha channel below it.

Finally, drag your filled color layer below your plant layer where it is needed, and things will look more normal.

## STEP 11: SAVE AS A TARGA FILE

Double-check that all your layers are visible, making sure the eye symbol shows on each of them. Go to the File menu at the top of the screen and click on Save As. In the window that comes up, you can name your file (see Figure 7-72). Name it as you will, probably using a different name than the file you just worked with in case you want to work again on that file in the future in a different way. Choose a location for your file, if you want to save it to a different folder, by clicking in the top box on Folders or the up-arrow folder at the top.

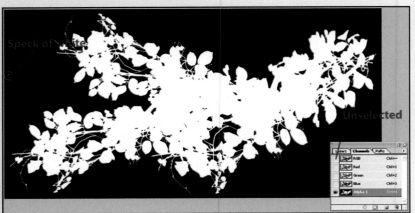

**Figure 7-70**
*Only the white-and-black alpha channel is shown.*

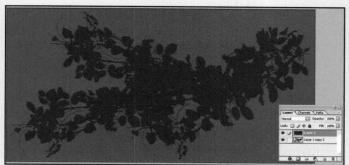

**Figure 7-71**
*Fill the new layer with a green.*

**Figure 7-72**
*Name your file and choose a file format.*

Click in the Format box to drop down a menu and choose a format. Click on the TARGA option. You will see a check beside Alpha Channels and an exclamation in a yellow triangle alerting you that the file must be saved as a copy. Click on Save.

Another window will present you with options for the kind of TARGA file you want. Check 32-bit and then click OK. Remember that when you see your texture in SL, it will look distorted, squashed down. Don't worry about this; you'll be texturing a prim that will have a narrow rectangular shape, and it will be proportional then.

# TUTORIAL: MAKING A PLANT WITH JULIA HATHOR

Plants are satisfying things to make in SL. Not only do they brighten up the world and satisfy a communal human need for something that speaks of our natural world, but they are also fairly easy to create. I will be using the texture called BlackBerryVineFinal for this tutorial as well as TotallyTransparent and am assuming that you know the basics of building.

If you did not build your own plant texture but want to build a plant, you can find the 100% transparent texture and the blackberry plant texture located at the in-world companion site in Humuli here:

 http://slurl.com/secondlife/humuli/222/123/29

## STEP 1: MAKE A FLAT PANEL

Start by rezzing a square prim on the ground. In the edit window, click on the Object tab, where you will enter these numbers into the Size parameters: X=0.02, Y=4, Z=1.5 You should end up with a flat plywood panel (see Figure 7-73).

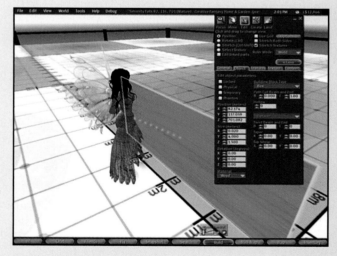

**Figure 7-73**
*The flat plywood panel.*

## STEP 2: TURN IT TRANSPARENT

With the edit window still open, click on the Texture tab. You will see two square boxes with the labels Texture and Color below them. Click on the square box labeled Texture, and it will then open the Pick: Texture window where you can find your texture (see Figure 7-74). Using the folder tree to the right, find the texture called TotallyTransparent, click to highlight it, and then click Select. The whole panel immediately turns invisible.

**Figure 7-74**
*The Pick: Texture window opens.*

Keep your edit window open; otherwise, you'll lose track of it! (However, if you do lose track of it, just go to the top of your screen and select View->Highlight Transparent, and it will become visible to you as a semitransparent reddish panel.)

## STEP 3: APPLYING YOUR PLANT TEXTURE

Toward the top of the edit window, click on the circle before Select Texture. Keeping the window open, click on the flat side of the panel that is before you. You will see some white markings appear on that side, letting you know that you have selected it. Find the texture named BlackBerryVineFinal in the Pick: Texture window and choose Select.

You should now have the texture of a blackberry vine on only one side of your flat panel. To minimize any image lines at the edges of your plant panel, you must make some numerical changes to the texture. Look below the two squares under the Texture tab, and you will see Repeats per Face, Horizontal (U), and Vertical (V) with numbers to the right. Change those numbers from 1.000 to 0.990 in both the Horizontal and the Vertical fields (see Figure 7-75). This will stretch the texture just a tiny bit.

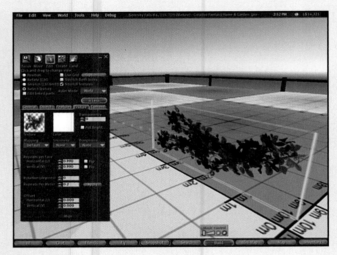

**Figure 7-75**
*Change the settings to 0.990 in both the Horizontal and Vertical fields.*

## STEP 4: MIRROR THE PLANT IMAGE

Ctrl+Alt+Click and orbit your view around to the other flat side of your panel. Then repeat the procedure, placing your plant texture on the opposite side, as in step 3. There's one extra step, however: Put a check in the Flip check box to the right of Repeats per Face, Horizontal (U) (see Figure 7-76).

Checking this setting will flip the texture, making it a perfect mirror of the texture on the opposite side. You should now have a panel that is textured on its two flat broad sides with a blackberry vine, while all the edges around it remain transparent.

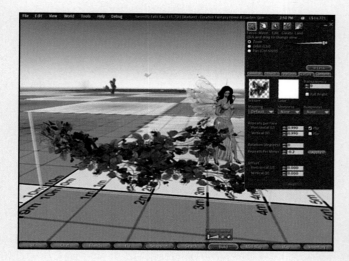

**Figure 7-76**
*Check Repeats per Face, Horizontal (U).*

## STEP 5: ROTATE THE PANEL

Click on the Object tab and then on Rotate. Look lower for the field called Rotation and place the value **270** in the X number field. Your panel will immediately flip so the vine is now vertical instead of horizontal (see Figure 7-77).

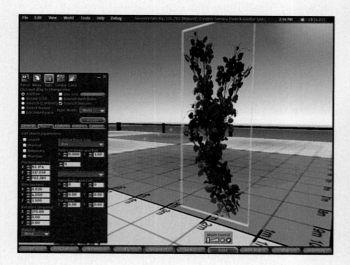

**Figure 7-77**
*Turning the panel 270 degrees flips it so it's vertical.*

## STEP 6: MAKE COPIES OF YOUR PANEL

Ctrl+Alt+Click and orbit your view so you're looking down at your panel from above (see Figure 7-78). Click on the Edit square, hold down your Shift key, and drag the

red arrow until you see a copy separating from your first panel. Press Ctrl+Z to return the copy to the exact position where it started.

Click on the Rotate button above and, highlighting the blue rotation band, rotate your copy panel around until the two panels intersect into an X (see Figure 7-79).

Click on the Position button and repeat this, creating a third panel. Try to have the three panels evenly spaced when you rotate them out, like cutting into a pie.

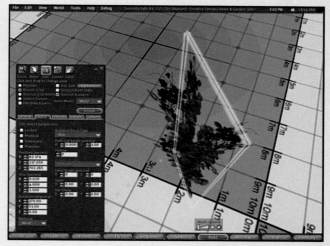

**Figure 7-78**
*You should be looking down at your panel.*

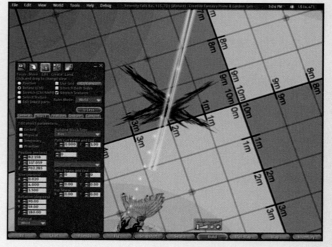

**Figure 7-79**
*Rotate the copy until the two panels form an X.*

## STEP 7: LINK THE PRIMS

Keeping the last panel highlighted, hold down Ctrl+Shift and click on the other two panels (see Figure 7-80).

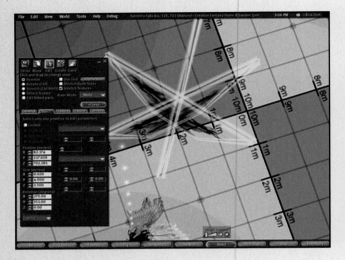

**Figure 7-80**
*Select all three panels.*

When all three panels are highlighted in yellow, press Ctrl+L. All the panels should link together; two panels will now have a blue, glowing edge, and one will still be yellow (the root prim). Under the General tab, name your creation **Blackberry Vine**.

## STEP 8: MAKE A POLE FOR YOUR VINES

Rez a cylinder on the ground. Then, on the Object tab, find the Size field and change the values to X=0.1, Y=0.1, Z=4. Click the Texture tab and then click on the left Texture box to bring up the Pick: Texture window.

Follow the folder tree to find a texture called Old Wood by following this path: Library>Textures>Wood>Old Wood. Click to highlight it and select. Of course, many times a texture doesn't look good at its default settings. The best way to get a feel for the Repeats per Face, Horizontal and Vertical settings is to play with them. Use the arrows beside the numbers or change the numbers themselves and see how your texture changes with them. For this pole, I set them to Horizontal=1.000, Vertical=0.200. Still

doesn't look right, does it? We also need to change the rotation of the texture on the prim to 90 degrees; then it's finished (see Figure 7-81).

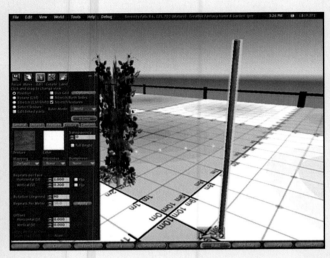

**Figure 7-81**
*The prim is now vertical.*

The easiest way to learn the texture controls is to play with them. Textures will react differently to different shapes of prims, to rotation, to the repeats per face, to the repeats per meter, and to the offset. Use different textures on different prims, such as a striped pattern on a sphere or a circle design on a square. Change the transparency. Experiment! Don't be afraid to use a texture that's clearly labeled for something else (like glass) on something it wasn't meant for (like texturing a waterfall).

## STEP 9: LINK THE POLE TO YOUR PLANT

With the edit arrows, move your pole to exactly in the middle of your intersecting plant panels. With the pole selected, select your plant, and then with the Ctrl key held down, press the L key to link it all. As your final steps, go to the General tab and name your creation; then go to the Object tab to check the Phantom box (see Figure 7-82). I check Phantom so that people don't get tangled up walking around plants; plus, I've been told that if an object is Phantom, it creates less lag.

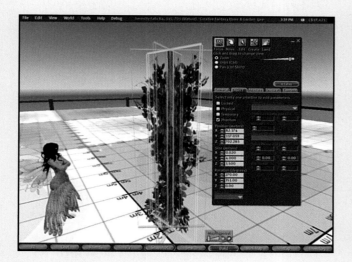

**Figure 7-82**
*Select Phantom.*

## STEP 10: PLANT YOUR PLANT SOMEWHERE

I have included a picture of how you can use your black-berry vine (see Figure 7-83), and you can see it in person at the Serenity Falls or Shadow Brook sims.

The Little Country Nook is made of simple shapes: a cut cylinder for the bottom, tori for pillows, squashed cylinders for the couches, and plain square panels to form the background.

**Figure 7-83**
*The Little Country Nook.*

The blackberry vines are made of the same blackberry plants you made, and the same texture is also placed on cylinders to provide depth but save on prims. Building in SL is a constant battle between creating a realistic appearance and saving on prims. Textures are our tools to help with this problem. Explore the Library Texture folders in your Inventory. They contain many treasures that a lot of residents never even discover and experiment with!

You can see and enjoy the Little Country Nook, which uses this plant, at Serenity Falls located at the following SLURL. Thanks, Julia!

SLURL **http://slurl.com/secondlife/Serenity%20Falls/
84/17/21/**

# TEXTURE TIPS AND TRICKS

To improve performance and save on uploads, you can create one texture image that contains several other textures. For example, a 512×512 pixel texture image may contain eight 64×64 pixel textures. Using the UV settings on the Texture tab, you can select parts of a texture image for use on different prims or different faces of the same prim.

It is often a trial-and-error process to pick the right piece of a texture image, particularly if you're using more of a texture collage instead of a specific texture grid.

Adrian Eisenberq (now Adrian Linden) created a nice little tool called the Texture Calculator that makes finding the UV texture settings easier. The tool's interface is shown in Figure 7-84 with a sample image from Julian Fate's great texture zone tutorial.

The tool can be downloaded from
http://www.purplestatic.com/texCalc.zip.

The tutorial on texture zones can be found here:
http://sldevelopers.com/blogs/julianfate/archive/
2006/03/29/168.aspx#comments.

You simply load a texture image, drag and select the piece you want, and then enter the offset and repeats on the Texture tab.

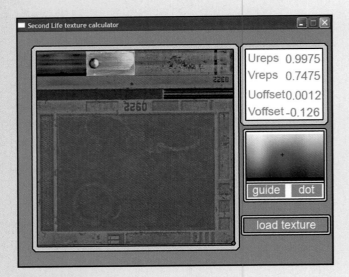

**Figure 7-84**
*The SL Texture Calculator.*

# AVATAR TEXTURING AND CLOTHING

Textures are also the secret sauce that makes avatar skins and clothing come alive. While you can do a lot with default clothing, you can't use transparency, and you don't have any control over where the texture is placed. As with all textures, clothing design in SL requires a working knowledge of a third-party program like Photoshop, Paint Shop Pro, or something similar.

The following sections introduce you to the basic concepts. If you're interested in more detailed information, particularly if your RL expertise is in 3D modeling/texturing, then you should check out both the SL forums (http://forums.secondlife.com/forumdisplay.php?f=109) and Robin Sojourner's in-world Texture Lab (more on this later) where more details are revealed.

## GETTING STARTED: LINDEN TEXTURE TEMPLATES (UV MAPS)

To design clothing, eyes, or skins in SL, you need to get ahold of a texture template so you can understand the places on a square texture that map to the points on the SL avatars. These "templates" are, in fact, UV maps for the head, upper body, and lower body of SL avatars. There are also templates for eyes, hair, and skirt.

To start, download the whole Linden template set from http://secondlife.com/downloads/templates.php.

You will also find a PDF file titled "Using the SL Fashion Design Templates." This is a must-read. In particular, make sure to hit the "Hints and Tips" section for invaluable advice.

The Linden-provided templates have several limitations, so two additional template sets are widely recognized by SL designers as the gold standards: one from Robin Sojourner and the other from Chip Midnight. Each one has certain advantages, so plan to use all of them if you get serious.

Robin Sojourner's set is available in various formats including JPEG, Photoshop, and a layered Photoshop CS2 with Vector Smart Objects. You can find it at http://www.robinwood.com/Catalog/Technical/SL-Tuts/SLPages/AVUVTemplates.html.

Another terrific set is available from Chip Midnight at http://www.slboutique.com/chipmidnight/.

Figure 7-85 illustrates the Linden templates and how they're mapped onto the SL avatar. The mapping is slightly different for male and female avatars.

The following sections discuss key considerations for each template. Significantly more detail on each of these templates and in-depth tips and tricks can be found in Robin Sojourner's excellent in-world Texture Lab (featured later).

## HAIR TEXTURING

The hair texture (see Figure 7-86) is used for texturing default hair in SL and has nothing to do with prim hair. I won't spend much time on this texture because prim hair is so much better than default hair that doing texture mapping for hair is not really worth the time IMO.

In Figure 7-86, note the green crosshairs in the middle, but offset to the right. This point represents the top of the head.

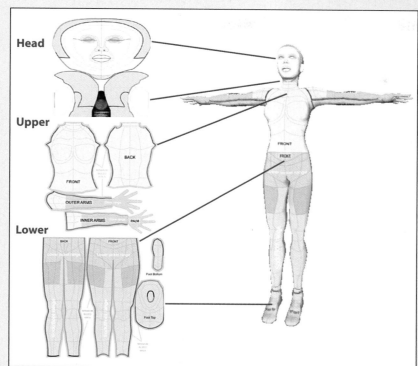

**Figure 7-85**
*How the Linden templates map onto an SL avatar.*

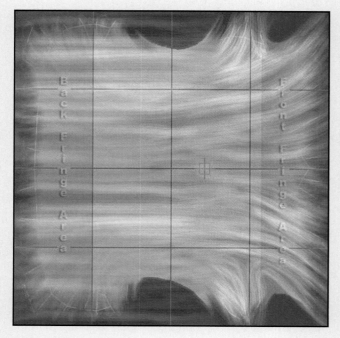

**Figure 7-86**
*Hair texture template.*

# EYE TEXTURING

The eye texture is used for the avatar's eyeball and is probably the easiest to work with. You can see the basic eyeball texture in Figure 7-87.

**Figure 7-87**
*The basic eyeball texture.*

If you want to create cats' eyes or other unusual effects, you create a texture for the eyeball.

One limitation in SL today is that this texture is mapped onto both eyes, so you can't have two eyes that are different colors without using attachments. In fact, they are identically mapped, so you can't have a texture that shows more pink near the nose (as is the case with a real human eye) because the pink will be on the side away from the nose of the other eye.

Robin notes this about the eye map in her tutorial: "[F]or some reason that defies all logic, the map is rotated. So, once you have your eyeball, you will need to rotate it 90 degrees counter clockwise before you upload it to SL, or it will appear sideways on your AV's eye."

Figure 7-88 shows a pair of Curious Blue Star Eyes that I bought.

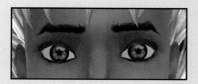

**Figure 7-88**
*Curious Blue Star Eyes.*

# HEAD TEXTURING

The entire AV head, with the exception of the eyeball, is included in the Face template. Included with your head are ears, mouth, teeth, eyelashes, and any facial tattoos.

The default Linden maps fall down here in a couple of ways. So, let's take a look at a sequence of images where I have mapped the default Linden and Chip Midnight's texture maps onto the default female avatar.

First, in Figure 7-89, shot from the front, you can see there is significantly more detail in the Chip Midnight maps.

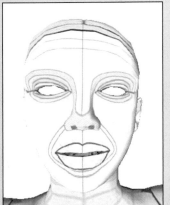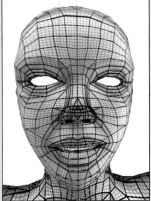

**Figure 7-89**
*The Linden and Chip Midnight facial texture maps displayed on avatars.*

In the side view shown in Figure 7-90, you can see it is much easier to line up details around the ear and side of the head using the Chip Midnight version.

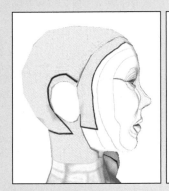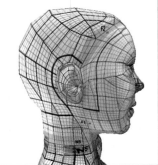

**Figure 7-90**
*The Linden and Chip Midnight side views.*

Finally, in the top view shown in Figure 7-91, you can really see that making a seamless texture across the skin of the scalp would be tricky using just the Linden templates.

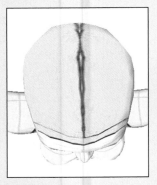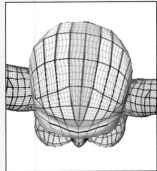

**Figure 7-91**
*Top view of template mapping on avatar head.*

Figure 7-92 shows the three templates used for the head. These flattened 2D images were applied to the 3D avatar shown in the preceding figures.

In 3D circles, this flattened view of 3D vertices is called a *UV map*. There are a few issues with these that you need to know if you're going to create your own skin textures. First, there is not enough room around the mouth section and back of the head, so if you're not very careful, you'll have a dark seam along the back side of the head. It is better to use a gap like the one shown in the second template from Robin Sojourner. In this case, any mistakes will show up inside the AV's mouth, which is not seen as often.

Of course, if you're wearing hair or prim hair, not to worry, but if you want to sell a high-quality skin, you need to pay attention to this kind of detail.

Second, you will notice that in the upper-right corner in both Chip's and Robin's templates there are the eyelashes. If you just paint this area out white or black, you'll end up with white or black or skin color eyelashes, so keep this point in mind.

With the appropriate transparency maps, you can easily make tattoos or makeup that overlays the default skin in SL, but most of the time when you're working with the head template, you're working on part of a new skin for your entire avatar.

More on skins later.

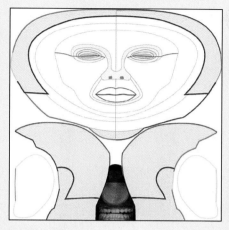
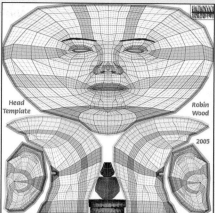
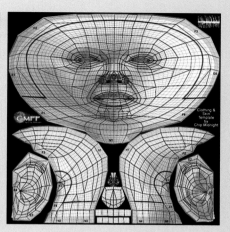

**Figure 7-92**

*Three head templates: Linden Lab, Robin Sojourner, Chip Midnight.*

# UPPER BODY TEXTURING

The upper body template can be used for upper body skin, undershirt, shirt, upper jacket, gloves, and tattoos (see Figure 7-93).

**NOTE**

If you have some experience with 3D modeling, you may have noticed by now that some of the mesh was split, like in the case of the arm, which means you have two seams to deal with instead of one. Annoying at best.

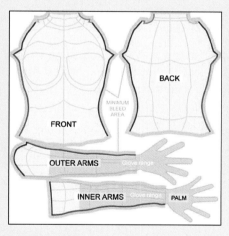
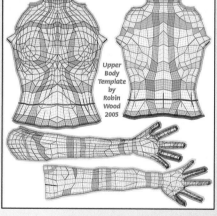

**Figure 7-93**

*Upper body templates.*

Shown here are templates from Linden and Robin. You'll notice a lot more color coding on Robin's, which helps in ensuring your textures are aligned. This is particularly important for skin, but also imagine you're working on a pair of gloves with a checkerboard pattern. Getting these patterns to align on the arm seams is a trick.

You'll also notice that there is only one arm, which is the right arm. The upper arm has the back of the hand; the lower arm, the palm of the hand. As Robin notes: "This arrangement means, of course, that the sleeves will always be identical, and that one will be the mirror image of the other. So much for having writing on the sleeves. You can't even work around it by using only a single sleeve, and putting reverse writing on an undershirt. They are both there, or both gone, locked forever in tandem."

Because every avatar can change its shape, there is no way to avoid some stretching of clothing in SL. You can, however, squash your textures where appropriate to compensate for the stretching that occurs. More details on how to do this and faults in the upper body UV map can be found at Robin's Texture Lab.

There is one more thing to say about this template: If you want to make an outfit that goes seamlessly all the way from shirt to fingertip, you should create one texture but then use that texture for both shirt and glove clothing items in SL. This texture will appear as a seamless piece of clothing on the avatar.

## LOWER BODY TEXTURING

The lower body template is used to create lower body skin, underwear, pants, the lower portion of a jacket, shoes, feet, and any private tattoos you may need!

Figure 7-94 shows the templates from Linden and Robin.

There are several things to note about the lower body template. First, there is only one foot, so again the texture you apply to one foot will also apply to the other. This symmetry in eyes, feet, and arms is really too bad. Second, the back is on the right versus the left, as in the upper body. Therefore, when you're creating jackets, watch out for this gotcha!

Robin notes this important point about the lower body texture if you're focusing on the feet: "The shape of the polys for the sole, at the upper right corner of the map, appear to be of a left foot. However, it's not. It's the right foot, and the big toe is to the right, in defiance of all logic and reason."

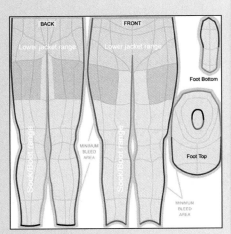
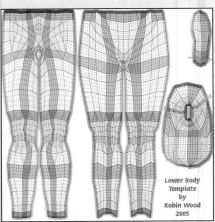

**Figure 7-94**
*Lower body templates from Linden and Robin.*

## SKIRT TEXTURING

Figure 7-95 shows the skirt template from Chip Midnight.

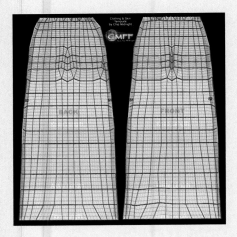

**Figure 7-95**
*Skirt template from Chip Midnight.*

This skirt template is likely the easiest to work with. Chip's template has some nice guides at the top that align with his upper body template, making it easier to position belts or other skirt accessories.

SL skirts, as we noted in the avatar section, are an additional mesh object. As of the introduction of flexi-prims into SL, the traditional skirt has really lost its purpose. Flexi-prims give much more realistic movement than the fixed skirt prim, but this template does make it easy to start making clothing and learn the basics before you move on to more difficult maps.

## MAKING SKINS AND JACKETS

If you're interested in creating a new skin or jacket, these are the two types of objects in SL that require you to use multiple templates/maps.

For a skin, you need the face, upper, and lower bodies. You need to ensure that the seams between these parts are perfectly aligned. You also should avoid using the "suggested alpha" on upload because this, at best, makes the seams slightly blurry and, at worst, will show a white chalklike halo. It's better to work to have a seamless texture that flows between templates.

Good skins, therefore, are quite hard to do, and you will find them to be more expensive than other items of clothing in SL. Remember, too, that "skin" is relative. I have seen some great avatars with scales, bark, and other textures instead of humanlike skin.

One more point to note is that the upper template has the front on the left side and the back on the right side, while in the lower template, this is reversed for some reason (see Figure 7-96). So, make sure you don't get confused on this point before you spend a lot of time aligning textures.

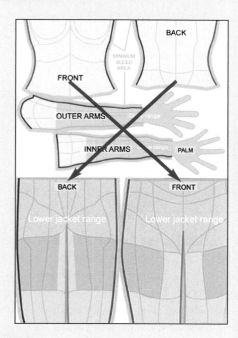

**Figure 7-96**
*The front and back are reversed.*

## SHOULD I WORK IN COLOR OR GRAYSCALE?

By habit, you may have started working on shirts, pants, or gloves in full color. In SL, however, you should consider whether you want to work in grayscale.

All SL clothing has an additional color "tint" that can be applied. This tint is added in addition to the color of the texture. So, if you're working purely in grayscale, then all the color in a texture will come from the tint. This allows

you to create a texture for some clothing and then to have multiple colors of that clothing without having to create and upload multiple textures. If you share articles with others and allow modify permissions, then they can pick the color of the clothing you have produced.

For some clothing, you will want to have very precise color control, and the obvious limitation here is that the cloth must have only one color. So, if an article of clothing has only one color and you want to support user-selected color, try creating your textures in grayscale.

## UPLOADING AND PREVIEWING TEXTURES

Getting textures just right can sometimes be painstaking work requiring further and further refinements. To avoid spending a ton of L$ uploading many textures only to find them lacking, you should try to preview these textures as applied to an avatar mesh before you finalize an upload.

I know of three ways to do this, and they are described in the following sections. Be aware, however, that none of these methods take into account the fact that most avatars will not have the default avatar shape, so you can expect some stretching and compression of textures when your clothing and texture are applied to avatars of varying shapes. If you want to have a product line that looks good on a wide variety of avatar shapes, you will ultimately need to upload it and try it out on various shapes yourself.

### Previewing on Upload

When you upload textures into SL, as discussed earlier, you can preview the upload. You will see a Preview Image As drop-down, which, by default, is set to Image. Use this drop-down to pick the avatar component you want to preview (see Figure 7-97).

Available options are Image, Hair, Female Head, Female Upper Body, Female Lower Body, Male Head, Male Upper Body, Male Lower Body, and Skirt.

You can control your view using the same camera controls available when building, so by all means, zoom in and have a closer look.

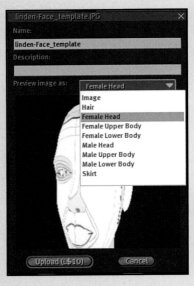

**Figure 7-97**
*The Preview Image As drop-down provides a number of options.*

## Previewing with 3D Modeling Software

You can download the default avatar mesh objects shown in Figure 7-98 from SL at http://secondlife.com/community/avatar.php.

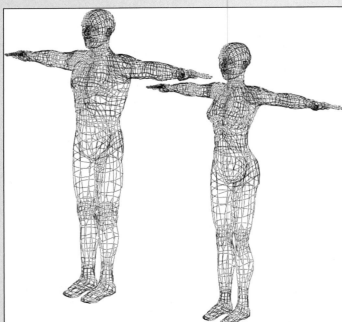

**Figure 7-98**
*The default avatar mesh objects.*

Included in this download are defaults for Curious Lab's Poser (which will also work in DAZ Studio) as well as .obj and .bvh files that you can use in 3D modeling tools like Maya, LightWave, and 3ds Max to test applying your textures to the default avatar mesh.

## Previewing with Johan Durant's Preview Texture Tool

If you get into clothing design seriously, and you can't afford or don't have time to learn some 3D modeling software, you should check out the excellent Preview Texture Tool by Johan Durant (see Figure 7-99). You can find more information about it in the Design and Texture forum. As of this writing, you can download it from http://www.fileden.com/files/2006/10/8/271989/slcp.zip.

**Figure 7-99**
*Johan Durant.*

Figure 7-100 shows the tool, where I applied the full set of Chip Midnight's templates. You can easily see how useful this tool is in getting the textures right, saving you upload costs. If you typically use the testing grid to avoid upload costs, this tool can also save you a lot of roundtrip time for uploads. A big thank you, Johan!

## USING YOUR NEW TEXTURES ON CLOTHING, SKINS, AND THE LIKE

After you upload your textures, you're ready to use them on an AV, as either a body part or as a clothing item. Open your Inventory and right-click on the folder where you want the article to be placed. That will open a menu that allows you to choose to create new things (see Figure 7-101).

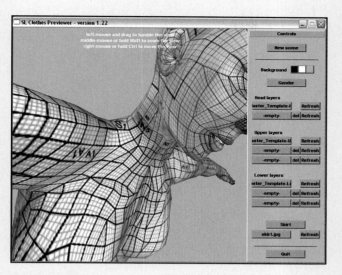

**Figure 7-100**
*Johan Durant's Preview Texture Tool.*

**Figure 7-101**
*New body part and new clothing inventory menus.*

Choose what you want from the menus by using the fly-out submenus in either category. For instance, to make a new skin, choose New Body Parts->New Skin. A new skin, with the default values, will appear in that folder. Another way to do this is in edit appearance mode.

It is important, however, that you create something new. If you don't—say you apply a texture to an existing piece of clothing—your name will not be listed as the creator. The creator will be the person who made the clothing you're modifying.

To add your new texture to the new article, enter edit appearance mode. From the thumbnails on the left side of the appearance window, you choose the textures. Drag

the texture you've made from your Inventory onto that thumbnail, or click that thumbnail and choose the texture from your Inventory.

Once you have made the article with your name as creator, you should name it and take it back into your Inventory. Your new article is now ready to show off, share, or sell.

Now it's time to put all this knowledge to use in one fantastic tutorial by Robin Sojourner.

# TUTORIAL: CREATING A CUSTOM T-SHIRT WITH ROBIN SOJOURNER

This tutorial teaches you how to use the Robin (Sojourner) Wood T-shirt template to put your own design on T-shirts for SL.

> **NOTE**
>
> To use this tutorial, you MUST download the Robin (Sojourner) Wood T-shirt file. You can find it here:
>
> http://www.robinwood.com/Catalog/Technical/SL-Tuts/SLDownloads/Robin(Sojourner)Wood_T-Shirt.zip

During the course of the tutorial, I refer to layers that I have built into this file and that you won't find in any other.

The templates provided by the Lindens, Chip Midnight, and my UV templates aren't really templates at all; they're simply UV maps.

This shirt is actually a template. The shirt is finished, including the alpha channel, so all you need to do is drop your design on the front or back, change the color, and upload. This tutorial explains how to do all of that and nothing more. It is not designed to teach you how to build any garment from scratch, although you may reverse-engineer it to figure that out.

You should be able to open the file in most graphics programs (Photoshop, Photoshop Elements, Paint Shop Pro, Painter, GIMP, etc.). The instructions are written for Adobe Photoshop (the screenshots are all from PS CS2 on a Mac) and assume that you are somewhat familiar with the workings of your graphics software.

Open the file. You'll notice that some layers are visible, and some are hidden.

For purposes of this tutorial, I'm going to assume that you have your image already prepared. I'm going to use a picture of my cat (see Figure 7-102), taken with a cell phone (so you know what kind of quality we're talking about here).

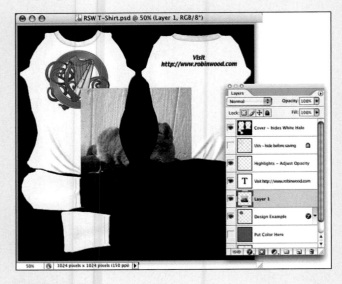

**Figure 7-104**
*Your picture will be on its own layer.*

**Figure 7-102**
*A cell phone picture of a cat.*

Open the image you want to use. Press Command/Ctrl+A to Select All and Command/Ctrl+C to copy the image. In the T-shirt window, click the Design Example layer to select it so the image will be pasted above this layer (see Figure 7-103).

Press Command/Ctrl+V to paste. Your picture will appear in the middle of the image on its own layer (see Figure 7-104). Because it's in the middle, it will be under the Cover layer and partially obscured, but that's okay. It's easy to reposition.

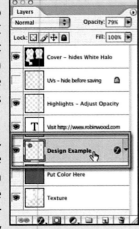

**Figure 7-103**
*Click Design Example.*

Reduce the opacity of your image. You can do so by dragging directly on the word *Opacity*, if you have PS CS2, to adjust it interactively, or you can type a new opacity setting into the text field (see Figure 7-105). I recommend between 60% and 70%. If you're typing, press Enter when you're done. That frees the keyboard so that you can use keyboard shortcuts.

**Figure 7-105**
*Set the opacity.*

Press the V key to get the Move tool (or select it from the toolbar) and drag the image into position in the middle of the shirt over the harp (see Figure 7-106).

If the image needs resizing, press the T key to move into free transform mode, or choose Edit->Free Transform. Now, hold down the Shift key to constrain resizing to proportional only and press the Option/Alt key to resize from the middle. Click one of the corner handles and drag inward, toward the center of the picture, to shrink it (see Figure 7-107). Drag outward, of course, if it's too small, and you want to enlarge it. When you're happy with the size, double-click inside the bounding rectangle to accept it or press Enter twice.

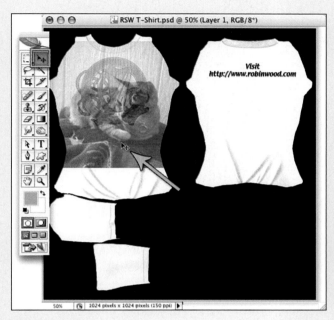

**Figure 7-106**
*Drag the image into position.*

**Figure 7-107**
*Drag inward to shrink, outward to enlarge.*

Adjust the placement with the Move tool, if necessary (remember, V brings it up).

Now, if you're happy with the T-shirt this way, you can change the opacity back to 100% (the quick way is to

press 0 [zero] on your keyboard or numeric keypad), click the Eye icon next to the Design Example layer (to hide it), and skip to the next page.

Now, I'm going to do a little more with it, just to show you what is possible.

First, we'll use a mask to make the image round. To do that, choose the Elliptical Marquee tool from the menu (see Figure 7-108). Or press M to choose the Marquee tool and Shift+M to toggle through the available tools till you get it.

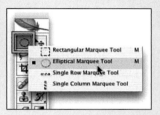

**Figure 7-108**
*Choose the Elliptical Marquee tool.*

Click where you want the center of the circle, hold down the Shift key to constrain the marquee to a circle and the Option/Alt key to make a marquee from the middle (notice a pattern here?), and drag the marquee out until it's roughly the same size as the circle around the harp (see Figure 7-109).

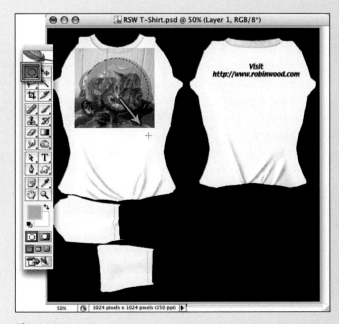

**Figure 7-109**
*Create the marquee.*

If the image is not centered, it's no problem. Switch fingers on the Shift key, reach over with your index finger, and hold down the spacebar too, and you can slide the marquee anywhere you want it while you're still sizing it. Yeah, it's a little tricky to do but well worth the effort of learning. If you drop a key, it's no problem, as long as you're still holding down the mouse button. Just press the keys again, and the marquee will spring back into shape.

When you have the image the way you want it, let go of the mouse button. Doing that will accept the circle. If you still need to tweak it, you can move it by just dragging with the Marquee tool or change it in other ways by choosing Select->Transform Selection from the menus.

Click the Make Mask button at the bottom of the Layers palette (see Figure 7-110) to mask the image.

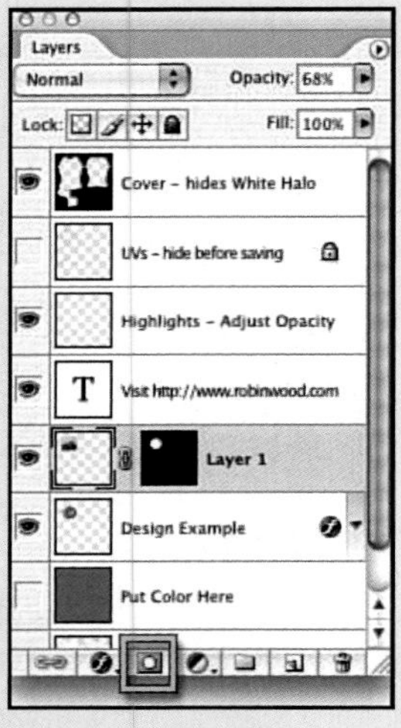

Press 0 to make the layer opaque and reposition it with the Move tool if desired.

Next, click the Eye icon for the Design Example layer to hide that layer (and get rid of the harp).

Now, let's add a layer style to the image to give it a little snap. Either double-click on the layer itself, or click the F (Effects) icon at the bottom of the Layers palette and choose a layer style.

**Figure 7-110**
*Click the Make Mask button.*

Either method will open the Layer Style dialog. The difference is that if you open the dialog through the icon, it will open to a style; otherwise, it won't. Personally, I find it easier to just double-click on the layer.

Choose a style by clicking on its name on the left side of the palette. When you do, the options for that style will fill the dialog. If you have the Preview enabled (on the right side of the dialog), you can see the results of the style as you play with the settings.

I'm using both a stroke and a drop shadow (see Figure 7-111). I'll just keep the defaults for the stroke. For the drop shadow, I'm going to use the settings shown here.

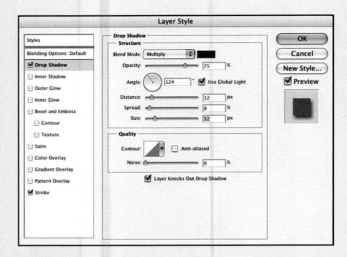

**Figure 7-111**
*Drop shadow and stroke are selected.*

If I wanted a white shirt (with an ad for this website on the back), I'd be done now. But let's say, for this example, that I want a burgundy shirt.

Begin by making the Put Color Here layer visible (see Figure 7-112), which instantly changes the shirt color to a deep blue. The reason is that the layer is filled with that color and set to Multiply for the Blending Mode.

Choose a new foreground color and fill the Color layer by either clicking on it with the Paint Bucket tool, or simply holding down the Alt/Option key and pressing Delete/Backspace. The shirt will take on whatever color you've chosen (see Figure 7-113).

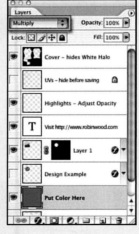

**Figure 7-112**
*Make the Put Color Here layer visible.*

That looks good, but the highlights are a little dim on the darker shirt. Let's brighten them up a bit.

If you click on the Highlight layer, you'll notice that the Blending mode is Screen. To get brighter highlights, just increase the opacity of this layer. Click on the word *Opacity* and drag to the right, or type in a slightly higher number (see Figure 7-114).

**Figure 7-113**
*Your shirt is now burgundy.*

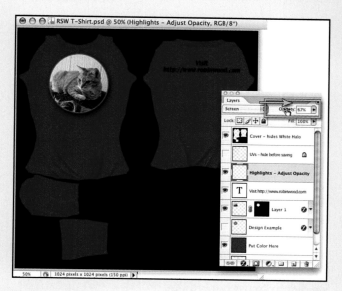

**Figure 7-114**
*Change the opacity level.*

Be careful and subtle here. If you make the colors too bright, they can look like chalk in SL. You want just enough that the folds and wrinkles look natural. I'm going with 67% for this color.

If your color is very light, you might want to decrease the opacity of this layer.

You'll probably want to change the text on the back, too. Or you may just want to hide that layer. If you want to change it, get the Text tool (T) and click five times to select the whole thing. Then just start to type (see Figure 7-115). If you want to change the color, font, or whatever, pick your choices from the Option bar at the top of the window in CS. With earlier versions of Photoshop, these options might be in a different palette.

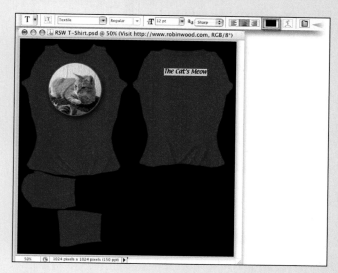

**Figure 7-115**
*Change the text.*

You can also highlight text and change any other attribute, but that's beyond the scope of this tutorial. Besides, you can probably figure it out for yourself.

OK! The design is done, and we're ready to prep the finished texture for uploading to SL.

The first thing we need to do is resize the image. Working at 1024×1024 is recommended, but it's *best to upload clothing no larger than 512×512*. But we also want to keep a copy of the layered file because it's much easier to tweak later.

So I'm going to teach you a trick that works only in Photoshop. (If you're using a different graphics program, you can save your layered file and then choose Save As with a different name instead.)

Look at the History palette. At the bottom, there are three buttons. Click the leftmost one, and you'll create a new document from the current document state (see Figure 7-116).

If it does, then go ahead and click the Upload button and pay your L$10.

I've included a hidden UV layer in the template, if that's what you'd like to do. The lines on that map correspond to the polygons in the model. Think of it as a wireframe. There will be forthcoming tutorials explaining exactly how to use the UVs if you find them confusing.

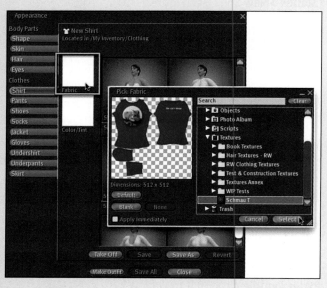

**Figure 7-122**
*The Pick: Fabric dialog appears.*

**Figure 7-123**
*The finished product.*

You can also increase the darkness of the shadows by duplicating the Texture layer. Select it and press Command/Ctrl+J, or drag it to the New Layer icon at the bottom of the Layers palette. Change the blending mode to Multiply (you know how to do that), and you'll effectively double the depth of the shadows. If that's too much, use the Opacity slider to make them a little lighter.

If it's not enough, duplicate that layer to make them even darker.

If you want to make a black shirt, by the way, I suggest that you use a dark gray, not black. That way, you'll be able to see the shadows.

Experiment with it! Try filling the Color layer with a pattern instead (choose Edit->Fill: Use Pattern and then pick one from the flyout menu). Try using different blending modes with the pattern. Change the opacity and see if you like that better. Add another layer and use color in one and a pattern in the other. Play with the blending modes and opacity of both of them.

Have fun with it! And if you make a particularly nice shirt, let me know.

If you would like to see the other tutorials in this series, try http://www.robinwood.com/Catalog/Technical/SL-Tuts/SLTutSet.html.

# THE TEXTURE LAB

The Texture Lab (see Figure 7-124) is an in-world location with a set of stations that cover more detail on textures than has been covered here.

**Figure 7-124**
*The Texture Lab.*

If you're serious about texturing, don't miss this spot. Robin Sojourner's shop is right next door, so walk through the one spot in the wall that has no supporting column over the pillars to find it.

 SLURL http://slurl.com/secondlife/Livingtree/ 126/101/25

## A VISIT WITH THE TEXTURE LAB'S CREATOR

*"I think that the reason this world works so well is that it has the three things that humans like best: discovery, creativity, and socialization."*
—Robin Sojourner

I chatted for two and a half hours with long-time SL resident and texture artist Robin Sojourner. What follows is a snapshot of our conversation:

```
[Ansel arrives in a small open area
next to a clothing store and the tex-
ture lab, there is a street here.
Across the street is a campfire. The
campfire is burning.]
```

**Ansel Gasparini:** *Hi Robin, so nice to meet you.*

**Robin Sojourner:** Hi Ansel. Nice to meet you, too. :D

*AG: Lumiere says your specialty is textures.*

RS: Yeah. It seems that it is. :D I built the texture lab, which needs to be updated at this point. But, except for the arrangement of the stuff in the Edit panel, it's still all sound.

*AG: So, take me back, how long have you been here, how did you find out about it, get attracted to it?*

RS: When I got here, you had to TP into a Telehub, and then fly to your destination. Sometimes over several sims. I've been here almost 2 years. Sept. 19, 2004. I found out about it because I was playing a game called "Journey to Wild Divine." http://www.wilddivine.com/ It's a single player bio-feedback game, and we were going to try to use this platform to do some multi-player stuff. But due to one thing and another, it didn't work out, and I wandered off and started to do my own stuff. :D

*AG: Do you think of SL as a game?*

RS: No. It's a multi-person environment. No more a "game" than RL is. More like a chat room on steroids. :D Shall we go across the street? I have a proto-fire circle there, and no one ever goes there. :D

```
[Ansel and Robin wander across the
road to sit by the fire]
```

*AG: so, how long before you decided to buy land?*

RS: I didn't buy land until I decided to open a store. I was lucky, and had friends who allowed me to live on their land from the very beginning. But land here changes hands so often; I got tired of having my work-room sold out from under me, and went and bought my own. :D

RS: That's what I have here, by the way. I don't have a house per se. I don't need to eat or sleep, you see. :D

*AG: Is your workshop around here?*

RS: It's a skybox. Not interesting at all, but we can go up there if you want. I did finally have to put a security thing there that keeps strangers from just plunking themselves in.

*AG: So, explain the skybox for me? How do you get one? How does it get up there? How do I get back down?*

RS: The skyboxes are what most people do here for privacy. Anyway, it's considered pretty rude to just go into someone's skybox without an invitation. Unlike their houses, which are mostly considered open, unless the doors are locked or something. So, when builders want someplace quiet and private to work, they set up a skybox.

*AG: So, how do you get an fully enclosed box up there and get inside/outside of it?*

RS: Teleport. You get it up there by making a platform, on land you own, and setting the Z axis value to something above 300 m.

AG: why 300m?

RS: 300 m is AV flight limit. You can't fly above that without a scripted device. Also, 300 M. is the top point to show on the map. If you put something 300 m or less, it shows up. That's new, too, since I got here by the way. The map didn't have any buildings on it when I arrived. But, mostly I do textures.

AG: So, textures mostly, which I associated with building, but they are intricately linked to clothing and skins as well aren't they?

RS: Yep. I've been doing 3D work for years, in the RL. Textures are, in fact, what clothing and skins are made of, mostly. So, when I got here, I went to the Ivory Tower, and it was wonderful, and I learned how to use the quirky prims and things, but the mapping and texturing were…odd, to say the least, coming from my background. And there wasn't anything to explain it. I also found that there were a lot of people delving quite deeply into 3D here who had never encountered it before

AG: I still find Z as up kinda hard to deal with LOL

RS: ROFL, Oh yeah. :D I work here for a bit, and then go to LightWave, and it's all backwards. :D Of course, I can build things in LightWave in a fraction of the time it takes to do it here. Sometimes, I'm afraid to say, I have to use LW just to remind myself that 3D isn't really frustrating. But, anyway, that's why I started to do the Texture Tutorials. Because there were so many people here who hadn't ever heard of UVs, and didn't know what they were, but were trying to work with them.

AG: cool, you teach in RL?

RS: I used to, long ago. Now I just teach like I do here. It's my nature, so I really can't stop doing it. :D I figure stuff out, and then I explain it. :D With Textures, you have to predict how they'll behave wrapped on a 3D surface. it's hardest for clothing and skins, I think. I've had tons of people tell me that they were having a hard time wrapping their heads around it.

AG: So, what advice would you have for newbies?

RS: Just say Thanks. :D Say, "Excuse me,…" It's just like Real Life. Be polite, and you'll get a lot farther. When you ask a question, listen for the answer.

RS: But I think that the reason this world works so well is that it has the three things that humans like best. Discovery, Creativity, and Socialization. Not necessarily in that order. :d there's always something new to discover and learn, and new people to meet, and you can make anything you can imagine, within the limits of the program. :D

# ON IMAGE DIMENSIONS AND UPLOAD DISTORTION

As mentioned earlier, SL supports a limited set of image sizes (the definitive list is coming up in the next section). Any image you upload that does not conform to one of these uniform sizes will be converted into that size and potentially distorted if it is not a power of 2. By *power of 2*, I mean that the width and height in pixels are, relative to one another, even multiples of 2, such as 8, 16, 32.

Figure 7-125 shows an image that is 300 pixels wide and 700 pixels tall. At 300×700, the width and height are not a power of 2. Instead, 400×800 would be a power of 2. I've created several perfect circles in this texture so you can see the impact of distortion on the upload. We will upload 400×800 and 300×700 versions of this texture so you can see the difference.

When you upload the images, you see the image upload preview (see Figure 7-126). The preview is displayed as a square (this is SL favoring square textures), and because of this, it is clearly distorted, but this does not necessarily mean your uploaded texture will be distorted. At this point, it is really hard to tell whether there will be any distortion or not.

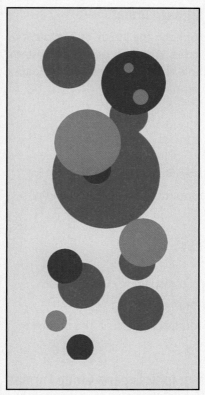

**Figure 7-125**
*A texture with perfect circles 300×700 pixels in dimension.*

pixel image. You can see it has some distortion (the circles are slightly flattened or stretched).

The easiest way to avoid distortion is to work in one of SL's default sizes. With that, on to some final details on texture size, pixel count, video memory, and file formats from Chosen Few.

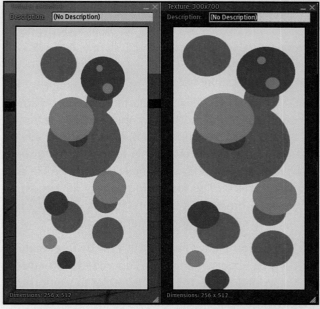

**Figure 7-127**
*Two textures forced to 256×512 pixels in dimensions, one distorted one not.*

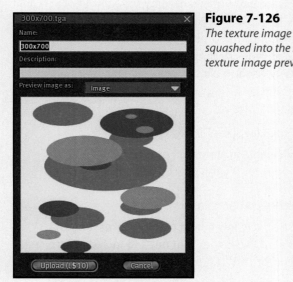

**Figure 7-126**
*The texture image squashed into the square texture image preview.*

In the final figure, Figure 7-127, you see the two texture images side by side after being uploaded into SL. If you look closely at the bottom of each, you will see the dimensions are the same 256×512 pixels. The first one (on the left) has perfect circles with no distortion. This image was originally 400×800. The second image is the 300×700

# TEXTURE SIZE, PIXEL COUNTS, VIDEO MEMORY, AND FILE FORMATS WITH CHOSEN FEW

The information in the following sections comes from a post I wrote for the SL texturing forum a while ago. At the time, there had been several recent questions from various SL users regarding file formats, the differences between file size and image size, and so on. I designed this brief informational resource as a kind of handy reference to help people make intelligent decisions when managing and creating textures in SL.

I've done my best to keep it simple, but some of the information is rather technical, so I don't necessarily recommend reading through all of it in one sitting. It's much more appropriate just to browse through it to get a grasp on the general concepts and then refer back to it as needed for specifics. Don't feel like you have to commit every last detail to memory to be a successful texture artist.

## IMAGE FILE FORMATS

SL allows you to use any of three different image formats as your source files for uploading: TGA, BMP, and JPEG.

### TGA: The TARGA File Format

TARGA (Truevision Advanced Raster Graphics Adapter) format, or TGA, is the most commonly used image format for texturing for 3D applications. It has certain advantages for this purpose over other formats, among them being it is lossless, it has an entirely predictable file size, and its simple bitmap formatting is easy for almost all programs to interpret. Of the three formats SL will accept, it is the only one that supports transparency.

The TGA file format was invented in 1984 by Truevision for TARGA graphics cards, and it was upgraded to its current version in 1989. It was the first file format to support true color on IBM-compatible PCs. Its characteristics include:

- Advantages:
  - High quality
  - Entirely lossless
  - Supports transparency
  - Entirely predictable file size (uncompressed)
  - Simple bitmap formatting is easy for all computers to read
  - Industry standard format for textures, also used extensively in video applications
- Disadvantages:
  - Large file size
  - Not readable by low-end graphics programs or by programs not intended for serious graphics work (you can't view a TGA in Windows Picture Viewer, for example)
  - Not well suited for printing

### BMP: The Windows Bitmap Format

BMP format was developed in the 1980s by Microsoft as an image standard for the Windows operating system. Today, it's used for simple things like desktop wallpaper images and not much else.

- Advantages:
  - High quality
  - Entirely lossless
  - Entirely predictable file size
  - Simple bitmap formatting is easy for all computers to read
- Disadvantages:
  - Large file size
  - Does not support transparency
  - Not well suited for printing
  - Not a common format of choice in the graphics industry

### JPEG: The Joint Photographic Experts Group Format

The JPEG format was invented by the Joint Photographic Experts Group in 1986. Today, it's the most commonly used image format on the Web, the last place where file size is still more important than image quality. It's also commonly used in digital cameras, but that's changing fast.

- Advantages:
  - Small file size
  - Viewable in almost all programs
- Disadvantages:
  - Lossy compression
  - Relatively low image quality makes it poorly suited for images that need to include sharp lines and/or text
  - Image quality degrades every time it's saved
  - Does not support transparency
  - Not well suited for printing

## FORMATS AND UPLOADING CONSIDERATIONS

When you upload an image to SL, it is stored on the server in JPEG2000 format, an optionally lossless type of compressed file. I won't bother providing much information about it, since SL's implementation of it is outside our control as users. If you're curious, you can read all about it at http://www.jpeg.org/jpeg2000/index.html.

For best results in SL, I recommend always using TGA as your source file format. It's the only format of the three that supports transparency, so for items like clothing, windows, and so on, you have no choice but to use it, and it's the industry standard for texturing.

I recommend not ever using JPEG for SL texturing. It's great for web pages, but it's not well suited to 3D work. Since the SL servers will store your images as JPEG2000 anyway, you don't need to be concerned about file size, which nullifies JPEG's one and only real advantage, leaving you with nothing but all the disadvantages. It's a lossy, low-quality format.

For SL texturing work, I always say, "Use TGA, every day, TGA all the way."

## FILE SIZE VERSUS TEXTURE MEMORY

It's not uncommon for those new to texturing to assume that they should use highly compressed formats like JPEG out of the mistaken belief that keeping file sizes small will increase performance. People usually come by this presumption as a result of everyday experiences using the Internet, where it's easy to see that web pages load faster with smaller image files than with larger ones. For the novice, the expectation that this same behavior would apply equally to graphics applications is logical, but it's incorrect.

The perceived correlation between file size and speed on the Web is actually an illusion that has nothing to do with graphics processing. Where the Internet is concerned, speed is primarily determined by the rate at which files can be sent from computer to computer. Since smaller files have less information to deliver, of course, they are delivered faster.

The rate at which graphical images are processed onscreen, though, actually has nothing whatsoever to do with file size. Graphics processing is all about texture memory, not about storage space.

Texture memory is always determined by the amount and depth of the actual pixels in the image, not the bits and bytes in which the file is stored. The number of pixels in an image times the number of bits in each pixel will always equal the amount of texture memory the image uses, no matter what. Its file size can vary depending on what format it's saved in, but its actual texture memory consumption when the image is in view will always be the same.

Why that's important to the SL texture artist is pretty simple. Knowing the rudimentary mathematical principles of how images affect performance enables you to optimize your textures so you can ensure your creations are as lag free as possible while also being as high in quality as they can be. The key to success in any real-time graphics application is always finding the right balance between detail and speed. Make your textures too big and you use too much memory, slowing down your frame rate (and everyone else's). Make them too small, and while your system performance will be relatively good, your imagery might look terrible.

File size is not part of the equation when thinking in this context. What's relevant to performance and visual quality are the actual images, not the files that store them on hard drives. Graphics performance is affected not at all by file size, but by texture memory consumption. Texture memory is determined by the number of pixels that make up each image and the number of memory bits in each pixel. That's it.

## HOW TO CALCULATE TEXTURE MEMORY

Determining how much texture memory an image will consume is fairly straightforward. It's basically a count of the total number of pixels in the image, multiplied by the number of bits in each pixel.

RGB color images without transparency have 24 bits per pixel, and those with transparency have 32 bits per pixel. So, for example, if you have a nontransparent color image that is 1024×1024 pixels, here's how the math would break down:

- 1024×1024 = 1,048,576 total pixels
- 1,048,576×24 bits in each pixel = 25,165,824 total bits in the image
- 25,165,824 bits / 8 bits in every byte = 3,125,728 bytes, or precisely 3MB

Pretty simple math. A 1024×1024 image (sans transparency) will always use exactly 3MB of texture memory. That's regardless of whether or not the file is compressed for storage. As far as the graphics card is concerned, an image is just a collection of pixels to be drawn, not a file to be saved.

Just for informational purposes, Table 7-1 presents a quick breakdown of some common texture sizes and their corresponding texture memory requirements. Note, by the way, that all the sample sizes are measurable in powers of 2. This is a requirement of OpenGL, the graphics language in which SL is written.

**Table 7-1    The Image Sizes SL Allows and Their Memory Consumption**

| IMAGE SIZE | TEXTURE MEMORY AT 32-BIT TEXTURE | MEMORY AT 24-BIT |
| --- | --- | --- |
| 1024×1024 | 4MB | 3MB |
| 1024×512 | 2MB | 1.5MB |
| 1024×256 | 1MB | 768KB |
| 1024×128 | 512KB | 384KB |
| 1024×64 | 256KB | 192KB |
| 1024×32 | 128KB | 96KB |
| 1024×16 | 64KB | 48KB |
| 1024×8 | 32KB | 24KB |
| 512×1024 | 2MB | 1.5MB |
| 512×512 | 1MB | 768KB |
| 512×256 | 512KB | 384KB |
| 512×128 | 256KB | 192KB |
| 512×64 | 128KB | 96KB |
| 512×32 | 64KB | 48KB |
| 512×16 | 32KB | 24KB |
| 512×8 | 16KB | 12KB |
| 256×1024 | 1MB | 768KB |
| 256×512 | 512KB | 384KB |

| IMAGE SIZE | TEXTURE MEMORY AT 32-BIT TEXTURE | MEMORY AT 24-BIT |
| --- | --- | --- |
| 256×256 | 256KB | 192KB |
| 256×128 | 128KB | 96KB |
| 256×64 | 64KB | 48KB |
| 256×32 | 32KB | 24KB |
| 256×16 | 16KB | 12KB |
| 256×8 | 8KB | 6KB |
| 128×1024 | 512KB | 384KB |
| 128×512 | 256KB | 192KB |
| 128×256 | 128KB | 96KB |
| 128×128 | 64KB | 48KB |
| 128×64 | 32KB | 24KB |
| 128×32 | 16KB | 12KB |
| 128×16 | 8KB | 6KB |
| 128×8 | 4KB | 3KB |
| 64×1024 | 256KB | 192KB |
| 64×512 | 128KB | 96KB |
| 64×256 | 64KB | 48KB |
| 64×128 | 32KB | 24KB |
| 64×64 | 16KB | 12KB |
| 64×32 | 8KB | 6KB |
| 64×16 | 4KB | 3KB |
| 64×8 | 2KB | 1.5KB |
| 32×1024 | 128KB | 96KB |
| 32×512 | 64KB | 48KB |
| 32×256 | 32KB | 24KB |
| 32×128 | 16KB | 12KB |
| 32×64 | 8KB | 6KB |
| 32×32 | 4KB | 3KB |
| 32×16 | 2KB | 1.5KB |
| 32×8 | 1KB | 768 Bytes |
| 16×1024 | 64KB | 48KB |
| 16×512 | 32KB | 24KB |
| 16×256 | 16KB | 12KB |
| 16×128 | 8KB | 6KB |
| 16×64 | 4KB | 3KB |
| 16×32 | 2KB | 1.5KB |
| 16×16 | 1KB | 768 Bytes |
| 16×8 | 512 Bytes | 384 Bytes |
| 8×1024 | 32KB | 24KB |
| 8×512 | 16KB | 12KB |

| IMAGE SIZE | TEXTURE MEMORY AT 32-BIT TEXTURE | MEMORY AT 24-BIT |
|---|---|---|
| 8×256 | 8KB | 6KB |
| 8×128 | 4KB | 3KB |
| 8×64 | 2KB | 1.5KB |
| 8×32 | 1KB | 768 Bytes |
| 8×16 | 512 Bytes | 384 Bytes |
| 8×8 | 256 Bytes | 192 Bytes |

Notice how much memory the larger textures demand. It doesn't take all that many textures to overwhelm a 256MB or 128MB video card. The biggest reason SL operates as slowly as it does is poor texture management on the part of resident content creators. Many people use textures that are simply way too big, and as a result, video cards choke.

The average video card can process only a few hundred megabytes' worth of textures at a time. Professional game artists are well aware of this, so they make sure to optimize all their textures to keep them as small as possible. SL, as a mostly amateur-created environment, does not tend to benefit from the same professional wisdom, and as a result, an average busy scene in SL can have literally gigabytes' worth of textures on display. Obviously, that's not a formula for effective real-time performance.

For everyone's sake, always keep all textures as small as they can be. I usually suggest as a rule of thumb that about 80% of textures should be 256×256 or smaller, about 15% should be 512×512, and about 5% should be 1024×1024. SL is extremely good at displaying small textures on objects at full screen size, better than just about any other program I've ever seen, in fact. It's quite rare that there's a legitimate reason to go much larger than 256×256.

## CHOOSING THE BEST TEXTURE SIZE FOR THE JOB

The two most important factors in determining what size to make a texture are how much screen real estate that texture is likely to occupy and how much fine detail it really needs relative to its size.

For example, if you're doing a life-size replica of the Sistine Chapel, with giant ceiling murals that are likely to fill the entire screen, and with lots of fine details that people are likely to zoom in on and study, go with 1024s by all means. However, for the parts that aren't likely to fill much of the screen, like your little donation box next to the front door that no one's gonna look at, use something MUCH smaller.

Of course, just because something will fill the screen doesn't automatically mean it demands a large texture. A brick wall, for example, is just a repeating pattern. The pattern itself doesn't need to be very big to be effective. You could paint just a few bricks in exquisite detail at maybe 128×128 and then repeat the texture across the wall surface many times via the repeat and offset settings inside SL.

If the wall needs other details embedded into it like windows, doorways, creeping vines, and so on, then it's no longer just a repeating pattern; it's a whole painting. In that case, you'll need to go larger with the texture to fit all those things in.

What you want to avoid is doing things like slapping a 1024×1024 texture on a little two-word sign that no one's ever gonna zoom in on. For that, something as small as 64×64 would probably be plenty. Always make every texture only as large as it needs to be, not one pixel more.

Again, it's all about finding the optimum balance between texture memory and texture detail. That means using good, sound judgment. Choose your texture sizes carefully. Make appropriate decisions.

## SUMMARY

We covered a lot of ground in this chapter. You learned how to texture primitives by applying the appropriate textures to all sides. You learned about advanced texture options such as mapping types, bump, and shininess. You also learned how to create your own textures, upload the textures, create textures with transparency, and create quite a few objects including a plant and T-shirt.

Texturing really creates a lot of visual magic in SL, and using good textures makes the difference between a good build and an awesome build. Try your hand at it and keep practicing. If it's not for you, don't worry; you can find free textures, buy textures at various places like LillyBeth Filth's Textures R Us, or find other resident texture artists to work with.

*You might be asking yourself if you can actually write useful scripts without spending four years earning a degree in computer science. Based on what I've seen and what I've read, you most certainly can.*

**—Jeffronius Batra**

# Making the Magic: Scripting Basics

# 8

## CHAPTER BY JEFFRONIUS BATRA

Scripting is what makes the magic in Second Life (SL). Teleport buttons, animations that come on when you sit down, fire, rain, smoke, vending machines, doors that swing open, dogs that follow you around, and vehicles all rely on scripting to make them work. The good news is, you don't need to be a developer or computer scientist to write scripts in SL. In fact, you don't have to write scripts at all to enjoy SL, but you can create some serious magic with just a few lines of the Linden Scripting Language (LSL). Jeffronius Batra kindly agreed to take us through the learning process. I'll let him take it from here.

## What You Will Learn

- The basics of the Linden Scripting Language
- The six stages of script mastery
- How to find and use scripts with no programming experience
- How to write your own scripts
- How to create a scripted door complete with sound and security
- How to create an object that gives a notecard when touched
- How to create an object that teleports your avatar when touched

# INTRODUCTION TO THE LINDEN SCRIPTING LANGUAGE

You've already learned how to create, sculpt, and texture prims. Now you're ready to take the next step: learning how to use a script to add some "magic" to your prims.

A *script* is a self-contained program that runs inside a particular prim. Scripts can initiate actions and respond to them. They can alter the size, position, shape, and other characteristics of the prim. They can even receive messages from SL users and from other prims and can respond with actions or messages of their own.

When placed inside a prim, scripts can control the behavior and appearance of that prim. Scripts can make objects move, communicate (listen/talk), or change their physical characteristics (color, texture, size, shape). Scripted prims can interact with avatars or with each other.

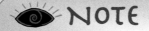

NOTE

An avatar can wear (or attach) a scripted object, but scripts cannot be placed inside an avatar.

If you're a professional programmer or if you have written code in JavaScript, Java, Visual Basic, or even C, then much of what you have already learned is relevant here. A lot of what you already know about data types, flow control, modular programming, and debugging is of use.

If you have not written any code before, don't worry. This chapter teaches you everything you need to know to start writing your own scripts. Before long you will have your prims dancing, singing, and responding to the environment in all sorts of interesting ways.

Writing scripts in SL's scripting language is actually a lot of fun. When compared to other programming environments, the commands are at a somewhat higher and more powerful level; in other words, a single command can do a lot. Because there is a physics engine at the heart of SL, you can even make your prims react to in-world physical actions such as being pushed, created, touched, or even stepped on. The prims can respond in realistic ways—falling down, moving, or changing shape—in response to these actions. Scripted prims can even animate avatars, by invoking animations!

As mentioned previously, the SL scripting language is called LSL, short for Linden Scripting Language. On the surface, it resembles procedural languages like JavaScript or Visual Basic. It has a full complement of data types and operators, includes decision-making capabilities, and features a full set of looping constructs. To this base, LSL adds advanced features that allow it to tightly integrate with the SL environment. Finally, LSL incorporates a unique state-driven processing model. This model simplifies the process of creating prims that mimic real-world objects.

## CATEGORIES OF SCRIPTED POWER

Because LSL is what is known to computer scientists as a *Turing-complete language*, it is actually impossible to create a full list of all the things it can do. Instead, let's take a look at some of the basic operations, which LSL calls *functions*. As you read the following list, you should let your mind start to imagine using any mix of these functions to accomplish your task. Indeed, one of the skills that you will develop over time is the ability to come up with a great idea and then deconstruct it into the LSL functions needed to make it happen. This is similar to the ability to look at a real-world object and to break it down (and then replicate it) using one or more prims.

Here's a list of the categories of functions available, along with a *sampling* of the kinds of functions in each category. These categories were taken directly from the home page of the LSL Wiki (http://www.lslwiki.net/lslwiki/wakka.php):

- **Agent/Avatar:** Control which avatars can be on a piece of land. Transfer money. Manage permissions. Attach and detach items from an avatar. Start and stop animations. Control sit behavior.

- **Camera:** Get or set the current camera position and rotation. Enter mouselook mode. Take or relinquish control of the camera.

- **Collision:** Detect and handle intersection of two in-world objects. Play sounds or emit particles. Receive information about the type, identity, direction, rotation, and speed of the collision.

- **Color:** Get and set a prim's color or set the color of a linked object.
- **Communications:** Pop up a dialog to ask the user a question. Listen to and originate chat messages from the user or from other prims. Encrypt and decrypt strings. Send and receive email messages. Use the HTTP or XML-RPC protocol to connect with external web services.
- **Controls:** Manage the camera. Take direct control of the keyboard or release it.
- **Detection:** Determine information about other objects and agents, as detected by sensors or events.
- **Dynamics/Movement/Physics:** Manage the physical properties of objects, including size, scale, rotation, mass, friction, rotational impulse, velocity, torque, buoyancy, and hovering.
- **Group:** Deal with group membership.
- **Inventory:** Accept inventory items. Give inventory items to others. Get information about inventory items and notecards. Create (*rez*) objects from inventory.
- **Land:** Get information about land. Manage the lists of avatars allowed on the land (the pass list) or not allowed on the land (the ban list). Eject avatars from the land. Get and also modify the height and shape of the land.
- **Light:** Get the sun direction. Get and set information about the light emitted by a prim.
- **Link:** Work with prims that are linked together. Break apart linked sets and link existing objects into a set. Set the local (root-relative) position and rotation of objects in a linked set. Handle collisions. Set color and alpha (transparency) properties of linked items.
- **List:** Manipulate lists, one of LSL's intrinsic data structures. Convert a list to and from other data types. Sort a list, randomize a list, access a single element of a list, or delete a portion of a list.
- **Math:** Compute standard mathematical functions such as log, sine, cosine, tangent, and square root.

- **Particle:** Create a particle system, a set of free-floating visual effects that can simulate special effects such as fires, explosions, steam, and even weather.
- **Primitive/Object:** Get and set the basic physical parameters that comprise a prim—size, alpha (transparency), color, and scale, along with other values such as floating text, names, and descriptions.
- **Script:** Get information about the script itself, control the script state (running or not), and deal with scripts in other prims (so-called remote scripts).
- **Sensor:** Locate (either once or on a continuous basis) other objects or agents that are nearby.
- **Simulator:** Get (and occasionally set) information about the current simulator (*sim*) including weather, simulator performance, time, sun direction, land shape, and water level. Manage playback of audio and video.
- **Sound:** Control playback of sounds (often done in response to various events).
- **String:** Manipulate strings of characters in various ways. Get the length of a string, get a portion of a string, or search for a string within another string. Convert a string to a list, and vice versa.
- **Teleport:** Show a particular location on the in-world map, set the sit target for a prim, or teleport an agent to his home location.
- **Texture:** Set textures and texture properties for all or for any face of a prim, including the texture itself, alpha level, texture rotation and offsets, and texture animation.
- **Time:** Get the in-world time and date in various formats. Arrange for periodic timer events.
- **Transformation:** Rotate, scale, and move objects in three dimensions.
- **Vehicle:** Make a primitive into an airplane, balloon, boat, car, or sled that can be controlled using the keyboard. Control a number of different vehicle parameters, each of which affects the physical properties of the vehicle in some way.
- **Video:** Play video on one or more faces of a prim.
- **Weather:** Get information about the clouds, wind, and sun at the current location.

## SIX STAGES TO SCRIPT MASTERY

If you have never written any code before, don't let all this talk of scripts and programming scare you away. The bar to entrance is very low. You can start by simply using scripts written by others. At first you can treat the contents of the script as a magic incantation that you simply utter exactly as written in order for it to have the desired effect. Before too long, you will find yourself wanting to do something better (or just different). At that point, you can take someone else's script, make a small change, and try it out to see what happens. Do this enough times, and you'll end up with a script that is almost all yours. From there, you'll be ready to create a script from scratch.

Put another way, mastery of scripting is attained in at least six stages:

1. Using existing scripted objects.

2. Using existing scripts, treating them as read-only black boxes.

3. Modifying existing scripts, using an understanding of what's inside and how it works.

4. Creating scripts from scratch.

5. Building scripts that are flexible, powerful, and general enough for other people (who may be at level one on this ladder) to use without modification.

6. Building scripts that are so useful and powerful that other SL residents will pay money to acquire them.

## CAN YOU WRITE SCRIPTS?

After reading this far, you might be asking yourself if you, possibly a nonprogrammer, can actually write useful scripts without spending four years earning a degree in computer science. Based on what I've seen and what I've read, you most certainly can. In much the same way that many web developers started out by writing HTML and then progressed to JavaScript, you can start your avocation as a SL developer by creating cool-looking prims and then proceed to bring them alive using a little bit of script.

What you'll find is that scripting is enjoyable, productive, and self-reinforcing. Your first little success with a script will give you the positive feedback and the additional self-confidence needed to try something just a little bit more complicated.

So my advice to you, dear reader, is to simply jump in. The water's fine and you'll be swimming before long.

## USING SCRIPTED OBJECTS

The easiest way to get started with scripts in SL is to simply use the scripted objects provided to you with your installation of SL. The Objects subfolder within the Library folder of your Inventory contains a number of interesting objects, many of which include scripts (see Figure 8-1).

**Figure 8-1**
*Scripted objects in the Library folder.*

Before going any further, you need to log in to SL and find an area that allows you to create your own prims and run scripts. All public sandboxes allow you to create your own prims, and most allow you to run scripts. Once you are properly situated, drag the Basic Chair to an empty space. Then right-click on the chair and choose the Sit option from the right-click pie menu. Figure 8-2 shows what I looked like after I did it.

At this point, you are probably wondering what (if anything) is so special here. The chair is actually made up of six distinct parts: four legs, a seat, and a back in a linked set of prims. The sitting position of a linked set is always specified relative to the root prim (which is always the last prim selected prior to the creation of the linked set). Without any script, a default seating position would be used. Depending on the orientation of the root prim of the linked set, this could leave me sitting upside down, sideways, or both. The script in the chair calls the `llSitTarget` function to set the avatar's position and orientation relative to the prim so that the avatar is properly situated on the chair. After changing a few of the parameters, I managed to create the (very silly) sit target shown in Figure 8-3.

**Figure 8-2**
*The result of choosing the Sit option.*

**Figure 8-3**
*The result of randomizing a few of the parameters in the Sit script.*

# USING EXISTING SCRIPTS

Another way to start working with scripts in SL is to use some existing scripts. In general, you can easily use these scripts with your own prims. In the following sections, you learn how to attach one or more existing scripts to a prim, and you also learn where to find lots of these scripts.

## DRAGGING SCRIPTS FROM THE SL LIBRARY

Once again, before going any further, you need to log in to SL and find an area that allows you to create your own prims and run scripts. The Scripts subfolder within the Library folder of your Inventory contains a couple of useful scripts (see Figure 8-4).

As you can see, I have anim SMOOTH, HoverText Clock, and Rotation Script in my Library. Your library might have additional scripts in it.

Create a prim and set up your camera so that you can see the prim and your inventory at the same time, as shown in Figure 8-5.

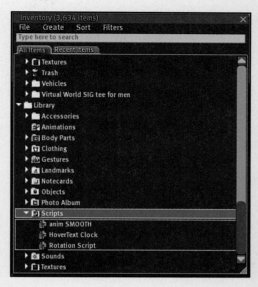

**Figure 8-4**
*Scripts in the Library folder.*

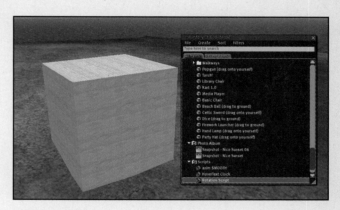

**Figure 8-5**
*View with both a prim and Script folder.*

Now drag the Rotation Script onto the prim. Put your mouse cursor over the words *Rotation Script* and mouse-down. Then drag the cursor over the prim (the edges of the prim light up, or highlight, to confirm that you're in the right place) and let go of the mouse button. After a short pause, the cube begins to rotate about the z axis in a counterclockwise direction. When you drag a script out of the Library and onto a prim, you are creating a new copy of the script inside the prim's contents section. Let's say that you create 10 prims and put the Rotation Script into each one. Later, a friend gives you a better version of the Rotation Script. You would need to replace the existing script in each prim with the new one to make use of the improved version. You can replace an existing script by simply dragging it into the prim as previously described.

A prim can actually run more than one script at a time! While the cube is still spinning, drag the HoverText Clock script onto it (see Figure 8-6). After another short pause, your cube spins (from the first script) and also displays a floating clock (from the second script).

**Figure 8-6**
*HoverTextClock on the cube.*

Although we could just delete the prim, let's learn how to manage individual scripts while we're here. Right-click on the prim and select the Edit action. Note that the cube stops rotating when you're in edit mode. Click on the Content tab (see Figure 8-7).

Select the Rotation Script in the Contents folder and hit the Delete key. The script disappears, and the cube no longer rotates.

> **TIP**
>
> If you open the Edit window and it doesn't have all the details shown in Figure 8-7, simply click on the button labeled >> More.

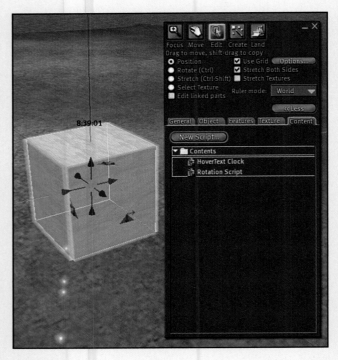

**Figure 8-7**
*The Content tab.*

At this point, you know enough to be dangerous! You can add scripts to your own prims, where they will start running at once. You also know how to remove scripts from your prims.

Let's cover a few more important scripting concepts before we wrap up this section.

Each script can be either running or not running. Nonrunning scripts are inert and lifeless; they cannot do anything. Running scripts have all the capabilities described in this chapter. You can set all the scripts in a prim as running or not running by simply selecting the object for editing and then choosing Tools->Set Scripts to Running in Selection or Tools->Set Scripts to Not Running in Selection.

Occasionally, you may find that a normally trustworthy script starts to behave a bit oddly. In many cases, you can bring it back to its senses by selecting the object and then choosing Tools->Reset Scripts in Selection. This selection brings each of the scripts in the object back to a known state.

Finally, scripts have a set of properties associated with them. These properties regulate the visibility of the code for the script, the set of users who can modify the script, and a set of options that control what happens when the script is sold or given away.

## FINDING AND REUSING GOOD SCRIPTS

Once you are familiar with the little collection of scripts that come in the SL library, you'll probably want to go find some more. A good place to start is the LSL Wiki at http://www.lslwiki.net. This Wiki contains two collections of scripts:

- **Script Library:** http://www.lslwiki.net/lslwiki/wakka.php?wakka=ScriptLibrary
- **Script Examples:** http://www.lslwiki.net/lslwiki/wakka.php?wakka=examples

The Script Library contains full scripts, whereas the Script Examples are generally fragments of scripts suitable for pasting into a script of your own.

You can also find a number of free and low-cost scripts at various in-world locations. Open the Search window, select the Places tab, and search for "script" to get started.

You need to know a bit more to get these scripts into your SL Inventory and from there into your prims. Let's walk through that process now, using the TextureSwitcher script from the LSL Wiki.

The TextureSwitcher script, when placed in a prim along with two or more textures, cycles through the textures, changing to a new texture every 30 seconds.

Open your SL Inventory and expand the My Inventory folder. Scroll down until you find the Scripts folder (see Figure 8-8).

Right-click on the Scripts folder and choose New Script (see Figure 8-9).

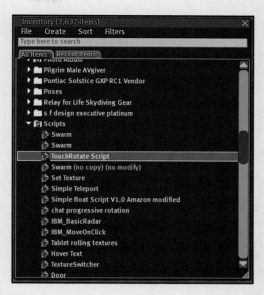

**Figure 8-8**
*The Scripts folder.*

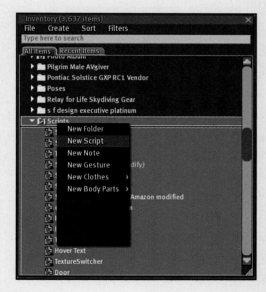

**Figure 8-9**
*Create a new script.*

When the New Script item appears in the Scripts folder, right-click on it, choose Rename, and type **Texture-Switcher**. Now double-click on TextureSwitcher to open the script editor (see Figure 8-10).

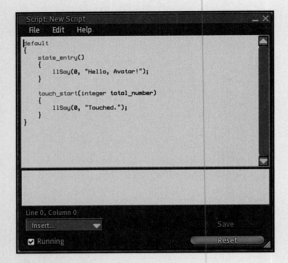

**Figure 8-10**
*Default new script.*

The script in there is a default script. Click in the editor window and then press Ctrl+A (Select All) and then Ctrl+X (Cut). Next, open the TextureSwitcher script (http://www.lslwiki.net/lslwiki/wakka.php?wakka=LibraryTextureSwitcher) and select the script (the section of the page inside the box), as shown in Figure 8-11. Now paste the script into the editor window.

You can use a similar sequence of Select/Copy/Paste operations to copy any LSL script from a web page into your Inventory and from there into a prim. You can also copy scripts directly into the prim. If you do this, take care not to delete the prim; otherwise, you lose the script along with it.

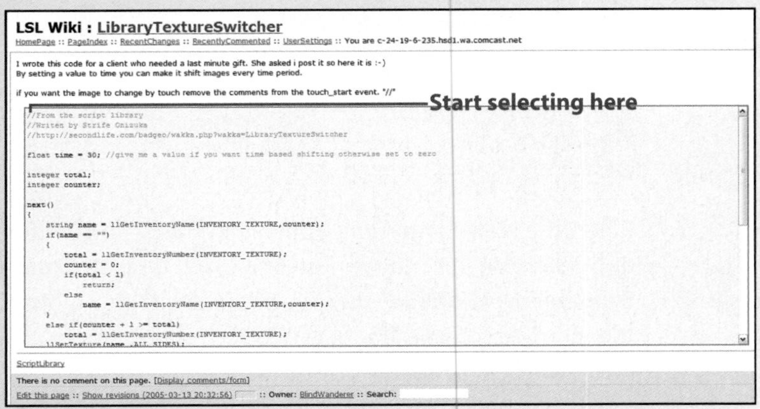

Take care to select only the actual script (the portion within the gray box). Switch back to SL and paste the contents of the Clipboard into the script editor. After you do so, it looks like the script in Figure 8-12.

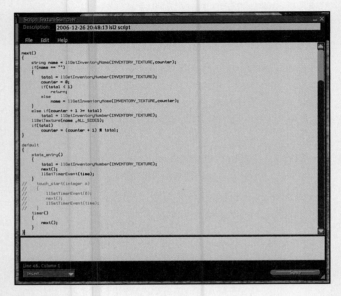

**Figure 8-12**
*The script in the script editor.*

Click the Save button, close the window, and your script is safely stored within your Inventory.

Now create a prim and add some textures to its inventory. To do this, simply open the prim's Edit window, switch to the Content tab, and drag some textures from your Inventory into the Contents folder (see Figure 8-13). If you don't have any textures of your own, scroll down to the Library part of your inventory and then open the Textures folder.

Now scroll up to your Scripts folder and drag the TextureSwitcher script into the Contents folder. Unselect the prim; then stand back and watch it do its thing (see Figure 8-14).

OK, that seems to work! Leave the prim where you created it; we return to it after we learn how to edit an existing script.

**Figure 8-11**
*Select the Texture Switcher script.*

**Figure 8-13**
*Drag some texture into the Content tab.*

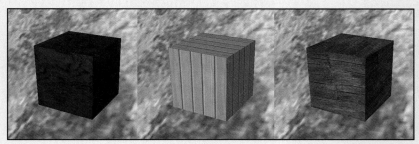

**Figure 8-14**
*The textures change over time.*

## MODIFYING EXISTING SCRIPTS

If you're at all curious, you probably scrolled through the TextureSwitcher script in an attempt to understand what it does and how it works. Let's change the script so that it changes the texture of a random face, rather than all the faces of this cube.

Right-click on the prim and choose Edit. Then open the Content tab and double-click on the TextureSwitcher script that's stored in the Contents folder. Scroll down a bit and look for the following piece of code:

```
llSetTexture(name ,ALL_SIDES);
```

This bit of code tells SL to set the texture of all the cube's sides to the texture denoted by the variable name. The value ALL_SIDES is a special constant value. When used in this context, it denotes that all the sides will be changed.

Instead of passing in this constant value, we can pass in a random value ranging from 0 to 5, denoting the various faces of the cube.

We're going to modify the script to randomly change the texture of one face at a time. For this, you cannot hard-code a fixed integer value. Instead, you modify the code to read as follows:

```
llSetTexture(name ,(integer) llFrand(6.0));
```

Make sure that you get the spelling, punctuation, and capitalization correct and then click the Save button in the lower-right corner of the script editor (see Figure 8-15).

**Figure 8-15**
*Click the Save button.*

When you click this button, the script is checked for errors and then saved. If you made any mistakes, you see some error messages in the bottom of the window. If all goes well, you see the messages shown in Figure 8-16.

Experienced LSL scripters generally make a habit of clicking the Reset button after they save their scripts after each modification. Clicking this button forces the script to "start over" and simplifies the process of creating, modifying, and debugging scripts.

**Figure 8-16**
*You should see these messages if the script saved successfully.*

> ## 👁 NOTE
>
> The code (integer) llFrand(6.0) returns an integer that is less than 6.0 (an integer between 0 and 5, inclusive), all with equal probability. The resulting, randomized integer is passed to the llSetTexture function (just as the ALL_SIDES constant was in the unedited script). As a result, the texture change occurs only on the face having that assigned integer value. If the integer returned is 0, the top face changes. If the integer is 5, the bottom face changes, and so on.

Close the Edit window and let the script run for a while. Mine looked like Figure 8-17 after 10 minutes or so.

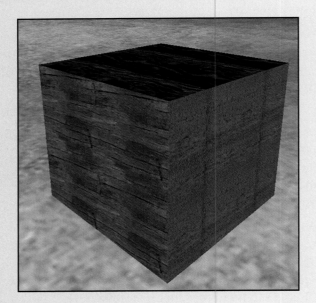

**Figure 8-17**
*My cube after 10 minutes or so.*

If you made any mistakes while you were editing the script, you get an error message when you try to save it. For example, using a capital *R* instead of a lowercase *r* when typing the name *llFrand* produces the message shown in Figure 8-18.

```
(24, 44) : ERROR : Name not defined within scope
Line 24, Column 44
```

**Figure 8-18**
*A script compilation error message.*

The values in the parentheses (24, 44) indicate that the error was detected on line 24, column 44. The error message is a clue (sometimes specific and sometimes frighteningly vague) as to what is wrong with your code. For extra credit, find the value in the code that sets the time interval between changes and reduce it to a second or two.

Modifying scripts written by others is a good way to ease into programming. If you've ever created your own web page, you're probably familiar with the View Source command. Using this command, you could look at the HTML, CSS, and JavaScript inside a web page, see how it worked, and then use what you learned as part of your own work. Once you start looking at other people's scripts, you're heading down a similar path, this time in SL.

Here are a few tips to make your exploration and modification more productive:

- **Be curious:** If you're wandering through SL and you see something unusual, stop and ask yourself if you know how to replicate the effect yourself. Think of what you already know how to do and see if it can be applied to this new situation. Consider asking the owner of the build for some information; build owners are often willing to give you a clue or even a complete copy of the script. It never hurts to ask, that's for certain.

- **Study:** Spend some time paging through the LSL reference section on the LSL Wiki. Visit other pages of the LSL Wiki and inspect some of the sample code. I have found that it is often worthwhile to read and then later reread the same language reference a couple of times. It is impossible to comprehend every detail on the first read-through, so simply read with the intention of getting an overview of the language and of learning just enough to get started. At this point, simply skip over anything you don't understand. Later, after you feel somewhat competent, read again, this time going a bit slower. You will find that a lot of the mysteries you encountered on the first read-through are no longer so mysterious.

- **Experiment:** Programming isn't supposed to be a trial-and-error proposition, but it never hurts to simply try out a few different things to see what they do. You aren't going to hurt anyone or break anything (although you can make people mad).

- **Participate:** You can often find some like-minded people hanging out at online developer forums such as the SL Scripting Tips forum at http://forums.secondlife.com/forumdisplay.php?f=54 or the SL Developer Forum at http://sldevelopers.com/forums/default.aspx . Read some postings to get an idea of what's going on, search around a bit to see if anyone else has asked a question similar to yours, and then jump right in and ask. Check back in a day or so, and there may very well be an answer there for you. If you find the forums useful, then you should, at some point, return the favor and start answering questions, too. At first, this may seem like an impossible task. Before long, however, you will find that you've actually learned quite a bit and that you do actually have the answers at your fingertips!

If you take an existing script and modify it in a useful and interesting way, consider sending the modifications back to the owner of the original script. In some cases, programmers are receptive to accepting changes from outsiders and incorporate your changes into their master copy. Don't be discouraged if this doesn't happen, however. Some programmers like to keep their own code pristine and would prefer not to take in changes from the outside. Sometimes this is done for legal reasons, sometimes it is a matter of ego, and sometimes there's no particular reason. If an author doesn't want your changes, ask her if she would allow you to distribute the modified version yourself. If you've added 5 lines to an existing 100-line script, this is probably not going to happen. However, if you've taken an existing script, hacked and slashed it so that the original is almost unrecognizable, and then cleaned it up, claiming it as your own (while acknowledging inspiration from the original script and author) may be the way to go.

# WRITING YOUR OWN SCRIPTS

At the point at which you can open the Content tab and confidently click the New Script button, you are ready to call yourself a real LSL developer. Let's get you to the point where you know the scripting system in enough detail so that you can get there in short order.

## SCRIPTS AND PRIMS

Let's begin by discussing the relationship between a prim and its scripts. A single prim can hold any number (zero or more) scripts. The prim is effectively a container for the scripts, and the scripts can operate on the prim. Many of the LSL functions operate on the prim itself. For example, there are LSL functions to rotate, move, and change the

size of a prim. Other LSL functions can operate on the linked prims associated with a root prim.

Scripts can indirectly operate on other, unrelated, prims. Doing this is a bit more complex, and it will take a little while to get you to the point where you can do this. Basically, one prim must send a message to another prim, asking it to make a change to itself.

The scripts themselves are isolated and self-contained. Scripts cannot call functions or reference variables in other scripts. In SL, unlike many other programming systems, there is no way to create a library of reusable functions in a single location and then allow any number of other scripts to call it.

## RUNNING SCRIPTS

The scripts in a prim run only when the prim has been materialized in-world. Scripts do not run when the objects are in Inventory. Also, inventoried scripts do not need to be inside objects; they can be standalone script files. Neither the script file nor the scripted object runs while in Inventory.

Scripts can exist in materialized prims in a nonrunning form. This is controlled by the Running check box at the bottom left of the Script window (see Figure 8-19). Just uncheck the box to stop the script from running.

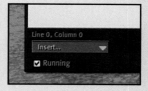

**Figure 8-19**
*The Running check box.*

If a script is saved with errors, it won't be running. Also, certain programming errors can cause a script to stop running. You can control the running mode of all scripts in a prim by using the menu options Tools->Set Scripts to Running in Selection and Tools->Set Scripts to Not Running in Selection.

## STATES

Each LSL script can also be in a particular *state*. A door might have an open state and a closed state. A car might be parked, idling, moving forward, or moving in reverse. Choosing the appropriate set of states will come naturally to you after a while. In most cases, the LSL state mechanism is a big help to you as you design and build your script. In a few cases, I have noticed that the state mechanism actually causes more problems than it solves and that writing scripts can be easier if you ignore it. The states are a programming convenience in LSL, and nothing forces you to use anything other than the default state.

It is important to realize that the scripts have states, not the prims. If we use several scripts to create a complex, drivable car with some doors, then the motion script has a set of states that are independent of the states used by the door script. The doors can be open while the car is in motion.

Each script has one initial state that is known as the *default*. If you don't create any more states, then your script remains in this state. If you create a prim with a script, store that prim in your inventory, and then create a fresh copy from there, then the script is reset to the default state. The scripts are also reset when they are saved after being edited. Note that the Tools menu contains the Reset Scripts in Selection Command. Simply select one or more scripted prims and then choose this command.

States are declared within the script as follows:

```
default
{
}

state Open
{
}

state Closed
{
}
```

## EVENTS

LSL allows you to write code to handle certain types of events that happen to the prim from in-world. Events are often used as triggers—for example, signaling to a script that an avatar has interacted with an object in-world. The code to do this is known as an *event handler*. The handlers exist within a given state; this allows you to easily customize the response based on the current state of the object. Returning to our door example, if the door is in the closed state and it is touched, it should open. If the door

is in the open state and it is touched, it should close. Of course, the event handlers should also alter the door's state to match its position. We will see how to do this before too long.

Here are some of the situations in which an event handler can be called:

- When an object is attached to or detached from an agent
- When certain attributes of an object are changed
- When an object collides with another object or with land
- When an object receives external data
- When an object receives email
- When an object hears a chat message
- When an object receives money
- When an object is created or creates another object
- When an object detects the presence of an avatar or another object nearby
- When an object is touched by an avatar
- When an object enters or exits a state
- When a certain time period has passed

Event handlers are created within the scope of a particular state. By creating them this way, you can have a distinct response for each event that is specific to a particular state. Here are some event handlers:

```
default
{
    touch_start(integer n)
    {
    }
}

state Open
{
    touch_start(integer n)
    {
    }
}

state Closed
{
    touch_start(integer n)
    {
    }
}
```

## DATA TYPES

LSL can store seven distinct types of data:

- Integers
- Floats
- Strings
- Keys
- Vectors
- Rotations
- Lists

Let's look at each one in turn. If you've written code in other languages, you are probably familiar with integers, floats, and strings. If you've studied advanced math, you may know about vectors and rotations.

**Integers** are whole numbers, stored with 32 bits of precision. They can range from approximately negative 2 billion to positive 2 billion. Here are some good integers: –100, 0, and 256.

**Floats** are decimal numbers, also stored in 32 bits. Floats can be negative or positive, with values that range from the very small ($1.1 \times 10^{-38}$) to the very large ($3.4 \times 10^{38}$). Here are some float values: –123.3, 0.0, 1E3, and 1000. Note that 1E3 and 1000 represent the same value, since 1E3 is a shorthand way to write the value $1 \times 10^3$, and $10^3$ is 1000.

**Strings** contain arbitrary sequences of characters, delimited by double quotation marks. The length of a string is limited only by available memory. The empty string is written as a pair of adjacent quotation marks. Here are some string values: `"Bob"`, `"1234"`, and `"Hello"`. Note that the string `"1234"` is not the same as the integer with the value 1234.

**Keys** are special strings known as GUIDs, or Globally Unique Identifiers. In this case, Global refers to the entire SL world. Every avatar, texture, and prim has a GUID all to itself. For example, my avatar's key is 2558a927-53cf-4a95-8baf-d5963cadc22f. The individual characters within the key are of no particular significance on their own.

A **vector** is made up of three float values named x, y, and z. A vector can represent a position, a direction, a force, a scale, a color, or a Euler rotation. Vectors are specified using the < character, three comma-separated floats, and then a final >. Here are some vectors: <–1.0, 2.0, –3.0>, <–10, –20, 300>, and <0, 0, 0>. The vector with the value <0, 0, 0> can also be written as `ZERO_VECTOR`.

A **rotation** is made up of four float values: x, y, z, and s. These four values specify the quaternion rotation of an object in three-dimensional space. Rotations are specified using the < character, four comma-separated floats, and then a final >. Here are some rotations: <0, 1.0, –2.0, 0.5>, <0.0, 0.0, 1.0, –0.25>, and <0, 0, 0, 1.0>. The final value can also be written as `ZERO_ROTATION`.

A **list** contains an ordered sequence of values. A list cannot contain another list as a member, but it can contain everything else. Each element of a list has a type of its own, so it is perfectly reasonable to have a list that starts with an integer, has a string in the middle, and then has a vector on the end. Such a list would be written like this: [123, "Four Five Six", <7.0, 8.0, 9.0>]. The [ character introduces the list, and the ] character ends the list.

## VARIABLES

Scripts use variables to hold information. Each variable has a name, a type, and a value. The name is often suggestive of what's inside. Speed, Cost, and Height are all good variable names, while X17, ZZZ, and Ooops are probably not. The name must start with an upper- or lowercase letter, followed by up to 254 more letters, digits, and the underscore (_) character. The case of the letters is significant; x and X are two distinct variables. Variables are of a particular type: integer, string, key, vector, rotation, or list.

Each variable must be declared before it is used. Declaring a variable specifies its name and its type, and can optionally specify an initial value. Here are some sample variable declarations:

```
integer a;
integer b = 10;

float c;
float d = 15.0;

string e;
string f = "I am F";
```

```
vector g;
vector h = <1.0, 2.0, 3.0>;

rotation j;
rotation k = <1.0, 2.0, 3.0, 0.5>;

list l;
list m = [b, d, f, h, k];
```

## PREDEFINED FUNCTIONS

As we discussed earlier in this chapter, LSL includes many predefined functions. These functions all have names that start with 11, for Linden Lab. All functions accept a list of inputs and can optionally return a value to the calling program. For example, the 11ToLower function accepts a single string as an argument and returns another string as its result. Here's how 11ToLower is called:

```
string U = "Hello How Are You?";
string V = 11ToLower(U);
```

Here's a little script that uses 11ToLower to display the name of the avatar who touched the prim:

```
default
{
    touch_start(integer n)
    {
        string AvName = 11DetectedName(0);
        string LowerAvName = 11ToLower(AvName);

        11Say(0, "Your original name is " +
            AvName);
        11Say(0, "Your lower cased name is " +
            LowerAvName);
    }
}
```

This code also uses the 11DetectedName function to get the name of the avatar on the other end of the "touch," and 11Say to send out a message on chat channel 0.

Here's the output I saw when I put the code into a prim, saved it, and then touched the prim:

```
[22:21]  Object: Your original name is
         Jeffronius Batra
[22:21]  Object: Your lower cased name is
         jeffronius batra
```

There are hundreds of LSL functions, and it doesn't make sense to list them all here. Instead, refer to http://www.lslwiki.net/lslwiki/wakka.php?wakka=functions for a complete and current list. You can also access a complete list of functions via the Insert menu found within the script editor.

## USER-DEFINED FUNCTIONS

You can also define your own functions. These are called, naturally enough, *user-defined functions*. User-defined functions are declared outside any particular state because they can be used from any state. You should use user-defined functions when you find yourself doing the same thing more than once in a single script. Instead of repeating the code several times, simply create a function. This approach has several benefits. First, any future changes need be made only once. Second, when compiled, your script occupies less space.

Here is a script with a user-defined function:

```
string MakeGreeting(string Name)
{
    string LowerName = 11ToLower(Name);
    string Greeting = "Hello " + LowerName + "!";

    return Greeting;
}

default
{
    touch_start(integer n)
    {
        string AvName = 11DetectedName(0);
        11Say(0, MakeGreeting(AvName));
    }

    collision_start(integer n)
    {
        string AvName = 11DetectedName(0);
        11Say(0, MakeGreeting(AvName));
    }
}
```

The function MakeGreeting accepts a single string as its argument, and it returns another string as its result. It takes the input string, converts it to lowercase, and then uses it to form a greeting. The resulting greeting is then returned as the function's result.

The function is called from two locations in the script. The touch_start event handler and the collision_start event handler are actually identical. Each one simply retrieves the name of the associated avatar, calls

`MakeGreeting` to create the greeting, and then displays the greeting. If we wanted to make a change in the displayed greeting (perhaps we want to show it in all uppercase instead), then we would change it in one place.

Now, you might look at the event handlers and realize that there's still some duplicate code. Great observation! We can further simplify the code as follows:

```
IssueGreeting()
{
    string AvName = llDetectedName(0);
    string LowerName = llToLower(AvName);
    string Greeting = "Hello " + LowerName + "!";

    llSay(0, Greeting);
}

default
{
    touch_start(integer n)
    {
        IssueGreeting();
    }

    collision_start(integer n)
    {
        IssueGreeting();
    }
}
```

As you write your first LSL scripts, you may often find yourself arranging and rearranging code throughout the process. This is a reasonable and natural thing to do. Quite often, you don't know how to best solve the problem until you are almost finished solving it. Your first few programs may look a bit battle-scarred as you cut, copy, and paste. As you gain experience, you will find that it is worth taking the time to neaten up your code as you go. Developing a sense of pride in the aesthetic and structural aspects of your code will come with experience. Code that looks neat and clean doesn't run any better, but your perception of the code as either clean and structured or messy and disorganized can undoubtedly affect your desire to continue working on it. If you find that your code has become a rat's nest, by all means take the time to clean it up.

# TUTORIAL: SCRIPTING A DOOR

This tutorial begins as a simple door script that opens and closes the door in response to a touch. We add features to it on a step-by-step basis until the door closes automatically after a predetermined time, plays sounds as it opens and closes, and also refuses to open for certain "bad guys."

## STEP 1: FIRST FIND OR BUILD A DOOR

We've got a nice wall with a door in it, and we want to make the door slide open and closed when the user touches it (see Figure 8-20).

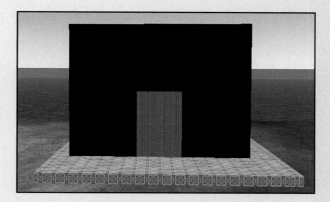

**Figure 8-20**
*The wall with the door in it.*

## STEP 2: PUT THE DOOR IN CLOSED POSITION

Start by putting the door into the closed position and recording its position. To do this, right-click on the door and choose Edit from the menu. Select the Object tab and then write down the three position values (see Figure 8-21).

**Figure 8-21**
*The three position values.*

In my case, the door's closed position is the vector <206.718, 149.262, 22.625>.

## STEP 3: PUT THE DOOR IN OPEN POSITION

Now, move the door until it is in the desired open position and then record the position. My door's open position is <206.718, 151, 22.625>.

## STEP 4: ADD A SCRIPT

Put the following script into the door, but edit CLOSED_POSITION and OPEN_POSITION to reflect your door. If you don't do this, your door will fly off into never-never land, possibly never to be seen again!

```
vector CLOSED_POSITION = <206.718, 149.262,
22.625>;
vector OPEN_POSITION = <206.718, 151, 22.625>;

default
{
    state_entry()
    {
        state Closed;
    }
}

state Closed
{
    state_entry()
    {
        llSetPos(CLOSED_POSITION);
    }

    touch_start(integer n)
    {
        state Open;
    }
}

state Open
{
    state_entry()
    {
        llSetPos(OPEN_POSITION);
    }

    touch_start(integer n)
    {
        state Closed;
    }
}
```

## STEP 5: TEST THE BASIC DOOR

Close the script editor and get out of edit mode. Touch the door and it opens (see Figure 8-22). Touch it again and it closes. Magic, isn't it?

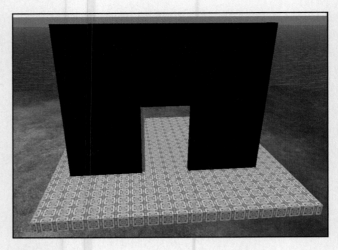

**Figure 8-22**
*The door opens and closes like magic.*

So what's going on here? Let's take this script apart piece by piece and see how it works. CLOSED_POSITION and OPEN_POSITION are effectively constant vectors; they are set once when the script starts and never changed.

The script has three states: default, Closed, and Open. Note that each script has a state_entry event handler. The handler for the default state simply sets the current state to be the Closed state. This causes the state_entry handler for the Closed state to be executed.

When this handler runs, it calls the llSetPos function to set the door's position to the value set in the CLOSED_POSITION vector. This is all that need be done to make the door appear to be closed.

Note that the Open and Closed states each have a touch_start event handler. LSL ensures that the proper handler is run, based on the current state of the script. If the door is closed, then the touch_start handler in the Closed block runs. If the door is open, then the touch_start handler in the Open block runs.

## STEP 6: ADD AN AUTO-CLOSE FUNCTION

Let's enhance the script so that the door doesn't stay open forever. If you have kids, you probably wish that your real-world house had some doors like this! We use a 10-second timer, activating it when the door opens. When the timer expires, the door is closed automatically.

Replace the existing code for the Open state with this new code:

```
state Open
{
    state_entry()
    {
        llSetPos(OPEN_POSITION);
        llSetTimerEvent(10);
    }

    touch_start(integer n)
    {
        llSetTimerEvent(0);
        state Closed;
    }

    timer()
    {
        state Closed;
    }
}
```

When the door is opened, llSetTimerEvent is used to start a 10-second timer. When the timer counts down to 0, the timer event handler is called. The handler simply sets the door to closed.

If the user touches the door to close it, the timer is canceled by calling llSetTimerEvent with a zero time. If we didn't do this, the timer would fire after the door was closed, and the door would simply close again. Not a big deal in this particular case, but cleaning up after yourself is always good programming practice.

## STEP 7: ADD SOUND!

If you've ever watched *Star Trek*, you might be thinking that it would be cool if the door made a whooshing sound as it opens and closes. Fear not; we can make it do that!

The SL Library includes a number of predefined sounds. For simplicity, we use a couple of these sounds. With a little more work, you can record, upload, and then use sounds of your own.

After some experimentation, I found that the sounds named Gasp Female and Gasp Male actually sound like an air-powered *Star Trek* door. It is a simple matter to play the appropriate sounds as the door is opened and closed. Here are the relevant parts of the script:

```
state Closed
{
    state_entry()
    {
        llSetPos(CLOSED_POSITION);
        llPlaySound("90dd885b-fb70-4857-bec6-
        252ec7a4f3d8", 1.0);
    }

    …
}

state Open
{
    state_entry()
    {
        llSetPos(OPEN_POSITION);
        llPlaySound("0107a560-e2c3-699b-0488-
                    1f63f7b06b76", 1.0);
        llSetTimerEvent(10);
    }

    …
}
```

All it takes is a pair of calls to llPlaySound—one when the door opens and another when it closes. The first value passed to the function is called the Asset ID. This is a value of type key. You can obtain the keys by right-clicking on the sound in the Inventory window and choosing the Copy Asset UUID command (see Figure 8-23).

**Figure 8-23**
*The Copy Asset UUID command.*

A simple Paste then inserts the Asset ID into the script.

## STEP 8: ADD A LOCK

Perhaps we want to stop certain avatars from opening the door. We can keep a list of bad guys (and gals) in the script and then check this list before opening the door. This is easy to do. First, we need a list of bad guys and a little function to see if a name is on the list:

```
list BadGuys = ["Amazon Link", "Yoz Linden"];

integer BadGuy(string Name)
{
    if (llListFindList(BadGuys, [Name]) != -1)
```

```
    {
        return TRUE;
    }
    else
    {
        return FALSE;
    }
}
```

The `BadGuy` function uses the built-in `llListFindList` function to search the `BadGuys` list for the given name. The function's second argument must be a list, so the string is converted to a list by enclosing it in square brackets as `[Name]`. Note that Yoz Linden is actually a perfectly nice guy; I just thought that it would be fun to stop him from opening the door.

If `llListFindList` returns a value other than `-1`, then the given name is on the `BadGuys` list, and the function returns the value `TRUE`. Otherwise, the given name isn't on the list, and the function returns the value `FALSE`.

Now, all we have to do is call the function when the user tries to open the door (the `state_entry` handler didn't change and is not shown):

```
state Closed
{

    ...

    touch_start(integer n)
    {
        if (BadGuy(llDetectedName(0)))
        {
            llPlaySound("ddab3fc2-2146-f866-734e-
            a6f99e2185c5", 1.0);
        }
        else
        {
            state Open;
        }
    }
}
```

If the user is a bad guy, then the door stays in the `Closed` state, and the indicated sound (a woman saying "Get lost!") is played. Otherwise, the door is set to open.

So let's say one of your so-called friends turns out to be a pest, and you want to keep him from opening the door. Simply add his avatar name to the `BadGuys` list:

```
list BadGuys = ["Amazon Link", "Yoz Linden",
"Cranston Ganache"];
```

If you need to block dozens or hundreds of people, you need to come up with a more sophisticated solution. Your door script could call out to an external web service. The web service could consult a database of bad guys and return an appropriate value to the program. This would also be a good technique to use if you had a number of doors and you didn't want to edit the script in each one of them to add another bad guy.

# TUTORIAL: GIVING A NOTE ON TOUCH

In this tutorial, we create a script that gives users a note-card when they touch the script's prim. You've probably seen scripts like this in action in stores and clubs. It is also useful for creating informational signs. A slightly more aggressive version can actually detect your presence and hand you the card without any action on your part. I actually consider this just a little bit rude, so this tutorial requires a touch!

## STEP 1: CREATE A DISPENSER PRIM

Begin by creating a prim of the desired shape, size, and texture. I made a tall pyramid (see Figure 8-24).

**Figure 8-24**
*A pyramid notecard dispenser prim.*

## STEP 2: CREATE A NOTECARD

Open your Inventory (Ctrl+I is a handy shortcut). Pull down the Create menu and choose New Note. When the new notecard appears, type the desired text and fill in the Description at the top as well (see Figure 8-25).

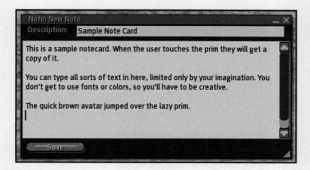

**Figure 8-25**
*A sample notecard.*

Click the Save button and then close the notecard by clicking on the X at the top-right corner.

## STEP 3: PUT THE NOTECARD INTO THE PRIM'S INVENTORY

Make sure that your Inventory window is open. Scroll down so that the Notecards folder is visible.

Right-click on the prim and choose Edit; then select the Contents tab.

Arrange the Edit window and the Inventory window to make it easy to drag items from one to the other (see Figure 8-26).

Now click on the new note (mine has the default name, New Note) and, without letting go of the mouse, drag the notecard into the Contents folder. Let go of the mouse, and the notecard is copied into the prim's inventory, as shown in Figure 8-27.

You can do further editing on the notecard by simply opening up the prim's inventory, double-clicking, editing, and then saving.

**Figure 8-26**
*Arrange the Edit window and the Inventory window so they are side by side.*

**Figure 8-27**
*The notecard is copied into the prim's inventory.*

## STEP 4: ADD A SCRIPT

Create the following script in the prim:

```
default
{
    state_entry()
    {
        llSetText("Touch The Pyramid for a
        Notecard", <0, 1.0, 0>, 1.0);
    }
```

```
touch_start(integer total_number)
{
    llGiveInventory(llDetectedKey(0),
llGetInventoryName(INVENTORY_NOTECARD, 0));
    }
}
```

This is a simple script. When the script is reset, the `state_entry` code is run. This code uses the `llSetText` function to create a text label that floats over the pyramid. The text for the label is specified in the first argument. The second argument (`<0, 1.0, 0>`) is a single element of type vector. This composite value specifies the text color in RGB format. This value specifies that the text will be displayed in blue. The third argument (`1.0`) specifies that the text will be fully opaque. When an avatar touches the prim, the `touch_start` code is run. Although this function has just one line of code, it actually calls three distinct LSL functions. Let's review them in the order that they are activated.

First, the `llDetected` key is used to return the key of the avatar who is doing the touching. Each and every SL avatar has a unique key that unambiguously identifies the avatar.

Next, `llGetInventoryName` is used to retrieve the name of the first notecard in the prim's inventory. If your application requires you to have more than one notecard in the prim's inventory, you would have to write a bit more code here.

Finally, `llGiveInventory` hands the notecard to the avatar. SL displays the notecard so the user can read it.

# TUTORIAL: TELEPORTING

In this tutorial, we create a script that will teleport an avatar from one place to another when a prim is clicked. A collection of such prims can be used to create a navigation system for a SL build.

The script that we use actually has the destination coordinates hard-coded inside and allows teleportation only within the bounds of a single sim. If you're creating a build that will use the script, be sure to finalize the positions of your teleport destinations before you start creating the teleporters.

## STEP 1: CREATE A TELEPORT PRIM

Begin by creating a prim of the desired shape, size, and texture. I was hungry, so I made a donut (see Figure 8-28).

**Figure 8-28**
*A donut prim.*

## STEP 2: SET THE PRIM'S ACTION TO SIT

Right-click on your prim, choose Edit, and left-click on the General tab. In the bottom left, select Sit on Object as the When Left-Clicked action (see Figure 8-29).

**Figure 8-29**
*Set Left-Clicked Action to Sit on Object. After you make this change, left-clicking on the prim is the same as right-clicking on it and choosing the Sit action from the menu.*

## STEP 3: DETERMINE DESTINATION COORDINATES

While staying within the bounds of the current sim, walk, run, or fly to the desired teleporting destination, and then record the coordinates. I walked over to the lamp, as shown in Figure 8-30, and then copied the coordinates out of the menu bar.

Figure 8-31 shows the menu bar.

My target coordinates are 234 (X), 135 (Y), and 21 (Z).

**Figure 8-30**
*I walked over to the lamp.*

Amazon Developers 1 234, 135, 21 (Mature) - Amazon Developer Island

**Figure 8-31**
*The coordinates in the menu bar.*

## STEP 4: ADD A SCRIPT

Put the following script into the Teleport prim but edit the Dest vector to reference your actual target coordinates:

```
vector Dest = <234, 135, 21>;

default
{
    state_entry()
    {
        float OffsetX;
        float OffsetY;
        float OffsetZ;
        vector Pos;

        llSetRot(ZERO_ROTATION);
        llSetSitText("Teleport");

        Pos = llGetPos();
        OffsetX = Dest.x - Pos.x;
        OffsetY = Dest.y - Pos.y;
        OffsetZ = Dest.z - Pos.z;
```

```
        llSitTarget(<OffsetX, OffsetY,OffsetZ>,
        ZERO_ROTATION);
    }

    touch_start(integer total_number)
    {
        llResetScript();
    }

    on_rez(integer num)
    {
        llResetScript();
    }

    changed(integer change)
    {
        if (change & CHANGED_LINK)
        {
            llUnSit(llAvatarOnSitTarget());
            llResetScript();
        }
    }
}
```

Test the script by clicking on the prim. Your avatar is instantaneously transported to the desired destination.

Although this is a fairly short script, it uses several SL features in nonobvious ways. Let's take it apart and see how it works.

The Dest vector specifies the target coordinates within the current sim.

When the script is reset, freshly rezzed, or touched, the state_entry function is called. The high-level goal of this script is to set the prim's sit target. The sit target is a point relative to the center of the prim that specifies where the avatar will be positioned when it sits on the prim.

Note that the sit target is a property of the prim. Once the script has run, the sit target remains set even if the script is deleted. If you change a prim's sit target and later find that you need to reset it, use this code:

```
llSitTarget(<0, 0, 0>, ZERO_ROTATION);
```

The teleport script begins by resetting the prim's rotation and setting the "sit text" to "Teleport." The sit text is displayed in the right-click menu for the prim (see Figure 8-32).

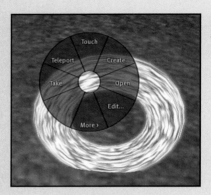

**Figure 8-32**
*Menu label changed to Teleport.*

**Figure 8-33**
*The avatar sitting.*

Recall from step 2 that we set the prim's left-click action to Sit on Object. When you left-click on the prim or when you right-click and choose Teleport, you are actually saying that you want to sit on the prim.

That's where the sit target comes into play. The sit target need not specify a position on the prim. In fact, the avatar can sit far away from the prim if necessary. The distance between the current location and the desired teleport destination is used as the sit target. This is computed as follows:

```
Pos = llGetPos();
OffsetX = Dest.x - Pos.x;
OffsetY = Dest.y - Pos.y;
OffsetZ = Dest.z - Pos.z;

llSitTarget(<OffsetX, OffsetY,OffsetZ>,
           ZERO_ROTATION);
```

Pos is the current position, and Dest is the desired position. Subtracting the current position from the desired position tells us how far from the teleport prim we need to place the sit target.

Once the sit target has been established, sitting on the prim places the avatar at the actual teleport destination. As far as SL is concerned, the avatar is logically sitting on the prim, even if the avatar is many meters away from it! Once you understand what is happening here, the entire script should begin to make sense to you.

Sitting is great, but we can't leave the avatar like it is shown in Figure 8-33. That looks silly, and it hurts my legs, too.

The changed event is used to return the avatar to its standing position. This event is invoked after the sit action is complete and the avatar is in the new position. The llAvatarOnSitTarget function is called to figure out the identity of the avatar, and then llUnSit is used to make him (or her) stand up! If you would like to experiment, comment out the call to llUnSit and try the teleport again.

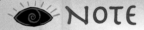

**NOTE**

This script was supplied by SL resident Peter Newell of Metaversatility.com.

## TELEPORTING TO OTHER SIMS

As of this writing, there's no way to create a script that can teleport the avatar to an arbitrary sim with a single click. The easiest way to implement this type of teleport is to use the llMapDestination function. This function highlights the desired destination on the SL map. The user can then click the Teleport button to go to the destination. This approach is not very elegant, but it definitely gets the job done.

# SUMMARY

Scripting is what makes the magic in SL. There are so many options and capabilities that there will surely be multiple books to come covering LSL in depth. In this chapter, we gave you an overview of LSL and how you can start using scripts without having any development background. We walked through several common applications of scripting in tutorials such as opening/closing a door, giving someone a notecard, and creating teleport buttons. We cover other scripting options such as Particles and Vehicles later in this book.

The key to getting started with scripting is to find scripts that are close to what you need and modify them to your own purpose. After studying and reusing scripts for a while, you'll be ready to write your own. So, get in-world and start creating some magic of your own!

*My first homes in SL were living with friends. I shared a home with one person, then split an apartment rental.*

**—Ceera Murakami**

# Land Ownership, Terraforming, and Landscaping

# 9

You can have a lot of fun in Second Life without ever owning land, but at some point the bug will catch you and you'll decide to set down roots. I have interviewed some who were here for months without buying land and others who bought something their second day. I myself lasted perhaps as long as two weeks.

This chapter helps you understand land sales and rental basics. It guides you in finding your first plot, and doing something with it that will please you even months later.

In my opinion, owning a piece of virtual land is one of the biggest pleasures available in SL. It's even more so when you can share it with your SL friends.

## What You Will Learn

- The advantages of owning land
- The differences between the mainland and estate land
- The difference between renting and buying
- How to go about locating a new piece of land
- How to terraform and landscape your new plot
- How to build a waterfall and pond to enjoy
- How to find your first house

**Figure 9-1**
*Julia Hathor.*

Julia Hathor (see Figure 9-1) had this to say on the topic:

**Julia Hathor**: I was landless for the first 6 months. In fact, when I started I told someone that I would never own land, I thought it was a stupid expense. It isn't. I can walk across this island and it is like meditating to me.

On the opposite end of this spectrum, I met Fabs McAlpine by accident as he passed through my land (see Figure 9-2). He emphatically stated *"I sleep on my horse's back."* There is no one right way to look at land ownership in SL, but I expect most of you will enjoy owning land, so let's get started.

Fabs McAlpine: I sleep on my horse's back

**Figure 9-2**
*Fabs McAlpine.*

# LAND OWNERSHIP AND THE SL ECONOMY

SL has an economy and a currency, the Linden dollar, or L$. There is an established exchange rate, which allows you to convert real-life money (US$) to SL money (L$) and vice versa. The exchange rate, since I have been here, has hovered between L$250–300 for US$1. So, for example, something in SL that costs L$250 will cost you one buck! This book is not about the business or economy of SL, so I won't go into any more detail other than to note that you can find ample economic data, charts, and graphs on the SL website if you're interested.

In SL, like RL, you can buy or rent land. The pros and cons are the same as in RL. When renting, you can just stop paying rent if you decide to move to a new location or leave SL. If you have purchased land, you will need to sell it should you decide to change locations or leave SL.

> **NOTE**
>
> You can easily abandon land, which returns to Linden Lab ownership if you like, but you're essentially throwing away money.

To become a land owner in SL, you buy the land using L$. After you purchase the land, there is typically a monthly fee associated with your land ownership. Usually, the more land you own, the more you pay. The cost per square meter goes down the more land you own.

Unless you're lucky enough to find some benefactor, *land ownership will put an end to your free SL existence*! Thousands (maybe millions) have purchased and own land in SL, and it is not really all that expensive compared to your cable or cell phone bills. Before you rush out and buy a plot of land, however, you should consider what you plan to use your land for; you also should take into account a few other key considerations, such as your budget:

- **Budget:** Think about how much you want to spend. If you want to buy land, there is an initial purchase price, plus reoccurring land-use fees. You may also need to upgrade to a premium SL account.

- **Size in square meters:** How much land do you need for your project?

- **Intended use:** Are you planning to use the land for commercial operations (a store), residential (a home), or both? Will the content and activities on this land be rated PG, or will you have mature content and activities?

- **Mainland versus private island/estate:** We will spend a lot of time on this choice, but basically do you want to own on the mainland and pay Linden Lab? Or do you want to own a private island or estate land and pay another SL resident or corporation?

- **Terraforming flexibility, such as height limits and texture:** What do you want the land to look like, and can you raise or lower it the amount you want? What texture is on the ground, and can you change it?

- **Degree of freedom:** What are the covenants or rental agreements? Are there any zoning issues, community codes of behavior, or role-playing restrictions you need to be aware of? Typically, you are mostly free to do what you want on the mainland.

- **Level of control:** Do you need to control parcel settings such as security, music (audio feed), parcel divide/join, no-flight, and so on?

- **Prim demands:** How many prims do you think you need for your build? How many prims does the land support? Is there other available land in the same sim that you could buy to support a higher concentration of prims?

- **Ease of moving/leaving SL:** If you want to leave SL or move to another location, how easy does it need to be to get out of your commitment?

- **Payment mechanism:** Fee payment may come in different forms, some of which work better for you. Consider, currency, PayPal requirements, L$ or US$, and so on.

There are two primary land ownership options available: owning land on the mainland and owning land on an island/estate. You may also choose to own an entire island estate, which is covered only briefly in this chapter.

With ownership on the mainland, you pay land-use fees directly to Linden Lab. With estate land, you pay land-use fees to another SL resident or corporation unaffiliated with Linden Lab. Let's look at each in more detail and explore the pros and cons. At the end of the chapter, we discuss rentals.

# MAINLAND LIVING

The mainland is a set of joined regions that form continents with lakes, rivers, and roads surrounded by seas. The mainland is under the control of Linden Lab, and land-use fees are paid directly to them. In the following sections, we discuss the requirements for ownership on the mainland (a premium account), mainland usage fees, the controls you have over mainland property you own, mainland prim limits, and how to buy mainland property.

## PREMIUM ACCOUNT REQUIREMENTS

Ownership on the mainland follows some clear guidelines. To own mainland property, you must have a premium account (http://secondlife.com/whatis/plans.php). As of this writing, this level of membership comes with a signup bonus, weekly stipend, and *the right to own mainland property*. To sweeten the deal, premium accounts are granted the right to own up to 512 square meters of mainland property, without incurring additional fees. Premium accounts as of this writing cost $9.95 if you pay monthly, less if you pay for the whole or a part of the year.

Linden Lab on premium accounts: "Well consider that the L$1200 stipend per month (around USD$4.50) plus 512m free tier per month (around USD$5.00) means that the monthly premium account essentially pays for itself."

Listen up! Paying for a premium account grants you only the right to own 512m of land. LL does **not** give the land to you. You must find and purchase the land on your own. Depending on where you buy, this can be expensive. As in RL, the most important factors are location, location, location.

## MAINLAND USAGE FEES (YOUR TIER)

By signing up for a premium account, you have the right to use up to 512m of land with no additional fees. However, the moment you own more than 512m of land, you will start paying an additional fee called your *tier*. This is also extremely important to understand! Tier is calculated based on the maximum amount of land you held at any moment during the previous 30 days. Say you hold 1024m of land on Sunday at 10 a.m. SLT. At 10:05 a.m., you buy another 1024m of land. Then at 10:10 a.m., you sell your original land. You will be charged a land-use fee for 2048m – 512m (premium account bonus) of land even though you held that much land for only 5 minutes!

Table 9-1 outlines the mainland-use fees as of this writing. You can find the latest information at http://secondlife.com/whatis/landpricing.php.

**Table 9-1    Mainland Usage Fees: Requires Premium Level Membership (05/26/2007)**

| ALLOWED HOLDINGS (M$^2$) | MONTHLY LAND-USE FEE |
|---|---|
| 512 m$^2$ | US$0 |
| 1024 m$^2$ | US$5 |
| 1536 m$^2$ | US$8 |
| 2,560 m$^2$ | US$15 |
| 4,608 m$^2$ | US$25 |
| 8,704 m$^2$ | US$40 |
| 16,896 m$^2$ | US$75 |
| 33,280 m$^2$ | US$125 |
| 66,048 m$^2$ | US$195 |

You can see the fees are graduated to offer a quantity discount as more land is acquired. If your holdings fall between two tiers, you'll be charged at the higher tier level.

## MAINLAND PARCEL PRIM ALLOWANCE

Another important point to know is that each plot of land can support a certain number of prims (refer to Chapter 6, "Building Basics"). Mainland regions are 16 acres (65,536 m$^2$). Each region is simulated by a single server that supports a maximum of 15,000 prims. These prims are evenly distributed across the region's area. The maximum prim load for any parcel, therefore, can be calculated by using the following formula (rounding down):

$$\text{Parcel Size} \ast [15{,}000 \text{ prims} / 65{,}536 \text{ m}^2] = \text{Prims Supported}$$

Table 9-2 does the math for common land parcel sizes.

**Table 9-2    Prims Supported Based on Parcel Size**

| LAND PARCEL SIZE (M$^2$) | PRIMS SUPPORTED |
|---|---|
| 512 | 117 |
| 1024 | 234 |
| 2048 | 469 |
| 4096 | 938 |
| 8192 | 1875 |
| 16,384 | 3750 |
| 32,768 | 7500 |
| 65,536 | 15,000 |

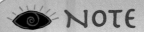 NOTE

You might be surprised to see 16m$^2$ parcels for sale. For what purpose would you want to own a property that supports only three prims? These areas are typically used as *ad farms*, which are tiny, side-by-side parcels displaying commercial advertisement. Some people consider these parcels a tremendous eyesore that ruins the SL landscape; others find them to be a great means to market their goods or services throughout the world. When you purchase on the mainland, you might just find them on a neighboring parcel.

To check the number of prims a land parcel supports, select World->About Land. Look at the Objects tab under Primitives Parcel Supports.

One final thing to know, if you own multiple parcels on the mainland *within the same region*, you can distribute your combined prim allotment in any manner you see fit. You can use prims from one parcel to supplement another. That is, you can exceed a parcel's prim allowance, provided you don't go over your total combined allotment for all parcels you own within that same region. It is *not* uncommon for players to buy land that they never develop but, instead, use the prim allowance to enhance a build elsewhere on the region.

## MAINLAND FREEDOM AND CONTROL

When you own on the mainland, there are no covenants zoning the use or resale of your property. You may sell it freely and use it for any purpose. You can set up ban lines to restrict others' access, control your own music stream, define your parcel as a "no fly" zone, prohibit visitors from running scripts or placing objects, subdivide the lot, construct a neon pink skypad, or whatever. As always, your behavior is bound to SL's Terms of Service and Community Standards (which include guidelines regarding decency in Mature/PG regions). Beyond that, this land is your land.

For this reason, the mainland offers the most freedom available in SL with the exception of buying an entire island or estate. Keep this flexibility in mind as you shop for mainland parcels and remember that your next-door neighbor has as much freedom as you do to set up a glitzy shopping mall next to your quiet homestead.

### BUYING ON THE MAINLAND

Clicking the Buy Land button (or placing the winning bid at a land auction) is a deceptively simple process. In so doing, you've essentially paid for the *transfer* of the land into your name.

Your land purchase will be paid from available L$ in your account. If your balance is insufficient to cover the costs and/or you haven't yet upgraded to a premium account, you'll be prompted to take corrective action. You will also be advised of your monthly land-use fee. The purchase price will be automatically paid to the existing landowner. Fees associated with account upgrade and recurring tier will be paid directly to LL (via your payment info on record).

### GROUP LAND AND DEEDING TO GROUPS

Even an SL group can "own" land. You can get together with a set of friends and buy land that you deed to the collective group. With group land, someone else can manage the land for you, or you can set up a nonprofit organization with a group of SL residents. Group land may be shared with group members who may not be premium account holders. The main point to understand is that you lose some control of the land, so make sure you're happy about deeding the land to the current group membership.

Wondering how to donate land and why to do it? See the following http://secondlife.com/knowledgebase/article.php?id=268.

## ESTATE LIVING

When you purchase property on an estate (or private island), Linden Lab is no longer part of the transaction. You own at the discretion and under the terms established by the estate owner. The estate owner is an individual or corporation that purchased a full private island/estate directly from LL. This has some critical implications for your purchase decision.

Remember the pricing structure and prim allotment detailed in Table 9-2? The freedom and control afforded you as landowner operating under no covenant? Those were LL's rules of the road for the mainland. They no longer apply if you're buying land on an island/estate.

The terms and conditions of estate land purchase and use are established at the discretion of the estate owner and are publicized in the covenant (World->About Land->Covenant tab). The covenant is a binding contract you enter with the estate owner. Don't purchase estate land if you don't understand and agree with the terms of the covenant.

**Kymber Schnook:** I watched some poor guy that only spoke/read Portuguese get his land yanked because he couldn't read the estate covenant (written in English) to know that ban lines were prohibited. After he put them up, he got three 'warnings' from the estate owner (in English and Babel-generated Portuguese), before his land was finally reclaimed. I'm sure the new buyer was completely perplexed that his house and all his belongings were returned and the parcel put back on the market.

## ESTATE LAND USAGE FEES (YOUR TIER)

Only mainland holdings are reflected in your SL account. Acquisition of estate land has no bearing on your tier. From Linden Lab's perspective, the tier is paid for by the estate owner. In fact, you only pay land-use fees with Linden Lab through ownership of mainland property. You don't need to have a premium account to own estate land.

Estate owners often develop their own land usage fee system, wherein you can expect to pay more for a larger-sized parcel or one that supports more prims. Unlike the LL system, in which you pay for the land usage in tiered blocks, estate owners commonly charge only for the actual space you occupy. Some estate owners charge less than LL's tier for the equivalent-sized space; some charge more.

Some estate owners defray their costs (or raise their profits) by selling the land initially at a premium price. Others emphasize a back-end strategy in their tier pricing such that you can acquire the land free or for a nominal setup cost. In any case, it pays to shop around and to consider both initial purchase price (to effect transfer of ownership) as well as ongoing fees for land use.

The covenant should detail the fee structure, the frequency of payment, currency accepted, the mechanism for this transaction, and any consequence for late- or non-payment. Some estate owners require their landowners to remit to a private corporation through automated monthly PayPal subscription in US$. Others will accept an in-world payment to the estate owner's avatar in L$. Missed or late payments may result in anything from IMs requesting prompt remittance to permanent banishment from the land.

Aside from understanding and abiding by the terms of the covenant, you will generally find it helpful to build rapport with your estate owner or his designee.

## ESTATE PARCEL PRIM ALLOWANCE

Identical to mainland regions, each estate region covers 16 acres ($65,536m^2$) that are simulated by a single server that supports a maximum of 15,000 prims. Unlike on the LL's mainland, however, an estate owner may elect *not* to distribute these prims evenly across the land. Your estate purchase could come with more (or fewer) prims than an equivalent-sized mainland parcel.

For example, an estate owner may reserve a disproportionate number of the region's prim allotment to support a prim-heavy common area, commercial district, elaborate mansion, and so on. If the balance of prims were equally distributed on the remaining parcels, they'd each have fewer than their mainland equivalent. Conversely, an estate owner might reserve land for low-prim landscaping, community gathering areas, or roadways. In so doing, the estate owners can effectively underbuild these areas and return the prim surplus to the landowners.

Always remember to check World->About Land->Objects tab->Primitives Parcel Supports. Any multiple of prims above the default distribution can be seen in the World->About Land->Objects tab->Region Object Bonus Factor.

## ESTATE FREEDOM AND CONTROL

The estate covenant (World->About Land->Covenant tab) defines the terms of land use and resale. Many covenants address such issues as building height restrictions, the use of security ban lines, owner terraforming, parcel subletting, and the bounds of neighborly behavior. Some go as far as to proscribe manner of dress, speech, and style of resident homesteads. Covenants can serve to protect the interests of estate owner and residents alike, reducing conflict (and often region clutter) through contractual agreement.

It's vital to keep in mind that covenants can change at the discretion of the estate owner. Your residential-only plot could, for example, be converted to commercial land overnight. Your land-use fee or prim allocation might be changed with little notice. An estate owner may opt to exit SL and close down her region altogether. This is another reason why it's important to establish rapport with your estate owner.

Whether on estate or mainland, you're obliged to follow LL's Terms of Service Agreement and Community Standards. The covenant is the estate owner's way of imposing further guidelines regarding your conduct (and that of your guests). Reports of covenant violations should be directed to the estate owner or her designee. As always, ToS and Community Standards violations should be reported via Help->Report Abuse. On estate land, however, your abuse report may not be directed to LL staff for their resolution. Instead, it may be directed to the estate owner. If that's the case, you'll see a message to this effect when you initiate a report.

## BUYING ESTATE LAND

Your land purchase will be paid from your available L$. If your account balance is insufficient to cover the costs, you'll be prompted to take corrective action. You'll be informed of your present monthly tier (if any) and the impact this new purchase will have on your LL mainland holdings (none!). You'll need to check a box to agree to the terms of the estate's covenant (prominently displayed). Your purchase price will go to the existing owner (sometimes the estate owner, sometimes not). It's your responsibility to follow up with appropriate tier payments to the party specified in the covenant.

## OWNING AN ENTIRE ISLAND/ESTATE

You may also decide for the ultimate in flexibility and control and become an estate owner yourself. Estate ownership brings with it many benefits such as defining your own land form using height maps, defining the textures of the land itself at various elevations, and having complete control over the sim behind your estate. For example, you have the ability to reboot the sim if it is having trouble.

As of this writing, setting up an island or estate costs US$1675. Once setup, it costs US$295 a month for land usage fees. The details of buying and building out an island estate will be left for another book, but you can read more at http://secondlife.com/community/land-islands.php.

# RENTING

Renting in SL is a bit of a misnomer, in that even when you buy land in SL, you are still paying monthly fees. The main distinction in SL is that when you rent, you do not appear as a land owner. Your freedom of control depends on what the landlord allows and should be spelled out in a rental agreement. The main advantage of renting is that you don't need to sell your land to leave SL or move from one location to another.

The second advantage to renting is that rentals are often made up of prebuilt, move-in-ready units (some furnished, some not). Some rentals are residential in nature, providing homes, skyboxes, or even tree houses. Other rentals are commercial, providing you space to sell your goods.

Rentals in SL come in all shapes, sizes, and prices, so you really need to use Search and do a lot of research to find the best value. These are the most important points to consider:

- Do you like the location, and will you enjoy spending time there?
- What do other renters have to say about the location and the landlord?
- How accessible is the landlord? Is the landlord friendly and does he give you the time of day, or are his IMs capped and he never gets back to you?
- How much land/rental property does the landlord own and how long has she been in SL?
- What is the proximity to neighbors (if you're sharing walls, you're sharing chat)?
- Do you have to fill out a rental application or agreement?
- What are the region settings (for example, no-fly zones, permit harm)?
- What are the terms of lease cancellation?
- Is the property "managed"? (How do you request help?)
- Can you buy extra prims?
- What are community amenities?
- Is there a security system (from door locks to visitor detectors to region patrols)?
- Do you have to belong to a group to be able to place objects (landlords forget this)?
- For audio and video systems, can you set your own audio or video streams?

- What happens if you go over your prim allotment?
- What happens if your rent is overdue?

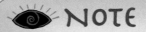

**NOTE**

Public chat travels 20m in all directions—even through walls! Think about a traditional RL apartment building in SL. If all the rooms are within 20m of each other, you will hear everything your neighbor says and vice versa. Look for rentals that have appropriate separation between units for privacy.

Use Search and classifieds to find rentals and ask around. Landlords with happy renters who have been around a while are certainly better than brand-new landlords who may decide next month to leave SL and leave you without your rental. When in doubt, go with known landlords such as Anshe Chung. Anshe is one of the most famous SL residents, having been the first to make over US$1 million in SL. She did it with land trading and rentals. See her site at http://dreamland.anshechung.com (see Figure 9-3).

**Figure 9-3**
*Anshe Chung Studios.*

When you find a place you like, make sure you take a close look at the rental agreement (if there is one). Trust me; this is important! These agreements are similar to estate covenants. They may be tricky when you're just starting, since they reference aspects of SL you know nothing about. Ask an experienced friend (if you've met one) for help.

There are short agreements and long agreements. I have included a good-sized agreement because it is reasonably representative of SL rental agreements and, while being a pretty fun read, it also highlights issues you may face when buying on the mainland where you do not have a landlord to protect a particular regional theme.

I have modified this agreement a bit to protect the landlord's privacy.

## Sample Rental Agreement

THIS LAND IS RENTAL PROPERTY—YOU ARE NOT PURCHASING IT.

This land is for rent. The "Purchase" price is a ONE TIME setup fee. It is NOT applied to your rent nor is it returned when you leave.

So—if this looks like a place you want to rent then this is how you proceed.

1) READ THIS COVENANT (Rental agreement) and be sure you understand it all.

2) "Buy Land" for L$1000. (REMEMBER—it is a setup fee not a real purchase).

3) Pay the rental box on the property (4 weeks rent minimum).

THAT'S IT! You can begin using the land immediately.

VERY IMPORTANT—PLEASE READ THE FOLLOWING CAREFULLY.

ONE IMPORTANT THING—MOST OF THE RULES HERE APPLY TO BELOW 400 METERS. Above 400 meters you can do NEARLY anything you want. More on this later.

Instead of making a list of rules I would prefer to present how I envision the atmosphere of this SIM.

First—just a little about me and my partner so you will understand where we are coming from. We both have been involved with Second Life (SL from now on and RL for Real Life) for over a year. We both greatly enjoy building and creating here. I spend nearly all my free time here and am happy to do so. Serenity Serpentine is my RL and SL wife. She is from Australia where I met her when I was living there. In SL we have lived on several mainland locations, each bigger than the previous one.

We ended up with a quarter SIM on the ocean. What we did not like was how any other SIM inhabitant was able to totally disrupt our experience with laggy scripts or really ugly structures adjacent to us. We figured that we are not the only ones who felt like this so we decided to go ahead and purchase an island. Our plan is to find residents who are looking for a nice place to live without all the anarchy of the mainland. (For the record—I enjoy that anarchy; I just don't want to live in the middle of it.)

Anyways—Serenity and I decided we would make the theme of our island that of a beach village. We are sticking to that theme and will strongly enforce it.

So that leads us to RULES. For the most part I hate rules but I am wise enough to realize that they are necessary. I am not going to make a huge list. I think that there are many people who don't need every little detail spelled out for them. Let's go over my short list and hopefully it will be sufficient for you to understand what we are aiming for.

HOUSES—They must fit in with the theme. I have several approved houses for sale that fit in perfectly. They are very reasonably priced and paid residents can buy them from me at 1/2 price. You can also buy your house elsewhere as long as it is a beach style and fits in the theme. Please don't hesitate to ask me before you buy something. You can also build your own house but again IT MUST FIT IN.

GENERAL APPEARANCE OF YOUR LAND—Keep it looking REAL and in theme. For example—don't keep a model of the titanic rezzed on your front lawn. Want to set up a surfboard with a seagull flying in the breeze, sure, that fits in; you would see that in a real beach neighborhood. Another example, no 30 meter high sculptures but yes to a trailered waverunner in your driveway. Most people should understand what I am getting at. Also keep it neat; keep your unfinished projects up in your sky platform.

LAG—It SUCKS but it can be prevented. One major cause of LAG is the scripts that run all the cool things in SL. SIM owners have the ability to see how much processor time each script on the island is consuming. Not all scripts are equal. Some scripts really hog the processor while others are relatively benign. If I see any scripts really hogging the resources I will let you know so you can correct it. For instance if your motorcycle is just some crazy resource hog but the SIM is relatively empty it probably won't have much effect. Put it away when you're done and I cannot imagine that I would bug you. If however it is Friday night and there are lots of people in the SIM your hog (pun intended) might push things over the threshold and I will ask you to put it away. Not the best example but I think most of you will get the idea. Final point—quantity of scripts also have a negative effect. If you have a tremendous amount of scripted items, so much so that it impacts the performance of the SIM I will let you know so you can correct it.

PAYMENTS—RENT is set in dollars but paid in Lindens. Let me explain. I pay Linden Lab a fixed fee each month for the SIM. That fee is in US dollars and always the same. Likewise when you rent my land it is based on a fixed US dollar amount. That weekly amount is displayed over the rental box. Also displayed is the conversion amount in Lindens. My rental boxes check the official exchange rate (with the Lindex fee included) and will convert your US dollar price into a Linden dollar equivalent. Your rent may vary in Linden dollars but the exchange value will always equate to the same dollar amount. This is fair to both of us. I will not try to profit in any way due to fluctuations in the exchange rate.

PAYMENTS ON TIME—I MUST make my payment to Linden Lab on time. I always do. In addition to automatic deductions from me I always maintain a credit balance with them. I don't take any chances in this respect whatsoever. LIKEWISE—I expect the same from the people who rent from me. The rental system allows you to pay up to 8 weeks in advance. If rent is overdue do not expect me to give more then 24 hours before I return all your items and reclaim the land.

NO BAN LINES—I REALLY HATE THESE. To me they are ugly, screw up flying and are rude. I am fully aware that this is JUST MY OPINION and others may feel differently. If you feel as strongly for them as I do against them then this is probably not a good place for you to reside. Unfortunately I do not have the ability to disable these. All I can do is reclaim the property and turn them off. If I must do this I will reset the property to be purchased again to only you. I will set the purchase price to 100 Linden. This is a fine. NO BAN LINES ALLOWED. Repeated violations and I will terminate your rental without refund.

MORE ABOUT BAN LINES—It may be confusing but ban lines show when you set up an access list in your land properties. For instance if you limit access to 5 of your friends then EVERY-ONE ELSE SEES BAN LINES. In contrast to confuse the matter if you ban 5 people that are griefing only they see the ban lines. You are allowed to ban specific individuals who are causing you problems. You cannot ban all your neighbors. If there are real griefing problems contact me and I can ban griefers SIM wide. Again—I am a reasonable person and will work with you if there are real problems.

SECURITY SCRIPTS—If you really MUST keep people off your land then purchase a security script. You must allow at least 20 seconds before you eject the people. Flying around SL is one of the great pleasures here. I really don't want to disrupt that pleasure.

HARASSMENT—I am not a police department nor judicial system nor family counselor. I really don't want to get involved in squabbles between neighbors. However if I am presented with evidence that one resident is actually harassing another I will ask them to knock it off or leave.

RESIDENTIAL ONLY—No vending machines, stores, clubs etc. No anything else that is not a residence. Don't have 20 people constantly at your house and call it just a party (every night!). I am not stupid; I can tell the difference between someone having an occasional party and someone running a club from their land.

COMMERCIAL PROPERTY—I will be setting up about 10—12 low prim shops on top of the big hill. Residents will have first shot at vender spots. I will only allow low lag vendors. If I see there is TOO much traffic I will take some sort of action to prevent disruption on the SIM. Don't let this worry you—if it becomes a problem I will fix it. Remember, I live here too.

BUILDING—Building is my favorite pastime in RL and SL. I make a mess. Projects in the works all over the place. BUT YOU WON'T SEE MY MESS. It is over 500 meters up and not visible from below. YOU CAN DO THE SAME. I am placing basic teleporters and platforms between 400 and 600 meters in the sky for each piece of land. I want to encourage you to build. You can of course replace them with your own platforms and teleporters if you like. As long as it is above 400 meters, above only land you own, not lagging the SIM, not breaking any Linden Lab Terms of Service rules you can do and build what you like (except Commercial things as stated above). You can run your business in the sense of building your products here. You just cannot set up your store here.

HELP IMPROVE THE SIM—If you have some good ideas to make the SIM more authentic then please let me know. I am up to my ears in projects already; if so it involves work and it seems to fit in I would consider letting you implement it. ALSO—Let's say you build some beautiful cafe or store or something of that nature then let me see it. If it fits in and I feel it is appropriate I might just put it out there (if you let me!). Just to clarify, when I say store or cafe I mean for visual enhancement only—not for real commerce.

FINALLY—I can change these rules at any time. I imagine I will try to clarify things as situations arise. If you have read everything up to here you probably have a good idea of what I am trying to accomplish on the SIM. I believe that most people will have no problems at all here. I know there are many people that will be happy to live in a nice place and also have the opportunity to build to their heart's content up in the sky. I reserve the right to terminate your rental at any time but will only do so under the gravest circumstances (by my determination). I will not give refunds.

Remember—IF IN DOUBT—ASK.

# FINDING AND ASSESSING THE LAND PARCEL

There are several ways to look for land—search, map, classifieds, and auctions. Let's take a quick look at each (more detail will be provided in the following tutorials).

- **Search:** Using Search->Land Sales, you can find land available for sale. There is a limited number of filters available to you such as mature/pg, parcel size, price, type (mainland, estate, auction).

- **World Map:** Another great way to search for land is to use the world map. I spent several hours going around the coast of the mainland one night to locate potential seaside property. You can turn on land sales, and they will be highlighted in yellow.

- **Classifieds:** Rentals are often listed under classified ads; you can find land sales here as well.

- **Auctions:** LL runs auctions a la eBay, and this is another place to find and bid on land (see http://secondlife.com/auctions/)

Once you find a place, you really need to visit the parcel yourself, just as you would tour a house in RL. Here are some things to consider (we will cover these points in more detail in the upcoming tutorials):

- Read the covenant (World->About Land, Covenant tab)! This is your *contract* for land use.

- Verify the area available: World->About Land, General tab, Area (m$^2$).

- Verify the prims the parcel supports: World->About Land, Objects tab, Primitives Parcel Supports.

- Determine the parcel boundaries (Ctrl+Alt+Shift+P).

- Hide existing objects (Ctrl+Alt+Shift+1) to see if there are cutouts within the boundaries.

- Look at land conformation and consider any terraforming limits (you can find a region terraformability list at http://secondlife.com/knowledgebase/article.php?id=235).

- Is the surrounding area to your liking? Is it low lag? (Over time, this too could change.)

- Given the size of your anticipated build, will you have enough space (>20m) from the next parcel

to avoid being overheard in chat (if privacy is a concern)?

- Is the asking price reasonable compared to current market data?

The remainder of this chapter takes you through finding land, buying it, planning a build, terraforming the land, building and buying what you need, landscaping, and finally enjoying your new home. So let's get busy.

# TUTORIAL: BUYING YOUR FIRST BIT OF LAND

This tutorial walks you through a reasonably safe approach to making your first land purchase in SL. If this seems overly analytical for you, then just go with your gut! There is no right or wrong way to find or purchase land in SL.

## STEP 1: CONSIDER MAINLAND OR ESTATE LAND

I will assume for the purposes of this tutorial that you want to own land versus rent. Renting is a perfectly great way to get started in SL if you want to have a virtual place to put down roots but don't want the risk of having to sell your land later to move or leave SL.

If you decide on mainland property, you will need to upgrade to a premium account (you can do this at the time you buy the land). Monthly tier payments are automatically made to Linden Lab, so you don't have to remember to make them. You will have a lot of flexibility and so will your neighbor.

If you decide on estate land, you don't need a premium account. You must ensure you are paying the estate owner on the schedule determined by the covenant. You will not have as much flexibility, but then again neither will your neighbor.

## STEP 2: CONSIDER SIZE AND COST

I recommend starting with 1024 square meters. It's a nice size and gives you room to breathe with 234 prims (verify the number of prims supported if you're buying estate land). If you buy on the mainland, the monthly cost of 1024m$^2$ is only US$5 a month in addition to your premium account fees. You may find more land for the same or less cost on an estate; just make sure to read the covenant.

## STEP 3: START SEARCHING FOR LAND

Either use the Search dialog and enter plot sizes or price limits that you want to set, or use the world map. Find an area you like—for example, near a friend, the water, or a road. Perhaps you just like the look or name of a certain sim. Zoom in on the world map and check the Land Sales box. All plots of land for sale will be highlighted in yellow (if you check this option on the world map), as you can see in Figure 9-4.

**Figure 9-4**
*Plots of land are highlighted in yellow.*

If you click on one of the $ tags, you will see how big the plot is and how much the owner is asking for it.

## STEP 4: TELEPORT TO POTENTIAL SITES

Once you find land that interests you, teleport there and have a look around. Pay particular attention to the property lines and what has been built up around this plot of land.

Figure 9-5 shows a blank plot of land. Most landowners will spruce things up a bit and put out some For Sale signs.

**Figure 9-5**
*A blank plot of land.*

Certain things make land valuable in SL, such as proximity to protected water or a roadway. You can determine whether land is protected by selecting a neighboring piece of land and looking at its properties. If it's owned by Governor Linden and indicates it is protected, this means LL will not build on this land or sell it.

There are also things that make land bad, such as being next to an extremely laggy dance club, a shopping mall, or an unsightly build. Remember that being next to a shopping mall may be good for you if you're building a store versus a residence.

In SL, just like in RL, it is all location, location, location.

## STEP 5: CHECK THE PROPERTY LINES

To see where the property lines are, go to the View menu and select Property Lines or press Ctrl+Alt+Shift+P (see Figure 9-6).

**Figure 9-6**
*Select Property Lines.*

A nice red/green border (see Figure 9-7) will surround everything (see Figure 9-8).

**Figure 9-7**
*The red/green border.*

**Figure 9-8**
*The property lines highlighted in red and green.*

## STEP 6: GET THE LATEST ECONOMIC DATA

You need two key pieces of data: the current exchange rate of US$ to L$ and the average L$ per square meter price for land. Try this URL for information: http://secondlife.com/whatis/economy-market.php.

You should see something like what is shown in Figure 9-9, which indicates that the average price paid was L$12 per square meter in January 2007. That same night I bought land at L$19 per square meter. Just remember that this is average and cost does not equate to good/bad land. As in any market, there are motivated sellers eager to dump land cheaply to get out of their next month's payments. There are also absurdly inflated land parcels.

| Land | | |
| --- | --- | --- |
| **Land Sales by Resident** | | |
| Month | Total Square Meters Sold by Residents | Avg L$ Paid Per Square Meter |
| December 2006 | 52,507,664 | 9.84 |
| January 2007 - MTD | 47,997,408 | 12.20 |

**Figure 9-9**
*Land sales by square meter and average cost per square meter.*

## STEP 7: DO THE MATH

OK, so how much is this land going to cost you? Remember, once you buy it, you own it. If you want to get rid of it without just giving it away (called *abandoning*), you will have to sell it. So, it's worth a bit of math to understand what you are committing to.

Here are the formulas:

- US$ Cost = L$ Price of Land / Currency Exchange Rate
- L$ per square meter = L$ Price of Land / Size of Land in Square Meters

Let's try an example. First, locate the current exchange rate at http://secondlife.com/whatis/economy-market.php. You should see something like what is shown in Figure 9-10. I usually use the best buying rate or last close. In this case it is L$266/US$1.00.

| Daily Summary | |
| --- | --- |
| *Last Close Date 2007-01-30* | |
| Best buying rate: | L$266 / US$1.00 |
| Best selling rate: | L$277 / US$1.00 |
| Last trade: | L$266 / US$1.00 |
| Last close: | L$266 / US$1.00 |
| Change: | L$0 / US$1.00 |
| Today's volume: | L$29,391,846 |
| Today's open: | L$266 / US$1.00 |
| Today's high: | L$277 / US$1.00 |
| Today's low: | L$266 / US$1.00 |
| Today's average: | L$269.1106 / US$1.00 |

**Figure 9-10**
*Daily summary of exchange rate.*

So, take the world map example shown previously in Figure 9-4: 512m for L$9999 per square meter = 9999 / 512 = L$19.5 per square meter. Given that the average is L$12, that's OK. Not great, but not bad.

Now how much will it cost me?

US$ Cost = 9999 / 266 = US$37.59

Yes, I am saying it will cost you $37.59 to buy this virtual piece of land! Consider that buying a private island today costs US$1,675. There is an active virtual real estate market in SL, so while virtual land is well, virtual, it still has value that people are willing to pay for. A large number of users are buying and selling land in SL, so you will not be alone.

If you don't want to do the math, don't worry; when you're ready to buy the land, all will be revealed to you before you click the Buy button.

## STEP 8: IM THE OWNER

I highly recommend IMing the owner of the land and asking her why she's selling and what she knows about the area. Also ask whether the price is firm or negotiable. Just like in RL, you may discover something bad or be able to negotiate a better deal.

## STEP 9: TALK TO YOUR POTENTIAL NEIGHBORS

Use the mini-map to see if there are residents nearby who are in the same sim. Fly or walk over and ask them what they know about the place.

## STEP 10: BUY IT!

What are you waiting for? If it all looks good, then you simply right-click to buy the land. If you don't have a premium account or you have insufficient funds, the UI will help you through these issues. It is, after all, in Linden Lab's best interest that you buy and stay awhile.

# PLANNING YOUR BUILD

So, now that you've bought or rented your first plot, what are you going to do with it? I suggest taking some time to study the land and maybe get to know your neighbors. What can you highlight? What should you screen out? What are you planning to use it for?

In Figure 9-11 I'm studying the plot with property lines enabled. For the purposes of this chapter, assume I'm going to build my first home in SL. I want a nice, peaceful place where I can hang out and maybe share with friends.

Figure 9-12 shows an overhead view.

I kind of like the stone wall on the right. It's not on my land, but I think I can take advantage of it. Below and to the left, there is a very large structure that I'm going to screen out. Above and to the left is another large structure. I figure if I place my house correctly, the back could face it.

**Figure 9-12**
*An overhead view.*

Figure 9-13 shows a quick sketch of my plan (I used a screen capture and MS Paint).

**Figure 9-11**
*The plot with property lines enabled.*

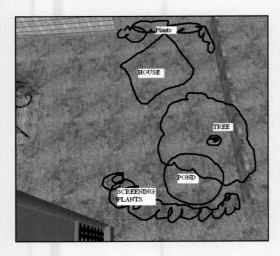

**Figure 9-13**
*A quick sketch of my plan.*

So, now that we have a plan, it's time to break ground.

# TERRAFORMING

Terraforming in SL refers to modifying the land itself; you can raise and lower land or make it rough or smooth. There are limits, however. For example, most regions in SL can be adjusted up or down by only 4m. Some older sims allow +/– 40m, and private islands allow for +/– 100m. Remember, your rental agreement or covenant may also limit what you're allowed to do.

To start editing, press Ctrl+5 or right-click on land you own and select Edit Terrain from the pie menu (see Figure 9-14).

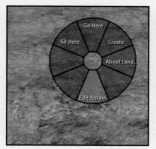

**Figure 9-14**
*Select Edit Terrain.*

Your land will be colored with green, and other land you do not own will appear in red, as shown in Figure 9-15 (group land where you are a member of the group shows in blue).

**Figure 9-15**
*Your land is green.*

The land editing dialog will also be displayed with the bulldozer in the upper corner and a set of editing tools below (see Figure 9-16). You can toggle the color coding on and off by checking or unchecking the Show Owners box.

**Figure 9-16**
*The land editing controls.*

Here's what the land editing tools do:

- **Select Land:** Allows you to select subsets of your land (useful for subdividing or joining large plots of land). This tool is also useful for terraforming selected areas. For example, to flatten an area quickly, first select the area using Select Land, pick Flatten Land on the editor dialog, and then click Apply To Selection a few times.

- **Flatten Land:** Makes the land more level or flat.

- **Raise Land:** Raises the land; click and hold the mouse to keep raising.

- **Lower Land:** Lowers the land; click and hold the mouse to keep lowering.

## WARNING

Before you begin working with these tools, I must warn you that the land as you bought it is probably not the same now as when it was originally created by Linden Lab. Chances are, it was edited by the previous owner(s). Once you start editing, there is no way to get back to the "current" state. You can revert back to the original Linden state, but again, this may not be the current land state.

- **Smooth Land:** Smoothes out bumps and makes transitions between high and low cleaner.
- **Roughen Land:** Enhances or emphasizes differences in height.
- **Revert Land:** Reverts mainland back to original default state and reverts estate land to its last saved state.

The sad fact is that you cannot experiment or learn on any other land (unless you find a real friend). So, as you learn to terraform, you will also make mistakes, and it's a bit of a pain to correct them because the terraforming tools are crude at best. SL's online help has this to say: "Be warned though, this reverts land to its original state, which may not necessarily be the state it was in when you bought it or when you began editing it. Only use Revert if you are very sure." And "very sure" means you have totally screwed up the land and you need to get it back into some shape. So, my main advice here is to go slowly, change a little bit, then close the land editing dialog, and walk around a bit to see what has happened. What appears, while editing, as a small change may, in fact, be a large and significant change.

You can edit land in one of two ways. The first is to use the bulldozer and your mouse to apply an effect such as Raise, Lower, or Smooth to the land. Second, you can select some part of the land (using Select Land), select an effect like Raise, and then use Apply To Selection to apply evenly to a selected set of land.

You can control the size of selection or amount of land influenced by the bulldozer by selecting the size of the cursor you will be using. There are three sizes: Small, Medium, and Large (see Figure 9-17).

**Figure 9-17**
*The bulldozer cursor comes in three sizes.*

The size simply relates to how big your cursor is or how much land is affected at once by your changes. Figure 9-18 shows a medium bulldozer. The small white dots represent the land area that will be modified when you left-click or left-click and hold.

**Figure 9-18**
*The bulldozer cursor (white dots) over the land.*

For our first plot of land, I selected the Lower Land option and a Medium brush, and then I focused on a spot to dig a hole (see Figure 9-19).

**Figure 9-19**
*I'm going to lower the land.*

From this view, it's hard to see how deep it is due to the green tint. But if you look at Figure 9-20, after I've closed the terrain editor, you can see that there is, in fact, a deep hole on my land.

**Figure 9-20**
*There is a hole.*

I climbed into the hole, as shown in Figure 9-21, and you can see it is a full 4m deep. This is a great start for a pond.

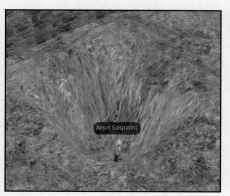

**Figure 9-21**
*The hole is 4m deep.*

To wrap this up, I smoothed out a section that will hold the house and roughed up the land a bit in between the house and the pond (see Figure 9-22). Now I'm ready to build and landscape.

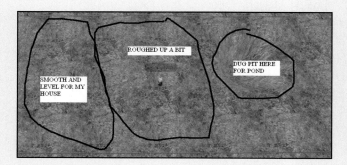

SMOOTH AND LEVEL FOR MY HOUSE

ROUGHED UP A BIT

DUG PIT HERE FOR POND

**Figure 9-22**
*Terraforming of the whole plot.*

## CREATING A BASEMENT WITH CEERA MURAKAMI

Here are some tips on making a basement from Ceera Murakami's (see Figure 9-23) post to the Build Forum:

**Figure 9-23**
*Ceera Murakami.*

> Making a basement requires 'digging' a hole under your build, which requires having terraforming rights. You must own the land, be an officer in a land group that owns the land, or for estate land, the estate owner must have extended terraforming rights to you.

> Be aware that the sides of this hole will always have a horizontal slope of at least 0.5 meters, because the grid points in the terrain are spaced in 0.5m intervals, and can't move sideways—only up and down. It is not possible to make a hole with vertical walls.

> So…you want to select an area that is smaller than your actual foundation, so the sloping sides don't show.

> Selecting land selects 4m x 4m squares, and again, you can't control where the corners of these squares are. It's locked into the terrain grid. So if you had a building with a 10m x 10m foundation, with a single prim for the foundation, you could right-click, edit land, select an 8m x 8m area, lower the land there by 3m or so, and then center your building over the resulting pit. Your 10m x 10m foundation should just barely cover it, because as the 8m x 8m selected area goes down, the surrounding land gets pulled down with it, like stretching a rubber sheet, to make the sloping sides.

> It is certainly possible to make holes in the land that are not locked to those 4m pre-assigned grid points. But doing so with the manual tools requires much more finesse and patience. My advice is to get the main hole by using the grid and 'lower land', then use the small selection tool to lower the edges as needed. I will warn you in advance that terraforming a hole is not for the

easily aggravated soul. The tools for terraforming are quite crude, and it takes time and practice to master them. Remember that "Undo" is your best friend, and all will be well.

# CONSTRUCTION: ADDING A HOUSE

Now that we have finished terraforming, the next step is to get the primary object onto the land, our house! You can build your own, but there are also some great freebies available at various locations. The most widely known freebies are at YadNi's Junkyard. The six houses shown in Figure 9-24 came from a $1L box labeled "11 Free Houses." The middle one on the bottom row has "some assembly required." The others are just rezzed out of the Inventory or a standard box.

I like the "low prim beach house," which is the upper middle. BTW, I found a sandbox to rez all of these things to see what they looked like, compare them, and walk around inside.

In Figure 9-25 I rezzed the beach house on my land and rotated it slightly. The problem here is this house is too big for my 512m plot.

**Figure 9-25**
*This house is too big.*

At this point, if you really love it, you can try shrinking the house, breaking it into pieces, and editing it using all the build tool know-how you gained in Chapter 6, "Building Basics."

You could also try a smaller house, which I will do here. For this build, I ended up going with "cabin" from the "11 Free Houses" box. If you can't get to YadNi's, try one of the Atoll huts from Library->Objects ->Atoll Continent Stuff.

I had to lower this thing into the ground, and then I rotated it a bit to get it into the position I was looking for (see Figure 9-26). Also, I decided to place it diagonally across from the pond. By putting something in place in SL you can walk around it and view it from different angles to see whether you like it.

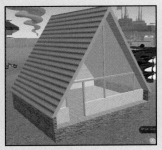
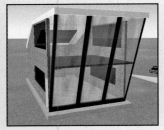

**Figure 9-24**
*Free houses.*

**Figure 9-26**
*The cabin in position.*

OK, to finish up with the "hardscape," I decided it would be nice to put in a little boardwalk/deck that ran next to the pond. The Library->Objects->Atoll Continent Stuff->Atoll-Wood Walkway Small works well for this.

I placed it next to the pond, but you will notice that in Figure 9-27 it is sitting off the ground. This does not make it easy to walk onto. If I lower it too much, though, several pieces go into the ground, so that won't work. This is where the terraforming tools come back into play. With a little "Raise" followed by some "Smooth," I created a smooth transition from land onto the deck/dock (see the after portion of Figure 9-27).

| Before | After |
|--------|-------|

**Figure 9-27**
*The walk before and after.*

Figure 9-28 shows the final land and buildings, ready to add a pond, waterfall, and landscaping.

**Figure 9-28**
*The final land and buildings.*

# TUTORIAL: ADDING A POND

In this section, we add a pond to the land. I drop into tutorial mode, but my descriptions are abbreviated. I'm assuming you have done some basic building and are familiar with the build tools covered earlier.

## STEP 1: REZ A CYLINDER

First, let's start with the pond. Rez a cylinder, flatten it, and resize it so that it fits the pond you created. Then lower it into place. The surface of the cylinder will be the surface of the water. It should look something like Figure 9-29.

While the texture is still plywood, it's a great time to shape up the edges. You may notice straight lines or a square pool, depending on how carefully you terraformed. Try using Raise, Lower, and Smooth in small quantities while the plywood pool is in place until you get a pleasing shape.

**Figure 9-29**
*The pond is on its way.*

## STEP 2: APPLY A NICE TEXTURE

Drag and drop the texture Library->Textures->Waterfalls->Water-Ripple Layer 1. Now adjust the size to your pond using Repeats per Face. Since my cylinder ended up being 10×10, I used 3h×2v Repeats per Face. Figure 9-30 shows the before and after.

**Before**

**After**

**Figure 9-30**
*Before and after pool textures.*

## STEP 3: ADD TRANSPARENCY

I ended up with 61% transparency, but you may have a different idea of what you want. The basic idea is that you should see a bit of the land underneath the water (see Figure 9-31).

**Figure 9-31**
*You can see a bit of land underneath the water.*

OK, this by itself is way cool! If you don't get a least a small kick out of this, then SL is not for you! But it only gets better.

## STEP 4: ADD MOVEMENT

Now we're going to make the water move, which is hard to show well in a book! This step is so simple and yet so cryptically obscured that it's not even funny! Locate a default script in Library->Scripts->anim SMOOTH. Drag this script from the library onto your object, and it should start moving!

## STEP 5: ADJUST THE SPEED

Next, we need to adjust the water's speed. Newbies commonly leave fast-moving water in place because they can't edit scripts. But do not fear, even if you've never done any coding in your life; you can handle this one.

Edit the pond object as if you were making a build change to it. Go to the Content tab. You should see the animSMOOTH script (see Figure 9-32).

**Figure 9-32**
*The animSMOOTH script.*

Double-click on the script and scroll down until you see a line like this:

```
llSetTextureAnim(ANIM_ON | SMOOTH | LOOP,
ALL_SIDES,1,1,1.0,1,0.25);
```

Simply change the 0.25 value up or down to get to the desired speed. Smaller values are slower. I changed mine to 0.05. After you make the change, click the Save button and wait. You should see two messages: "Compile successful, saving…" and then "Save complete" (see Figure 9-33). After that, you will probably have to wait a moment for the change to take effect.

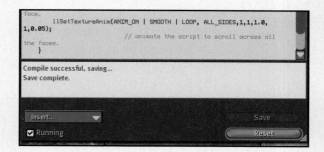

**Figure 9-33**
*You should see two messages.*

## STEP 6: ROTATION ANYONE?

If you feel that your pond is flowing like a river versus pooling like a pool, try adding a script that rotates the texture. Here's a basic sample:

```
float rotate;
default {
    state_entry()
    {
        rotate = 0;
        llSetTimerEvent(.1);
    }
    timer()
```

```
    {
        rotate = rotate + .01;
        if (rotate==10.1)
        {
            rotate = 0;
        }
        llRotateTexture(rotate,ALL_SIDES);
    }
}
```

## STEP 7: ENJOY THE POND!

I can't show you your pond in action, of course. But Figure 9-34 shows the pond as seen from the cabin.

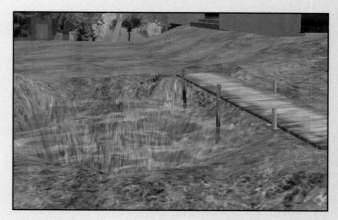

**Figure 9-34**
*The finished pond.*

# TUTORIAL: ADDING A WATERFALL

OK, the pond is great, but we want to really WOW our guests. As Julia Hathor noted in Chapter 6, *"One person showed me how simple it was to create a waterfall and OMG I was hooked after that!"*

Julia walked me through the process one evening, and I'll walk you through it here. I'm assuming you've done some building at this point and have the basics down, so things will move a bit faster here.

Figure 9-35 is a quick sketch of what we're going for.

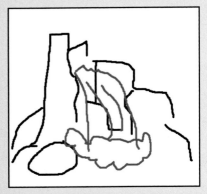

**Figure 9-35**
*A quick sketch.*

## STEP 1: BUILD OUT A ROCK BACKDROP

Again, since we're all new, we'll turn to the library for some objects to help us get started. Alternatively, you can create your own rocks as you did in Chapter 6, in the section "Tutorial: Creating a Rock."

Look under Library->Objects->Landscaping. You should find four different rocks there. Drag some in, resize, move, and play around. You're creating a waterfall here! Have fun, but remember prim counts; you probably want to use only four or five rocks. Figure 9-36 shows what I ended up with.

First, hollow out the cylinder as far as possible: 95%. Then cut a good-sized chunk out of it. Finally, rotate and resize it to fit. Figure 9-37 shows my plywood cylinder in place and ready to be turned into running water.

**Figure 9-37**
*The plywood cylinder ready to be made into running water.*

**Figure 9-36**
*The finished rock structure selected and unselected.*

## STEP 2: REZ A CYLINDER

To add water to the waterfall, you need to create a cylinder and do some serious "prim torture." Prim torture refers to the process of taking an innocent prim and twisting, turning, cutting, and bashing it into the shape you want.

OK, if you haven't been building stuff for a while, this will be a bit challenging. If you're whimpering right now, just open the Search dialog and type in **waterfall** under Places. You can probably find something you like.

If you're still going strong, here are a few tips:

- You want the water coming out of a seam in the rocks.
- You need the water to touch or go beneath the pond layer.
- You can move or resize the rocks as well as the water.

## STEP 3: ADD THE TEXTURE

The best free texture for waterfalls is located under Library->Textures->Waterfalls and is named Waterfall-Dense Layer 1. Drag it onto your waterfall prim now.

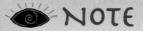

**NOTE**

The ideal approach here is to apply a totally transparent texture to the waterfall prim so it is invisible and then to apply this texture to the front and back sides. Since there is no totally transparent texture in the library, you will have to search one out or make one. You can get one from Robin Sojourner's Texture Lab (noted in Chapter 7, "Advanced Textures and Clothing"), or I have made a totally transparent texture available at the in-world companion site. Also worth knowing is that animated textures do not keep their sizing without a special script. You can find it at the in-world site as well.

**SLURL** In-world book companion site:
**http://slurl.com/secondlife/humuli/222/123/29**

## STEP 4: GET IT MOVING

Just as you did with your pond, apply the animSMOOTH script from the library to your waterfall. If your waterfall is flowing in the wrong direction, just change 0.25 to –0.25 and remember this setting controls the speed. I slowed mine and reversed it to –0.15. And there you have it, waterfall, pond, and all (see Figure 9-38).

**Figure 9-38**
*My waterfall.*

# TUTORIAL: LANDSCAPING— GREENING IT UP

This section is about adding the color, plants, trees, ground cover, and so on. Perhaps first we should take stock as to where we are.

We found some land, we planned our layout, we terraformed a bit, and we added a house and dock/deck. Then we added a pool and created a waterfall to arrive at the scene you see in Figure 9-39.

**Figure 9-39**
*What we've done to this point.*

It's nice, but it's not green! Creating trees, bushes, and grass is easy in SL. One way to approach this is to use the Create tools.

As you may recall from Chapter 6, we skipped over the Tree and Grass buttons.

## STEP 1: ADD SOME GROUND COVER

One thing you may want to add is ground cover. Select the last build tool, as shown in Figure 9-40. Then click on the ground somewhere to create a ground cover.

**Figure 9-40**
*Select the last build tool.*

Figure 9-41 shows before and after shots.

**Before**

**After**

**Figure 9-41**
*Before and after application of ground cover.*

Yes, one click will create all that. A single ground cover object will have many components that spread across a relatively large area (hence, the name ground COVER).

Ground cover objects have several unique attributes. Even though they look fairly complex, they're counted only as one prim. They cannot be rotated, or raised or lowered. Their height is determined by the land. However, they can be moved around on the x,y axis, and they can be proportionally scaled.

I don't recommend using the build tool as we did for the purpose of creating ground cover because the type of ground cover will change as you click. You might get prairie grass on one click and kelp on the next. A much better approach is to drag the ground cover you want from your library onto the ground so you will always get the one you want.

## STEP 2: ADD SOME TREES

I like to add the big pieces or anchor pieces before I start to add all the bushes and other plants. You could just add trees like we did with ground cover from the Create menu, but this technique can be troublesome. As with ground covers, and I'm not sure why, the build tool picks trees and bushes randomly from the library. While this is

fun to play around with, it's hard to get what you want. Figure 9-42 shows the results of four clicks—four very different trees:

**Figure 9-42**
*Four clicks and four different trees.*

Better to go to Library->Objects->Trees, Plants, and Grasses. There you will see all the Linden landscaping objects available. These are all great because they are high detail, sway in the breeze, and count as only one prim against your quota.

I ended up adding one cypress tree and one eucalyptus tree (see Figure 4-43). Both of these are large trees that have good cover.

**Figure 9-43**
*A cypress tree and a eucalyptus tree.*

## STEP 3: ADD A PRIVACY SCREEN

I wish there had been someone around to tell me about this technique early on. If you spend much time in SL, you will see some "bad builds." These are things people erect nearby or next to your land that you really wish were not there. Sometimes rather than building a big wall, you're better off just providing a gentle plant screen. That's what we'll do here.

I like to use the Plumeria under Library->Objects->Trees, Plants, Grasses. It somehow reminds me of a rhododendron.

Figure 9-44 shows before and after shots.

**Before**

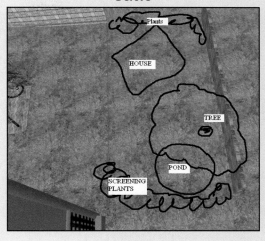

**After**

**Figure 9-45**
*Aerial pictures before and after.*

**Before**

**After**

**Figure 9-44**
*Before and after shots.*

## STEP 4: SCATTER SOME PLANTS ABOUT

Since each Linden plant is only one prim, you can scatter a few around and make a dramatic impact. Figure 9-45 shows the before and after aerial pictures. Figure 9-46 shows the view from my living room. All that remains is to get some furniture and invite a few friends over.

**Figure 9-46**
*The view from the living room.*

The completed project has been re-created for your viewing pleasure with all items available to copy freely at the in-world companion site. Go behind the main build and take a closer look.

 **http://slurl.com/secondlife/humuli/222/123/29**

## STEP 5: BONUS STEP: ADD SOME WILDLIFE

Now my good friend Julia would say, "It looks great, but there is no wildlife." Well, a perfect addition would be a few Koi in the pond. You can find birds, fish, crabs, dolphins, killer whales, spiders, and even a pet dog in SL. Use Search to find the latest. I searched for "Koi" and came up with nine different locations.

Instead of checking out one of these locations, I headed over to a store I know. Kaikou Splash's place, Splash Aquatics, has a great aquarium and some fishing stands where you can fish for a free fish.

You can find Splash Aquatics at

 **http://slurl.com/secondlife/Gooruembalchi/ 112/192/70/**

In Figure 4-47 you can see the Koi I bought, Koi "Florence," for L$50 and Koi Florence deployed in my pond.

**Figure 9-47**
*Florence, the Koi, moves from tank to pond.*

When you're ready for some more plants besides the Linden plants, take a look at Heart Garden Center, at

 **http://slurl.com/secondlife/Plush%20Iota/ 143/108/22/•**

You can find a free cutting garden where you find freebie

plans and "cut" them using Take Copy at

 **http://slurl.com/secondlife/Serenite/86/228/23/**

# PRIMS REPRISE: WHY YOU REALLY DO CARE!

Maybe I haven't gotten through yet why you should care about prims, so here is the reprise of our build (if you've seen the HGTV cable show *Design on a Dime,* you'll appreciate this). Our budget for a 512m land plot is 117 prims. Table 9-3 shows how it broke down.

**Table 9-3    Prim Build Breakdown**

| ITEM | NUMBER OF PRIMS |
| --- | --- |
| House | 35 prims |
| Pond | 1 prim |
| Waterfall | 1 prim |
| Rocks | 5 prims |
| Plants | 20 prims |
| Swimming Koi | 2 prims |
| Dock | 13 prims |
| Total Used | 77 prims |
| Remaining Available | 40 prims |

I have 40 prims remaining. I think I'll try to stick to 20 prims of furniture and save myself 20 prims to rez various things on my land. And remember, once you get into building, you may want to buy more land in the same sim to add to your prim quota!

Tess Whitcroft posted this query (http://forums.secondlife. com/showthread.php?t=122300) to the Build Forum a while back with several questions relevant to the prim topic. I've summarized (and in some cases, augmented) the responses here:

- Is 234 prims the correct amount for a 1024m parcel?

  Yes, this is the correct number of prims on the mainland. It may or may not be the case for estate land.

- How many prims should I look for in a house, and how many prims should I leave for furnishings?

  This is a personal choice, but with only 234 prims, the recommendation is 40–80 prims for the house and to pay attention to any furniture you buy. Zayante Hegel said, *"There are couches and then there are couches. Low prim couches can be only a few…5 or 6. Hit the item, click Edit, and you'll see its prim usage. You won't believe how many prims some things are. My wife has a sofa that is 45 prims. Jeez!"*

- How many (if any) prims should I leave unused?

The number of prims you leave unused depends on how often you rez other things. If you want to rez a vehicle, for example, you should have 31 prims free. Zayante Hegel again, *"I've gone down to one prim, but then if you want to open a nice object that you just bought you might not be able to. Or if one of those fancy wedding invites come, you have to go to a sandbox to open your invite. Bah. I don't know that there is a rule, but I like to have a few left for the unexpected."*

- Do the prims in my (and my visitors') hair/clothes count against the total on the parcel?

No. Prims that are attached to your avatar do not count against any land use unless you take them off and drop them on the ground.

- Do the prims in a skybox (if I had one) count against the total?

Yes, a skybox is just like a house, only it is floating. All prims will count against your quota.

- What about my neighbor's tree that seems to be mostly in my yard?

If the tree is in your yard, it counts against your prims. Most Linden trees have a large radius of foliage that often spills over if your neighbor placed the trunk right on the property line. You can check your land settings to determine whether someone else has prims on your property. This is true for all objects; the center point of the object determines what land it is on, so just because some object overlaps your land does not mean it necessarily counts against your prim limit.

- Is there any way to get more prims for my parcel?

Buy more land in the same region. It doesn't even have to be joined to the same parcel; it just needs to be in the same region. If you are renting or own estate land, check with the landlord or estate owner and see if you can purchase more prims.

# A TALK WITH PEAS IN A POD LANDLORD ARIES MATHILDE

I bought some land from Aries Mathilde (see Figure 9-48). She was a landlord who rented condos to around 18 tenants and was moving her operation elsewhere. We ended up discussing rentals as we talked about the land sale. I think there are some interesting tidbits to be gleaned from our conversation.

**Figure 9-48**
*Aries Mathilde.*

***Ansel Gasparini:*** *Since you rent property, I would like your perspective on what a newbie should know?*

**Aries Mathilde:** if you remember I started out with the apartments but those had privacy issues you could hear everyone else talking LOL or doing what ever it was that they were doing so I went to skyboxes. I call them condos LOL

*AG: I guess they need to be more than 20m apart to avoid that issue?*

AM: Yes there has to be at least 20m clearance on each side some people don't want to mess with land use fees and I don't blame them if they are just here to play, then I understand but I know that I wanted a place to call home

AM: When you buy its all yours when you rent, its yours, but at the whim of someone else. I mean, if I was rude, I could boot everyone out and build a casino not that I would I like my tenants I get to meet all kinds of new people

*AG: yes, that is a good point*

AM: I try to at least meet all of my tenants at least once newbies need to read things that are given to them like I give out notecards when they first rent there is detailed information in them in general newbies should understand that the rules that apply in RL also apply here. Be nice to others

AM: When renting, they need to remember that they need to like the place and that asking questions is ok, understanding prims seems to be a big issue and unfortunately, there is no prim counter that I can set for each person that counts them so I need to cleanup and look around every couple days

*AG: I really appreciate your time*

AM: no its all good! have a good one!

# SUMMARY

In this chapter you learned about SL real estate, the advantages of owning land, the difference between renting and buying, and the differences between mainland and estate land. You discovered how to locate land that is for sale and how to terraform and landscape your new plot. You also did some more building, creating a waterfall and pond and home to enjoy.

Remember that you can view the sample build shown in this chapter in-world along with freely available objects and textures at

 **http://slurl.com/secondlife/humuli/222/123/29**

Next up, we'll step off the deep end and introduce some of SL's more advanced building topics.

*SL's major advantage over other online worlds is the fact you can make almost anything you want, but to DO anything you want you need an animation for whatever IT is.*

**—Craig Altman**

# Particles, Vehicles, Animations, and Sculpted Prims

# 10

WITH JOHAN DURANT, CHOSEN FEW, AMANDA LEVITSKY, JOPSY PENDRAGON, AND CUBEY TERRA

This chapter introduces the advanced building features of SL: particle systems, animations, vehicles, and sculpted prims. Using these features requires that you are already familiar with camera controls, basic building, texturing, and scripting.

To cover this material in a single chapter, I depart from the more comprehensive approach of previous chapters and provide basic knowledge, a starter tutorial or two developed by experts in each area, and pointers where you can learn more. Believe me; if I had the time, I would have written an entire chapter on each of these fantastically fun topics!

If you're very new to SL, you may want to skim this chapter and come back to it later after you've improved your basic building, texturing, and scripting skills.

## What You Will Learn

- How to use and create particle systems
- How to use and create poses and poseballs
- How to animate objects
- How to create vehicles
- How create and use sculpted prims

My deepest thanks to all the SL experts who have shared their knowledge with me and helped make this chapter possible, most notably Craig Altman, Johan Durant, Chosen Few, Amanda Levitsky, Jopsy Pendragon, and Cubey Terra.

# PARTICLE SYSTEMS BASICS

Particles really bring SL alive with visual effects that would not otherwise be possible. Flames, candles, smoke, fireworks, fog, falling leaves, dripping water, and "bling" (an effect that simulates flashes of light reflecting off jewelry/sunglasses, and so on) are all examples.

Particles are not created like prims. They are generated by using one LSL function named `llParticleSystem()`. The following sections give you a high-level overview of what particles are and how they work. My deepest thanks to Jopsy Pendragon and his Particle Lab for providing the structure and information that form these sections.

Details about this function are available on the LSL wiki at

https://wiki.secondlife.com/wiki/LlParticleSystem

## THE ANATOMY OF PARTICLES

A **particle** is basically a two-dimensional image that is always seen straight on by any given avatar. You'll never see a particle at an angle. If a particle were a prim sign, for example, it would rotate as you walked around it so that it was always facing you (perpendicular to your vantage point).

Particles emanate from the geometric center of a prim that contains a script which calls the `llParticleSystem()` function. This prim is known as the **particle emitter**. The script contains special attributes that control more than two dozen particle parameters.

All particles are short-lived; each one dissipates after no more than 30 seconds. They may be no larger than 4×4 meters. Particles are not prims.

The SL viewer (client) is responsible for creating and displaying particles, and as such SL creates particles directly on the SL client (your desktop/laptop), and as such particles do not contribute to network or sim lag. They do require some graphics horsepower on your client, however. Because particles are client-side, no two people will see particles in exactly the same way.

To create particles, you need the following items:

- A particle emitter. A particle emitter may be created using any prim shape, except grass or tree prims. Once you add a particle script to a prim, you can see the particle emitter by selecting View->Beacons-> Particle Sources.
- A script that calls the `llParticleSystem()` function placed in the Inventory of the particle emitter prim.
- A texture (optional). A particle system may optionally specify a texture. If you don't apply a texture, the particle resembles kind of a round, fuzzy ball.

When choosing a prim for your emitter, consider size, rotation, and shape. Jopsy notes the following:

Use small with small and big with big. Tiny particle effect? Pick tiny particles and tiny prims. BIG particle effect? Pick BIG prims and BIG particles. A prim's particles won't be seen until the prim can be seen. Some "angular" particle displays are sensitive to the rotation of their source prim. Some prims, like Sphere, Torus, Ring and Tube are created turned on their side.

The particle effect for any prim is defined using a script and a call to the `llParticleSystem()` function. A prim may have only one particle system active at a given time, and particles are always emitted from the center of the prim.

Particles are viewable by SL clients by default. They can be disabled (View->Beacons-Hide Particles) or tuned to show more or fewer particles. You set the total number of particles you can see at any given time by selecting Edit->Preferences->Adv. Graphics->Max. Particle Count. This is the total number of particles for all emitters in your sight.

> 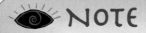 NOTE
>
> The particle system is a property of the prim itself. You use `llParticleSystem()` in a script to set those properties. If you delete the script, this will not change the current particle system settings on that prim. To turn off a particle system, create an empty script with this line:
>
> `llParticleSystem( [ ] );`

Some avatars may not see particles when you do because they have this number dialed back or because they are too far away to have the particle emitter prim in viewing range.

The `llParticleSystem()` function is a monster, as I previously noted. It has more than 20 different parameters that control various aspects of particles. Jopsy Pendragon has broken them down into four manageable categories:

- **Appearance:** Scale, color, transparency, glow, texture
- **Flow:** Count, rate, age, life
- **Placement:** Patterns, angles, radius, rotation
- **Movement:** Speed, acceleration, wind, bounce, relative and targeted movement

The following sections cover each category briefly. There are many particle script samples available all over the place. Some are more complex than others. If you'd like to learn more, here are some places to look:

- The old LSL wiki at http://rpgstats.com/wiki/index.php?title=ScriptLibrary. See ones by Ama Omega and Keknehv Psaltery.

- In-world at the Particle Lab (see "The Particle Lab" later in this chapter).
- In-world at the companion book site at

 http://slurl.com/secondlife/humuli/222/123/29

## PARTICLE APPEARANCE

The first step in defining particles is determining how they'll look. You can control the color, size, transparency (or alpha), glow, and texture of the particles in the system.

For many of these properties, you can control how they change over the life span of each particle. For example, a particle may start off blue but end up red. Or it may start off solid but end up totally transparent. The key settings for appearance are covered in the following sections.

### Scale

Scale sets the particle's height or width from 0.04 to 4.0. There is no depth to a particle, as it is always facing the viewer, so the Z component of the scale vector should be left 0.0. If you want to have a particle change size from the time it is first brought to life to when it dies, set `PSYS_PART_INTERP_SCALE_MASK` to `TRUE` and use both `PSYS_PART_START_SCALE` and `PSYS_PART_END_SCALE` scale settings.

### Color

Color sets the color of the particle (or tint, as with textures). If you set `PSYS_PART_INTERP_COLOR_MASK` to `TRUE`, then it will interpolate between the start and end colors. `PSYS_PART_INTERP_COLOR_MASK` also needs to be set if you want to use beginning and ending transparency.

Colors are set in `llParticleSystem` using an RGB vector with values from 0.0–1.0 as compared with integer values 0–255. To get from a 0–255 RGB value to a vector value, simply use the formula

$$Y = (X+1) / 256 \quad \text{(note if X=0, Y=0)}$$

where Y is a 0–1 value and X is the 0–255 value. For example, 127 = 0.5.

The `llParticleSystem` values for start and end color are `PSYS_PART_START_COLOR` and `PSYS_PART_END_COLOR`, respectively.

### Transparency (Alpha)

`PSYS_PART_START_ALPHA` sets the transparency of a particle. A value of 1.0 is fully opaque (or not at all transparent), while 0 is totally transparent (not visible). Water spray is a great example of something that starts more solid and fades away in the breeze. You must set `PSYS_PART_INTERP_COLOR_MASK` to `TRUE` if you want to use both `PSYS_PART_START_ALPHA` and `PSYS_PART_END_ALPHA`.

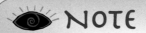

**NOTE**

`PSYS_PART_START_ALPHA` is ignored if it is less than `PSYS_PART_END_ALPHA`. In other words, due to a bug, particles can only fade out, not fade in.

### Glow

The `PSYS_PART_EMISSIVE_MASK` setting enables or disables a particle glow effect. If it is enabled, particles are full bright and unaffected by global lighting. If it is disabled, particles use ambient light.

### Texture

By default, particles resemble fuzzy white balls. You can override this appearance by applying a texture. If you have ever been griefed by a Mario Brothers bomb, that is an example of a textured particle. The emitter script must reference the texture by either its UUID or name. (If by name, the texture file must be placed within the particle emitter's Inventory.)

## PARTICLE FLOW

Flow settings control how many particles are produced (`PSYS_SRC_BURST_PART_COUNT`) per burst, the time interval between bursts (`PSYS_SRC_BURST_RATE`), how long each particle lives (`PSYS_PART_MAX_AGE`), and how long the particles are produced (`PSYS_SRC_MAX_AGE`).

### Count

Count (`PSYS_SRC_BURST_PART_COUNT`) determines the number of particles per burst (1–4096).

### Rate

The rate is the time, in seconds, between particle bursts set by the `PSYS_SRC_BURST_RATE` parameter.

### Age

Age determines the particle age, in seconds (a max of 30 seconds).

### Emitter Life

`PSYS_SRC_MAX_AGE` is the time, in seconds, that the prim emits particles (once it comes into view range or the function is executed). Specify 0.0 for never-ending particles.

When you're creating particle displays, it's pretty important to try to use the minimum number of particles required to achieve the desired effect. The maximum number of concurrently visible particles an emitter produces can be computed by this formula:

Total # of Concurrent Particles = (AGE / RATE) * COUNT

Note that this is not necessarily the maximum number of particles that will be displayed (a setting that is controlled by each user in her client properties).

## PARTICLE PLACEMENT

Particle placement determines where new particles are created relative to the center of the prim. Different particle patterns can be achieved using these settings.

### Pattern

You must set the pattern to one of four pattern types:

- `PSYS_SRC_PATTERN_DROP` particles appear or are dropped at the source position with no initial velocity.

The drop pattern is the simplest. Particles are created at the center of the prim with no initial velocity or direction. They will not move unless you apply some movement controls. They're good for droplets or for glow trails left behind by moving objects. When you use the drop pattern, the following parameters are ignored: `PSYS_SRC_BURST_RADIUS`, `PSYS_SRC_OMEGA`, `PSYS_SRC_ANGLE_BEGIN`, `PSYS_SRC_ANGLE_END`, and `PSYS_SRC_BURST_SPEED_MIN` and `PSYS_SRC_BURST_SPEED_MAX`.

- `PSYS_SRC_PATTERN_EXPLODE` sends particles in all directions.

  The explode pattern creates particles that head out in all directions from the center of a prim. The explode pattern usually requires a lot of particles to create a good effect.

- `PSYS_SRC_PATTERN_ANGLE` uses `PSYS_SRC_ANGLE_BEGIN` and `PSYS_SRC_ANGLE_END` parameters to emit particles across a 2D arc.

  The angle pattern creates a flat fan-shaped burst of particles. The width is controlled by `PSYS_SRC_ANGLE_BEGIN` and `PSYS_SRC_ANGLE_END`. `PSYS_SRC_OMEGA` will cause the direction of the spray to rotate around the center of the prim after each burst of particles. Figure 10-1 is a little busy, but the light blue particles are coming from one of the garden sprinklers, showing how the angle pattern can work.

- `PSYS_SRC_PATTERN_ANGLE_CONE` uses angle settings to emit particles in ring or cone patterns.

  The angle cone pattern creates a 3D ring or cone-shaped burst of particles (see Figure 10-2). The width is controlled by `PSYS_SRC_ANGLE_BEGIN` and `PSYS_SRC_ANGLE_END`.

Next are the additional parameters used for particle placement.

## Radius

`PSYS_SRC_BURST_RADIUS` is the distance between the emitter's center and each new particle's creation. `PSYS_SRC_BURST_RADIUS` is ignored if you use `PSYS_PART_FOLLOW_SRC_MASK`.

**Figure 10-1**
*Particle Lab angle pattern sprinkler display.*

**Figure 10-2**
*Particle Lab angle cone display.*

## Angle

PSYS_SRC_ANGLE_BEGIN and PSYS_SRC_ANGLE_END set the width for both the angle and angle cone patterns. Values are between 0 and PI.

## Rotation (Omega)

PSYS_SRC_OMEGA determines how much to rotate the emitter around the x-, y-, z-axes after each burst. Set PSYS_SRC_OMEGA to 0.0 to disable it.

# PARTICLE MOVEMENT

Movement properties determine how the particles move after they're created. Movement parameters include

- Speed

  PSYS_SRC_BURST_SPEED_MIN,
  PSYS_SRC_BURST_SPEED_MAX

- Acceleration

  PSYS_SRC_ACCEL

- Wind

  PSYS_PART_WIND_MASK

- Bounce

  PSYS_PART_BOUNCE_MASK

- Relative Movement

  PSYS_PART_FOLLOW_SRC_MASK,
  PSYS_PART_FOLLOW_VELOCITY_MASK

- Targeted Movement

  PSYS_SRC_TARGET_KEY,
  PSYS_PART_TARGET_LINEAR_MASK, PSYS_PART_
  TARGET_POS_MASK

## Speed

PSYS_SRC_BURST_SPEED_MIN sets the minimum speed of a particle. The slowest speed for a new particle is 0.01.

PSYS_SRC_BURST_SPEED_MAX sets the maximum speed of a particle. PSYS_SRC_BURST_SPEED_MIN and PSYS_SRC_BURST_SPEED_MAX are ignored for the drop pattern.

## Acceleration

PSYS_SRC_ACCEL specifies each particle's directional acceleration (along region coordinates). Use small values here for long-lived particles. Units are meters/second and the maximum value is 100.

## Wind

If PSYS_PART_WIND_MASK is set to TRUE, the particles will be affected by the wind in a sim. Note that the wind direction and force are different between sims, so be aware of this when you're placing particles near sim boundaries.

## Bounce

PSYS_PART_BOUNCE_MASK makes particles bounce off the z-axis of the emitter. If you place the emitter in a table top or just underground, you'll get the right effect.

## Relative Movement

Setting PSYS_PART_FOLLOW_SRC_MASK to TRUE will make the particles move relative to the emitter's position. This setting is useful for vehicles or moving objects where you want the particle effect to remain local, such as a vehicle that leaves a plume of exhaust behind it. Using this setting disables PSYS_SRC_BURST_RADIUS.

Setting PSYS_PART_FOLLOW_VELOCITY_MASK to TRUE causes particles to rotate toward the heading of the emitter.

## Targeted Movement

With targeted movement, you can have particles target an object in the world. To do this, you need the UUID key of the object to be targeted. llGetKey() will return the key of the emitter itself, allowing particles to return to their source. llGetOwner will target the owner of the particle emitter. It is also possible, using message passing, to ask for and get the key of another object if you want to target something else. PSYS_PART_TARGET_POS_MASK must be set to TRUE to enable this feature. Set the target object with PSYS_SRC_TARGET_KEY. Then use the undocumented feature PSYS_PART_TARGET_LINEAR_MASK to make particles move toward their target in a straight line.

Now let's get past the theory and create a particle system!

# TUTORIAL: OCEAN SPRAY USING PARTICLES

Before you begin this tutorial, I suggest you pick a particle project that really interests you versus following this tutorial exactly. You'll have more fun and learn more. You can follow along this tutorial loosely, and it'll take you through the right order of events. In this tutorial, we travel to the Particle Lab and acquire a starter script. We then play with the settings and try to produce an ocean spray, like you might see when waves hit a break wall.

## VISIT THE PARTICLE LAB AND GET A STARTER SCRIPT

This tutorial is made easier if you get a starter script. You can find such scripts all around, as previously noted, but this tutorial starts with a visit to the Particle Lab.

### Step 1: Teleport to Teal and the Particle Lab

Search for the Particle Lab in Places or use the SLURL in the section "The Particle Lab." You'll arrive in a square and see a large balloon (see Figure 10-3); you use this balloon to ride up to the Particle Lab.

**Figure 10-3**
*Balloon ride to the Particle Lab.*

### Step 2: Learn a Little

Figure 10-4 shows a view of the entire Particle Lab. Spend some time reading the first few stations and trying out some of the stand-on displays. They kind of look like a large scale, and when you stand on them, the particles will turn on.

**Figure 10-4**
*A view of the entire Particle Lab.*

### Step 3: Get a Starter Object with Script

Walk around the perimeter of the Particle Lab, and you'll come back near where you started and see a practice area (a grassy area near the middle). Just outside this area are three objects (see Figure 10-5) that you can copy by right-clicking and then selecting More->Take Copy. Each object contains starter scripts. I recommend starting with Jopsy's Particle Script for Beginners because it has more comments.

**Figure 10-5**
*Starter particle script objects.*

## Step 4: Extract the Script

At this point, you'll see a new object in your Inventory, as in Figure 10-6. If you just drag this object out and start going to town, you'll have an object that indicates it was created by Jopsy Pendgragon. Jopsy doesn't want this and neither do you. You need to extract the script from this object and put it into your library so you can use it on your own objects.

**Figure 10-6**
*The scripted object in your Inventory.*

To do this, drag the object for which you made a copy in the previous step onto the practice area or some other area. Edit the object and go to the Content tab. You should see the script sitting there. Now open your Inventory and drag the script into it. The Scripts folder is a logical choice (see Figure 10-7).

**Figure 10-7**
*Extracting the script from the object.*

## CREATE AN EMITTER PRIM AND ADJUST THE APPEARANCE

In the remainder of this tutorial, you create a particle emitter by adding the script you retrieved to a new object. Then you learn how to adjust the appearance of the particles.

### Step 5: Create a Particle Emitter Prim and Add the Script

In Figure 10-8 I created a new cone, and then I dragged the script from my Inventory onto the Contents tab. Already, I've got some nice particle action.

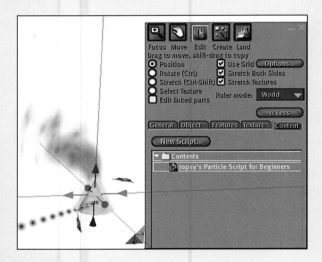

**Figure 10-8**
*Creating a particle emitter prim.*

### Step 6: Play with the Appearance

Next, I changed the start color and end color to the following:

- `START_COLOR = < 0.0, 0.1, 0.9 >;` // A Dark Blue
- `END_COLOR = < 0.4, 0.9, 0.9 >;` // A Light Blue

Remember, these are red, green, and blue settings from 0.0 to 1.0. To get a precise color you want, use something like MS Paint and get the RGB values, which will be between 0 and 255. As discussed previously, divide by 255 to get the value you want. For example, 0 = 0.0, 255 = 1.0, 128 = 0.5, and so on. Figure 10-9 shows the particles before and after changes to the color values.

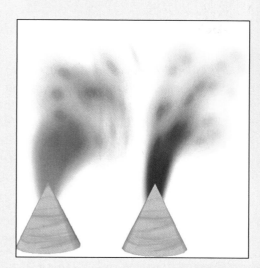

**Figure 10-9**
*Changing the color of particles.*

## Step 7: Play with the Flow

Well now, it gets kind of tricky to show in a book, but I played with these flow settings (see Figure 10-10). Now I'm getting a burst followed by a pause—unlike the original, which had a steady stream of particles, very flame like.

- AGE = 3.00; // particles last 3 seconds
- RATE = 2; // particles produced in 2-second bursts
- COUNT = 20; // 20 particles per burst

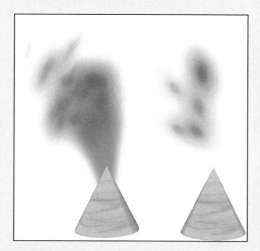

**Figure 10-10**
*Flow changes to my particle emitter.*

## Step 8: Play with Placement

For Figure 10-11 I increased COUNT to 200 and increased the ANGLE_END placement to 2.00 for a broader distribution. You can see we're starting to get a nice ocean wave spray!

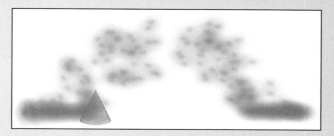

**Figure 10-11**
*Placement change to my particle emitter.*

## Step 9: Play with Movement and Fine-Tune

At this point, I started playing with movement settings. I changed SPEED_MIN to 1.5 and SPEED_MAX to 2.0. I had to dial the ANGLE_END back to 1.00 and also set the initial alpha to 0.9. The results are shown in Figure 10-12.

**Figure 10-12**
*A nice particle-bursting pattern.*

## Step 10: Tune the Texture

Finally, I purchased the JP Particle - Cloud v2 texture at the Particle Lab. Either you can get the unique ID of a texture, or you can place the texture in the same object as your emitter.

I did a bit more playing and a lot of placement work, and you can see the subtle surf spray in Figure 10-13! I ended up starting the alpha at 0.5, changing the color to be more white, with less variation. Finally, I placed the object down low so the initial burst of particles is not seen from this vantage point.

**Figure 10-13**
*Ocean-side surf spray particle effect.*

# THE PARTICLE LAB

As alluded to earlier, the definitive in-world source for learning particles at your own pace is the Particle Lab in Teal (see Figure 10-14).

**Figure 10-14**
*A balloon ride to the Particle Lab in Teal.*

It is truly an indispensable resource with many stations that demonstrate visually how particles work.

Of the three main in-world self-paced learning centers, this one is particularly well suited for its subject because the visual displays make it much easier to understand how all the settings work. Take your time; you won't get through it all in one go.

I also highly suggest having in mind a project you want to work on before you go there; it will help focus your learning at the Particle Lab.

 http://slurl.com/secondlife/Teal/180/74/21/

## A VISIT WITH THE PARTICLE LAB'S CREATOR

*"If there's a single mantra that should be chanted with regards to prims and particles...for a BIG particle display use BIG prims and BIG particles. For a SMALL effect, use SMALL prims and SMALL particles. Don't mix."*

*—Jopsy Pendragon*

Jopsy Pendragon (see Figure 10-15) was kind enough to spend some time with me answering questions about SL and particles. A summary of our conversation follows.

**Figure 10-15**
*Jopsy Pendragon.*

```
[You arrive at the floating citadel
(see Figure 10-16), a tower-like
structure hundreds of meters above
the Particle Lab. Ansel Gasparini is
here. Jopsy Pendragon is here.]

Ansel Gasparini: Hello!

Jopsy Pendragon: Hello :)

AG: So, you want to talk here?

Object whispers: Yes, Ansel Gasparini

JP: ah.. hmm.. we should probably
step away from pythia a bit or she'll
keep nattering at us. ;)

AG: who is pythia?

JP: The 2nd floor of the tower here
has a 'bot' like construct that
responds 'pithily' to questions. :-)
```

**Figure 10-16**
*Jopsy Pendragon's Floating Citadel.*

```
AG: ha

JP: a partial import of a chat bot I
was working on for tinymuds ages ago
```

**Ansel Gasparini**: *How did you hear about SL?*

**Jopsy Pendragon:** a friend tried several times to get me to try out SL...but I kept resisting, in part because it didn't look (from the screen shots) much better than old VRML worlds...and in part because I'm a control freak, used to owning my own servers. ;)

*AG: What was your initial impression of SL?*

JP: Hm... I'd have to say my first impression was that it had a lot of potential, but was still a bit on the rough side. My first avatars were embarassingly hideous looking...It was a few short weeks before I picked up some land (just below us and slightly west), and started building. I'd done rendering and modelling in other programs prior...it was nice not to have to publish to the web to share things. I've also been a developer type, so scripting comes natural ...

*AG: Was the Particle Lab the first thing you built when you got here?*

JP: oh no...I didn't start on that until nearly may of 2004 ...I'd started teaching classes. I wasn't working during my first 5 months or so here, so had a lot of free time to play. But, I got an offer I couldn't refuse and knew that I'd have to fade from SL for a while as I spun up to the new job. Before I started work I converted my class materials into self-paced lab materials...in the first incarnation of the lab :-)

*AG: So you were teaching about particles in-world?*

JP: Back then it was all about getting dwell income...teaching particle classes once or twice a week put my land in Teal up in the top 30 or so most popular fairly often back then. :-) There was certainly no LindeX back then, the idea of buying L$ was somewhat alien to me. I was hoping to leave the [particle] lab as a 'dwell magnet' while I was away for my new job, so that when I got back I could afford more land and such.

*AG: When dwell ended, how did it impact you?*

JP: Hmm...it was sort of a sad thing for me...but not devastating...I'd started selling a few odds and ends which seemed to do reasonably well with the traffic going to the lab...wasn't break even, but it helped. When I wasn't working I was more conscious of my tier payments. With an RL job, I can afford to hold more land ... I just have less time to play with it. folks have been very generous towards the lab, buying textures and such, it breaks even most months now. :-)

*AG: For a new resident, what are the best things to use particles for and what should they avoid using particles for?*

JP: Good question. Best thing for newbies to use particles for is usually 'bling' or 'glow' effects on personal attachments, they really give things a nice pop, especially if the effect isn't completely "common"...using particles to create "big" effects, like massive amounts of fog, or weather, isn't something I'd recommend new scripters try...it can generate a lot of rendering lag.

I have a 'sample' bling script in the lab now, there's a library of "basic particle patterns" all use the default particle texture. Another one I get asked for often is rings or jet flames…they're in there too.

*AG: Since particles are displayed client side, how is the world starved for particles?*

JP: The client is limited as to how many particles it can draw at one time. The default is 4096, you can double that if you're equipment is up for the challenge. It's not hard to make one emitter create 4096 concurrent particles and if you have many emitters…the displays start looking rather 'thin' as particles drop out

```
[Jopsy pulls out a few cones which
start emitting particles]
```

*AG: wow, nice effect (see Figure 10-17), are they following the wind?*

JP: Yep! This emitter is great for showing wind currents in the sim :-) It's amusing to see them cross sim boundaries… wind is not consistent from sim to sim…so particles will suddenly swerve and go a different way as soon as they cross into a new region. :-)

*AG: what are the number one mistakes newbies make with particles?*

JP: The number 1 mistake is using too many particles. What I often find newbies doing with particles is trying to create a fire effect made up of thousands of tiny particles rather than just a few that behave a little better …using bunches of tiny particles instead of slightly larger ones can really waste huge numbers of them. Another common mistake newbies make is not understanding that particles are based on the PRIM…scripts set the prim attributes that control particles…once the particles are turned on though, the script really isn't needed anymore. Deleting the script WON'T STOP PARTICLES. Probably the most frequent question I get. "But …I deleted the script! They won't stop!!!"

*AG: Are some prims better than others for particles?*

JP: Well, tree and grass prims can't be used…they won't accept scripts. Ring, Torus, Sphere…are created turned 90 degrees sideways … this confuses people trying to use angle patterns, so some care should be used picking those. Like SitTarget(), sometimes it's easier just to rotate the prim instead of trying to force something that's hard to do. If there's a single mantra that should be chanted with regards to prims and particles … it's BIG BIG BIG or SMALL SMALL SMALL. For a BIG particle display use BIG prims and BIG particles. For a SMALL effect, use SMALL prims and SMALL particles. Don't mix.

The reason I recommend small prims for small displays is that MOST small prims don't get communicated or seen by the client until the avatar is rather close to them. (usually 28m or less). And if the client doesn't "see" the prim, the avatar won't "see" that prim's particles. Which means more particles not in use unnecessarily. (a small effect could be something like a candle in someone's house or such) you're not going to see that more than 28m away, most likely.

*AG: Any other advice for new people getting into particles?*

JP: Practice practice practice … :-). Particles 'work' better if a person has a short draw

**Figure 10-17**
*Particles that respond to the wind.*

distance, I often keep my own at 64 for just that reason. It's more to reduce competition for particles from other nearby displays (the short draw distance that is).

JP: Pardon me a moment…laundry going into the dryer.

AG: Thank you again for the time and all the knowledge

JP: Sounds good! If you have any other questions feel free to IM me anytime…:-)

# ANIMATIONS, POSES, AND POSEBALLS

This section provides you with the basic information about SL animation and how to bring your avatars and creations to life. It also includes a great tutorial from Johan Durant on creating a basic sit animation and how to use that animation in a poseball.

## WHAT ARE POSES AND ANIMATIONS?

Avatars can be made to perform different movements in SL. One of these is called an **animation**. For example, you may swim, dance, or just sit on a couch. An animation in which the avatar does not move is called a **pose**. Poses require two frames, the first of which is never seen.

When you walk or run in SL, your avatar is using a certain animation to make it look as though it is walking or running. Animations and poses may be part of an object and used to pose or animate avatars sitting on or wearing these objects (for example, part of a couch or a pair of shoes).

You may also see gestures in SL. **Gestures** group chat text, sounds, pauses, poses, and animations into a sequence that can be replayed together. Gestures can include just one, two, or all of these types of items. Gestures cannot be part of an object; they are triggered by avatars by typing something like **/clap** (see Figure 10-18), as we saw in Chapter 3, "Communication and Social Networking."

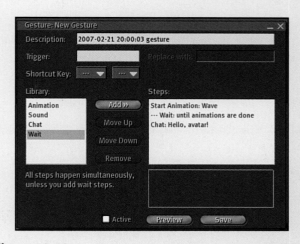

**Figure 10-18**
*The Gesture Editor.*

## WHAT CAN I DO WITH POSES AND ANIMATIONS?

Basically, you can do about anything with poses and animations! You can make your avatar walk the way you want it to walk. You can create custom furniture that, when used, the avatar will sit or lie on more realistically. You can create cool dance moves. You can even make two avatars hug, dance together, and, yes, have sex as well!

## HOW DO I CREATE POSES OR ANIMATIONS?

Just like creating textures, creating poses or animations is something you do outside SL. You'll need some animation software to create them. The software you choose must be able to output to the Biovision Hierarchical Data (BVH) file format.

There are a lot of tools available that support this format. Popular choices include Poser, DAZ|Studio, QAvimator, and Maya, among others. Throughout the following sections, I focus on QAvimator, a free SL-specific utility, and Poser, an inexpensive commercial animation program.

### QAvimator

QAvimator is a simple, open source piece of software that was designed specifically for use with SL. If you don't want to invest any money in animation creation, then QAvimator is for you.

The original version, Avimator, was discontinued as of this writing and replaced by QAvimator. QAvimator supports Windows, Linux, and Mac clients. See the QAvimator site for download and details: http://www.qavimator.org/.

Figure 10-19 shows the QAvimator interface.

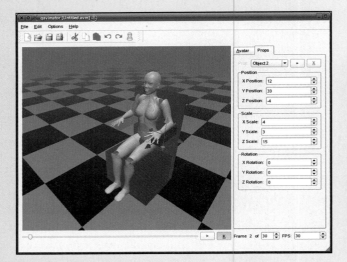

**Figure 10-19**
*The QAvimator interface.*

## Poser

Poser is an extremely powerful and yet easy-to-learn commercial software package originally designed for animating human figures. Currently at version 7, it is published by e frontier. You can buy it at http://www.e-frontier.com/.

## DAZ|Studio

Also worth checking out is DAZ|Studio, which is a free 3D modeling package with some basic animation support. You can download it from http://www.daz3d.com/.

## HOW DO I LOAD SL AVATARS INTO POSER?

QAvimator, because it was designed for use with SL, already has the default SL female/male avatars loaded. For Poser, however, the default figure is a Poser figure. To create animations for SL, you need to download and install the SL male or female avatar **mesh,** which is the data that represents the male and female base avatars in SL. I won't go into all the gory 3D details of what a mesh

is here, so trust me (see http://en.wikipedia.org/wiki/Polygon_mesh if you're interested in more details).

Download the zip file from http://secondlife.com/community/avatar.php and unpack it. The Readme.txt file explains how to get the meshes into Poser. Even though this file was written in January 2005, I tried the instructions for Poser 6 with good results: Figure 10-20 shows the main Poser interface with the SL male avatar loaded.

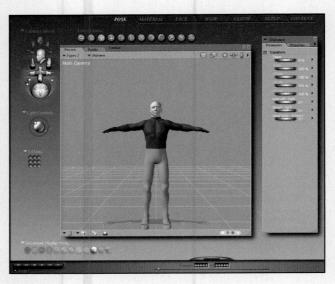

**Figure 10-20**
*Poser 6 with SL male avatar ready to pose.*

Before we start, let me give you one quick tip: If you're using Poser 6, you need to download the latest service release to resolve a bug. Specifically, when you try to upload your animation, you'll see this error: "Unable to read animation file can't get rotation values". See this forum post for answers (thanks to Seagel Neville): http://forums.secondlife.com/showthread.php?t=79269. This problem is resolved in Poser 7.

## WHAT IS A BVH FILE?

Biovision Hierarchy is a motion-capture or "mocap" file format that stores information about an animated character in simple text form. It is commonly used throughout the 3D industry. BVH is certainly not the only mocap format out there, but it happens to be the only one that SL can read at this time.

When you create a pose or an animation for SL in Poser, QAvimator, or in any other suitable animation program, you'll export the animation as a BVH file and then upload the file to SL. Once the file has been uploaded, your avatar will be able to use it.

## CAN I JUST BUY AN ANIMATION OR POSE?

Sure, you can! Just use Search and look for terms like "poses," "poseballs," "animations," or "gestures."

Here are a couple of spots I know of:

Bits and Bobs by Craig Altman

 **http://slurl.com/secondlife/The%20Island/237/131/22/**

The Motion Merchant by Johan Durant

 **http://slurl.com/secondlife/Gnoma/164/183/62**

Abranimations

 **http://slurl.com/secondlife/Abranimations/128/128/0**

## ANIMATION OVERRIDES

Every avatar has a default set of animations such as walking, running, flying, jumping, and crouching. You can override these animations by using something called an **animation overrider** (AO or ao). An AO is basically an object you attach to your avatar that contains scripts and animations to override the default animations. AOs allow you to have a sexy saunter or macho strut; they also allow for other interesting options like movement while pregnant, animal movement, movement while drunk, and the like.

AOs come in a wide variety of forms, such as cell phones, necklaces, invisible cubes, and even shoes. There are several good ones for sale that include very cool animations. You can also find freebies at YadNi's Junkyard.

YadNi's Junkyard can be found at

 **http://slurl.com/secondlife/leda/210/28/54/**.

Also check out

 **http://slurl.com/secondlife/Animation%20Island/16/6/322/**.

How each AO works depends on its creators, and there are no standards. Many listen to their owner on the main chat channel for commands; others are HUD driven. At a minimum, there is usually a command to turn the AO on and off such as /ao on or /ao off. There may also be commands to show or hide the AO, making it visible or invisible.

You may also be able to copy your own animations into the AO. Make sure to read carefully any notecard that comes with your AO. Also be aware that some high-lag places may require you to turn off or remove your AO (see Chapter 12, "Practical Matters: Under the Hood of the Metaverse").

## AN INTERVIEW WITH CRAIG ALTMAN OF BITS AND BOBS

Craig Altman (see Figure 10-21) is a busy guy. He is best known for his couples' animations, which can be found at his chain of stores Bits and Bobs. I exchanged questions and answers via notecards with Craig; here's what he had to say on animation in SL.

**Figure 10-21**
*Craig Altman.*

**Ansel Gasparini**: *How did you get into the Animation business?*

**Craig Altman:** SLs major advantage over other online worlds is the fact you can make almost anything you want, but to DO anything you want you need an animation for doing whatever it is. At the time there were animations to do lots of things, but there were things I wanted that I could not find, I thought it would be great if I could have things exactly as I imagined them, and the only way to do that really is to make it yourself.

CA: I went and got a trial version of Poser to see if I could do it, of course as with most things, its not as easy as you might think and it was very slow progress, I think it took me 5 weeks to make a single 2 second animation, but it was great to see it in world, and to show others, it was really the encouragement of others and Jenny which kept me doing it.

*AG: Did you have RL experience that carried into SL?*

CA: Well with animations anything that I do in RL is easier to make an animation of, other things like complex dances etc. I must watch on video in fine detail in order to make, certain things you can picture in your mind, with romantic animations you just *know* when a thing looks right and when it doesn't, I have in the past completely remade ones that didn't have the feeling I was going for. I think anyone can look at a film or animation and just *know* if it captures something.

*AG: How would you recommend a new resident get started if they want to create animations?*

CA: Well there are free animating programs that were not around when I started, I have not used them because I'm a bit set in my ways now, but I have heard they are very good, of course its an advantage to be used to 3d programs like this but by no means essential, I was not.

Probably the biggest thing is to not see what others do and assume that's what you must do, make whatever it is you personally want to see, you may find a lot of people want to see it too, also make sure the end result is truly the best you can do, don't ignore parts where you know its not as you wanted it thinking "oh well, no one will notice", as I mentioned before, people know.

Apart from anything else you will look back and wish you had taken the time later, I have re-made a number of my very old ones, simply because I know more than I did then, they were the best I could make at the time, but now they could be better, if they can be they should be.

*AG: What advice can you offer new builders who want to add an animation to a bed/chair?*

CA: Well this actually comes more into the area of scripting than animating, many people confuse the two things, unless you are running an animation inworld by clicking on anims in your Inventory, all objects in world using animations must also be using a script to trigger and stop the animation, the script also controls where the animation is placed relative to the prim the anim and script are in.

The basic poseball method of putting animations in furniture is annoying to some because of the extra prim used and the general appearance of poseballs, but it does allow for easy adjustment for different avatar shapes and sizes, it also makes it easier for people to sit in a certain place they want on a piece with more than one seating position.

The method with the script and animation inside the furniture piece is tidier I think, but can lead to problems with shorter or taller avatars than the one for which the script was set up for. But as I said, Im not a scripter so there could well be a better way where you can have all these things

## WHERE CAN I LEARN MORE?

If you're serious about building your own poses and animations, the best resource is the SL Animations Forum located at

SLURL **http://forums.secondlife.com/ forumdisplay.php?f=52**

Start with Strife Onizuka's FAQ for Animators at

SLURL **http://forums.secondlife.com/ showthread.php?t=107495**

# TUTORIAL: CREATING A SITTING POSE WITH JOHAN DURANT

To give us a quick tutorial on how to use Poser to create a basic sitting pose and poseball, I have turned to Johan Durant (see Figure 10-22), owner of The Motion Merchant. Johan is also well known for his freely available clothes-making tool, SL Clothes Previewer (information can be found in Chapter 7, "Advanced Textures and Clothing"). Take it away, Johan!

This tutorial is an explanation of how to create a pose for sitting down and how to use that pose with a piece of furniture in SL. I picked this subject matter to focus on because it's of general usefulness to SL content creators and because it covers most of the SL-specific animation issues. I won't cover how to animate, and thus the "animation" is just a static pose without any movement.

**Figure 10-22**
*Johan Durant.*

## STEP 1: OPEN YOUR ANIMATION TOOL

To begin, first open your animation tool. I use Poser, and that's what's depicted in Figure 10-23.

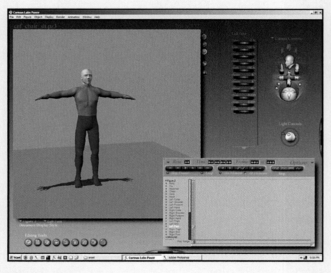

**Figure 10-23**
*e frontier's Poser interface.*

## STEP 2: CREATE YOUR POSE

If you don't already have it set up, download the avatar model from the SL website and use that instead of Poser's default figure. There are a couple of little gotchas to keep in mind when making animations for use with SL. The first little detail to remember is that the first frame is not part of the motion. SL uses the first frame as a reference for how the character is set up. That can be useful for some tricks with animation, but for now, just note that you want

to leave the first frame in the default T pose and work only on the second frame onward. Of course, in the case of a static pose, there is only one frame for the "movement," so you'll be working only on frame 2 in your animation tool.

To work in frame 2, change the frame at the bottom of the Poser interface. Working on frame 2, I moved the body parts around and created the sitting pose in Figure 10-24.

**Figure 10-24**
*A sit pose defined.*

## STEP 3: APPLY ANIMATION TO ONLY POSED PARTS

Now, this step illustrates another oddity about SL. Notice how the head is facing down? I don't actually want the head facing down, but rather I want to keep the head free for the software to control. In short, I want the avatar to look around as normal. I just make sure not to apply any animation to the head or neck, and those body parts are controlled normally by SL. Take a look at my Animation Palette (Window->Animation Palette), shown in Figure 10-25, and you can see I have not applied key frames to the head or neck.

**Figure 10-25**
*Poser Animation Palette.*

The implication here is that the converse is also true: To make sure a given body part is controlled by your animation and not, as it normally would be, by SL, make sure to apply animation to that body part. Once you get your avatar into the right place, remove any key frames from elements you want controlled by SL.

## STEP 4: EXPORT A BVH FILE

The next step is to export a BVH file of the animation. If you're using QAvimator, this step is unnecessary because QAvimator saves to the BVH file format natively. Using Poser, however, you have to export to that format. Just select File>Export>BVH (see Figure 10-26). You'll be prompted to indicate whether you want to scale the motion capture data. It's important that you select Scale Automatically.

**Figure 10-26**
*Export menu in Poser.*

## STEP 5: UPLOAD YOUR ANIMATION

Once the BVH file is created, you can upload the animation into SL. Fire up SL and log in. Under the File menu, choose Upload Animation (see Figure 10-27).

**Figure 10-27**
*Upload Animation menu option.*

## STEP 6: SELECT OPTIONS IN UPLOAD PREVIEWER

When you choose the Upload Animation option, it will open the Upload Previewer (see Figure 10-28). Here, you can view the animation applied to an SL avatar and monkey with a few options and settings. The first setting to adjust is Priority. In SL, the priority of an animation determines what is seen if multiple animations are playing simultaneously. Basically, the higher priority animation is the one you actually see.

>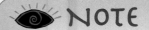
> **NOTE**
>
> Animation priority levels determine which animation trumps any others that are triggered. For example, if I'm slow dancing with my partner and I want to chat, I *don't* want my AV to break from the embrace so that I can type (the priority level for the slow dance is higher than the priority level for SL's internal *typing* animation). Priority level is assigned at upload. There are five levels (0–4). Higher priorities levels outrank lower. If priority levels are identical, the latter-playing anim gets priority. For a helpful reference, see http://wiki.secondlife.com/wiki/Internal_Animations.

Also check the Loop option. Sometimes you want an animation to play through once and then end, in which case don't check this option. Other times, however, you want the avatar to keep playing the animation over and over; that's called **looping**. For a static pose, you want to loop over and over on the one frame you set. Alternatively, don't check Loop, but set In% to 100 and Out% to 100, to lock into the last frame.

Finally, once looping is set, you can adjust the Ease In/Out values. They determine the smoothness of transitions when the avatar starts and ends this animation. Just set both to 0.3, a relatively ordinary level of smoothness.

With those settings done, click Upload to bring the animation into SL.

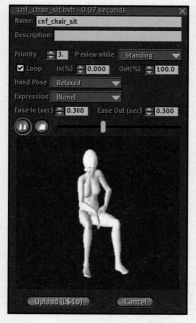

**Figure 10-28**
*Second Life Upload Previewer.*

## STEP 7: TEST THE ANIMATION

Once the animation file is finished uploading, you'll find it in your Inventory under the Animations folder. Double-click it to bring up the playback buttons and click Play Locally. Check out Figure 10-29; I'm sitting!

You can either choose Play In World, which will show your animated avatar to everyone around you, or Play Locally, which will just play the animation on your own client so that no one sees it (great for testing)!

**Figure 10-29**
*Testing an uploaded animation.*

At this point, however, the animation isn't really much use as a sit pose. Playing the animation file directly, you won't be positioned correctly for sitting on anything and will simply be sitting on thin air. To overcome the positioning issue, you typically use poseballs. In a nutshell, **poseballs** are small spheres that contain both the animation and a script that plays the animation when you sit on the poseball.

## STEP 8: CREATE A POSEBALL

To make a poseball, the first step is to create a sphere. Blank its texture and set its size a little smaller so that it doesn't dominate the scene. I like to set my poseballs to 0.2 meters, as shown in the edit window (see Figure 10-30).

**Figure 10-30**
*Creating a poseball.*

## STEP 9: ADD THE ANIMATION AND POSE SCRIPT

Now add to the contents of the poseball prim. Click the Contents tab in the edit window to view the poseball's Inventory. Next, drop your animation into the poseball. Then click New Script, double-click the script to edit it, and overwrite the script with the following. Alternatively, pick up a copy at the in-world site.

```
string ani = "cnf_chair_sit";
default
{
state_entry()
{
    llSitTarget(<0,0,-0.1>,<0,0,0,1>);
    llSetSitText("Pose!");
}

changed(integer change)
{
    if(change & CHANGED_LINK)
    {
```

```
key avataronsittarget =
    llAvatarOnSitTarget();
if( avataronsittarget != NULL_KEY ) {
    llSetAlpha(0.0, ALL_SIDES);
    if ((llGetPermissions() &
        PERMISSION_TRIGGER_ANIMATION) &&
        llGetPermissionsKey() ==
        avataronsittarget) {
        llStopAnimation("sit");
        llStartAnimation(ani);
    } else {
        llRequestPermissions
        (avataronsittarget,
        PERMISSION_TRIGGER_ANIMATION);
    }
    }
    else{
        llSetAlpha(1.0, ALL_SIDES);
    }
    }
}

run_time_permissions(integer perm)
{
    if(perm) {
        llStopAnimation("sit");
        llStartAnimation(ani);
    }
    }
}
```

**Figure 10-31**
*Finished pose—sitting in a chair.*

## STEP 10: CHANGE THE NAME OF THE ANIMATION

On the first line of the script, you define the name of your animation. Just change the part inside the quotation marks to whatever your animation is named. This script is designed so that the poseball disappears when sat upon and reappears when you stand.

## STEP 11: TRY IT OUT!

With that script in the object, just link the poseball into a piece of furniture and sit on the poseball (see Figure 10-31). Lookin' good!

# ADDING MOVEMENT TO OBJECTS IN SECOND LIFE

Objects can be made to move in SL. They may move on their own or react to physical forces such as a push, gravity, or the wind. A robot can patrol your land, butterflies can hover over a bush, a dolphin can jump through the water, waves can roll onto the beach, logs can tumble downhill, a familiar can follow you around, and an elevator can carry you up to the top floor at the push of a button.

How an object moves depends on what type of object it is. With respect to movement, objects can be considered one of three classes: nonphysical, physical, and vehicular.

- Nonphysical objects are objects that do not react to the SL physics engine.
- Physical objects are objects that do react to the SL physics engine.
- Vehicles are physical objects that can be driven, flown, sailed, or whatever by an avatar using avatar movement controls.

The following sections discuss moving objects as well as the SL physics engine. Vehicles are discussed in the section "Finding and Using Vehicles."

# NONPHYSICAL OBJECTS

Most things you see in SL are nonphysical objects. Nonphysical objects defy gravity, and if pushed, they do not respond.

To see how they work, create a sphere and drag it up into the air. Now close your editing tools. What happens? Nothing, right? The plywood sphere just hangs there in the air defying gravity! Gravity, you say, what's this about gravity? Well, just hang on a second.

Next, left-click and drag on the sphere (without using the editing tools). Does it move? No, nope, nada, nothing. It doesn't respond to your pushing on it. It is just a nonphysical object after all.

Earlier, we made objects sway, flap, or twist by making them flexible (see Chapter 6, "Building Basics"). Flexible prims are not actually moving; that is, their location in-world (their x, y, z coordinates) does not change. So, even though they flex, flexible primitives are still nonphysical objects.

You may also recall that we made a waterfall in Chapter 9, "Land Ownership, Terraforming, and Landscaping," in the section "Tutorial: Adding a Waterfall." In that case, we used an animated texture that gives the appearance of movement. The nonphysical object, however, is not moving at all.

So, what if you want to make an nonphysical object move? These are the key LSL functions involved:

- llSetPos(): Sets a nonphysical object's position or sets it moving toward that position. There is a limit on this function of no more than 10 meters (per call) away from the current position.

- llSetRot(), llLookAt(), llRotLookAt(): Set a nonphysical object's rotation or the direction in which it's facing.

- llTargetOmega(): Causes the object to spin.

- llSetLocalRot(): Establishes the rotation of a child prim relative to the parent.

# PHYSICAL OBJECTS AND THE SL PHYSICS ENGINE

SL has a physics engine that simulates gravity and other physical forces like wind. An object may be made "physical" and will interact with the world if it's pushed or thrown.

Let's do the same exercise as we did in the nonphysical object section. First, create a sphere and drag it up into the air. Now, select the check box named Physical under Object Parameters, as seen in Figure 10-32. Then exit your editing tools and watch what happens!

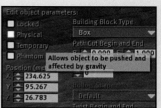

**Figure 10-32**
*Physical object check box.*

If you did things right, the sphere will drop out of the sky and roll around on the ground (see Figure 10-33). If you're on a slope, it may actually roll away from you. That's gravity for you!

**Figure 10-33**
*Nonphysical and physical spheres.*

Now, left-click and drag on the sphere and then let go. You should see it move and then go rolling away as if pushed! In fact, that is what you did—pushed the sphere. It moved because it is now physical.

For some beach-side fun, find Philip Linden's beach ball in the library under Library->Objects->Beach Ball (see Figure 10-34).

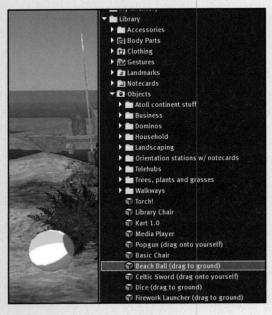

**Figure 10-34**
*Beach ball rolling on the ground.*

Check out the beach ball script and the contents (see Figure 10-35) of the object to see how the sound effects work, how you set buoyancy, and how you can apply a little force to a physical object.

**Figure 10-35**
*Beach ball content.*

# FINDING AND USING VEHICLES

Vehicles in SL are highly scripted objects that take over input and movement control from the avatar who is driving. They are available either free or to purchase all over SL and can be a lot of fun. As you'll see in the next section, "Tutorial: Using a Vehicle (Kart 1.0)," you already have a vehicle in your library.

Vehicles are typically cars, motorcycles, jetskis, boats, and planes, but they can also be flying carpets, surfboards, a dragon, or a winged horse.

Vehicles are built by all kinds of people and have various levels of quality. Some are hard to control, some have trouble crossing sim boundaries, and so on. It's best if you test drive a vehicle before you buy, particularly if it's an expensive one. Also, remember to carefully read the instructions (usually on a notecard) that come with the vehicle because they don't all operate the same way. It is often useful to use mouselook when driving a vehicle.

# TUTORIAL: USING A VEHICLE (KART 1.0)

When you arrive in SL, you already have a fine starter vehicle in your Inventory. This tutorial shows you how to locate and use it. The scripts are freely editable, so this is a great place to start if you want to tinker with a car-style vehicle.

## STEP 1: FIND KART 1.0

Open your Inventory and look in the library for Kart 1.0 (see Figure 10-36).

**Figure 10-36**
*Kart 1.0 in the library.*

## STEP 2: REZ THE KART

Drag Kart 1.0 from your Inventory onto the ground somewhere to rez the Kart (see Figure 10-37). You'll be given a notecard with a set of instructions.

## STEP 3: GET ON THE KART

Right-click on the Kart to bring up the pie menu (see Figure 10-38). There, you'll see the Ride option. The word used here is set in the vehicle's script; other vehicles may use different words like "Sit," "Sail," "Board," or "Drive."

Figure 10-39 shows me sitting in the driver's seat ready to go.

**Figure 10-37**
*Kart 1.0 rezzed on the ground.*

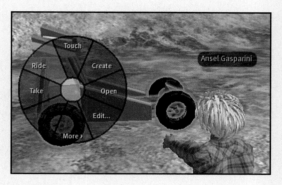

**Figure 10-38**
*Ride pie menu.*

**Figure 10-39**
*Ready to ride Kart 1.0.*

## STEP 4: DRIVE THE KART

Now you're ready to go. With vehicles, the controls you normally use to move your avatar will move the vehicle. Try the arrow keys or WASD keys to accelerate and turn. You'll quickly find that Kart 1.0 is tricky to handle but great for off-roading.

I found myself at the bottom of the sea pretty quickly, as you can see in Figure 10-40. Look at your Kart 1.0 instructions for a nifty feature to right yourself when you tip over.

**Figure 10-40**
*Wrecked underwater in Kart 1.0.*

## STEP 5: GET THE HANG OF IT

After a bit, you'll get the hang of driving. In Figure 10-41, I'm taking my Kart out for a spin down a local road. Next, you can edit the script to tweak how Kart 1.0 behaves. You might also try using this script in your own vehicle.

> 👁 **NOTE**
>
> If you're riding in a vehicle and want to get out or stop using it, click the Release Keys button at the bottom of your display. The Release Keys button is used the same way for vehicles as the Stand Up button is for sofas.

**Figure 10-41**
*On the road in Kart 1.0.*

# BUILDING VEHICLES

The subject of creating and selling vehicles really deserves an entire book, and I'm sure there will be one before long. Until then, this section introduces you to a few basic concepts, but expect to do a lot of your own research and study existing freebie vehicles if you really want to create your own. Kart 1.0 and Cubey Terra's Do-It-Yourself plane kit offer great starting scripts, as does the LSL Wiki.

Vehicles have the following properties in SL:

- They are physical objects.
- They must be 31 or fewer primitives (–1 prim for each passenger).
- They contain a lot of scripts.

If you've never done any scripting in RL or in SL, then I suggest you try your hand at a few more basic projects before you dive into vehicle creation. In the following sections I'm going to assume you have some level of familiarity with basic building techniques and basic scripting.

Scripts are placed in the root prim of a vehicle. Typically, vehicle scripts do the following:

- Provide a sit target and name such as "Ride," "Drive," or "Sail." When you right-click on the vehicle, this is how you board it.
- Provide some level of owner security; typically, only the owner is allowed to drive the vehicle (and commonly passengers cannot "sit" until the driver's seated).
- Define a startup function that sets the camera position, changes the vehicle to physical, and sets other vehicle parameters.
- Define a source of power, a linear or angular motor, sometimes both, and sometimes more than one.
- Define how friction impacts the vehicle, if at all.
- Define whether the vehicle hovers, and if it does, how it hovers, at a certain height over water or land or at a global height regardless of terrain (think Luke Skywalker hovercraft versus hot air balloon).
- Define the banking characteristics such as when an airplane, boat, or motorcycle turns versus a sled or car.
- Define how the vehicle is controlled; for example, do you move it with standard movement keys and can you steer it in mouselook?
- Possibly contain animations and sounds. Scripts can activate these animations and sounds at the right time, such as idling the motor when a car comes to a stop.

The best approach to getting good at vehicle creation is to spend some time on the wiki and find something free that you like and try improving or adding to it before you build something from scratch (http://www.lslwiki.net/lslwiki/wakka.php?wakka=TutorialVehicle).

If you're itching to get started, and you have some basic building skills, then the next tutorial is a real gem and has a huge payoff at the end.

# TUTORIAL: ASSEMBLING A KIT AIRPLANE WITH CUBEY TERRA

For this tutorial, you should set aside about an hour (yup, this is in the advanced section). It's helpful if you have some experience with building, linking, and using scripts, but not required.

A big thank you to the master of SL aeronautics, Cubey Terra (see Figure 10-42), for the use of the class material for the do-it-yourself (DIY) airplane repurposed in this tutorial. Before you begin, you'll need to find your way to Abbott's Aerodrome to retrieve your DIY airplane kit.

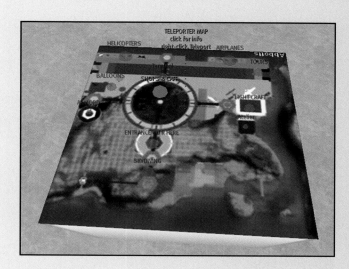

**Figure 10-43**
*Teleport map of Abbotts Aerodrome.*

**Figure 10-42**
*Cubey Terra.*

At this point, I'll turn you over to Cubey Terra. Let's get started!

## STEP 1: TELEPORT TO ABBOTTS AERODROME

You should know by now how to use Search to find a location and TP there. Search for "Abbotts" and teleport in. The Abbotts entry location changes sometimes, but as of this writing you'll find a cool mini-teleport map when you arrive (shown in Figure 10-43). Teleport to the Shop and Cafe.

## STEP 2: GET A FREE COPY OF THE DIY PLANE KIT

Find your way to the "flight shop" in a wide open space. On one of the tables, you'll find the DIY plane kit (see Figure 10-44). Yup, it's small, but there is a whole airplane waiting to be built.

Right-click and select Buy from the pie menu (see Figure 10-45). I can hear you now, "You said it was free!" Well, just trust me.

**Figure 10-44**
*DIY plane kit on table.*

**Figure 10-45**
*Buy the DIY plane kit.*

At the top of the display, notice the message that you're buying the "Terra DIY Plane Kit." But below, it says "Buy for L$0 from Cubey Terra" (see Figure 10-46).

Yes, you can buy something for FREE in SL.

**Figure 10-46**
*DIY plane contents.*

## STEP 3: FIND A PLACE TO BUILD YOUR DIY PLANE

You should see in your Inventory the DIY plane kit, as shown in Figure 10-47. You'll need to find a place where you can build your plane. Sandboxes are great if you don't own land, but make sure the sandbox you pick allows vehicle testing.

**Figure 10-47**
*DIY plane kit in your Inventory.*

Drag your "Terra DIY Plane Kit" onto the land. When you open this kit (in the next step), you see the following parts:

- A notecard
- Two scripts: "Terra DIY - Plane 1.0" and "Terra DIY - Second seat"

- Terra DIY - Fuselage
- Terra DIY - Horizontal stabilizer
- Terra DIY - Landing gear L
- Terra DIY - Landing gear R
- Terra DIY - Pilot's seat
- Terra DIY - Passenger seat
- Terra DIY - Propeller
- Terra DIY - Vertical stabilizer
- Terra DIY - Windscreen
- Terra DIY - Wings

## STEP 4: ADD THE PLANE PARTS TO YOUR INVENTORY

You'll see the DIY kit on the ground. At this point, select Open (see Figure 10-48).

You'll have the option to copy the contents to your Inventory. Select Copy To Inventory, and all the parts will be loaded into your Inventory (see Figure 10-49).

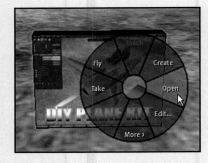

**Figure 10-48**
*Opening the DIY plane kit.*

## STEP 5: REZ PARTS ON THE GROUND

Simply drag all the components of the plane (except for the notecard or scripts) from your Inventory onto the ground in something like the configuration shown in Figure 10-50. See the parts list and make sure you have all of them.

**Figure 10-49**
*Copy the DIY parts to your Inventory.*

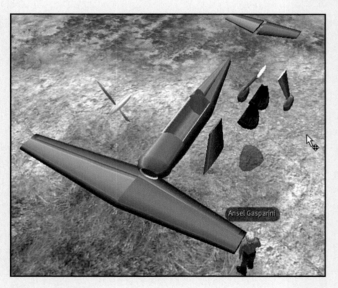

**Figure 10-50**
*Rezzing the parts on the ground.*

## STEP 6: GET STARTED WITH THE FUSELAGE

Drag the fuselage to a spot with enough room to build and lift it up off the ground a little (see Figure 10-51).

**Figure 10-51**
*Rezzing the fuselage.*

## STEP 7: POSITION THE HORIZONTAL STABILIZER

Drag the horizontal stabilizer into position at the tail end of the fuselage (see Figure 10-52). The lines on the stabilizer should be just behind the end of the fuselage. Vertically, it should be around the middle. Eyeball its placement and adjust it to suit.

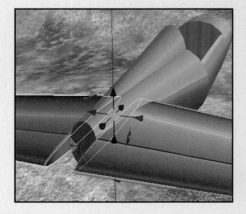

**Figure 10-52**
*Adding the horizontal stabilizer.*

## STEP 8: POSITION THE VERTICAL STABILIZER

Drag the vertical stabilizer into position at the tail end of the fuselage. Position it as you did the horizontal stabilizer (see Figure 10-53).

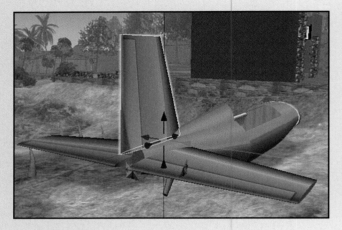

**Figure 10-53**
*Positioning the vertical stabilizer.*

## STEP 9: POSITION THE WINGS

Drag the wings into position. Vertically, they should be located near the bottom of the fuselage. The front/back position should be near the forward end of the cockpit, but not in front (see Figure 10-54).

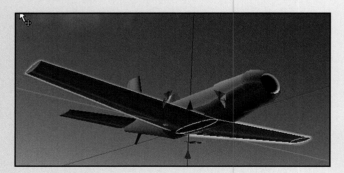

**Figure 10-54**
*Positioning the wings.*

## STEP 10: POSITION THE RIGHT LANDING GEAR

Drag the right landing gear under the plane. Position its top forward edge so that it touches the leading edge of the wing, where it meets the fuselage (see Figure 10-55).

**Figure 10-55**
*Position the right landing gear.*

> 🖐 **TIP**
>
> If you position your landing gear too far back, your plane might tip forward on takeoff or landing.

## STEP 11: POSITION THE LEFT LANDING GEAR

Drag the left landing gear under the plane and position it as you did the right landing gear. Remember to make sure the landing gear is aligned on the x- and z-axes. That is, the left and right gear should have the same height and forward/back position (see Figure 10-56).

**Figure 10-56**
*Position the left landing gear.*

## STEP 12: ADD THE SEATS

Locate the passenger seat and sit on it. Drag it into position inside the cockpit so that the seat back touches the back of the compartment. Vertically, adjust it so that it's just high enough that your feet don't stick out the bottom of the plane. Add the pilot's seat so that the chair back touches your knees (see Figure 10-57).

**Figure 10-57**
*Adding the seats.*

## STEP 13: ADD THE WINDSCREEN AND PROP

Next, drag the windscreen and propeller into position (see Figure 10-58).

**Figure 10-58**
*Adding the windscreen and propeller.*

## STEP 14: LINK THE PLANE PRIMS

It's time to link everything together. Stand up first and then select all parts, making sure that you SELECT THE PILOT'S SEAT LAST. This ensures that the pilot's seat becomes the parent prim. This step is very important. Press Ctrl+L to link the parts together (see Figure 10-59).

**Figure 10-59**
*Linking all the parts.*

## STEP 15: RENAME THE PLANE

Rename the plane (see Figure 10-60). Be creative.

You've now finished assembling the airplane model. Next, you add the scripts!

**Figure 10-60**
*Naming your plane.*

## STEP 16: ADD SCRIPT TO PASSENGER SEAT

In the edit window, choose the Edit Linked Parts check box and then click the passenger seat. The passenger seat is selected in the edit window. Next, click the Content tab, which lists any items inside the currently selected prim. It's empty at the moment. Drag the script Terra DIY - Second seat into the Content tab (see Figure 10-61).

**Figure 10-61**
*Adding a script to the passenger seat.*

## STEP 17: ADD PLANE SCRIPT TO PILOT SEAT

Now click the pilot's seat to select it and drag the script Terra DIY - Plane 1.0 into the Content tab (see Figure 10-62).

**Figure 10-62**
*Adding a script to the pilot seat.*

## STEP 18: TAKE A COPY INTO YOUR INVENTORY AND FLY

Right-click your plane and choose More->Take Copy. Now you have a backup copy in case something goes horribly wrong. DONE! You've built the plane and added the scripts. Hop in and fly!

## STEP 19: NEXT STEPS

The scripts and parts are all fully modifiable, so if you want to improve the script, you can.

I hope to see people modding, sharing, and maybe even selling this plane. See you in the skies!

# ABBOTTS AERODROME

No chapter on vehicles would be complete without a discussion of Abbotts Aerodrome (see Figure 10-63). Abbotts Aerodrome was founded by Cubey Terra and Apotheus Silverman and is the second airfield they have constructed. It's a great place to go skydiving or test drive one of the many aircraft Cubey has produced. If you're into aircraft design, this is a great place to hang out and meet like-minded residents.

Abbot's Aerodrome can be found at

 **http://slurl.com/secondlife/Abbotts/160/160/70**

## A VISIT WITH ABBOTTS AERODROME'S FOUNDER

*"We wanted a place where aircraft designers can meet and exchange ideas. Collaborate on projects. Play."*
*—Cubey Terra*

Figure 10-64 is a picture of Cubey Terra. See Cubey's website at: www.cubeyterra.com.

I sat down for a chat with the cofounder of Abbott's Aerodrome, Cubey Terra (see Figure 10-65). What follows is a summary of our conversation.

**Figure 10-63**
*Abbotts Aerodrome from the air.*

**Figure 10-64**
*Cubey Terra.*

**Figure 10-65**
*Cubey Terra and Ansel Gasparini interview.*

[Ansel arrives in a skybox hanger. There is an orderliness about the place. There are two chairs in front of a stage reminiscent of a talk show. In the hanger are various aeronautical projects underway. Cubey Terra is here. Ansel Gasparini is here. A purple fish swims around Ansel's head.]

Cubey Terra: howdy fishhead!

Ansel Gasparini: hello

Ansel Gasparini: Yes, I got this fish a couple nights ago

Ansel Gasparini: Kinda a memorial to Starax

Cubey Terra: I have a gold one somewhere

Ansel Gasparini: Thanks so much for taking the time

Cubey Terra: no problem!

Cubey Terra: Where shall we start? :)

**Ansel Gasparini**: *How did you come into SL? And what is your past history with on-line worlds?*

**Cubey Terra:** hm. First, the how … I saw an article about SL on Wired.com in 2003. At the time, my computer was incapable of running SL, so I missed out on the beta. Months later, as soon as I upgraded, I tried SL. That was September 2003. I was addicted right from the start. I'd never tried a multiplayer virtual world before. I was a big fan of the Myst games, and liked the idea of a world that you explore instead of blow up.

*AG: So, tell me how Abbotts came about?*

CT: Abbotts is the 2nd airport I helped build…First, there was Zoe Airfield …

at the end of 2003, I was a bit bored and looking for something interesting to do. I ran into Apotheus Silverman—another newbie—who was building an airstrip on the east side of Zoe. In a kind of random collaboration, I asked if I could build a hangar beside his airstrip. That evolved into a small, but popular, airport.

But…we had growth problems. Zoe was too small and too laggy. So we closed shop and bought about a quarter of Abbotts at auction as soon as it came online. We had big plans right away, but it's taken us since Feb 2004 to grow it to ALMOST the entire sim. 1 parcel at a time. The idea behind Abbotts Aerodrome … is not just a bunch of shops. We wanted a place where aircraft designers can meet and exchange ideas. Collaborate on projects. Play. It's also a public attraction. We want anyone to be able to drop by and have fun.

*AG: How should someone new to SL approach playing at Abbotts?*

CT: Teleport in, find a plane that you want to try and click the TEST DRIVE button. Away you go! You don't have to buy anything if you don't want to. There's also skydiving. Free parachutes and public skydiving pods. The whole skydiving craze started in 2004 sometime. Can't remember specifically when.

*AG: So, unlike a boat or motorcycle, seems like you need a runway for a plane, do people keep their planes here?*

CT: Well…you don't really need a runway. SL planes can usually take off within 20 meters. the runway is more for show. Runways are symbolic of aircraft. More of an esthetic feature than a functional one. Before you start building, you need to learn a bit about the nature of vehicles in SL…physical objects with a script. If you're not clear on what a "parent" or "root" prim is, you'll need to learn. It's key to making a vehicle model. If you already know…let's move on.

*AG: It determines the orientation of the entire object right?*

CT: exactly

*AG: What do you think about the exponential growth of SL residents? Does this change things for Abbotts or present new challenges?*

CT: Certainly, in terms of running a business, population growth means not only more customers, but more competition. There are dozens of aircraft makers in SL now. Abbotts stays afloat in part because of the aircraft sales. If we can stay in the virtual spotlight, Abbotts will be around for along time. There's a danger, though…we aren't the first big airport in SL. There are and were others. Some folded…some linger, like ghost towns. The key, I think is to attract the active SLers with interesting and fun things to do. Gray Field for example—the Kazenojin home base—is an amazing build that's been around forever, it seems.

But it's usually empty. We'll have to work hard to keep Abbotts interesting and populated.

*AG: What advice do you have for new residents?*

CT: Explore and meet people first. Find places that excite you and you'll find people with similar interests.

Ansel Gasparini: Well thank you so much for your time, this has been very informative

Cubey Terra: It's my pleasure.

# SCULPTED PRIMS

Learning to create sculpted prims (or sculpties) will garner you the most freedom and control over the shaping of prims in SL. Compared to the basic prim types (box, sphere, torus, and so on), sculpted prims allow you to create more organic and intricate shapes. Sculpted prims are not meant to completely replace regular prims in your SL building and modeling efforts but rather to supplement them. At the time of this writing, you can find the main online source of information about sculpted prims at http://wiki.secondlife.com/wiki/Sculpted_Prims.

To give you an idea of how powerful sculpted prims are, Figure 10-66 shows a comparison of a bottle created using basic prims and a similar bottle created with a single sculpted prim. From this close, you can see the sculpted prim is not as precise (more organic); however, the sculpted prim bottle consumes only one prim as compared to the regular prim bottle's five (each colored differently in Figure 10-66). Consider the prim savings if you created a bucket of beers for your backyard BBQ.

**5 Prim Bottle    1 Prim Sculptie Bottle**

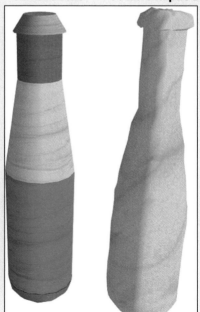

**Figure 10-66**
*Traditional prim bottle compared to a sculpted prim bottle.*

To focus only on saving prims, however, would really be to sell sculpties short. The real innovation is in organic shape control. There are three objects to be aware of if you want to tame sculpted prims:

- **Sculpt Prim:** A sculpted prim is a prim just like any other that you create in SL using the build tools. However, the sculpted prim geometry uses a 3D mesh of vertices as opposed to a shape extruded on a path, as is the case for other prim types.

- **Sculpt Texture:** The sculpt texture (sometimes referred to as the sculpt map) is a 2D image that defines the shape of the sculpted prim using an innovative technique. To create sculpt textures, you must use an external tool. LL plans to provide in-world build tools for sculpted prims in the future.

- **Texture Image:** In addition to the sculpt texture, a sculpted prim has a regular texture just like any other prim to provide the visual appearance of the prim's surface.

The following sections discuss sculpted prim basics, how to create sculpt textures, and how texture images are applied to sculpted prims. For these sections, I assume you have some basic 3D modeling experience and understand concepts such as RGB color channels, 3D space, vertices, edges, and how they form 3D meshes.

## CREATING SCULPTED PRIMS

To create a sculpted prim, first rez a cube (or any type of prim other than bushes or trees). Open the More>> dialog and change the prim type to Sculpted using the Building Block Type selection box. The default sculpt texture used is the shape of an apple (see Figure 10-67).

You can change the position of a sculpted prim, change its size (scaling), rotate it, and set its material. However, unlike other prims where you have a set of parameters to control aspects of the prim's shape (for example, taper, twist, hollow), the sculpted prim has only a sculpt texture (or a sculpt displacement map really) that defines the shape itself.

If you're just interested in using sculpted prims, the quickest way to start is to find freebie sculpt textures or buy sculpt texture packs. You can then assign the sculpt texture to create the shape you want.

However, I'm assuming you want to know how to create your own sculpties' shapes. To do that, you need to know how to create sculpt textures.

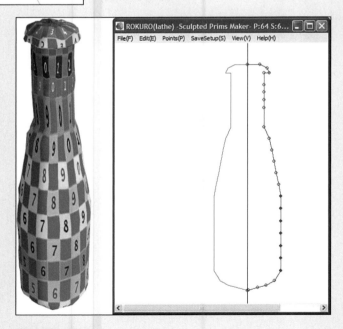

**Set the building block type to sculpted**

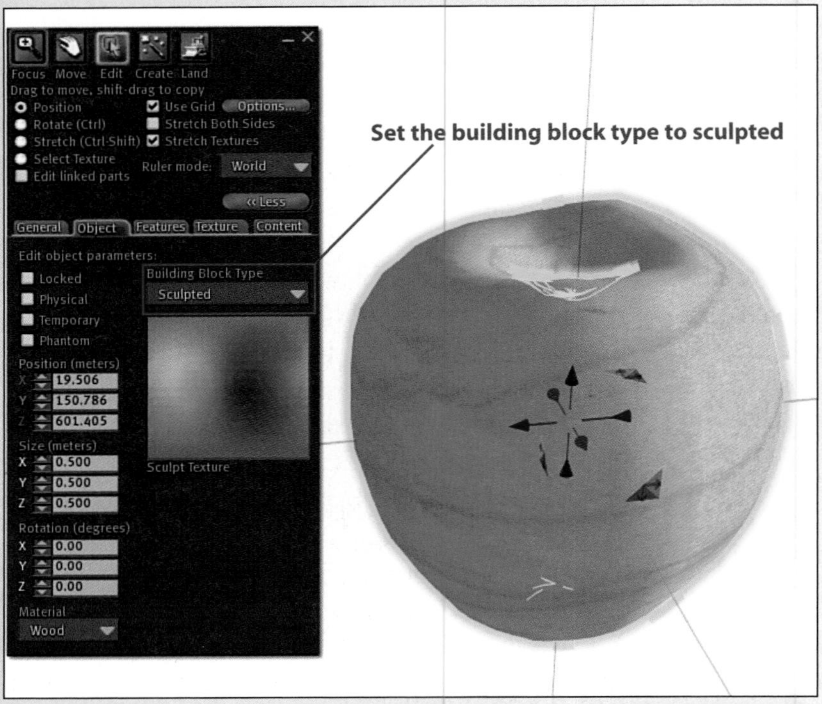

**Figure 10-67**
*Creating a sculpted prim.*

## CREATING SCULPT TEXTURES

To create your own sculpt textures to form unique sculpt prim shapes, you need to use software outside SL, typically a 3D modeling package. You also need some way to export the 3D model to a sculpt texture or have a tool that allows you to manually configure it to create your sculpt texture.

The first exporter available for this task was a MEL script for Maya. You'll see how to find and use this in the first sculpted prim tutorial. The second sculpted prim tutorial covers how to do this for Blender. Other modeling products such as Wings3D, LightWave, and 3ds Max may also be used to create sculpt textures as well (some with exporters, some with manual steps). See the wiki for a 3D software guide for sculpted prims at http://wiki. secondlife.com/wiki/Sculpted_Prims:_3d_Software_ Guide.

What if you've never done any 3D modeling and you don't have time to learn? Well, you're in luck because several residents have built simple sculpt creation tools. The full list is also available on the sculpted prim wiki under the 3D software guide. These tools typically have much less capability than the 3D modeling packages but also a much lower learning curve.

For example, see nand Nerd's sculpt texture generator website (http://www.nandnerd. info/sculpty.php) where you don't even need to download any software to generate your own sculpt textures. I love Yuzuru Jewell's lathe (ROKURO) tool (http://www. kanae.net/secondlife/) where you just define a profile shape by moving points, and it spins out a sculpt texture for you (see Figure 10-68).

The future of sculpted prim creation tools in SL may resemble something similar, but who knows what LL will cook up that will allow us to collaboratively author sculpted prims in-world.

**Figure 10-68**
*Using the lathe sculpted prim maker.*

# HOW DO SCULPT TEXTURES WORK?

A sculpt texture defines the shape of a sculpt prim. This is done with an innovative approach that uses the RGB color values of a 2D image to indicate x, y, z displacement values from the center point of a sculpted prim (see Figure 10-69). As alluded to earlier, calling sculpt textures *sculpt displacement maps* would be a more accurate description.

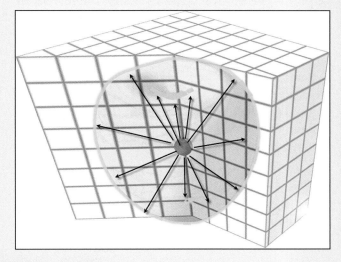

**Figure 10-69**
*Sculpt texture used for displacement.*

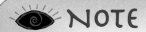

Linden Lab could have taken a different approach, but the 2D sculpt map/texture approach allows for the complete reuse of existing, well-exercised infrastructure that is already available for texture images.

You may be wondering how a 2D image can be used to define a 3D shape like this? Well, a digital image is essentially just rows and columns of data. Traditionally, this data (a pixel) defines a color (RGB values), and the result is what looks like a picture. However, there is no reason the data in this format needs to be related to color. So an image file makes a convenient package in which to store vertex placement information on a sculpted prim.

Every pixel in a 24-bit image stores 8 bits of information for the red, green, and blue colors (RGB). This gives you data values ranging from 0–255.

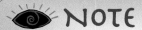

Be aware that 32-bit images have an additional alpha channel used for 8 bits of transparency data. Sculpt textures will ignore the alpha channel.

Instead of these values representing colors, the values for each pixel are used to represent relative displacement values for the corresponding vertex in the sculpt prim. Let's look at how we get from 0–255 color values to displacement values in meters.

An RGB value of 127,127,127 (flat gray) represents no displacement at all. That is, any vertex with a corresponding RGB value of 127,127,127 will be located at the center of the sculpt prim. So, if you were to create a sculpt texture that was a solid gray (127,127,127), you would get a sculpt prim with all vertices located in one single point at the center of the sculpt prim.

The displacement values are defined relative to the sculpt prim's local coordinate system. Red is the x-axis, green is the y-axis, and blue is the z-axis. Pure white (255,255,255) represents the top-right front corner. Pure black (0,0,0) is the bottom-left back corner. A few other colors are also shown in Figure 10-70. The red channel defines the x-axis displacement, the green channel defines the y-axis displacement, and the blue channel defines the z-axis displacement.

The displacement amount in meters depends on the size of the sculpted prim itself. For example, consider a sculpted prim that is 1m × 1m × 1m (the default size). A displacement color value of 255 would represent +0.5m from the center, whereas a color value of 0 would represent –0.5m from the center for a total range of 1m (see Figure 10-70).

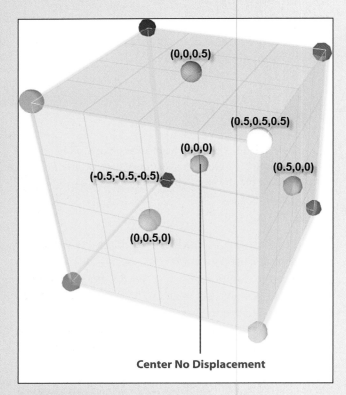

**Figure 10-70**
*Vertex displacement values scale with prim size.*

So it all makes sense, right? OK, maybe not. In any case, you don't create a sculpted texture by using Photoshop to paint various pixels the displacement colors; that would be truly onerous. Instead, you use 3D modeling tools to create the shape you want and either export the model to a sculpt texture or set up the tools to create a sculpt texture for you.

## SCULPT TEXTURE CONSIDERATIONS

Sculpted prims allow for an unprecedented level of control over a single prim. However, they do have several issues you should understand. Sculpted prims only approximate the shape you have created using your modeling tool of choice due to three primary factors: displacement precision, lossy storage format, and level of detail. Let's hit each one of these.

First, displacement precision is limited to 256 increments because we have only 8 bits of precision in a 24-bit image. The sculpt texture exporter must convert from the vertex

positions in your modeling package to these approximate RGB displacement values. You may lose some precision during this conversion.

Second, all images uploaded to SL are converted to JPEG2000 format, in a somewhat "lossy" implementation. That is, there may be compression artifacts and some data loss on upload. Because of this, it is recommended that you create sculpt textures that are 64×64 so that when they're downsampled to 32×32 for the 32×32 mesh, these artifacts are reduced or eliminated.

Finally, as we discussed previously, the level of detail in the mesh will change from 32×32 to 16×16 to 8×8 as a sculpted prim is further from the viewer. You don't have direct control over how the mesh is reduced, so the shape of a sculpted prim up close with 1024 vertices may appear very different than the shape of the same sculpted prim from a distance with only 64 vertices.

The only control that you do have is to dedicate more vertices to a single area where you want to retain detail. Using multiple vertices in one location is also how you create sharp edges in a sculpted prim (if you model using NURBS, you may be familiar with this concept).

> **TIP**
>
> If your sculpted prim seems inside out when you're using certain sculpt textures, the UV map may be reversed. Flip the image horizontally in an image editor. This may correct the problem.

## TEXTURING SCULPTED PRIMS

Sculpted prims have both a sculpt map texture and a regular texture that define the visual surface of the prim. You apply textures to sculpted prims just like you do regular prims with all the scaling, rotation, and positioning controls being available. Sculpt prims have only one face. In Figure 10-71, I have applied the texture test pattern we used in Chapter 7 to the default apple prim and rotated a couple of copies so that you can see the apple's top and bottom.

Like all prims, sculpt prims offer default and planar mappings. The planar mapping is not so useful, just as with spheres, tori, and other curved shapes. The main point to understand is that the default mapping uses the same image for vertex mapping as is used in the sculpt texture. That is, the UV map of the texture image is pinned in the same places as the vertices of the sculpt mesh. This is great news for 3D modeling/texture artists because it makes it much easier to create custom textures that correct for any UV distortion as compared to default prims.

**Figure 10-72**
*Chosen Few.*

Sculpted prims are unique building materials in Second Life. Unlike the regular primitives SL has always used for building blocks, sculpties are not entirely parametric. LL has cleverly come up with a way to use RGB channel data in an image to map vertex placement from a 3D mesh model onto a prim object in SL. The result is a wealth of organic, inorganic, and complex geometry that was never possible before without investing huge numbers of prims to form the shape of an object, or in many cases, not previously possible at all.

Sculpties allow greater artistic control over 3D models at the vertex level that is not possible with regular prims. As already mentioned, the use of SL's sculpted prim capability is not without a few caveats:

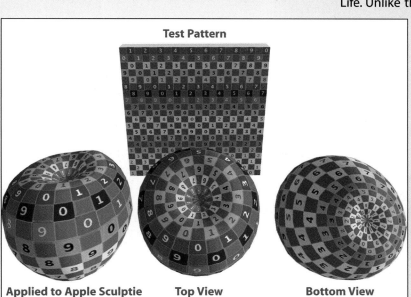

**Test Pattern**

**Applied to Apple Sculptie**   **Top View**   **Bottom View**

**Figure 10-71**
*Applying textures to sculpted prims.*

To wrap up, I've gathered two great tutorials for creating sculpt textures. The first, which uses Maya, was written by Chosen Few. The second, which uses Blender, was written by Amanda Levitsky. Thanks to both of them for sharing this knowledge.

# TUTORIAL: GETTING STARTED USING SCULPTED PRIMS WITH CHOSEN FEW

Chosen Few (see Figure 10-72) is your guide through this excellent tutorial.

- **Sculpties cannot be created directly in SL.** At least at the time of this writing, you need a third-party 3D modeling application. Popular choices include Maya, 3ds Max, Blender, and Wings3D, among others. LL has announced that it's working on a system to create sculpties entirely in-world, without the need for any third-party programs, but at the time of this writing, a separate 3D modeling app is a must.

- **You cannot turn arbitrary 3D models into sculpties.** SL requires that the model be constructed in a specific way. Advanced methods can be employed to convert other models into sculptie-compatible models, but those are beyond the scope of this tutorial.

- **Not everything in SL can or should be made from sculpties.** The purpose of sculpties is not to do away with regular prims. They are simply another tool in your repertoire.

For this tutorial we'll be using Autodesk Maya, as it's the program sculpties were first invented on, and the one for which LL has written a sculpties exporter. Exporters for all other programs have come from enterprising SL residents. Maya is an expensive, professional-grade program, and I realize not everyone reading this will have access to it. Maya also happens to be my favorite 3D program in existence, and since I'm the one writing this, I get to have my pick. If you prefer a different modeling program, no problem; what you'll want to take away from this tutorial are the underlying principles behind how sculpties work, not necessarily the specific procedures and techniques.

For the scope of this tutorial, I assume you have some basic Maya knowledge already. If you're new to Maya, watch the quick introductory training videos that come with it and run through the "Using Maya" tutorials in the Help file. Specifically, you'll want to go through Basics, Polygonal Modeling, and NURBS Modeling. I'll do my best to make everything here as newbie-friendly as possible, but if you find I'm using terminology you don't understand, consult a good book on Maya (there are hundreds) or look it up in Help.

Let's get started.

if nothing else. Instructions beyond that will obviously vary from program to program.

At the time of this writing, the MEL exporter script is located at http://wiki.secondlife.com/wiki/LlSculpt_mel (see Figure 10-73). Copy all the text from the script and paste it into a text editor of your choice (Notepad is fine). Save your text file and name it **LlSculpt.mel**.

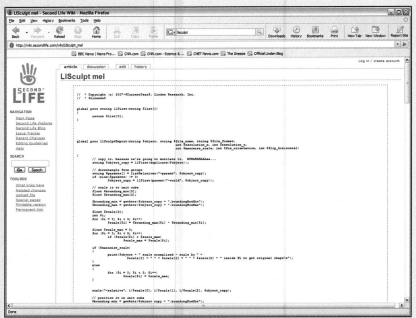

**Figure 10-73**
*The MEL script.*

## STEP 1: GET THE EXPORTER (MEL) SCRIPT

First, you need to get your copy of Maya set up to export sculpt map images for SL. For this, you'll need the exporter mentioned earlier, which is a Maya Embedded Language (MEL) script. Now, remember how I said that certain things here would be Maya-centric, and certain things would be universally applicable? Here's a good example of both. Obviously, this particular script was written directly for Maya, and the instructions I'm about to explain for how to integrate it into the program will be entirely Maya-specific. However, for whatever program you're using, you're going to need an exporter of some sort. So the main principle of "install the sculptie exporter" is what you'll want to take away from this part,

## STEP 2: OPEN THE SCRIPT IN MAYA

Now, start Maya and open the Script Editor. You can do this either by selecting Window->General Editors->Script Editor or clicking the little button in the bottom-right corner of the Maya interface, the one that looks like three stacked rectangles.

In the Script Editor, choose File->Open and open your LlSculpt.mel file. You'll see the script laid out under the MEL tab in the lower pane of the Script Editor window (see Figure 10-74).

You can now either run the script directly from the editor or make it into a button on your Maya shelf so that you don't have to go through all these steps every time. I suggest the latter.

**Figure 10-74**
*MEL Script Editor.*

## STEP 3: MAKE THE SCRIPT INTO A BUTTON ON YOUR MAYA SHELF

Let's start by making a new tab on the shelf, so your new button will have a place to go. To do this, open the Shelf Editor by selecting Window->Settings/Preferences->Shelf Editor. Note that this is done from the main Maya window, not from the Script Editor.

Now, in the Shelf Editor, click on the Shelves tab (see Figure 10-75) and then click on the New Shelf button toward the bottom. In the Name field, type **Second Life** and press Enter, click on Save All Shelves, and then on Close.

You should see a new tab on your shelf called Second Life. Click on that tab now.

**Figure 10-75**
*Create a new Second Life Shelf.*

OK, back to the Script Editor. In the MEL pane, select all the text in the script (by pressing Ctrl+A). Now choose File->Save Script To Shelf. In the dialog that pops up, name your new shelf item **LlSculpt** and click OK (see Figure 10-76). Then close the Script Editor.

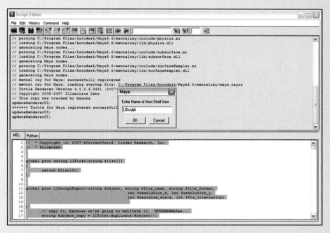

**Figure 10-76**
*Save the LlSculpt.mel script to the shelf.*

You should now see a new button called LlSculpt under your Second Life tab (see Figure 10-77).

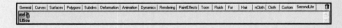

**Figure 10-77**
*LlSculpt button.*

## STEP 4: TEST THE LLSCULPT BUTTON

If you click on LlSculpt, you'll see that it opens a dialog called Export Sculpt Texture (see Figure 10-78). Your sculptie exporter is now installed and running, so you're ready to begin modeling.

By the way, everything we just did was a one-time operation. Since you saved the script to your shelf, you'll never have to go through these steps again (unless a new version of the script is released, in which case you'll want to replace your existing button with a new one). After you close Maya, the button will still be there the next time you use it. So, from now on, all you need to do is click the button to open the exporter, and that's it.

OK, enough of this technical prep stuff; let's move on to modeling.

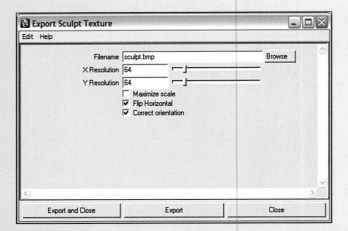

**Figure 10-78**
*Testing the Export Sculpt Texture button.*

NURBS display. You can switch between them very easily simply by selecting a NURBS object onscreen and pressing 1, 2, or 3 on your keyboard. A setting of 1 is the lowest level of detail and will produce an angular look with straight lines connecting each of the vertices, similar to the way polygonal geometry is typically displayed. A setting of 3 produces the highest detail, with finely smoothed curves interpolated between the vertices. What we want here is 2, the medium detail level. A setting of 2 corresponds very well with the way SL interpolates sculptie geometry. So select your sphere and press 2.

## STEP 5: BEGIN YOUR SCULPTIE—CREATE A NURBS SPHERE

All sculpties in SL are essentially modified spheres, meaning they are all singular, closed surfaces. So for best results, start with a sphere and sculpt it into the shape you want to make by moving the vertices around. I suggest using NURBS, but you can use polygons if you like. Just be aware that Maya, by default, maps polygonal spheres differently than SL requires, so you'll need to do a little extra labor to make it work. NURBS surfaces are good to go, right off the bat. For this tutorial, we'll be using NURBS.

Every sculpted prim in SL is constructed from a grid of 32×32 vertices. So, we'll want to give our NURBS sphere 16 sections and 15 spans at a maximum. Less than that is fine, but don't go higher (see Figure 10-79).

Before we go any further, take a minute to make sure that what you're seeing in Maya matches what you'll be seeing in SL. First, work in smooth shading mode (press 5 in any Maya viewer pane or select Shading->Smooth Shade All).

Second, it's a good idea to set your NURBS display detailing in Maya to match the way SL will display the prim. Maya, by default, has three selectable levels of detail for

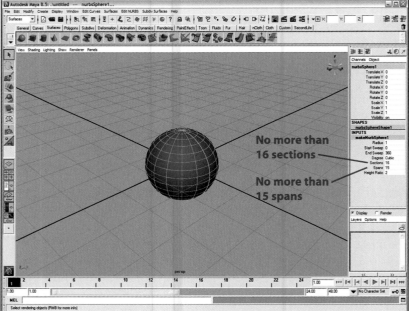

**Figure 10-79**
*Starting with a NURBS sphere.*

## STEP 6: MODEL YOUR SCULPTIE—MODIFY THE SPHERE'S SHAPE

So, what should we make? Well, we can deform this sphere into any object we can dream of that fits within the 32×32 vertices requirement. There are only a few simple rules:

- Don't tear the surface. Whatever happens, make sure the surface remains closed and that it has two distinct poles. No matter how much you deform it, it has to remain one contiguous surface.

- Don't let the distance between any two points ever get greater than 10 units. Remember, SL can't make prims bigger than 10×10×10 meters.
- Keep the object's pivot point located at (0,0,0). You can move the individual CVs anywhere you want within a 5-unit radius, but make sure the object itself is centrally located at (0,0,0).

As this tutorial is about sculpties themselves, not about any particular modeling techniques in Maya, let's start with something extremely simple that just about anyone, regardless of level of Maya expertise, should be able to make. Let's go with a fruit bowl.

Push and pull the sphere's vertices and hulls around until you have something that looks like a bowl (see Figure 10-80).

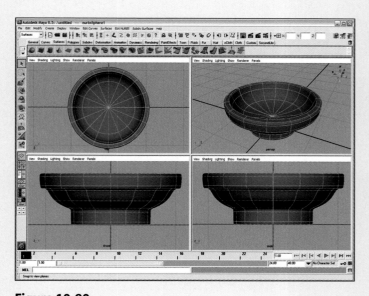

**Figure 10-80**
*Basic bowl modeled in Maya.*

## STEP 7: EXPORT YOUR SCULPT MAP TEXTURE

When you have your model the way you want it, go to the Export Sculpt Texture dialog by clicking the LISculpt button we made earlier. Click the Browse button, choose a location for your texture, and give the file a name (see Figure 10-81). For this tutorial, call it **sculpt_bowl_1**. For file type, choose TGA. The dialog will offer you every type of file Maya is capable of generating, but remember, most of those are not usable by SL. When you're ready, click

Export to close the Browse dialog and return to the main Export Sculpt Texture dialog.

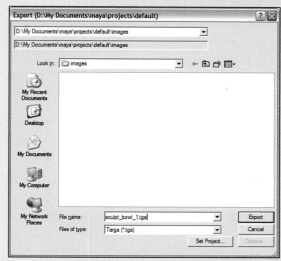

**Figure 10-81**
*Saving the sculpt map texture as a TGA file.*

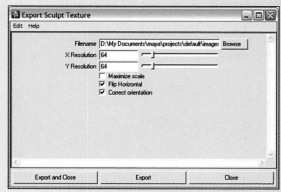

**Figure 10-82**
*Export Sculpt Texture dialog.*

Next, set the texture's size or resolution (see Figure 10-82). By default, it will be at 64×64. This is the recommended size and is fine in most instances. As a rule, keep your sculpt map as small as possible. Just as is the case with every texture, the larger the sculpt map, the more taxing it will be on every SL user's resources.

At the time of this writing, the Export Sculpt Texture dialog includes three check boxes underneath the area where you set the resolution. I won't take the time to explain what they all do, as I suspect they probably will be removed in future versions. For now, I suggest the following settings: Keep Maximize Scale turned off and keep Flip Horizontal and Correct Orientation turned on.

When everything's set the way you want it, click Export to generate your sculpt map.

## STEP 8: UPLOAD THE TEXTURE TO SL AND APPLY IT TO A PRIM

In SL, upload sculpt_bowl_1.tga the same way you'd upload any other type of image (File->Upload Image). This will cost you L$10, just like any other texture.

Now, create a prim, and on the Object tab in the editor, change the prim's Building Block Type to Sculpted. You'll see that many of the normal prim parameters disappear and are replaced by a large image field labeled Sculpt Texture (see Figure 10-83). Drag the sculpt_texture_1.tga from your Inventory onto that field, and you'll see your prim change shape to become your bowl (see Figure 10-84).

**Figure 10-84**
*The sculpted prim awaiting textures.*

**Figure 10-83**
*The uploaded sculpt texture applied to a sculpted prim.*

From here, you can treat the bowl just like any other prim. You can size it, move it, rotate it, and texture it—anything you want.

Happy sculpting!

## TUTORIAL: SCULPTED PRIMS USING BLENDER WITH AMANDA LEVITSKY

A big thank you to Amanda Levitsky (see Figure 10-85) for putting together this excellent Blender sculpt prim tutorial. The latest version of this tutorial can be found at http://amandalevitsky.googlepages.com/sculptedprims. Take it away, Amanda!

**Figure 10-85**
*Amanda Levitsky.*

This tutorial describes one way to make sculpt textures from a mesh for use as sculpties in SL using Blender 2.43. If you've never used Blender before, consider looking at the many starting tutorials on the Web to familiarize yourself before diving into this task.

The method described here has been pieced together from discussions on the SL wiki and by trial and error.

## STEP 1: CREATE A CYLINDER TO USE AS THE MESH

The first step is to create a cylinder to use as the mesh. The default 32 vertices works well (see Figure 10-86).

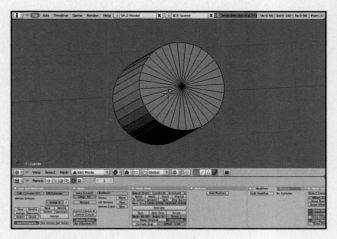

**Figure 10-86**
*Default cylinder in Blender.*

## STEP 2: DELETE THE SINGLE VERTEX AT THE TOP AND BOTTOM ENDS OF THE CYLINDER

Next, delete the single vertex at the top and bottom ends of the cylinder. If you're using Blender 2.44, you can also skip this step by choosing not to cap the ends when creating the cylinder (see Figure 10-87).

The UV mapping for a sculpt texture must be a regular grid and must fill the entire texture exactly from edge to edge. This conforms with a cylinder that has no end poles (if you visualize this mesh being cut and unrolled and flattened, you can see that it forms a rectangle). Currently, all sculpties conform to this cylindrical topology, which means that certain shapes (such as shapes with holes) cannot be made. Other topologies are expected to be supported in a future version of SL.

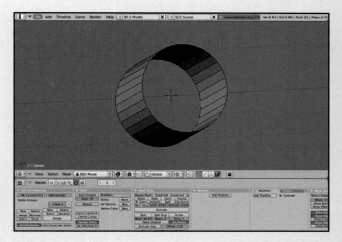

**Figure 10-87**
*Cylinder end vertices deleted.*

## STEP 3: SELECT THE VERTICES AT THE TOP END AND MARK THEM AS A SEAM

Select the vertices at the top end and mark them as a seam by pressing Ctrl+E. The seams tell Blender how your mesh should be sliced up and "unrolled," as we'll see later when the UV mapping is created by unwrapping the mesh (see Figure 10-88).

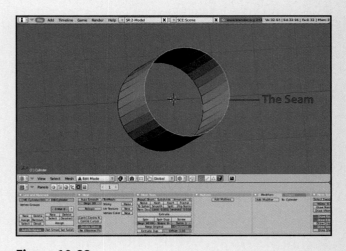

**Figure 10-88**
*Marking the top vertices as a seam.*

## STEP 4: MARK AN EDGE AS A SEAM

Select one of the top vertices and the vertex at the bottom connected to it; then mark that edge as a seam by pressing Ctrl+E (see Figure 10-89).

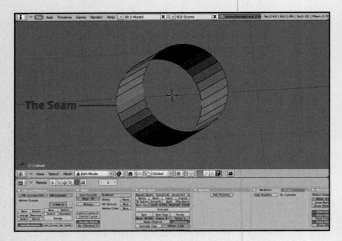

**Figure 10-89**
*Marking an edge as a seam.*

## STEP 5: SUBDIVIDE THE CYLINDER HORIZONTALLY

Subdividing the cylinder horizontally adds some vertices to work with (see Figure 10-90). The Loop Subdivide tool (Ctrl+R) is useful for this. The vertices of the original cylinder give you the vertical vertex positions in the sculpt texture. The vertices created here provide the horizontal vertex positions. Together, they give you a grid of vertices, which you can later move around as you please to mold into any shape you like, provided you don't add or remove any vertices. One way to think of this resulting cylinder is as a 3D representation of your sculpt texture; moving the vertices around will eventually result in colors in the sculpt texture changing.

## STEP 6: UNWRAP THE UV COORDINATES

Open the UV/Image Editor, enter UV Face Select mode, select all the faces (A), and then Unwrap the UV coordinates (U) (see Figure 10-91).

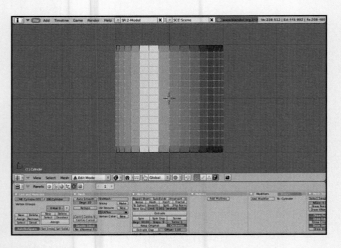

**Figure 10-90**
*Subdividing the cylinder horizontally.*

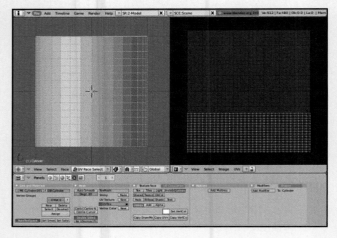

**Figure 10-91**
*Unwrapping the UV coordinates.*

UV mapping is a way to map between 2D images and 3D shapes. Each vertex in your 3D mesh will have a corresponding 2D UV coordinate, the total of which is represented by the grid of UV coordinates in the UV window.

Every viewing area in Blender can be split and set to show another window type. To split a viewing area, right-click on a border of the viewing area and select Split. Then move the split line that appears to wherever you would like the split to be made and click. You can then set each viewing area independently to another window type by using the drop-down button on that area's toolbar.

## STEP 7: MOVE AND SCALE THE UV COORDINATES

Move and scale the UV coordinates so that they fit as well as possible into the image square (see Figure 10-92). Because the sculpt texture is a result of the UV mapping of your mesh, the more accurate your UV coordinates are, the more accurate your resulting sculptie will be. Ideally, your UV coordinates will be as evenly spaced as possible, aligned neatly without any jagged coordinates, and fit from edge to edge.

Selecting UVs->Layout Clipped To Image Size can make adjusting the UV coordinates easier by confining movement and scaling to the UV image area.

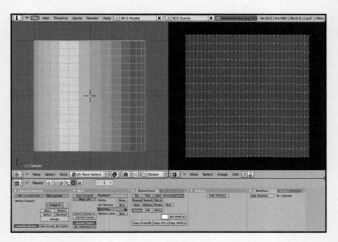

**Figure 10-92**
*Moved and scaled UV coordinates.*

## STEP 8: CREATE A NEW IMAGE FOR THE UV TEXTURE

Create a new 64×64 image for the UV texture in the UV/Image Editor (Image->New). You might want to adjust the UV coordinates here so that everything is straight and neatly lined up (see Figure 10-93).

Sculpties are currently limited to 32×32 vertices, which for various technical reasons are achieved most accurately using a 64×64 sculpt texture. Using a higher resolution texture will not result in more detailed sculpties because the sculpt textures are downsampled to 64×64 when they're rendered in SL.

Selecting UVs->Snap to Pixels will cause the UV coordinates to snap to the nearest texture pixel when moved. This capability is useful for ensuring your UV coordinates are lined up exactly at the edges of the texture and in rows horizontally and vertically.

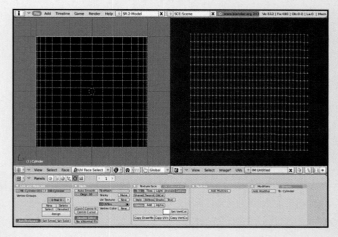

**Figure 10-93**
*Creating a new image for UV texture.*

## STEP 9: ADD A MATERIAL TO THE CYLINDER

Add a material to the cylinder and set the VCol Paint mode for the material (see Figure 10-94). VCol Paint causes the object to be rendered using its UV texture instead of normal shading.

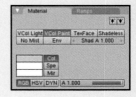

**Figure 10-94**
*Setting VCol Paint for material rendering.*

## STEP 10: ADD THREE TEXTURES FOR THE MATERIAL

Add three textures and then set the Texture Type for all three to Blend (see Figure 10-95). A sculpt texture is a texture where the red, green, and blue components map to the x, y, and z coordinates of each point on an object. To achieve this, we create three textures that we'll later set to map between each axis and color. The Blend mode means that the color value of each texture will blend smoothly from one side of the object to the other, which corresponds to mapping the furthest and closest points of the x, y, and z coordinates for the object to 0.0 and 1.0 for each color.

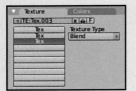

**Figure 10-95**
*Setting texture type to blend.*

## STEP 11: SET THE INPUT AND OUTPUT PARAMETERS FOR THE THREE TEXTURES

The important settings are the axis mappings on the input and the colors and Add mode on the output (see Figure 10-96). Now, set each of the textures created in the previous step to map from one axis to one color: red to represent x, green to represent y, and blue to represent z.

You can set sliders in Blender by clicking and dragging on the handle, clicking on either side of the handle to cause the value to "jump" by a step higher or lower, or holding down Shift while clicking to directly type in the value.

By selecting the Neg option for the red/x texture, you will find that the resulting sculptie appears to be inside-out. NightShade Fugu has found a use for this as a way to achieve better-looking transparent objects, like glass, by setting the transparency of the "inside-out" sculptie in SL to something higher than 0. This produces objects that have a two-sided appearance while still appearing translucent (compare this to a semitransparent box prim, in which the faces closest to your camera appear transparent, but the backs of the opposite faces do not appear at all). Note, however, that transparency rendering issues in the viewer are still being addressed, and a future viewer fix may cause this technique to no longer work.

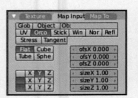
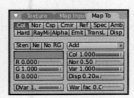

**Figure 10-96**
*Setting input and output parameters for each texture.*

## STEP 12: SCULPT YOUR MESH AS DESIRED

Blender's sculpt mode is lovely for organic shapes (see http://www.blender.org/features-gallery/features/feature-videos/?video=sculpt_two).

In Figure 10-97 I've unimaginatively created a vase. Note that while the cylinder mesh appears to be more like a tube and lacking a top and bottom, when it's rendered in SL, the top and bottom will be closed (though ugly; for better control you may want to scale the top and bottom rings of vertices down to one point and shape the ends yourself, perhaps bringing them into the body of the vase to create a true hollow).

When you're building your model, it's a good idea to first move more of the vertices to the areas that will have the most detail. In Figure 10-97, you can see that the region in the middle of the vase has only one row of vertices, while the curved neck has many more. This prioritization of vertices is what gives you fine control over the detail in a sculptie. Note that the UV coordinates in the sculpt texture do not move and remain as a regular grid.

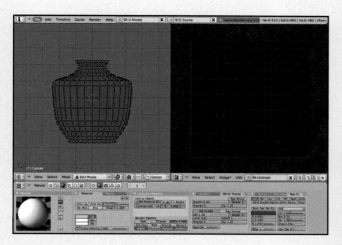

**Figure 10-97**
*Modeling a 3D vase.*

## STEP 13: SWITCH TO THE SCENE PANEL AND BAKE THE TEXTURES

On the scene panel, bake the textures into the UV image. If, after baking, you notice aliasing artifacts in the baked image, try increasing the margin by 1 or 2 (see Figure 10-98).

As a separate trick, using the Ambient Occlusion mode instead of the Textures mode will allow you to bake a shading/lighting texture that shadows the corners and crevices of your object quite naturally. This can then be applied to the sculptie as a regular texture to add shadowing. If you want to do this, consider using a higher resolution for the UV image when baking the ambient occlusion map, and a 64×64 resolution when baking the sculpt map.

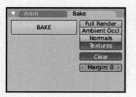

**Figure 10-98**
*Baking the textures.*

## STEP 14: SAVE THE UV IMAGE

Select Image->Save from the UV/Image Editor to save your image. Preferably, use a lossless format like TGA rather than JPEG (see Figure 10-99).

In fact, don't ever save sculpt textures as JPEG. Lossy JPEG compression will mean that your carefully placed, highly accurate vertex coordinates come out slightly less accurate when decoded as an image, which is then made worse when SL converts it into JPEG2000 format upon uploading. Save and upload sculpt textures as TGA instead (compressed TGA is fine, since it is lossless).

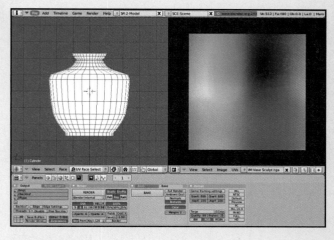

**Figure 10-99**
*Saving your sculpt texture to TGA.*

## STEP 15: UPLOAD THE IMAGE TO SL AND CREATE A SCULPTIE

Upload the image to SL. Create a prim, set it to Sculpted Prim Type, and then set the sculpt texture to your upload. See Figure 10-100 showing a sculpted vase!

**Figure 10-100**
*Sculpted vase awaiting a nice texture.*

## STEP 16: APPLY THE TEXTURE AND SCALE THE PRIM

Try applying different textures and scale to see what you can achieve (see Figure 10-101).

You can find the Blender file used in this tutorial at http://amandalevitsky.googlepages.com/Scupted_Prim_Example.blend.

Also check out Pavcules Superior's sculpties file repository for Blender and non-Blender sculpties-related resources at http://pkpounceworks.sljoint.com/index.php?option=com_remository&Itemid=28&func=select&id=2.

**Figure 10-101**
*Some vase sculpted prims.*

## SUMMARY

Well, I don't think I pulled any punches in this chapter. We looked at SL particle systems, what they can be used for, and where to learn more about them. In addition, we discussed one of the most basic things in SL animation, which is a decent sit pose and how to get it into your new chair.

We also covered SL physics, vehicles, and steps for creating our own airplane! You may realize now that vehicles are near the top of the SL creative hierarchy. You need to know texturing, building, animations, and scripting to pull off a good vehicle. Or maybe you just need the right mix of friends.

Finally, we covered sculpted prims and how to create sculpt textures using 3D modeling tools like Maya and Blender.

Because there is so much more to learn about these topics, pick one or two and go practice, practice, practice. I can't wait to hear about what you've created!

*SL launched me! It got me an interview with Wired and Rolling Stone magazine. I also got interviewed side by side with Suzanne Vega.*

**—JueL Resistance**

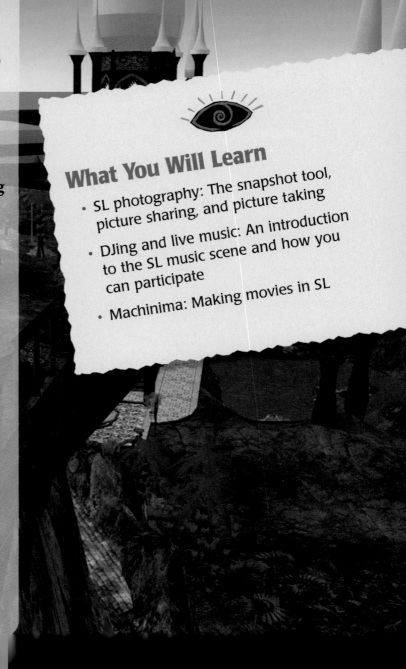

# Photography, Music, and Movies

# 11

In Second Life you can take pictures, attend or perform in live music events, DJ at a club, and be the director in your own movies with your own cast. This chapter covers the basics and provides pointers on where to learn more on these topics.

When I lived in Boston, I used to hang out at a small bar called Toad in Porter Square. It had live music playing every night, and for the price of a pint, you could sit and decide for yourself whether you should order another. It had great variety, great music, and easy access.

SL offers this and something more. The access is easy, the musicians can be anywhere in the real world, and you don't have to pay pub prices for your brew. Even more than that, you can be surrounded by your friends in a cool SL venue even when they themselves are located all over the real world.

## What You Will Learn

- SL photography: The snapshot tool, picture sharing, and picture taking
- DJing and live music: An introduction to the SL music scene and how you can participate
- Machinima: Making movies in SL

I hadn't planned this chapter when I started working on this book. It evolved from various sections elsewhere in the book, and the topics called out for more coverage. I wish I had the time to cover the topics here in as much depth and detail as prior chapters, but as with all writing projects, particularly ones involving SL, you have to stop somewhere. I hope you, my dear reader, can forgive me for all the references to additional resources.

# PHOTOGRAPHY: SNAPSHOT TOOL

Picture taking in SL, as in RL, can range from casual snapshots all the way up to professional lighting rigs and fantastic compositions. All you have to do is take a look at some *Second Style* magazine covers (http://www.secondstyle.com; see Figure 11-1), and you get an idea of what's possible.

SL photography has some really great advantages; for example, you can control the time of day by selecting World->Force Sun to Sunrise, Noon, Sunset, Midnight. In Figure 11-2 you can see a picture I took of myself at a really nice bay on an island owned by Jacqueline Trudeau, a famous SL yacht builder. I forced the sun into position so I could see it reflected on the water.

**Figure 11-2**
*Calm Bay, picture taken with forced sunset.*

With local lighting, it's possible to re-create studio lighting effects as well. You can place lights as carefully as in RL, but without the need for lighting stands, power boxes, and so on. See the section "Let There Be Light" in Chapter 6, "Building Basics," for information on how to create local lights. What about backgrounds, smoke effects, and fog? The answer is yes, yes, and yes! See Chapter 10, "Particles, Vehicles, and Animations," for information on how to create these effects. You may need to buy or build a studio for yourself, but that can also be fun.

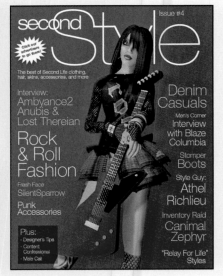
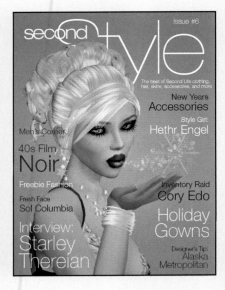

**Figure 11-1**
Second Style *magazine covers.*

As you might imagine, you can perform screen captures as you usually would (Fn->Prnt Scrn) or use software such as SnagIt (www.snagit.com), but SL has a built-in tool for taking snapshots that helps streamline a few sharing and usage options for your images. You bring this up by selecting the Snapshot button at the bottom of your main display or, better, by pressing Ctrl+Shift+S, which helps you avoid the problem of your avatar's head following the cursor around.

You will see the dialog shown in Figure 11-3. Directly from this tool, you can email a picture (Send a Postcard), upload it (for a nominal fee) so you can use it in SL, or save it to your hard drive.

**Figure 11-3**

*Snapshot Preview tool.*

The guide "Capture the Moment: Guide to the New Snapshot Preview", at http://secondlife.com/knowledgebase/article.php?id=176, takes you through the Snapshot tool in detail, so I will not do so here.

Following are two of the Internet picture-sharing tools used quite a bit by SL residents:

- **Snapzilla:** http://www.sluniverse.com/
- **Flicker:** http://www.flickr.com/

You can find some additional advanced photography tips in the video tutorial from Torley Linden, "Advanced Snapshot Magic Video Tutorial," at http://secondlife.com/knowledgebase/article.php?id=393.

I watched it and extracted the following key points:

- Press Ctrl+Alt+D to toggle the Client menu on and off (it includes extra features).
- When you take a snapshot in SL, it makes a sound; you can turn off this sound by enabling Client-> Quiet Snapshots to Disk.

- If you want to be able to zoom more freely, try selecting Client->Disable Camera Constraints.
- To enhance local lighting effects at night, select Edit->Preferences (or press Ctrl+P), go to the Advanced Graphics tab, and increase the number under the Nighttime Brightness setting. The default is 1, but it can go up to 4. The best way to tune this is to go to an area with local lighting and set the Sun to Midnight. Then play with the control.
- Many RL photographers angle the camera slightly for a more dynamic image (that is, the horizon line is no longer perpendicular to the frame). You could do this by post-processing the image in Photoshop, for example, but another approach is to sit on a prim box and then rotate the box. Use mouselook and take your shot.
- If you're using local lights but don't want to actually see the primitive that is giving off the light, you need to use a totally transparent texture. Such a texture is available from many locations including the in-world companion site. See Chapter 7, "Advanced Textures and Clothing," for more information. You also can make transparent objects visible to find the light. To do so, choose View->Highlight Transparent (or press Ctrl+Alt+T).
- Finally, and this is so cool, try selecting Client-> World->Mouse Moves Sun. Then go into mouselook and you can actually drag the sun around to get it into just the right spot (see Figure 11-4). Now that is god-like!

**Figure 11-4**

*Mouse moves the sun.*

Here are a few other tricks of the trade:

- To capture a snapshot on a moving subject, Alt+click on it, and the camera will track.
- Experiment by selecting Client->Rendering->Types (or pressing Ctrl+Alt+Shift+X) to show/hide various common world elements (and Avs!)
- Another goodie: selecting Client->Rendering->Features->Fog (or pressing Ctrl+Alt+6) eliminates all fog.

If you love photography in RL, you'll love it in SL as well. There are many SL jobs related to photography, such as art, fashion, weddings, events, portraits, commercial art, advertising/promotions, studio rentals, backdrop/mural art, and portrait pose animation.

# SL MUSIC, MUSICIANS, AND DJS (SL AUDIO)

Music is an extremely important element of SL. Without it, the nightclubs would not be hopping, the dance parlors would not be swinging, and you would not be able to enjoy the cool licks of jazz on your cheek as you watch the sunset from your beachfront home.

Even more importantly, SL represents a new way for musicians to get their music out to a large, diverse, and international audience cheaply and without going through record labels, radio, and TV. More than just having a website with MPEGs available for purchase or download, SL offers musicians venues to play live and connect directly with an audience, much as they do in RL.

A long-time resident, musician, and well-known live music promoter, Circe Broom, had this personal note on why she is here in SL, *"For the music and to help musicians get a break. I was there once and I love music. They need and deserve some help and it makes me feel good!"*

## WHAT MUSICAL JOBS ARE AVAILABLE?

There are five broad types of things you can do involving music in SL. You do **not** need to pick one! In fact, most people do several, such as club owners who play at their own place.

**NOTE**

The following sections are focused on music in SL, but many of the concepts apply to SL audio in general. For example, meetings or classes as well as music can be delivered over audio streams.

- **Disc Jockey (DJ):** DJs in SL are just like DJs in RL. They spin records, do some voice-over between songs, and take a crowd on a ride. DJs usually play nightclubs and other dance venues.
- **Play live:** Musicians play live music from wherever they are in RL. Their music is heard at a venue in SL by avatars who are there in near real-time. Venues can be clubs, watering holes, stadiums, or even on the beach by a campfire. Typically, the musician is playing/singing while his avatar is in SL at the same place doing the same.
- **Own a club or venue:** Club/venue owners hold musical events that showcase DJs or musicians. Typically, owners want to attract other avatars to their location. Owners typically like to find and help new musicians in starting their careers in SL.
- **Organize musical events:** Event organizers may be club owners or even musicians, but they focus on coordinating musical events for a group of people who appreciate their tastes. One night it may be blues in an undersea aquarium and the next night ballroom dancing to classical licks in an upscale lounge. Event organizers like to lead the pack, and their followers enjoy the diversity and camaraderie involved.
- **Participate! (Dare I say groupie or roadie?):** Well, let's face it; many of us music buffs are in SL. We love to listen and dance to the music and go with our favorite friends to see our favorite performer at our favorite spot. It's not so much a job as it is the desire to be with friends and listen to the music you like after a hard day in RL.

Figure 11-5 shows a great billboard that gives you a picture of the various roles. It combines a venue (Ripple), artist (Komuso Tokugawa), promoter (Nancy Lei), and event host (Azheni Something).

**Figure 11-5**
*Komuso Tokugawa billboard by Azheni Something.*

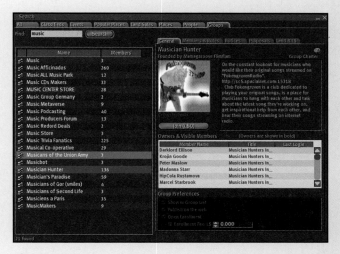

**Figure 11-6**
*Searching for live music venues.*

## HOW DO I ENABLE MUSIC IN SL?

The first stop you should make if you're into music and SL is to enable audio! Go to Edit->Preferences->Audio & Video tab. Deselect Mute Audio and select Play Streaming Music When Available. When you're on land that has an audio stream enabled, you'll see a small control in the center of your client just above the chat bar labeled Music. Here, you can turn on sound and control the volume. Also, make sure the sound is not muted on your computer.

The SL Knowledgebase article "How to Play Streaming Music in SL" (http://secondlife.com/knowledgebase/article.php?id=376) provides great step-by-step instructions on how to ensure your options and client are set up so that you can hear music playing in SL.

## HOW DO I FIND MUSICAL VENUES?

The best way to find musical venues is to use Search (see Figure 11-6). Look for live music or the type of music you want to see under Events. You can also search for groups and join the ones that have an interest in your type of music. Many good groups are mentioned in the interviews that follow.

## HOW DO I PLAY MUSIC OR BECOME A DJ HERE?

Music in SL is streamed from a streaming server to your SL client. Oddly enough, it does not pass through the Linden Lab servers. What stream you hear in SL depends on where you are in the world. That is, it depends on the land on which you stand. If you walk from land to land, you will hear different music, depending on what that landowner has set up.

If you're a DJ, you'll want to stream audio files from your machine to the streaming server. If you're a musician, you'll want to use a microphone to perform live and have the digital bits sent to the streaming server. In either case, you need some software installed (at a minimum) that will take a microphone feed or local MP3 file and send it to a streaming server.

To get really good sound, SL musicians strongly recommend augmenting the software with an external mixer and a good microphone. See Astrin Few's "Guide to Second Life Music" at http://secondlife.com/knowledgebase/article.php?id=320 for some good tips.

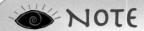 NOTE

If you don't have a great deal of bandwidth and a fixed IP address, it is not pragmatic to use your own machine as a streaming server.

Now, once your live performance or MP3s get to the streaming server, the music is available to anyone on the Internet via a URL such as http://TheSongster.server-room.us:9362.

To get it into SL and down to the land, you need to enter the streaming server URL into your land's properties (see the section "How Do I Play My Music on My Land?").

At this point, anyone on that piece of land with sound turned on will hear your music from the stream.

## DO I NEED MY OWN STREAM TO PLAY MUSIC OR DJ IN SL?

The answer to whether you need your own stream to play music or DJ in SL is no. If you play at a club or other venue, the owner of that venue may have a stream you can use. The upside is that you don't need to own land or pay for a stream. The downside is that you will need to configure your broadcasting gear for each streaming provider, which may be different from event to event.

If you want more control and less hassle, then owning your own stream is the way to go. You can set this up yourself if you have a good server, fixed IP address, and some technical know-how. You can also pay for a subscription or rent a stream. The most popular software and streaming services for use in SL today are Shoutcast, Icecast, and Simplecast (from Spacial Audio). If you're on a Mac, check out Nicecast.

- **Shoutcast:** http://www.shoutcast.com
- **Icecast:** http://www.icecast.org
- **Simplecast:** http://www.spacialaudio.com
- **Nicecast:** http://www.apple.com

## HOW DO I PLAY MY MUSIC ON MY LAND?

Each parcel of land in SL can support a music stream that can be set by hand. To set it, select About Land, Media tab and set the Music URL field. Type in a URL to stream, wait a second, and Voilà!

You can also buy a radio (or find a freebie). Radios offer a quick way to rotate through a set of channels when clicked without having to perform manual edits. I picked up a free radio from Diones Designs-JZ Corporation. This

radio basically changes the stream on your land through several hard-wired streams whenever it's touched. Diones has one of the most extensive sets of audio and video products I have found. Check it out at

 **http://slurl.com/secondlife/Diones%20Designs/129/45/21/**

> ## TIP
>
> If you're experiencing problems, make sure your computer is not on mute and audio is enabled. The Music URL can be MPEG audio and Ogg Vorbis streams. If the URL is bad, you just won't hear anything; you won't get any kind of error message. There is not yet support for playlist files.

## AN INTERVIEW WITH LIVE MUSICIAN JUEL RESISTANCE

JueL Resistance is a live musician in SL. I knew JueL (see Figure 11-7) for quite a long time before we had a chance to do this interview. We met after one of her shows (see Figure 11-8), and this proved to be a great choice because the founder of Vampire Empire and owner of the Peg Leg Saloon (see Figure 11-9), Obscuro Valkyrie, also sat in. Figure 11-10 shows JueL and Obscuro after the show at the Peg Leg.

The following chat is extracted from our discussion. (Visit JueL's RL website at http://www.myspace.com/7juel.)

```
[You have arrived at the Peg Leg
Saloon in Transylvania. Obscuro
Valkyrie is here. He is talking
to his radio. There are vampires
around.]

Land Streaming Radio v2.05: Ready.
Click me to start. Type 'station
help' for commands

Obscuro Valkyrie: station 19

Land Streaming Radio v2.05: Changing
stations to [19 of 20] 'Juel' [URL:
http://slmusic.info:8920/]
```

```
[Juel Resistance goes up on stage and
starts her show. People shout. People
start dancing.]

ima Narcissus: woo hoooo

leyla Christensen: Hoooo! there you
go juels!!!

Seiko Cao: go juels.

leyla Christensen: LOVE YOU JUELS!!!!

Obscuro Valkyrie:
V^OOOOooooooooo000000^V

[Obscuro Howls.]
```

And so the show begins.

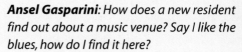 **http://slurl.com/secondlife/Transylvania/96/23/26/**

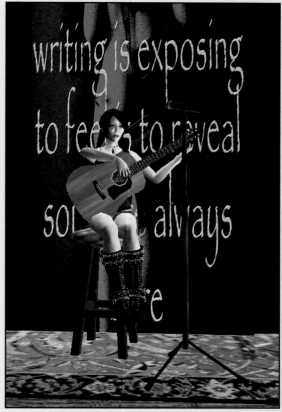

**Figure 11-8**
*JueL Resistance performing.*

**Figure 11-7**
*JueL Resistance.*

**Ansel Gasparini:** *How does a new resident find out about a music venue? Say I like the blues, how do I find it here?*

**JueL Resistance:** Ansel the best way, use search… and word of mouth, ask others where they go, who they listen to, what they like. It gives you more perspective. For ex. like tonight, you come to hear Nance, you hear me, or you hear me and hear Ricardo or go to Ricardos show and hear sCylindrian. It's a giant web of live music here.

**Figure 11-9**
*The Peg Leg Saloon in Transylvania.*

**Figure 11-10**
*JueL Resistance and Obscuro Valkyrie in Vampire Empire.*

*AG: How many music venues do you think are stable here? How many do you think come and go over time?*

JR: oooooo, they all come and go from what i see. I have been here at peg leg 4-5 months, it is one of the ones i've seen stay

**Obscuro Valkyrie:** she came here by my request. I saw her play, I loved her

*AG: Are there any good groups for newbies to join if they are interested in live music?*

JR: Live Music Enthusiasts, Independent Musicians and of course my group (plugs self a bit) Living room VIP. Ansel when i first joined SL in 2003 there was no live music

OV: nope was none

JR: So of course i quit LOL

*AG: How are SL live music venues different from RL venues like open mike night at a local pub for example?*

JR: Ansel not a lot of difference

OV: she can play topless at home and tease us

JR: LOL OBS ok so there is a diff. SL doesn't pay nearly as much as RL or SL Corporate RL gigs do, but the AUDIENCE IN SL is DIVERSE and GLOBAL and that is a PLUS

I just went to NC to meet 5 other SL musicians because of our global outreach in SL and People from SL came from diff states, flew or drove to see us it was amazing experience.

*AG: Are crowds more or less responsive in SL?*

JR: Crowds are MORE Responsive in SL I think. I thought RL would be, but it depends where you are. But Ansel, just like in RL we [musicians] feed off what we see. So if audience is NOT responsive we need to re direct our set going by SET lists, in my opinion…is lame. Go with the feeeeeel, follow the feel of audience not your 'list'

*AG: What is the difference between a musician here and a DJ?*

JR: a musician is performing all live NOT mp3's. DJ's are live, but they are spinning tunes like any dj does. Live Music is just that. Making mistakes in their songs, laughing and CONNECTING with audience a dj does the same

*AG: Obscuro, how do you decide who plays at the peg leg?*

OV: actually the ppl do if they play here and suck we don't have them back, simple. Well maybe thats a little harsh.

JR: LOL yeah

OV: let me rephrash

JR: LOLOLOL

OV: not the type of artist to support this crowd

*AG: What are the most annoying things a newbie does at their first live music event that they should not do?*

OV: be naked with a huge penis slapping everyone. It happens here

JR: cough in mic, leave lots of dead air, bad stuff. Ansel, i think a key in live music is to feel, if an artist does not feel what they perform, whether it be original or cover, it shows thru

*AG: Where do you think Music in SL is going?*

JR: Ansel i used to think it was moving forward, still do, but right now it feels kinda at a stand still…if a club hires you for $1000L that is like 4$ in USD, insulting. BUT ANSEL more corporates are comming to me and paying 100-300$ usd cash thru paypal

## AN INTERVIEW WITH MUSIC PROMOTER CIRCE BROOM

*"To ME, music is the most important part of SL!"*

**—Circe Broom**

Circe Broom is a tireless promoter of great musicians in SL. She owns her own sim and stream supporting several different venues for live music. You can always count on a crowd and great music if you attend one of her shows. She agreed to sit down with me and discuss the topic of SL music at the Pyramid of Cairo (see Figure 11-11), one of her many music venues. You can get into Circe's Circle at SL Group: Circe's Circle.

The Pyramid in Cairo can be found at

 **http://slurl.com/secondlife/Laurel/154/65/50/**

```
[You have arrived at the Pyramid in
Cairo. Live music is playing. People
are dancing. Circe Broom (see Figure
11-12) is here. The sounds of Silas
Scarborough playing curl through the
air.]
```

**Circe Broom:** hi Ansel

**Ansel Gasparini:** Hi Circe

CB: come sit in a booth with me

*AG: Is this your main spot?*

CB: no, I have four on this island alone. They are all my main spots. I am also in partnership with Elliott Eldirch on…Club Egret. See, Ansel, to ME, music is the most important part of SL! this is true enjoyment, and a chance for many of us to hear the kind of shows we just can't get to in RL. and for the artists, a chance to be heard WORLDWIDE

**Figure 11-11**
*Circe Broom and Silas Scarborough at Pyramid in Cairo.*

**Figure 11-12**
*Circe Broom.*

*AG: The global reach and ability for artists to connect with their audiences without record labels, TV, radio, seems like a huge thing here.*

CB: Yes, but you will find that here—is a microcosm some of the same stuff that goes on in RL, happens in here too like MANAGERS. I find myself gritting my teeth more and more

*AG: How do I find live music events and what are good groups to join?*

CB: Live Music ENthusiasts is a great one and of course, Circe's Circle is a great one, as I only use the BEST musicians, so you know the announced shows will be really good. You can find out what's going on by going to SEARCH/EVENTS/live music and just seeeeee more and more musicians coming in every day

*AG: How can I play my own music on my land?*

CB: you get a STREAM and play on the STREAM whatever you want!

*AG: What are the best stream sources for SL?*

CB: some little ones are quite cheap, like $15 a month, I hear. SHOUTCAST is great. I actually prefer IceCast servers but too many musicians are not technically oriented and it takes one more step to connect to IceCast servers although I have to say, this Shoutcast server is doing me quite well. Mine as a member of the Stream Team, is much more than the usual stream. It has a 1000 listener capacity (typically streams support 20–100 max). Professional musician should consider at least purchasing a Simplecast or Nicecast broadcaster at $40 a month.

```
[Silas Scarborough, wraps up his set
and strolls over to the booth.]

Circe Broom: Applause!!

Circe Broom: c'mon hommmmmmmee

Circe Broom: thank you, Silas

Ansel Gasparini: thanks man, great!

Silas Scarborough: Thank you Circe

Silas Scarborough: Thanks Ansel :)

Circe Broom: I can always depend on
Silas for goood music and no pissing
and moaning

Silas Scarborough: I don't get the
moaning—lol

Circe Broom: ooh

Circe Broom: I moan at some of your
tunes, Silas…they get to me. :)

Silas Scarborough: woohoo!

Ansel Gasparini: lol

Silas Scarborough: Now that kind of
moaning definitely works!

Circe Broom: come sit with me, Silas?
```

*AG: Is there a difference between a venue owner and event organizer?*

CB: well, many event organizers are also the venue owners me, I do those plus host, plus provide the stream!

*AG: How do you decide who plays at your spots?*

CB: I decide by how GOOD they are. I dont, cant deal, with the backyard playing variety. That might be fun for other people but if I'm paying for it I want as good as I could hear on a CD I buy so that' is what I go for, that is what I get. I have people like SIlas, RIch DeSoto, Ricardo Sprocket, Melvin Took, Kirsten Corleone, Slim Warrior, on and on, GREAT TALENTS!

*AG: How many avies can SL support in one sim?*

CB: I've had 103 in here, and still could move, if barely

## WHERE TO LEARN MORE

- **Some RL URLs and SL Groups for SL Musicians**

  - **Charles Bristol:**
    http://www.myspace.com/charlesbristol
    **SL Group:** Charles E. Bristol Blues Project

  - **Nance Brody:** http://www.n-a-n-c-e.com
    **SL Group:** NANCE's Fan Club

  - **JueL Resistance:** http://www.myspace.com/7juel
    **SL Group:** Living Room VIP Lounge

  - **RoseDrop Rust:** http://www.rosedropmedia.com/
    **SL Group:** Rusty Nails

  - **Sila Scarborough:** http://myducksoup.com/silas/
    **SL Group:** Silas Scarborough Rocking Fan Club

  - **Ricardo Sproket:** http://www.richpetko.com

  - **Komuso Tokugawa:** http://music.sonicviz.com
    **SL Group:** Komuso's Fans of the Blues

  - **Slim Warrior:** http://www.myspace.com/slimmie

- **U2inSL:** http://www.u2insl.com/
  **View concert:**
  http://www.youtube.com/watch?v=Mro9Qzv—k8
- **Overview of Music in Second Life**

  http://secondlife.com/knowledgebase/
  article.php?id=083
- **Linden Lab Community Music Page**

  http://secondlife.com/community/music.php

# SL VIDEO

Video can be streamed into SL as well. As with music, each plot of land can be set to one video stream. You can place the stream onto a prim's surface to form a screen, or you can buy some pretty cool flat-panel TVs in SL (as usual, freebies exist, but higher-end models offer hundreds of preset channels).

Jeffronius Batra had his SL moment when he watched the launch of a space shuttle with a large group of avatars that were, of course, all there for a common interest but located physically all around the globe.

Video in SL is still in its infancy, and SL is way too interesting to sit around in and watch TV. I was unable to find many pointers on how to get video into SL. However, I did locate this text deep in the online help under how to enable streaming video:

> In the Media tab of your About Land window, you can enter a URL for streaming video. The URL must be to a stream that is Quicktime compatible, which includes .mov files, and various other formats too.

> To be able to see the movie stream you selected, Second Life has to know which surface you want to display it on. This is done by designating a texture as the 'Media texture' in the Media tab of

your About land window. Be sure to select a texture that you don't use elsewhere on the same land because any surface set to display that texture will also become a movie screen when one is playing. Once the Media texture is set in the Media tab, all that's left to do is apply the same texture to an object that you want to use as the movie screen, and it's ready to play!

With a streaming movie URL set, a small Play button with volume slider will appear at the bottom of your screen, just above the Build button. Once you press Play your screen should play the movie for you. Do be patient, sometimes it can take a little while to get started. If you are having trouble, try testing the URL outside of Second Life in the Quicktime player itself. If it works in Quicktime player, it really should work in-world too.

This Knowledgebase article discusses how to stream video from SL: http://secondlife.com/knowledgebase/article.php?id=431

## USING THE FREE SL MEDIA PLAYER

Here is a quick tutorial on using the Media Player provided free in the library. You must have QuickTime installed on your computer (download from http://www.apple.com/quicktime/download/).

### Step 1: Enable Streaming Media

Select Edit->Preferences (or press Ctrl+P). On the Audio & Video tab, look for Streaming and check Play Streaming Video When Available.

### Step 2: Pick a Stream to View

The stream must be QuickTime compatible. It is best, I've found, to test this in a browser first before putting it into SL just to make sure it's working. To set the stream, right-click on your land and select About Land. Then go to the Media tab (see Figure 11-13).

**Figure 11-13**
*Free MediaPlayer and Video Stream Setup.*

## Step 3: Rez Library->Objects->Media Player

The stream needs to be rezzed on land you own, so select Rez Library->Objects->Media Player. The screen does not appear until you click the Play (green) button.

## Step 4: Click the Play Button

After you click the Play button, you should see a screen rez and the stream start playing shortly. If you have issues, check the stream in a browser outside SL and remember that you need to have QuickTime installed. I resized the screen in Figure 11-11 because the stream was in HD format.

## MACHINIMA

Machinima is all about making movies in a virtual environment such as SL. It requires building sets, costumes, props, sound effects, and any other special effects that may be required. It also involves being a director and coordinating and collaborating with other avatars in-world to achieve the scenes for your movie.

If you want to try your hand at directing and have a great idea for a movie, then SL is a great environment in which to try your hand.

Here are some links to get you started in SL Machinima:

- **SL Machinima Home Page**

  http://secondlife.com/showcase/machinima.php

- **Tips and Tricks: Ten Tips on Creating Machinima in SL**

  http://secondlife.com/knowledgebase/article.php?id=280

- **Eric Linden's Making Machinima in SL Whitepaper**

  http://s3.amazonaws.com/static-secondlife-com/_files/making_machinima.pdf

- **Video Machinima Tutorial**

  http://static.secondlife.com/downloads/advanced_machinima_tut.zip

- **Share Videos with Other Enthusiasts**

  http://www.secondlifevideo.com/

- **Video Tutorials on Machinima**

  http://wiki.secondlife.com/wiki/Video_Tutorials

## SUMMARY

In this chapter, you learned about several of SL's audio and video features. You now have references to SL photography, music, and movie-making (machinima) resources. While this chapter covers a lot of ground, it also leaves a lot of ground uncovered.

The best way to learn in SL is by doing, so get in-world and try your hand at any of these things. You'll quickly find something that you're passionate about, and with that, you will find a group of SL residents who are passionate about the same things as you. Together, you will learn and take SL creation to the next level.

*Change is SL's greatest strength*
*and its greatest weakness.*

**—Julia Hathor**

# Practical Matters: Under the Hood of the Metaverse

# 12

Second Life is an exciting new world where the culture and technology are rapidly evolving hand in hand. When complex technology is combined with explosive population growth, it should come as no surprise that you will face some technical and social challenges in SL.

This chapter covers my number-one suspects in each area. The most common technical challenge you're likely to face is dealing with lag. Put another way, the most common technical challenge is that of troubleshooting performance issues. To understand what you can and cannot do about lag, you first need a basic understanding of how the SL Viewer interacts with SL servers and other external servers.

## What You Will Learn

- How SL works
- How to troubleshoot SL bottlenecks
- How to deal with griefers
- How to tame your SL inventory

The most common social challenge you're likely to face is dealing with a class of residents known as griefers. Understanding what griefing behavior is and how it affects you will help you handle these encounters positively and not let them ruin your SL experience.

Finally, the chapter finishes with a great blog post from Willow Zander on managing your Inventory. The more time you spend in SL, the more stuff you'll acquire and the harder it will be to find things unless you think about Inventory organization.

Let's dig into the details of the last and final installment for this book.

# HOW SL WORKS (A TECHNICAL PRIMER)

SL is a resource-intensive product. That is, it will push the limits of your computer, the network connection you have, and even the SL servers themselves. It is highly likely that you'll face situations in which SL seems slow or seems to perform in unusual ways.

Common resident usage identifies these issues as **lag.** In addition to a noun, the term has become a verb and adjective—for example, "I'm lagging bad tonight" or "This sim is laggy right now." Traditionally, lag is related to network latency (the time it takes for data to travel from one end of the network to another), but in SL, the term seems to be used to refer to almost any performance-related problem, whether it's connectivity or something else.

To understand the different types of lag and how to address them, you must first understand the basic components of SL, what they do, and how they interact. Specifically, we focus on the SL Viewer and its interaction with other servers. The following sections provide the basics. For more detailed information, refer to the SL technical resources listed later.

# A SIMPLIFIED TECHNICAL OVERVIEW

You access SL using a software application called the **SL Viewer,** which is installed on your desktop or laptop computer. Think of the SL Viewer as a really complex web browser (such as Internet Explorer or Firefox) for the 3D world of SL versus the 2D world of the Internet.

The SL Viewer communicates with a wide variety of servers over the Internet (see Figure 12-1). The main set of servers the SL Viewer interacts with are the **SL Grid Servers.** These servers simulate each region (or sim) in SL. Several additional servers that support SL are discussed in the section "Supporting Servers." Some servers that the SL Viewer interacts with are not owned by LL at all. They are discussed in the section "External Servers."

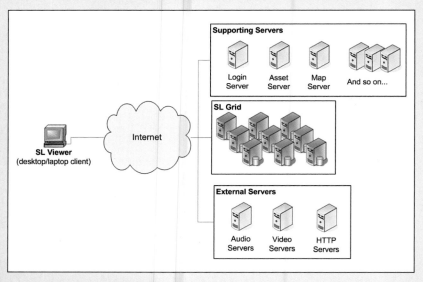

**Figure 12-1**
*High-level SL architecture.*

# THE SL GRID

We start our exploration of SL architecture with the grid.

## What Is the SL Grid?

You will hear the term *the grid*, which is used to refer to all the servers whose job is to simulate the SL landscape. In general, a grid server or **sim** simulates a **region** (256×256 square meters of land).

## What Is the Job of a Grid Server?

The job of a grid server is to maintain a common world state for a region that all the SL Viewers share. If you and I are looking at the same object (whether or not we're in the same region), it should appear in the same place for both of us.

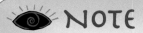

Interestingly, objects may not look exactly the same to both of us depending on our viewer preferences and what type of object it is. Whether an object has bumpy or shiny properties is an SL Viewer property. Flexprim objects and particles are managed by each client, so they may not appear identically to both of us.

Other than maintaining the location of all the objects in the region, a grid server is also responsible for handling the physics engine, performing collision detection, and running LSL scripts. The grid server sends updated information to the SL Viewer as needed when objects change location. So, for example, if a region has a lot of moving objects, there will be more network traffic between the grid server and the SL Viewers than if there were no moving objects in a region.

There is wind in SL, and another function of a grid server is to manage each region's wind speed and direction. Interestingly, wind in each region is independent of the other regions (very unlike real life). This is important to SL sailors because, as you sail from one region into another, the wind speed and direction may change radically.

## Understanding Regions and Boundary Crossing

The SL Viewer may be getting information from more than one grid server. Imagine that your avatar is standing at the intersection of four regions. You're standing in one but looking out onto the others. The grid servers simulating those other regions will be sending your SL Viewer information about the location and movement of objects in those other regions. In this way, the SL world appears (well, mostly appears) seamless to you.

## The Three Main Types of SL Grids

There is more than one SL grid in existence. There are, in fact, three different grids available to the public:

- **The Main Grid:** The, well…main grid for adults 18 years old or older.
- **The Teen Grid:** A grid for teens 13–17 years old (see http://teen.secondlife.com/). If you're a parent, check out http://teen.secondlife.com/parents.
- **The Beta Grid:** A much smaller SL grid running experimental server software. You are also required to install a companion Beta SL Viewer to use this grid.

For the most part, you'll be using the main grid.

## THE SL VIEWER

The following sections briefly discuss the SL Viewer.

## What Is the SL Viewer?

The SL Viewer is a program running on your computer that is your interface into SL—just like a web browser is a program running on your computer that is your interface into the Web. You download the SL Viewer and install it on a Windows, Mac, or Linux machine. The SL Viewer and a basic avatar account are free to use. See Chapter 1, "Welcome to Second Life," for more details on getting started in SL.

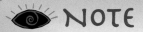

The SL Viewer source code has been made available to the open source community. Linden Lab will continue to provide the officially supported viewer, but it will be interesting to see what kinds of applications evolve due to the availability of this source code. See the section "SL Technical Resources" for more information.

## What Does the SL Viewer Do?

The SL Viewer is quite complex and does a surprising amount of work. The SL Viewer does the following (and this is by no means a definitive list):

- Draws the world. That is, it handles the visual representation of objects and their location and keeps them up-to-date, interacting with the graphics card on your machine. The SL Viewer uses OpenGL to do this.
- Communicates your requests and/or actions to the appropriate servers based on what you're trying to do in SL.
- Does some simple physics estimation to keep things moving between updates from the grid servers.
- Handles all movement of flexprim objects.
- Handles all rendering of particle systems.
- Handles all local lighting effects.

## The Four Main Types of SL Viewers

Four main types of SL Viewers are available. The first three can be downloaded from http://secondlife.com/community/downloads.php:

- **Latest Released Viewer:** This is the SL Viewer you're most likely to use.
- **First Look Viewer:** This test viewer is compatible with the main grid. You can use it to try new viewer features that do not require any server-side changes. The First Look Viewer may not always be available. News of new First Look Viewer releases typically is made available on the main SL blog (http://blog.secondlife.com).
- **Beta Viewer:** This test viewer requires server-side changes, so it works only against the beta grid.
- **Open Source Viewer(s):** As of this writing, the SL Viewer source code has been released. It is therefore possible for anyone to build his own SL Viewer and modify the code to do different things. These viewers are not supported by LL. If you're a developer interested in building your own viewer, try https://wiki.secondlife.com/wiki/Open_Source_Portal.

## SUPPORTING SERVERS

In addition to the grid servers, there are several servers that provide back-end support for SL (see Figure 12-1). See https://wiki.secondlife.com/wiki/Server_architecture more information on these servers.

For the purposes of understanding lag, the main point is that more than one server is involved with the SL environment, so it's possible that some parts of SL may be experiencing problems while the rest are working normally.

What does this mean for you? It means that some days teleport may be broken, but everything else is working. Other days, it may seem as though textures are downloading really slow, but once they're downloaded, everything works fine. You might be able to search for events but find yourself unable to move in a crowded sim.

In short, the SL Viewer may become partially disconnected, leading to strange results. Relax! Everyone experiences this. Try logging in again and see if that addresses the issue.

## EXTERNAL SERVERS

Finally, and this is important, some servers outside SL get involved with the SL Viewer as well. They are typically audio- and video-streaming servers. Audio and video streams come directly to your SL Viewer without passing through any LL servers.

For example, if you're on land that has audio or video streaming enabled, your SL Viewer will connect directly to those streams (if you have audio/video streaming enabled in your SL Viewer preferences).

Streaming audio or video does not pass through an LL-managed server, so if an audio stream becomes overwhelmed at a big event, you may experience audio problems that have nothing really to do with SL at all.

SL also interacts with web servers, sometimes by bringing up websites in embedded browsers.

## SL TECHNICAL RESOURCES

As mentioned previously, the SL Viewer has been released as open source, but most of the SL architecture remains proprietary. If you're interested in a further exploration of SL technology, the following resources may help:

- **SL Client (a.k.a. Viewer) Architecture**
  https://wiki.secondlife.com/wiki/Viewer_architecture

- **SL Server Architecture**
  https://wiki.secondlife.com/wiki/Server_architecture

- **SL Viewer Open Source Project**
  https://wiki.secondlife.com/wiki/Open_Source_Portal

- **The LibSecondLife Project**
  http://www.libsecondlife.org/wiki/Main_Page

- **Video of Philip Rosedale and Cory Ondrejka speaking at a Google TechTalk on March 1, 2006**
  http://video.google.com/videoplay?docid=-5182759758975402950

- **Zero Linden** (in-world office hours)
  "Come talk about the technology that runs Second Life." Zero's office hours begin at 1 p.m. on Tuesday and 7:30 a.m. on Thursday.
  SLURL You can find Zero at **http://slurl.com/secondlife/Grasmere/165/109/**.

# TROUBLESHOOTING SL PERFORMANCE PROBLEMS (A.K.A. LAG)

SL is a cutting-edge application that will push your hardware and network connections to their limits. Even though your machine may be performing well, a grid server may be heavily loaded when a large number of avatars decide to get together. Learning how to detect lag issues and understanding what you can and cannot do to address them can greatly improve your SL experience and reduce unnecessary frustration.

I don't have enough pages left in this book to include a primer on network bandwidth versus latency, describe the difference between a CPU and a GPU, and the like, so I'm going to assume you have some familiarity with these concepts. If you don't, ask a friend in SL. Many people are happy to help.

*Lag* is the term commonly used by SL residents to describe an SL performance or bottleneck issue, even though it may not be related to network latency, as the term is traditionally used.

If you think you're having an issue with SL performance, you can take a series of simple troubleshooting steps to determine where the problem likely resides. Once you know the problem, you can take corrective action, or if no corrective action is possible, you can at least grin and bear it.

Here are seven troubleshooting steps:

1. Check your computer's configuration.
2. Check your computer's network connection.
3. Check the SL grid status.
4. Check the SL network connection.
5. Check your region's grid server status.
6. Check your draw distance setting.
7. Check your computer's GPU performance.

## CHECK 1: YOUR COMPUTER'S CONFIGURATION

The LL minimum system requirements can be found at http://secondlife.com/corporate/sysreqs.php. You should, however, consider these requirements the bare minimum needed to make SL work. If you want a good SL experience, you're going to need more horsepower.

I cannot stress this point enough: The better the hardware you have, the better your SL experience is going to be.

### CPU

Your CPU will get a workout while you use SL. I suggest you get at least a 2 GHz processor. If your CPU is running at 100% at any point, verify that it's just SL using the CPU and not other processes on your machine. In general, you should not try to run any other CPU-intensive processes at the same time you're running SL.

If you think CPU is your bottleneck, check the Task Manager and see what is consuming CPU cycles; if it's something other than the SL Viewer, shut it down while you're using SL.

## Memory

You should have at least 1GB of memory if you expect to run SL smoothly. If you find your hard drive light is frequently on while you're using SL, you may be swapping to disk (although this is not a reliable indicator, as SL is constantly reading and writing from the cache files). Check your Task Manager and make sure that the SL Viewer is the main consumer of memory. If other applications are using large amounts of memory (for example, Outlook, Internet Explorer), close them while you're running SL. If you're only at 512MB, consider a memory upgrade.

## GPU (Video Card)

Your graphics card really gets exercised with SL, constantly drawing objects and loading and unloading textures. You should verify that you're running with a supported graphics card. Also, check to see that your graphics card has the latest drivers installed.

Later we discuss what you can do with SL preferences to make it easier for your graphics card.

## Hard Drive Speed and Health

Hard drive specs make a difference, as well as general hard drive health. There is a noticeable difference between a 7,200 RPM drive and a 10,000 RPM drive. The faster you can physically access your cache, the more smoothly SL will run. Because SL is constantly reading and writing files, it can contribute to fragmentation issues as well. Have you defragged lately?

## CHECK 2: YOUR COMPUTER'S NETWORK CONNECTION

Officially, SL is not compatible with dial-up connections, satellite (dish), or other wireless Internet services with limited bandwidth/reliability. Email and web browsing may be working fine, whereas SL may not work at all. You need either a DSL or cable connection. I use a direct connection to the Internet whenever possible, but I have also had reasonable success using wireless in low-lag environments.

Of all SL problems, network bandwidth and latency are by far the most likely culprits and the most resolvable of the issues, but you need to make sure your connection is good and that you're not using it to perform other tasks while you're using SL. For example, don't start downloading a 30MB YouTube video just before launching SL.

If you think you're having a network problem, test your connection without SL running. Various websites offer this service (search for "Internet speed test") or try the following link:

> http://www.speakeasy.net/speedtest/

Here are a few data points for Seattle to San Francisco:

- Comcast Cable, directly connected (5759kbps download, 374kbps upload)
- VPN into my corporate network (798kbps download, 788kbps upload)
- Wireless from a local coffee shop (1284kbps download, 752kbps upload)

You want to see at least 300kbps; less than that and you're going to have to dial things back in your SL preferences (more on this later).

Other sources of connectivity issues may be your firewall, which is blocking some traffic; active antivirus software that is checking everything that comes in; and fair/poor wireless connections.

## CHECK 3: THE SL GRID STATUS

If you're experiencing unusual issues with SL, you may want to see if there is some known problem going on rather than something isolated to your machine or one region in the grid. You do this by checking the current grid status at http://secondlife.com/status/. You can also check for scheduled grid downtime, which is announced on the LL blog at http://blog.secondlife.com. Finally, the problem may be really obvious when you try to log in, as you can see in Figure 12-2.

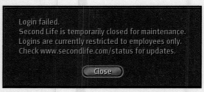

**Figure 12-2**
*Login failure message when SL is down for maintenance.*

If your computer is in great shape, you have verified that you're getting consistent and decent network bandwidth, and the SL grid appears to be up and problem free, then it's likely you're experiencing an SL network-specific problem, you're experiencing a regional or simulator problem, or your graphics card may be maxed out managing a particular area of SL.

Let's move on to the next topic, which is network connectivity between your machine and the SL servers.

## CHECK 4: THE SL NETWORK CONNECTION

If you're experiencing the following, you may be having connectivity or bandwidth issues:

- There is a delay between when your avatar starts moving and when you press a movement key.
- Your avatar keeps walking after you stopped pressing a movement key and then seems to snap back to a prior location.
- Chat you typed takes awhile to appear in the chat history window after you have pressed Enter, or your lines of chat appear out of order.

Assuming you've already determined that you have a well-powered computer, you're using a good network connection, and the SL grid is up with no known issues, you can make the assumption that the problem exists with one of three things: the problem is with the network connection between your machine and the region's simulator, the region's simulator itself is overworked, or your own computer is overworked for some reason.

To do the next level of troubleshooting, you need to log in to SL and use the statistics bar. You access the statistics bar from the menu by selecting View->Statistics Bar or pressing Ctrl+Shift+1.

The statistics bar provides a lot of detailed performance information about what's happening with the SL Viewer, the network, and the region you're in. It's divided into three sections: Basic, Advanced, and Simulator. You can see the bar with only the Basic section expanded in Figure 12-3.

**Figure 12-3**
*Statistics bar with Basic section expanded.*

The Basic and Advanced sections have information related to your SL Viewer performance and your connectivity to SL servers. The Simulator section has information about the region (or sim) you're currently in. I will not cover all the settings in the statistics bar here; for a detailed rundown on the statistics bar, try http://secondlife.com/knowledgebase/article.php?id=091.

To see whether your connection with the simulator is the problem, bring up the statistics bar and look at the Basic section. You need to check four settings: Bandwidth, Packet Loss, Ping Sim, and Ping User.

### Bandwidth

Bandwidth should be greater than 0 and jumping around a lot between 20 and 200kbps. The bandwidth shown in Figure 12-3 is the bandwidth being used versus the available bandwidth of your connection.

A bandwidth of 0 is bad; it means you're not connected or only partially connected to SL. Recheck your network connectivity again and try logging back in to SL.

One potential lag problem is if your bandwidth settings are too high in your preferences. Try starting with the setting (Edit->Preferences, Network tab, Maximum Bandwidth) between 300 and 500kbps.

You can readily see the Bandwidth indicator bar (which changes color) in the upper-right corner of your screen display. Rest your cursor over it to get details of bandwidth and packet loss.

### Packet Loss

Packet Loss should be 0.0%. If your Packet Loss is not zero, then things are not going well. If Packet Loss is greater than 10%, recheck your network connection and try logging back in to SL.

## Ping Sim/Ping User

Ping Sim and Ping User should be less than <100ms. These settings indicate how long it takes for data to travel from your machine to the region's simulator (Ping Sim) and how long data takes to travel from the simulator to your machine (Ping User).

While in New York staying at the Sheraton Manhattan, I was experiencing extreme lag with 6000+ms for both user and sim. After making several calls, I found out there were 126 guests connected sharing one T1 line. If you do the math, that's about 12kbps per guest! No SL for me that night.

If it seems like you're having a networking problem, one thing you can do to reduce network traffic is to disable audio or video streaming in your preferences (select Edit->Preferences or press Ctrl+P). On the Audio & Video tab, uncheck both Play Streaming items. Also, verify that you're not uploading or downloading anything large. For example, don't start uploading a bunch of pictures to Shutterfly and then log in to SL!

If everything checks out and you still see problems like those mentioned in this section, the region simulator may be overloaded or having an issue. You may, in this case, see Ping Sim being high, while Ping User is low. Let's move on to checking the region status also using the statistics bar.

## CHECK 5: THE REGION'S GRID SERVER STATUS

Regional lag depends on load on the region itself as it performs all its tasks. You may experience great performance in one SL region and very bad performance in another. The easiest way to check whether a problem you're experiencing is a regional issue is simply to go somewhere else and see if you still have the problem.

One of the main sources of regional lag is a crowed sim with a lot of avatars. Older sims on the mainland are good for only about 20–30 avatars. New island estates have reported crowds over 100 that did not crash, although you couldn't move around much.

Checking the mini-map can give you a clue as to how many avatars are on the simulator. In Figure 12-4, you can see there's a crowd. You can also just look around you. Look at Figure 12-5. Is it crowded? You tell me.

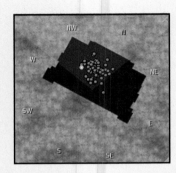

**Figure 12-4**

*Mini-map showing a crowded simulator.*

**Figure 12-5**

*An SL crowd—expect to lag.*

To find out exactly how many avatars are using sim resources, bring up the statistics bar again, and this time look under the Simulator section. You are looking for two items: Main Agents and Child Agents (see Figure 12-6).

Main agents are avatars who are connected to the same region as you. Child agents

| Simulator | |
| --- | --- |
| Time Dilation | 0.97 |
| Sim FPS | 43 |
| Physics FPS | 42.6 |
| Agent Updates/Sec | 4.0 |
| Main Agents | 2 |
| Child Agents | 2 |
| Objects | 10861 |
| Active Objects | 571 |
| Active Scripts | 3338 |
| Script Perf | 14001 ips |
| Packets In | 40 pps |
| Packets Out | 57 pps |
| Pending Downloads | 0 |
| Pending Uploads | 0 |
| Total Unacked Bytes | 0 kb |
| Time (ms) | |

**Figure 12-6**

*Statistics bar: Simulator section.*

are avatars in nearby regions who can see things in your region. Main agents and child agents add load to the sim. If you see numbers higher than 30, the region may be running slowly due to how many people are in or around the region at the time.

If the number of agents is low, and you still suspect the sim is having a problem, there is one more easy check. Under the Simulator section of the statistics bar, click on Time (ms) to open more data. Look for Total Frame Time.

David Linden has this to say from this Knowledgebase article (http://secondlife.com/knowledgebase/article.php?id=273):

> **Total Frame Time**—This measures how much time it takes the simulator to run everything that the simulator is trying to do each frame.
>
> - < 22 ms—the simulator is healthy, everything is running as fast as it can, and more scripts can be added without reducing the performance of individual scripts.
> - approx. 22 ms—the simulator is healthy, but there are probably a lot of scripts and agents on the simulator, meaning that script execution is being slowed down in order to maintain the simulator frame rate.
> - > 22 ms—the simulator is experiencing severe load, either due to physics or a large number of agents, such that even by slowing down script execution it is impossible to compensate. The simulator frame rate has been reduced as a result.

If the network checks out, and the simulator looks good, then you may be pushing your own computer to some limit. The first thing you can do to decrease load on your computer, the network, and grid servers in SL is to adjust your draw distance.

## CHECK 6: YOUR DRAW DISTANCE SETTING

Checking your draw distance setting is so important that I have put it into its own step. If you're experiencing poor SL performance for any reason, this is the one thing you can change that is likely to improve your situation.

Before I get into why this technique works, let me tell you how to change the setting. Bring up the Preferences panel by selecting Edit->Preferences or pressing Ctrl+P. Then go to the Graphics tab. Near the bottom, you will see Draw Distance. Set this to 64 or 96.

So, what is draw distance? The draw distance sets how far away you will be able to see objects in SL. Shorter distance settings will result in only close-by objects being drawn. Larger distance settings will result in more objects being drawn (assuming there are more objects further away). The more objects that need to be drawn, the more objects need to be downloaded to your machine, the more textures that need to be downloaded, the more textures that must be loaded onto your graphics card, and so on.

By drawing less, you reduce the number of network, CPU, and GPU resources across the board that SL requires to show you what you want to see. The trade-off is basically how much you can see into the distance. See Figure 12-7 through Figure 12-10 at Serenity Falls. I shot the same image using draw distance settings of 64, 128, 256, and 512, respectively. You'll note how a kind of fog seems to clear as you increase the draw distance and more and more distance details are revealed. For example, in Figure 12-7, there is no indication of distant mountains that you can clearly see in Figure 12-9.

**Figure 12-7**
*Serenity Falls draw distance of 64m.*

**Figure 12-8**
*Serenity Falls draw distance of 128m.*

**Figure 12-9**
*Serenity Falls draw distance of 256m.*

**Figure 12-10**
*Serenity Falls draw distance of 512m.*

So, if you've adjusted your draw distance to 64 and things are still slow, there is one more thing left to check.

## CHECK 7: YOUR COMPUTER'S GPU PERFORMANCE

For this section, I'm assuming you have already verified that you have hardware that exceeds the SL minimum requirements and that you're not experiencing a CPU or memory issue. Graphics in SL can challenge even the latest graphics cards, so sometimes you need to dial back the details that you see.

One quick way to check whether you're seeing graphics issues is to look at the FPS value at the top of the Basic section of the statistics bar. FPS stands for frames per second. Hollywood movies play in theaters at 24 FPS, meaning the appearance of a moving picture is created by displaying a sequence of 24 still images (frames) every second. Why 24? Well, just because. It's simply an arbitrary standard that was adopted many years ago by the industry. By comparison, North American broadcast television and video operate at 30 FPS. Computer video games operate "just as fast as they can," often at speeds of 50–60 FPS or higher.

In SL, frame rates tend to be more modest than in video games because SL is a highly resource-intensive application, and your computer can do only so many things so fast. Generally speaking, the more powerful your computer, the faster SL will run for you, but your actual FPS will depend on many factors.

Understand that unlike with video or movies, there is no standard whatsoever for how many frames per second you *should* be getting in SL. Users with ultra-high-end gaming rigs have reported frame rates well into the hundreds. Those on less powerful machines like business grade laptops tend to get twenties, teens, or even single digits. Most people fall somewhere in between.

Many SL users will tell you that should your FPS drop below about 10–15 or so, the world will start to look jerky to you. You may get the feeling that things are constantly jumping around, as the world seems momentarily to freeze and then jump ahead with each passing frame. If this is happening to you consistently, there are only three solutions: reducing your draw distance (as you saw earlier), lowering your graphic detail settings in your SL preferences, or upgrading your computer.

One way to reduce the load on your graphics card is to reduce the number of things it has to draw (lowering your draw distance), as you saw earlier. Several other settings in your display also can be tuned downward. Changing some will make the world look noticeably worse, so play with them to try and get the right combination of visual appeal with good performance.

Open the Preferences window (by selecting Edit-> Preferences or pressing Ctrl+P) and go to the Graphics Detail tab. Try doing the following and dial things back up as you see fit:

- Disable Vertex Shaders.
- Disable Bumpmapping and Shiny.
- Disable Ripple Water.
- Change Avatar Rendering to Normal.
- Set Lighting Detail to Sun and Moon Only.
- Set Terrain Detail to Low.
- Dial all Mesh Detail sliders to the left.

On the Advanced Graphics tab, you can dial back the maximum particle count if you're in an area with a lot of particles and they appear to be affecting your performance, or you can disable their display entirely. Just select View->Beacons->Hide Particles (or Client->Rendering->Types-Particles or press Ctrl+Alt+Shift).

Odds are, the world is not looking as good as it did before, but if you have a less-than-adequate graphics processor, this may be your ticket to getting around. Try turning on the things that are important to you one at a time until you find the right balance. You can learn all about SL preferences at http://secondlife.com/knowledgebase/article.php?id=335.

## TIPS FOR ATTENDING POPULAR EVENTS

Lag at highly popular events is just a fact of life in SL. Julia Hathor had these tips to offer on how you can help reduce overall lag at these events. Some event organizer may insist that you follow a set of rules that help reduce lag so that the venue can support more avatars. Be considerate of others and comply with local lag reduction rules (for example, leave the Animation Overiders [AOs] behind!).

- Remove attachments—the more the better!
- Take off/detach AOs; don't just turn them off.
- Wear jewelry based on a textures rather than a lot of prims.
- Wear low-prim shoes or clothing.
- Allow absolutely no poofers (particle effects triggered on teleporting in/out of a location)!
- If you're holding an event, consider planning it as informal. People are less likely to wear all those very high prim dresses, hair, shoes, and so on, to an informal event. If you have a wedding, make it a beach wedding where guests can come barefoot and in bikinis. Only the bride and groom need to dress up!
- Take off all weapons and other scripted objects.

## ADDITIONAL LAG/SL PERFORMANCE RESOURCES

Here are some additional resources:

- **Second Life Help on Lag**
  http://wiki.secondlife.com/wiki/Help:Lag

- **Second Life Preferences Guide**
  Many of the things you can do about lag require modifications to your preferences. You can find a complete guide to SL Viewer preferences at http://secondlife.com/knowledgebase/article.php?id=335

- **Statistics Bar Guide**
  http://secondlife.com/knowledgebase/article.php?id=091

- **I have a lot of lag; how do I stop it?**
  http://secondlife.com/knowledgebase/article.php?id=273

- **Guide to Improving Mac Performance**
  If you're a Mac user, you may want to look at http://secondlife.com/knowledgebase/article.php?id=088

- **Poor Performance Due to Dual Processors**
  http://secondlife.com/knowledgebase/article.php?id=303

- **How do I clear the Second Life cache?**
  (It can help find "lost" Inventory.)
  http://secondlife.com/knowledgebase/article.php?id=328

# WITH GRIEFERS…BE A TREE

*"Don't respond or react. Griefers don't shoot trees because trees don't shout "Ouch" or "F\*\*\* off!" Trees are boring. Be very, very boring…."*

**—Starax Statosky**

A **griefer** is an individual whose enjoyment of SL is enhanced by negatively affecting the experience of other SL residents. There will always be individuals who enjoy making life unenjoyable for others, and SL is no different.

Let me relate this story:

I was reclining on the couch in my living room contemplating my next build when the front door opened and in walked an avatar dressed in a gray ninja outfit, wielding a sword. The avatar's first name was MrGrieferBanMe. I raised a virtual eyebrow.

After assessing the situation, Mr. Griefer drew his weapon and proceeded to slash away at me as I relaxed on the couch. Despite the volumes of particle blood that sprayed everywhere, my carpet remained unstained, and my avatar remained unscathed (my home being in a no damage area).

I stood up.

"'Tis but a scratch," I exclaimed in the best Monty Python accent I could muster in chat. He redoubled his efforts. I walked outside, and he followed, hacking away the entire time.

Once outside, I remembered the advice Starax Statosky had given me: "Be a tree." So, I stood there and did my best bark impersonation. Seeing that I was not going to flame out, ban, or otherwise try to do anything about him, he let loose a giant burst of laughing and giggling Mario Brothers particles that surrounded me for several seconds.

When the Marios cleared, he was gone.

This was my first real griefing experience in SL. Others have had much worse. I will say this: It is one thing to be a tree when it's just you and another thing when the griefer is attacking an individual in a group setting or attacking your date!

Griefing behavior in SL typically takes the form of the following activities:

- Pushing other avatars, either by physically moving their avatar against yours or through the use of scripted devices or guns
- Creating scenes of blood and violence like the one described in my own story
- Displaying or chatting offensive material
- Repeating annoying, repetitive, or adult sounds
- Using particle system attacks to simulate explosions or obnoxious Mario Brothers displays

So, what can you do if faced with a griefer attack?

Read on….

## THE BASICS OF DEALING WITH GRIEFERS

If you're experiencing a griefer attack on land that you do not own, remember that you are in control, not the griefer. There are several things you can do in order of escalation:

- Be a tree.
- Sit down.
- Mute the griefer.
- Leave the area.
- File an abuse report.

First, be a tree; in other words, ignore the griefer. This approach can be very effective because most griefers want you to get pissed off, and if you don't, they may move on to more fertile targets.

Second, if you're being pushed (forcibly moved) by being shot or caged, just sit down on something. If nothing is available, create a prim box and sit on it. You will now be unmovable and can return to ignoring the griefer. Trust me; ignoring griefers bugs the hell out of them.

Third, you can mute the griefer. At some point in your SL experience, you'll discover someone who is extremely annoying, maddening, and perhaps, more likely, offensive. Linden Lab has provided the Mute tool (see Figure 12-11), which stops communication between you and the other avatar.

**Figure 12-11**
*Muting another resident with the Mute tool on the pie menu.*

Simply right-click over the griefer's avatar and select Mute from the pie menu, as shown in Figure 12-11. If the avatar is not immediately around, you can mute it from the IM dialog or directly from the griefer's profile. It is also possible to mute offending objects (yes, scripted objects can become annoying as well).

Fourth, you can always leave the area, either teleporting away or logging out entirely.

Finally, you can file an abuse report. See the section "The Official Word on Griefing from Linden Lab" for how this is done. If you decide to file an abuse report, having others who experienced the same event also file an abuse report is helpful.

## DEALING WITH GRIEFERS AS A LANDOWNER

If you're a landowner, you may have more at stake when a griefer strikes. The good news is you also have more extreme measures available to you that you can use to address griefing. They come in the form of tools such as Freeze, Eject, and Ban.

It doesn't make much sense for LL to provide an SL police force to deal with griefers. The strategy, which I believe is the correct one, is to provide landowners with the tools they need to deal with griefers as they see fit. Freezing, ejecting, and banning are the tools du jour available for landowners.

When you **freeze** avatars on your land, they are unable to move their avatar or chat. This usually stops the attack. They are able to send and receive IMs. This gives you a means to have a private conversation with the individuals about their behavior.

If this discussion does not go well, you can **eject** griefers. Ejecting them removes them from your land, but they can

always come back unless you **ban** them. Banned individuals will not be able to enter your property from ground level up to 200m. However, they can still come back and shoot at you from the land next door if they're bent on being annoying.

The Knowledgebase article "Guide to Freezing, Banning, and Ejecting" explains how to freeze, ban, or eject an individual (http://secondlife.com/knowledgebase/article.php?id=265).

I spoke with Jade Steele, shown in Figure 12-12, about griefers. She owned a nightclub for a while and now runs Midian City, and here is how she dealt with them at her club.

**Figure 12-12**
*Jade Steele.*

**Ansel Gasparini:** *What equates to a security problem in SL?*

**Jade Steele:** Usually one of two things. A griefer who is shooting or bombing the club or someone who is being offensive and abusive to someone. Standing up here is nice because you can observe things without being right in the middle of it.

[Ansel looks down at the ceiling under his feet. The flat club roof is semi-transparent. Inside the club, however, the ceiling looks solid, kind of like a giant one-way mirror.]

*AG: What can you do about griefers?*

JS: Well I personally can do this...Try to move...

[Ansel tries and fails, his avatar has been frozen.]

JS: That is because I own the land. You can't say anything in chat right now. So that is my first approach. I'll IM them and try to nicely talk to them about whatever the problem is. If I can't resolve the problem then eject and ban as needed.

*AG: And do you have someone here at the club all the time?*

JS: Yes I have security who deals with people and they can use our security orb to eject and ban people if needed, sometimes I have to step in though. Like the other night. We have a no guns policy and a guy had invisible guns in his hands. Security IMed and said that they had asked him several times to take them off but he refused. So I froze him and IMed him. I kindly asked him to remove them, to which he says he didn't have any. Maybe he didn't realize, I'm not sure, but I told him how to view transparent objects and then sure enough he took them off, and then even joined our VIP group.

JS: Unless they are a griefer just out to cause trouble, most people will comply once you nicely explain things.

## THE OFFICIAL WORD ON GRIEFING FROM LINDEN LAB

Reducing griefing incidents is clearly in the interest of LL because griefing behavior may cause some people to abandon SL altogether. LL defines abuse as "when anyone violates the Terms of Service (TOS) or the Community Standards (CS)." LL suggests you and everyone who has witnessed the event file an abuse report: "Whenever you see one of these rules being broken, and you believe it to be intentional or malicious, then everyone present at the incident should file an abuse report."

Following are several links to Knowledgebase articles related to abuse and griefing. If you plan to submit an abuse report, I suggest you read the second one listed here:

- **Abuse and Griefing Knowledge Articles**

  http://secondlife.com/knowledgebase/
  category.php?id=56

- **A Guide to Filing an Abuse Report**

  http://secondlife.com/knowledgebase/
  article.php?id=085

**NOTE**

When you file an abuse report on an island estate, the estate owner may handle abuse reports directly.

Finally, if you're interested in abuse and what action LL is taking, check out the police blotter at http://secondlife. com/community/blotter.php. The blotter includes the date, violation, region, description, and action taken on abuse reports.

## GWYNETH ON GRIEFERS

If you've been in the SL blogosphere for even a brief moment, you have heard of Gwyneth Llewelyn (see Figure 12-13). I'm going to let her close out this discussion on griefers with a summarized piece from her blog post on SL society. The full text is available at http:// gwynethllewelyn.net/articlecategory/sl-society/.

**Figure 12-13**
*Gwyneth Llewelyn.*

Second Life has an interesting catalyst for many sociopaths to come to it: it doesn't actively enforce (almost) anything. Griefers go mostly unpunished—they simple log off with an account and log back in with an alt [another account under a different name]. On the mainland, you can't even touch them—if you do, a clever griefer will file an Abuse Report on you instead.

The public Help Island is a notorious place where people are completely at the mercy of griefers, and they know that very well. The new users will be too confused to be able to react. The griefers, with returning alts, will be able to do whatever they please.

There are tricks and strategies to deal with this kind of borderline behavior, but they're not easily applied—it takes some training and some skill as well. Most people are simply unprepared to confront griefers—because in real life, if you're harassed, you go to the police. In SL there is no police, no justice, no laws, no enforcement. This is very hard to accept for many, who are used to living under democratic institutions and a code of law—and naturally, it's only when you miss those that you understand how important they are.

Sociopaths are actually dangerous for a virtual world that touts "social interaction" and a "collaborative environment," especially if they are allowed (as they are) to roam the world unchecked. It means that sooner or later you'll meet them, but you have to understand their psychological traits and not let them affect your enjoyment and participation in SL.

Too many people get such a strong reaction against griefers and leave, never to return. This is actually the wrong approach; one should stay and ignore the griefers, since the more they're ignored (something which can be very difficult for some), the faster they will go elsewhere, where they can be the focus of attention. Griefers, unable to deal with social relationships, only know one way of gathering attention: by disrupting social networks. If you prevent them from doing that, they'll leave.

# TAMING YOUR SL INVENTORY

Objects you own in SL exist in one of four places: in your Inventory, attached to your avatar, rezzed in-world, or inside another object. The vast majority of the objects end up in your Inventory. The SL Inventory is analogous in RL to all your closets, cabinets, attic, garage, storage units, Mom and Dad's basement, and the trunk of your car. In SL, however, there is no limit to how much you can keep in your Inventory. It's no wonder that the contents of your SL Inventory can quickly get out of control.

The most annoying part of an unorganized Inventory is the time it takes you to find things. Being able to find things quickly will enhance your SL experience, and the reverse is also true. You may want to make a quick clothing change before accepting a teleport, or you may want to rez that new surfboard you bought to go surfing with friends.

Let me just say for the record that SL does not make it easy to keep an organized Inventory. There are many reasons for this, but the basic issue is that objects get into your Inventory in various ways, and you don't have any control over where they go. Here are a few examples:

- A friend offers you an object and you accept it. It goes into your Inventory somewhere, typically under the Objects folder.
- If you're building something and you right-click Take Copy or Take, it goes into your Inventory somewhere, typically under the Objects folder as well.
- If you create a Landmark, it goes into your Inventory under the Landmarks folder.
- If you buy something from a shop, it is placed in your Inventory somewhere based on the seller's decision, typically a folder in your root directory.

I could go on with examples, but basically, SL tries to organize for you by placing certain types of objects in certain places. This capability works for a few objects, but it falls apart quickly once you start to really collect a bunch of stuff. Then you'll end up spending time in SL organizing things rather than having fun.

Willow Zander has more objects in SL than anyone I know. She kindly allowed me to share her organizational strategy here. Read more from Willow at http://www.styledisorder.com/.

Take it away, Willow.…

**Figure 12-14**
*Willow Zander.*

# WILLOW ZANDER'S INVENTORY POST

Now, I understand we *all* have our inventories organized in completely different ways. But let's face it, who likes a messy Inventory, where you can't find your ass from your head? No one!

Or at least no one in their right mind! I have over 49,000 objects (see Figure 12-15) in my Inventory and that's with a complete ton boxed up. Trust me; I am the asset server's biggest abuser, and I am slowly going through and deleting what I don't use and/or need, excluding hair, clothes etc. I hoard those, and I am DAMN proud! So…when it all started to get a bit too much, I decided to start organizing it! I have included a snapshot reel here, as I didn't want to spam up the page with snapshots, so please feel free to look at the examples :D

**Figure 12-15**
*Willow Zander's 49,777 item Inventory.*

First. I started with just your plain old folders like

> My Inventory>Clothing>Pants
>
> My Inventory>Clothing>Skirts
>
> My Inventory>Clothing>Tops

But I soon realized this wasn't good enough. I mean if I had 200 shirts, did I really want to scroll through them ALL to find one I want? So I started organizing as so:

> My Inventory>Clothing>Pants>ABC
>
> My Inventory>Clothing>Skirts>ABC
>
> My Inventory>Clothing>Tops>ABC

Here ABC, DEF, are folders which represent the designer's label name (see Figure 12-16). For those of you with favorite shirts/designers, a name like *FAVES is your friend! Of course, you don't have to call it that; just use an asterisk as the first character so it stays at the top and you're away! HURRAH! My outfits folder was a bit harder because, like everyone, I have a ton of outfits and, of course, I have my favorites, so how was I to organize this?

**Figure 12-16**
*Skirts organized using alphabetic folders.*

This time *FAVES doesn't quite cut it, so I introduced a designer subfolder element: *Dazzle, *Starley, *Cani. Of course, we also have *Midnight>Torrid or *Midnight>Camie because sometimes I find so many fab clothes in one sim! I like to have a sim folder. (Anyone think I'm crazy yet? Or did I lose you all a while ago?)

So now we have an outfit folder…how do we organize that?! How do you define a set that has both pants and a skirt in it? Well, if you're me (and sensible), you would define it as the set you would wear most. If you think you will make more use out of the pants, define it as pants! If you are a skirt lover, define it as a skirt set!

Easy peasy, so if you follow those rules, you should have something similar to this:

> My Inventory>Clothing>Outfits >
> Skirt Sets>*Dazzle>ABC
>
> My Inventory>Clothing>Outfits>
> Pant Sets>*Cani>DEF

Of course, you can make the ABCs into ABCDEs if you like; I know I have, depending on how much stuff there is or I think there might be in the future! I also have a folder called Hats N Stuff.

Inside Hats N Stuff I have many folders, including Jewelry, Butt (Tails! I swear, and belts and things), Hands, Head, etc.

Inside Jewelry I have more subfolders. I have Rings, Earrings, Collections, etc. all in subfolders and then folders inside those with more subfolders until you finally get to what you want! Fallingwater has *Fally folders, as I have a LOT of her stuff and I need to find them fast!

Now, take my hair folder, for example; I have so much hair it is *not* funny, but I wear ETD more than I do any other, so I made three folders: Accessories, ETD, and Others:

Accessories

ETD

Others>Panache>Zyrra>ABC

Others>Panache>Hosie

Others>Starley

Others>Toast

It just makes sense for me to have the hair I wear most at the top. Inside the ETD folder, there are three subfolders: New, Old, and Hats. New for the new textures, Old for the old textures, and Hats for fish. Fish, of course, being Hats (I'm trying to keep you interested here!). I found it easier to separate the Old and New textures instead of rifling through 50 billion folders (Elika has done LOTS of hair, you know!). So, let's look inside the New Folder, and what do we see?

New>ABC

New>DEF>Flirty

New>DEF>Flirty>Blondes

That's right; I, of course, have the Willow pack in ALL styles that it comes in, old and new. So I had this dilemma the other day, scrolling through at least 60 hairs to find a color I wanted, so I decided to make more subfolders, so now each folder contains

New>DEF>Flirty>Blondes

New>DEF>Flirty>Browns

New>DEF>Flirty>Blacks

New>DEF>Flirty>Reds

New>DEF>Flirty>Colours

New>DEF>Flirty>Grays & Whites

Doesn't that look fab! I think it does anyway! I know what you're all thinking now. GAWD how much time!? Honestly, it took me about two or three days, that's it, and in that time I binned SO much stuff that I had from my noob days or gave it to friends, I even did a yard sale! Yes, I'm evil; sue me :P.

You are probably also thinking, GAH, I don't want to scroll through 50 folders to get to what I want, but it's your choice, 50 folders or 500 items? Which is better to scroll through?

Finally, I have a folder I keep at the bottom of my basic Inventory list called Willow <3 (see Figure 12-17). It contains the following subfolders: Attachments, Elika, Gala, and Starley.

**Figure 12-17**
*Willow's Quick Change Avatar Organization.*

This is because when I want to quick change, I throw on one of these folders. I have Gala and Starley folders because they are the main skins I wear and I find that I have to change my face slightly between skins, so it's a lot easier than rifling through my shapes folder (don't even ASK why I have a ton of those!).

The Elika folder is for my modeling. If I am dressed as a goat or a pixie (I'm not odd, honest) and Elika needs me to model, I just throw on my Elika folder, which is just basically shape, hair, no attachments, and some clothes so she doesn't have to avert her eyes while TPing me in.

Attachments is exactly what it says—different attachments I wear. Subfolders in attachments are

- **Base Jewelry:** The jewelry that I always wear.
- **Jewelry:** Other jewelry I wear some of the time that I don't want to go rifling through folders to find.
- **Lashes:** Lashes are because I LOVE my lynnix lashes, but I have so many different ones I like to vary :D
- **Others:** Just my kitty ears and my wings, LOL, in case I'm feeling particularly feline or angelic :P

It is not just my clothes and attachments I organize; I have to keep my Objects folder organized too, or it drives me bloody insane. I have four main folders in my Objects folder:

- **Boxes:** Boxes that I have packed and my fav furniture!
- **Clothes to Unpack:** Clothing I have yet to unpack.
- **Modelling/Poses:** My modelling stands, backdrops, etc.
- **Stuff to Sort:** Random stuff to sort out.

I find this structure easier than having a lot of lil cubes staring at me every time I open my Object folder!

I hold my hands up, my snapshots are a complete MESS. I just keep adding a new folder and shoving them all in there, hoping that one day the magical Inventory fairy will come and organize them for me!

Don't leave ANY of your folders like that; you'll never find a thing, you'll buy doubles, and it's just NOT good! Not good at all! If you have a lot of textures/pictures, invest in a good texture sorter. There are several out there, and yes, I do own them—I just get lazy sometimes. And hey! what is more important, my clothes or my pictures? Pfft! I know which folder I delve into most!

I guess I've rambled, and you are probably reading this thinking, Why doesn't the girl just use the Search Inventory function? I ask you this: Have you ever, *ever* used that tool? Lordy, I know my Inventory is huge and that must have an impact, but gawd, I always have to relog after I search, because I can't move for like 10 centuries afterwards. Even then a simple relog takes about 5 mins for SL to actually close down, and then it takes an eon to get back in!

OK, I (Ansel) can't help but step in and say I find the Search Inventory function invaluable! If you name objects sensibly (to you), you can use this feature to find them regardless of what folder they're stored under.

I really do find this the most effective way to organize my Inventory. It's simple, effective, and once you have it in place, it's so easy to maintain as long as you keep on top of it. Give it a go! Don't go clubbing and lag yourself to death. Don't spend all your Lindens because you are bored. *Organize your Inventory! Do it today!*

So, I hope this may have helped in some way. I don't expect you all to want to organize yours the way I have organized mine. I only hope that this article has given you ideas on where to start. Two final tips:

- You can open multiple windows on your Inventory at the same time. Use two (or more) windows whilst sorting. It is way easier!
- Empty your trash, daily. Honestly, it makes SO much difference :D

Let me emphasize Willow's last point: Empty your trash and empty your Lost and Found folder on a regular basis. Doing this can cut your Inventory substantially and help clean up and improve performance for everyone in SL.

## OTHER INVENTORY LINKS

Here are a few Knowledgebase articles where you can find more information about your Inventory. Make sure to learn about the Recent Items tab and Inventory filter; they are invaluable tools.

- **You've Got Inventory: Inventory Inbox Tips**
  http://secondlife.com/knowledgebase/article.php?id=074

- **How do I find things in my Inventory?**

  http://secondlife.com/knowledgebase/
  article.php?id=138

## SUMMARY

In this chapter we discussed the basics of how SL works. You learned tips for troubleshooting and resolving SL performance issues. You also learned about griefers and how to handle them. Finally, you learned how to organize your Inventory so you can find things quickly.

One final aspect of change in SL that I must mention is that the world is easily modified. This may seem trivial on the surface, but it has broader-reaching implications. One of my favorite builds to explore and show new residents was the Cliffs at Bonny Doon (see Figure 12-18). This was a huge, expansive build with caves, cliffs, waterfalls, and the like.

One day I teleported in and found myself falling in mid-air. The cliffs were gone! In RL, something of this size could never disappear overnight without fanfare or at least an exciting display of demolition. To this day, I do not know who created the cliffs, but I am hopeful that someone reading this book will inform me.

Imagine if Google, Comcast, Yahoo!, Amazon, or AOL disappeared? How would that loss affect you?

## SL PREFERENCES

There are so many cool SL features that are disabled until you discover the SL Preferences panel. For example, things are shiny in SL if you have your preferences set properly. The Preferences panel is worth a visit. You can find a handy guide to setting preferences in SL at http://secondlife.com/knowledgebase/article.php?id=335.

**Figure 12-18**
*The Cliffs at Bonny Doon.*

## IN CLOSING

We have covered a lot of ground together in the exciting and rapidly evolving world of SL. I hope by now you call yourself an SL resident and are enjoying all SL has to offer. I also hope you share the struggle to explain SL to others.

As I said in the opening of this book, SL is a new frontier, sometimes thrilling, sometimes lawless, and sometimes exasperating. One thing it is not is short on opportunity and entertainment. I hope this book has added to your enjoyment and your success whether you were a newbie or a long-timer!

I hope to see you in-world!

Ansel Gasparini

# INDEX

# Q–R

# X–Z